Carpentry and Joinery for Advanced Craft Students: Purpose-made Joinery

Peter Brett

Brooklyn College, Birmingham

Stanley Thornes (Publishers) Ltd

Originally published in 1985 by Hutchinson Education
Reprinted, revised 1986 1988 (twice)

Reprinted in 1990 by:
Stanley Thornes (Publishers) Ltd
Ellenborough House
Wellington Street
CHELTENHAM GL50 1YD

Reprinted 1992
Reprinted 1995

British Library Cataloguing in Publication Data

Brett, Peter
   Carpentry and joinery for advanced craft students:
   purpose-made joinery
   1. Carpentry   2. Joinery
   I. Title
   694   TH5604

ISBN 0 7487 0297 0

Typeset in Times
Printed and bound in Great Britain at
The Bath Press, Avon

Contents

Seasoning of timber – Protection of seasoned timber and joinery components
– Decay of timber – Preservation of timber – Adhesives – Mechanics –
Glue-laminated timber – Mechanical fasteners for structural work –
Self-assessment questions

Preface

This book is designed to cover the City and Guilds of London Institute Carpentry and Joinery 585 Advanced Craft Certificate course. The course is aimed at students who, having obtained their craft certificate, wish to develop their knowledge and understanding of craft processes, technology and associated subjects, and the interrelationship of their craft activities with the industry as a whole. This will enable them to become fully skilled in their craft and also to form a foundation for further study and possible career progression.

At the advanced craft stage students are required to specialize in a particular aspect of their craft. The two specialist options that are available for study in most colleges are:

Site practice
Purpose-made joinery

In addition there are core topics which are common to all carpentry and joinery advanced craft students irrespective of the chosen option. These core topics consist of a study of general carpentry and joinery processes. Each course is divided into ten equal units which are allocated to the following sections:

Core topics	3 units
Specialist option	3 units
Practical activities	4 units

The core topics and one specialist option are covered in this book. In addition, a brief revision of certain craft-level topics and associated studies have been included where required as an aid to a fuller understanding of the subjects.

Each of the following chapters begins with a list of learning objectives and ends with a series of short-answer self-assessment questions, the answers to which are contained within the text. This will enable students to evaluate their understanding of the relevant chapter and to check their progress through the course. The last section of the book deals with examination and study techniques.

The City and Guilds of London Institute examination at advanced craft level consists of a college assessment of practical work and two written papers, one covering the specialist option and the other the core topics. Examples of each examination paper have been included in the examination and study techniques section.

Acknowledgements

The author wishes to thank the following for supplying technical information and photographs for inclusion in this book:

Agrément Board
American Plywood Association
Brick Development Association
British Industrial Fastenings Ltd
British Standards Institution
British Woodworking Federation
Building Centre
Building Research Establishment
Cement and Concrete Association
Chipboard Promotion Association
Copper Development Association
Council of the Forest Industries of British Columbia
Cuprinol
Dominion Machinery Co. Ltd
Elu Machinery Ltd
Erskine Systems Ltd
Fibre Building Board Development Organization
Finnish Plywood International
Fosroc Ltd Timber Treatments Division
Lawtons Ltd
Lead Development Association
Norton Construction Products
Protimeter plc
Sachs Dolmar (UK) Ltd
Swedish and Finnish Timber Council
Timber Research and Development Association
Wadkin plc

The forms shown in Figures 6, 7, 8, 9, 10, 11, 12 are reproduced with permission of The Controller of Her Majesty's Stationery Office who reserves Crown Copyright.

Specimen examination papers are reproduced with the kind permission of the City and Guilds of London Institute. Any worked examples or typical answers given in this book are the author's own and cannot be attributed to the Institute.

My sincere thanks go to my colleagues for their assistance and encouragement, in particular Derek Crafts.

Finally I would like to dedicate this book to my wife Christine and two children James and Sarah, without whose help, patience and encouragement, little would have been achieved.

chapter 1

Sources of technical information

After reading this chapter the student should be able to:

1 Define the need for up-to-date technical information.
2 Identify the most appropriate source or sources of information relevant to a given task.
3 Define the main function of given organizations.
4 Define the main purpose of given documents.

It is not possible to absorb and remember all the information required for a particular job; even if it were, it is essential that this information is regularly updated to take account of changes in legislation and technology.

Throughout your working life from apprentice-student to various levels in industry, you will have to make decisions and solve problems. To do this effectively, various sources of information will have to be consulted. Specialist information may be obtained from the following sources as well as from textbooks. Copies of the publications produced by the various information sources listed are normally available for student reference in most college libraries.

1 Building Regulations
2 British Standards Institution
British Standard Specifications and Codes of Practice
3 Building Research Establishment
BRE Digests, information papers and current papers
4 Research, manufacturers and trade development associations:

Agrément Board
American Plywood Association
Brick Development Association
British Woodworking Federation
Building Centre
Cement and Concrete Association
Chipboard Promotion Association
Copper Development Association
Council of the Forest Industries of British Columbia
Fibre Building Board Development Organization
Finnish Plywood International
Forestry Commission
Lead Development Association
Swedish and Finnish Timber Council
Timber Research and Development Association
etc.

Building regulations

The system of Building Regulations as we know them today stems from the Industrial Revolution. Development at this time was taking place rapidly, although as it was largely unplanned and uncontrolled by local authorities, it resulted in appalling housing conditions.

The Public Health Act of 1875 allowed local authorities to make local by-laws to control the planning and construction of buildings. As these were local there were many anomalies, what might be permitted in one authority could be prohibited in another. Therefore the Minister of Housing and Local Government was given under the 1961 Public Health Act powers to prepare a national system of building regulations. The Building Regulations 1965 replaced the local by-laws and were applicable to work in England and Wales, with the exception of work in Inner London which was controlled by the London Building Acts 1930 to 1978.

In 1984 a new building act was approved by Parliament. The Building Regulations 1985 which were made under this act apply to all building work carried out in England and Wales, including inner London. (Similar controls and regulations exist for building work in Scotland and Northern Ireland.)

The main purpose of the regulations is to provide safe and healthy buildings/accommodation for the public and to conserve energy. They do this by laying down minimum acceptable standards of building work and materials.

Copies of the Building Regulations 1985 and their supporting approved documents can be obtained from Her Majesty's Stationery Office (HMSO), Publications Centre, PO Box 276, London SW8 5DT.

British Standards Institution (BSI)

The BSI was granted a Royal Charter in 1929, its main purpose being to produce voluntary standards in consultation with all interested parties and to promote their use. The scope of these standards include:

Glossary of terms
Definitions and symbols
Methods of testing
Methods of assembly or construction
Specifications for quality, safety, performance or dimensions

The BSI publishes over 7000 publications of which around 1500 are related to the construction industry. The majority of these publications take the form of a British Standard Specification (BS) or a Code of Practice (CP)

Basically, British Standard Specifications deal with materials and components and Codes of Practice cover the design and workmanship of a whole process. Other publications include Drafts for Development (DD), Published Documents (PD) and Promotional Publications (PP).

A kitemark approval scheme is operated by the BSI. The presence of a BSI kitemark indicates that the BSI is satisfied that the product has been made in accordance with the relevant British Standard Specification.

Up-to-date details of BSI publications can be obtained from their year-book or sectional lists, which are available for reference in many libraries, or from: British Standards Institution, 2 Park Street, London W1A 2BS.

Building Research Establishment (BRE)

Founded in 1921 to carry out research and development for the government and construction industry. The BRE is a group of four laboratories within the Department of Environment. These four laboratories are:

The Building Research Station, Hertfordshire
The Fire Research Station, Hertfordshire
The Princes Risborough Laboratory (timber and wood-based materials). Buckinghamshire
The Scottish Laboratory (research relevant to Scotland), Glasgow

Note: The Scottish laboratory is concerned with research relevant to Scotland. This is because different solutions to problems are often required to cope with the effect on building materials of the climate.

The main activities of the BRE include:

Research into current practical problems facing the construction industry, covering environmental design, structural design, materials, production and development
Advice with the preparation of BS, CP, and Building Regulations
Investigation of new building products
Answering technical enquiries

The BRE present the results of their research in various forms:
BRE News
BRE Digests
Current papers
Information papers
Films and educational packages

Details of current publications, films and services, many of which are free of charge, are contained in an information directory which is published annually by the BRE and can be obtained from the following address: Distribution Unit, Building Research Establishment, Bucknalls Lane, Garston, Watford, Hertfordshire WD2 7JR.

Research, manufacturers and trade development associations

The objectives of these associations will be individual to each organization, but in general they will include:

Research and development of materials and construction techniques
Prevention of waste
Safety
Source of technical information
Technical advisory service
Means of communication between members, industry and the general public

Note: Details of free and priced publications can be obtained from the relevant association.

Agrément Board
Founded in 1966, the Agrément Board is sponsored by the Department of Environment. It is principally concerned with the testing, assessment and certification of normally new or innovatory products for the construction industry. An Agrément Certificate gives an independent opinion of the performance in use of a product, component, material or system, when used and installed in the specified manner. This facilitates their acceptance by architects, specifiers, local authorities, building contractors and consumers. Information can be obtained from: The Agrément Board, PO Box 195, Bucknalls Lane, Garston, Watford, Hertfordshire WD2 7NG.

American Plywood Association (APA)
The American Plywood Association is a non-profit trade association that represents the softwood plywood manufacturers of America. The Association carries out research and development, offers technical advice and publishes product guides and brochures. Information can be obtained from: American Plywood Association, Index House, Ascot, Berkshire SL5 7EU.

Brick Development Association (BDA)
A trade association formed in 1945 to promote all aspects of the brick industry, including research and development, manufacture, sale and use. All areas of bricks and brickwork are catered for in the wide range of technical publications produced by the BDA. Its address is: Brick Development Association, Woodside House, Winkfield, Windsor, Berkshire SL4 2DP.

British Woodworking Federation (BWF)
A trade association formed by the amalgamation of two associations in 1976. Through its six specialist sections, which are:

Architectural and general joinery
Kitchen furniture
Doors and doorsets
Timber frame construction
Laminated structures and timber engineering
Windows

It represents and promotes the interests of manufacturers of timber components for the building industry. The British Woodworking Federation produce on their members' behalf a wide range of technical and promotional literature which can be obtained from: British Woodworking Federation, 82 New Cavendish Street, London W1M 8AD.

Building Centre
The Building Centre, established in 1931, is part of the Building Centre Group, which in addition to the London centre includes regional centres in Bristol, Cambridge, Durham, Glasgow, Manchester and Southampton. They display building materials and components and provide a product and technical information service for the building industry and the consumer. In addition the centres in London, Manchester, Bristol and Cambridge house branches of the Building Bookshop which stock a vast range of building and architectural books, pamphlets, BSI and HMSO publications. The London address is: Building Centre, 26 Store Street, London WC1E 7BT.

Cement and Concrete Association (C&CA)
An association financed by Portland Cement producers and founded in 1935. It provides

technical information to cement users and promotes high standards of concrete design and construction. The Cement and Concrete Association produces a wide range of technical publications, films and slide sets, details of which are contained in their catalogue. Its address is: Cement and Concrete Association, 52 Grosvenor Gardens, London SW1W 0AQ.

Chipboard Promotion Association (CPA)

The Chipboard Promotion Association is a manufacturers' association which provides technical information on the correct use and potential of wood chipboard to specifiers and users of the material. Its publications include technical notes, data sheets and general advisory brochures, and can be obtained from: Chipboard Promotion Association Limited, 7a Church Street, Esher, Surrey.

Copper Development Association (CDA)

A non-trading organization founded in 1933. It is sponsored by the world's copper producers to encourage the use of copper and to promote its correct application. The Copper Development Association services include the publication of information sheets and priced technical notes, and these can be obtained from: Copper Development Association, Orchard House, Mutton Lane, Potters Bar, Hertfordshire EN6 3AP.

Council of Forest Industries of British Columbia (COFI)

The Council of Forest Industries is an organization which was set up by the major timber and plywood producers of British Columbia. Their objective is to promote and extend the use of their members' products in both Canada and other export markets around the world. They operate a technical advisory service, a film and video library and publish product and application literature. Information can be obtained from: Council of Forest Industries of British Columbia, Tileman House, 131–133 Upper Richmond Road, London, SW15 2TR.

Fibre Building Board Development Organization (FIDOR)

This is a non-trading information body that promotes and develops the use of fibre building boards in the UK. FIDOR operates a technical advisory service and publishes a range of data sheets, technical bulletins and sitework recommendations applicable to the building industry, and can be obtained from: Fibre Building Board Development Organization Limited, 6 Buckingham Street, London WC2N 6BZ.

Finnish Plywood International

Finnish Plywood International is concerned with the development of unsurfaced and surfaced Finnish plywood, blockboard and laminboard for applications in building and construction. It provides technical information on the use of its materials in the building industry. Copies of publications can be obtained free of charge. The organization also provides technical advice. Its address is: Finnish Plywood International, PO Box 99, Welwyn Garden City, Hertfordshire AL6 0HS.

Forestry Commission

The Forestry Commission set up in 1919, promotes the development of forestry and also carries out research of forestry in order to ensure the best use of the country's forest resources. A range of leaflets, guides and information pamphlets (details of these are contained in their catalogue of publications) are available from: Forestry Commission, 25 Saville Row, London W1X 2AY.

Lead Development Association (LDA)

Set up in 1953, the LDA is a non-trading body supported by leading producers and manufacturers of lead products. The Association provides authoritative information on every aspect of lead to users and potential users worldwide. A number of publications aimed at the building industry are available from: Lead Development Association, 34 Berkeley Square, London W1X 6AJ.

Swedish Finnish Timber Council

This is a technical organization which promotes the use mainly in the construction industry of Swedish and Finnish timber. Details of the Council's various publications are contained in the technical publications list, and can be obtained from: The Swedish Finnish Timber Council, 21/25 Carolgate, Retford, Notts. DN22 6BZ.

Timber Research and Development Association (TRADA)

TRADA, established in 1934 as the Timber Development Association (TDA), is an independent research and development organization. It is jointly financed by firms and individuals in the timber trade, professions and industry and grant aided by the Department of the Environment. It employs architects, engineers and technicians all working in the interests of timber users and specifiers. Research and development carried out by the Association has made important contributions to the use of timber in housing and building, timber engineering, industrial applications, fire research, timber drying, stress grading and the testing of structures, components and finishes. The results of TRADA's work are made available through its advisory service and its many publications including technical brochures, leaflets, teaching aids and information sheets. These can be obtained from: Timber Research and Development Association, Stocking Lane, Hughenden Valley, High Wycombe, Buckinghamshire HP14 4ND.

Other information sources

Much useful information can be obtained through reading various trade periodicals, for example, *Building Trades Journal*, *What's New in Building* etc. In addition many trade periodicals operate a reader's enquiry service whereby technical brochures and information can be obtained from various manufacturers and suppliers.

Self-assessment questions

1 Explain the purpose of the following
   (a) British Standards
   (b) Building Regulations
   (c) Codes of Practice

2 Define the main function of the following
   (a) Timber Research and Development Association
   (b) Building Research Establishment
   (c) Agrément Board

3 Technical information concerning the use of plywood is required. List *three* possible sources of reference.

4 Identify the various organizations from the following list of abbreviations

   (a) TRADA
   (b) CPA
   (c) C&CA
   (d) BWF
   (e) HMSO

5 Briefly explain why it is necessary to regularly update technical information.

chapter 2

Building control

After reading this chapter the student should be able to:

1 Define the main areas of building control and state their purpose.

2 State the procedures involved when applying for planning permission or Building Regulations approval.

3 Explain the role of the Health and Safety Executive.

4 Define the main duties under the Health and Safety at Work etc. Act 1974 of:
   (a) Employers
   (b) Employees
   (c) Self-employed
   (d) Designers, manufacturers, suppliers

5 Name the relevant statutory safety regulations applicable to a given situation.

There are three main areas of building control, these are illustrated in Figure 1.

Planning permission
Building Regulations
Health and safety controls

In brief, planning controls restrict the type and position of a building or development in relation to the environment, whereas the Building Regulations state how a building should be constructed to ensure safe and healthy accommodation and the conservation of energy. Both of these forms of control are administered by the relevant local authorities, to whom an application must be made and permission received before work is started. Health and safety controls, on the other hand, are concerned with the health and safety of building site workers, visitors and the general public. These controls are administered by the Health and Safety Executive under the Health and Safety at Work etc. Act 1974.

Planning permission

All development is controlled by planning laws, which exist to control the use and development of land in order to obtain the greatest possible environmental advantages with the least inconvenience, both for the individual and society as a whole. The submission of a planning application provides the local authority and the general public with an opportunity to consider the development and decide whether or not it is in the general interest of the locality. The key word in planning is development. This means all building work, other operations such as the construction of a driveway, and a change of land or building use, such as running a business from your home. Certain developments are known as 'permitted developments' where no planning approval is required. These permitted developments include limited extensions to buildings and the erection of boundary fences and walls within certain height limits. The two main types of application are:

Outline planning permission
Full planning permission

Outline planning permission
This enables the owner or prospective owner to obtain approval of the proposed development in principle without having to incur the costs involved with the preparation of full working

TOWN AND COUNTRY PLANNING ACT 1971 APPLICATION FOR PERMISSION TO DEVELOP LAND	BRACKENDOWNS BOROUGH COUNCIL

| Building Control Dept Council Buildings Brackendowns Bedfordshire BR1 4AC | **For office use only** Borough ref. _____ Registered no. _____ Date received _____ |

1 APPLICANT

Name _____

Address _____

_____

_____ Tel. no. _____

AGENT (if any) to whom correspondence should be sent

Name _____

Address _____

_____

_____ Tel. no. _____

2 PARTICULARS OF PROPOSED DEVELOPMENT

(a) Full address or location of the land to which this application relates and site area (if known).

(b) Brief particulars of proposed development including the purpose(s) for which the land and/or buildings are to be used.

(c) State whether applicant owns or controls any adjoining land and if so, give its location.

(d) State whether the proposal involves: State Yes or No

(i) New building(s) _____ [ ]

If 'Yes' state gross floor area of proposed building(s). [ ] m^2/sq ft*

If residential development, state number of dwelling units proposed and type if known, e.g. houses, bungalows, flats. [ ]

(ii) Alterations _____ [ ]

(iii) Change of use _____ [ ]

(iv) Construction of a new access to a highway } vehicular _ [ ] pedestrian [ ]

(v) Alteration of an existing access to a highway } vehicular _ [ ] pedestrian [ ]

If 'Yes' state gross area of land or building(s) affected by proposed change of use (if more than one use involved state gross area of each use). [ ] hectares/acres/m^2/sq ft*

*Please delete whichever inapplicable

3 PARTICULARS OF APPLICATION

State whether this application is for: State Yes or No

(i) Outline planning permission _____ [ ]

(ii) Full planning permission _____ [ ]

(iii) Renewal of a temporary permission or permission for retention of building or continuance of use without complying with a condition subject to which planning permission has been granted _____ [ ]

(iv) Consideration under Section 72 only (Industry) [ ]

If 'Yes' delete any of the following which are not reserved for subsequent approval

1 siting   3 external appearance

2 design   4 means of access

If 'Yes' state the date and number of previous permission and identify the particular condition (see General Notes)

Date

Number

The condition

Figure 2 *Planning application form*

Outline planning permission

This enables the owner or prospective owner to obtain approval of the proposed development in principle without having to incur the costs involved with the preparation of full working drawings, thus leaving certain aspects of the development for later approval.

Full planning permission

After obtaining outline planning permission and when full details of the development have been decided, an application for full planning permission can be made. Alternatively an outline application can be dispensed with and full planning permission sought at the outset. An application for full permission must normally include four copies of the typical form shown in Figure 2, and four copies of plans and drawings as follows.

A plan must be provided, drawn to a scale of not less than 1:2500, which shows the site shaded in red and its relationship to adjacent properties.

Further drawings should be produced that give a clear picture of any new building as well as the existing features of the site including trees. These drawings, normally of a scale not less than 1:100, must clearly indicate the position of the proposed development within the site and the amount of floor space to be used for each purpose. In addition the types and colours of materials for the external walls and roof should be indicated together with the proposed access to the site and the type of fence or wall surrounding the development.

After considering these details, which are also open to public inspection, the planning committee can either:

Grant permission
Grant permission with certain conditions
Refuse permission

Where permission is refused or given conditionally the committee must give their reasons for the decision. Applicants can then modify the proposed development and resubmit their application, or appeal against the decision to the Secretary of State for the Environment.

Building Regulations approval

Whenever anyone wishes to erect a new building or extend or alter an existing one or put an existing one to a different use, they will probably have to apply for building regulations approval.

The Building Regulations 1985 are supported by a manual to the regulations and a set of approved documents. The manual sets out the type of work to which the regulations apply; it describes the two alternate systems of inspection/control and contains the regulations themselves along with explanatory notes. In addition the manual also contains details of facilities for disabled persons.

The approved documents are intended to give practical guidance to ways of complying with the Regulations. When designing a building, you are free to use the solutions given in the approved documents or devise your own solutions providing you show that they meet the requirements of the Regulations. The following approved documents (AD) are available:

Part A   Structure
Part B   Fire
Part C   Site preparation and resistance to moisture
Part D   Toxic substances
Part E   Resistance to the passage of sound
Part F   Ventilation
Part G   Hygiene
Part H   Drainage and waste disposal
Part J   Heat producing appliances
Part K   Stairways, ramps and guards
Part L   Conservation, fuel and power

Building Regulations application

Certain classes of building are exempted from the Regulations, these include:

Class 1:   Buildings controlled by other legislation, e.g.
Explosive Acts.
Nuclear Installations Act.
Ancient Monument and Archaeological Areas Act.

Class 2:   Buildings not used by people, e.g. A detached building where people can not or do not normally go.

Class 3: Glass house and agricultural buildings.

Class 4: Temporary buildings and mobile homes. (Temporary buildings are defined as those which are intended to remain erected for less than 28 days.)

Class 5: Ancillary buildings, e.g. Temporary building site accommodation.
Any building other than a dwelling used in connection with a mine or quarry.

Class 6: Small detached buildings, e.g. A detached building of up to 30 m² floor area which does not contain sleeping accommodation.
A detached building of up to 30 m² floor area designed to shelter people from the effects of nuclear, chemical or conventional weapons.

Class 7: Extensions (of up to 30 m² floor area), e.g.
The ground floor extension to a building by the addition of a greenhouse, conservatory, porch, covered yard or covered way; a carport which is open on at least two sides.

In addition, certain organizations are exempted from the need to comply with the Regulations. These are organizations who can be trusted to build to at least the standards of the Regulations or where the Regulations are inappropriate to the types of building constructed. The main organizations exempted are:

The Crown; who under the Building Act can dispense with or relax the requirements of the Building Regulations for its own buildings

The Department of Education and Science; who have always been exempted from Building Regulations for the construction of educational buildings.

Statutory undertakers; (gas, electricity and water, etc.) who are exempted for their operational buildings but not their offices and showrooms, etc.

Local authorities; who are exempted from the

procedural requirements (application and inspection, etc.), but not the technical ones, e.g. they must still build at least to the minimum standards set out in the Regulations.

When building regulations approval is required the building control section of the relevant local authority must be notified of your intentions in one of the following three methods:

Deposit full plans
Issue of Building Notice
Appoint an Approved Inspector

Full plans (Figure 3)

Application using the full plans method can be made by depositing in duplicate full plans of the proposed works. These shall consist of:

A statement that the plans are deposited in accordance with the Building Regulations 1985
A full description of the proposed work (specification)
Details of the surrounding area (block plan)
The intended use of the proposed building
Drawings to a scale of not less than 1:1250 showing the size and position of the building, its boundaries and relationship to adjoining boundaries (site plan and general location plans)
The number of storeys in the building
The provision made for drainage
Details of any cavity wall insulation and its installer
Details of any unvented hot water system
Any other details or plans if required to show that the work will comply with the regulations.

These plans and details will be examined to see if they comply with the regulations, a decision will be made within five weeks or two months if you agree to an extension of time. The plans may be rejected on any of the following grounds: the plans show a contravention of the regulations; the plans are defective (they fail to show compliance with the regulations); they contravene or show insufficient detail with regards to one of the local authority's functions under the Building Act (e.g. drainage, water supply, public buildings and local legislation).

BRACKENDOWNS BOROUGH COUNCIL
BUILDING CONTROL DEPARTMENT

The Building Act 1984
The Building Regulations 1985
The Building (Prescribed Fees) Regulations

FULL PLANS NOTICE

PART 1.   TO BE COMPLETED IN ALL CASES

a)	Name and Address of Owner	a)	MR. W.H.WHITEMAN, WHITEMAN ENTERPRISES, ENGINEERING HOUSE, BEDFORD.
			Telephone No. 0641293
b)	Name and Address of Agent, if any	b)	B.B.S. DESIGN, SARBIE HOUSE, BRACKENDOWNS, BEDS.
			Telephone No. 0581 423
c)	Address or location of the building to which this notice relates.	c)	PLOT 3, HILLTOP ROAD, BRACKENDOWNS, BEDS.
d)	Description of the building work	d)	NEW DETACHED HOUSE AND GARAGE
e)	Present use of building	e)	NOT APPLICABLE
f)	Proposed use of building	f)	PRIVATE DWELLING
g)	Do you agree to the plans being passed subject to conditions?	g)	YES / ~~NO~~
h)	Is a new crossing over a footway required?	h)	YES / ~~NO~~

PART 2.   TO BE COMPLETED IF AN UNVENTED HOT WATER STORAGE SYSTEM IS TO BE INSTALLED

a)	Name and Type of System	a)	NOT APPLICABLE
b)	Agreement Certificate Number	b)	
c)	Name and Address of Installer	c)	

PART 3.   BUILDING (PRESCRIBED FEES) REGULATIONS – COMPLETE 'a', 'b' or 'c' and 'd'

a)	New Dwellings:– (enter number)	i)	Number of dwellings to which this notice relates	ONE
		ii)	Number of dwellings with floor area over 64m²	ONE
		iii)	Total number of dwellings in 'multiple work scheme'	
b)	Garage, Carport, or Domestic Extensions:– (tick as appropriate)	i)	Detached garage/carport with floor area under 40m²	
		ii)	One or more rooms in roof space	
		iii)	Domestic extension with floor area less than 20m²	
		iv)	Domestic extension with floor area 20–40m²	
c)	All other building work or Material Changes of Use:–	i)	Total estimated cost of work to which notice relates	£
		ii)	Aggregate total estimated cost of all buildings in 'multiple work scheme'	£
d)	Plan Fee calculated in accordance with the current Building (Prescribed Fees) Regulations:–	i)	Plan Fee	£ 39
		ii)	Plus VAT at current rate	£ 5.85p
		iii)	Total Enclosed	£ 44.85p

PART 4.   DECLARATION

This notice and duplicate copies of the relevant plans and particulars in relation to the above mentioned building work, are deposited in accordance with Building Regulation 11(i)(b).

The Plan Fee shown above is enclosed and I acknowledge that the relevant Inspection Fee will, upon demand after the first inspection, be payable to the Council by the person by whom, or on whose behalf, the work is being carried out.

Date 2nd MARCH 1986   Signed R.D.Paull.   Agent

P.T.O.

Figure 3   *Building application form*

BRACKENDOWNS BOROUGH COUNCIL

BUILDING INSPECTION NOTICE

Plan no.B _____ Date _____

Nature of works _____

Address of works _____

The undermentioned works will be ready for inspection on _____

_____ Signature of builder

_____ Address of builder

1 Commencement	5 Oversite Concrete
2 Foundation Excavations	6 Drains under Test
3 Concrete Foundations	7 Back filling of Drain Trenches
4 Damp Proof Course	8 Completion

Note (a) Strike out words not applicable.

Figure 4 *Building inspection notice*

Where an application is refused or the applicant and the local authority are in dispute, there is an appeal procedure to the Secretary of State for the Environment.

Note: The local authority has the power to relax or dispense with certain requirements of the Building Regulations.

Building Notice

Application using the Building Notice method can be made by depositing a Building Notice and limited accompanying information (e.g. specification, block plan, site plan and general location plans). In addition the local authority may request further information as the work proceeds, in order to show compliance to specific items which cannot be inspected on site (e.g. structural calculations, material specifications, etc.).

Note: You cannot use the Building Notice method when erecting shops or offices.

Approved inspector

Application using the Approved Inspector method can be made by you and the inspector jointly, by depositing an initial notice, limited plans and evidence of their insurance cover to the local authority. The local authority must accept or reject this initial notice within ten working days. Once accepted, their powers to enforce the Regulations are suspended and the Approved Inspector will carry out the building control function and issue a final certificate to you and the local authority when the work has been satisfactorily completed.

Inspection of building work

When either the full plans method or the Building Notice method has been adopted the local authority's Building Control Officer will inspect the work as it proceeds. The builder must give the local authority written notice of the following building stages (this notice need not be in writing if the local authority agrees) (see Figure 4 for a typical Building Inspection Notice):

At least 48 hours before the commencement of work

At least 24 hours before the covering up of any excavation for a foundation, any foundation, any damp proof course or any concrete or other material laid over a site

At least 24 hours before haunching or covering up any drain

Not more than seven days after laying, concreting or back filling a drain

Not more than seven days after completion of building work

Where a builder fails to notify the local authority of any stage as required, the local authority has the power to require them to 'open up' or 'pull down' part of the work at a later date to enable inspection. After inspection by the Building Control Officer, the local authority may require modifications or additional work to be carried out in order to comply with the Regulations.

Where an Approved Inspector has been appointed she or he will be responsible for inspecting the work as it proceeds. They may also require the builder to notify them of commencement and/or particular stages of building work.

The local authority will charge a set fee for considering an application and inspecting the work as it proceeds. If an Approved Inspector is appointed she or he will negotiate their fee with you.

Note: In addition to planning permission and Building Regulations approval an application must also be made to the local authority (highways officer) for permission to deposit a rubbish skip or erect a hoarding or scaffold on or partly on the highway (road, footpath or verge).

Health and safety controls

In 1974 the Health and Safety at Work Act (HASAWA) was introduced. This Act became the main statutory legislation completely covering the health and safety of all persons at their place of work and protecting other people from risks occurring through work activities. All of the existing health and safety requirements operate in parallel with the HASAWA until they are gradually replaced by new regulations and codes of practice etc. made under the Act. The main health and safety legislation applicable to building sites and workshops is indicated in Table 1.

The four main objectives of the HASAWA are:

1 To secure the health, safety and welfare of all persons at work.
2 To protect the general public from risks to health and safety arising out of work activities.
3 To control the use, handling, storage and transportation of explosives and highly flammable substances.
4 To control the release of noxious or offensive substances into the atmosphere.

These objectives can only be achieved by involving everyone in health and safety matters.

Table 1   **Health and safety legislation**

Acts of Parliament	Regulations
Control of Pollution Act 1974	
Explosives Act 1875 and 1923	
Factories Act 1961	Abrasive Wheels Regulations 1970
	Asbestos Regulations 1969
	Construction (General Provision) Regulations 1961
	Construction (Lifting Operations) Regulations 1961
	Construction (Health and Welfare) Regulations 1966
	Construction (Working Places) Regulations 1966
	Construction (Head Protection) Regulations 1989
	Diving Operations Special Regulations 1960
	Electricity (Factories Act) Special Regulations 1908 and 1944
	Highly Flammable Liquids and Liquified Petroleum Gases Regulations 1972
	Lead Paint Regulations 1927
	Protection of Eyes Regulations 1974
	Woodworking Machines Regulations 1974
	Work in Compressed Air Special Regulations 1958 and 1960
Fire Precautions Act 1971	Fire Certificates (Special Premises) Regulations 1976
Food and Drugs Act 1955	Food Hygiene (General) Regulations 1970
Health and Safety at Work etc. Act 1974	Hazardous Substances (Labelling of Road Tankers) Regulations 1978
	Control of Lead at Work Regulations 1980
	Safety Signs Regulations 1980
	Health and Safety (First Aid) Regulations 1981
	Control of Asbestos at Work Regulations 1987
	Control of Substances Hazardous to Health Regulations 1988 (COSHH)
	Reporting of Injuries, Diseases and Dangerous Occurences Regulations 1985 (RIDDOR)
Mines and Quarries Act 1954	
Offices, Shops and Railway Premises Act 1963	

This includes:

Employers and management
Employees
Self-employed
Designers, manufacturers and suppliers of
equipment and materials

Employers' and management's duties
Employers have a general duty to ensure the
health and safety of their employees, visitors
and the general public. This means that the
employer must:

1 Provide and maintain a safe working environment.
2 Ensure safe access to and from the workplace.
3 Provide and maintain safe machinery, equipment and methods of work.
4 Ensure the safe handling, transport and
storage of all machinery, equipment and
materials.
5 Provide their employees with the necessary
information, instruction, training and supervision to ensure safe working.
6 Prepare, issue to employees and update as
required a written statement of the firm's
safety policy.
7 Involve trade union safety representatives
(where appointed) with all matters concerning the development, promotion and maintenance of health and safety requirements.

Note: An employer is not allowed to charge an
employee for anything done or equipment
provided to comply with any health and safety
requirements.

Employees' duties
An employee is an individual who offers his or
her skill and experience etc. to his or her
employer in return for a monetary payment. It is
the duty of every employee while at work to:

1 Take care at all times and ensure that his or
her actions do not put at 'risk' himself or
herself, workmates or any other person.
2 Co-operate with his or her employer to

enable them to fulfil the employer's health
and safety duties.
3 Use the equipment and safeguards provided
by employers.
4 Never misuse or interfere with anything
provided for health and safety.

Self-employed duties
The self-employed person can be thought of as
both his or her employer and employee;
therefore the duties under the Act are a
combination of those of the employer and
employee.

Designers', manufacturers' and suppliers' duties
Under the Act, designers, manufacturers and
suppliers as well as importers and hirers of
equipment, machinery and materials for use at
work have a duty to:

1 Ensure that the equipment machinery or
material is designed, manufactured and
tested so that when it is used correctly no
hazard to health and safety is created.
2 Provide information or operating instructions as to the correct use, without risk, of
their equipment, machinery or material.

Note: Employers should ensure this information
is passed on to their employees.

3 Carry out research so that any risk to health
and safety is eliminated or minimized as far
as possible.

Enforcement
Under the HASAWA a system of control was
established, aimed at reducing death, injury and
ill-health. This system of control is represented by
Figure 5. It consists of the Health and Safety
Commission which controls the work of the
Health and Safety Executive (HSE). The
Executive is divided into a number of specialist
inspectorates or sections which operate from
local offices situated throughout the country.
From the local offices, inspectors visit the
individual workplaces.

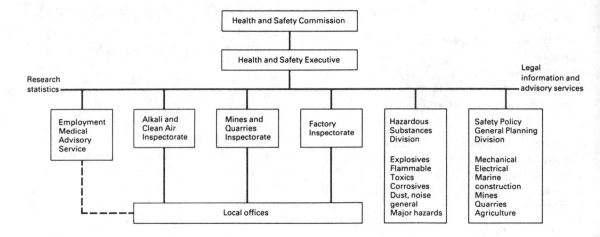

Figure 5   *Health and safety control*

Note: The section with the main responsibility for the building and construction industry is the factory inspectorate.

The health and safety inspectors have been given wide powers of entry, examination and investigation in order to assist them in the enforcement of the HASAWA and earlier safety legislation. In addition to giving employers advice and information on health and safety matters, an inspector can:

1 *Enter premises*   In order to carry out investigations including the taking of measurements, photographs, recordings and samples. The inspector may require the premises to be left undisturbed while the investigations are taking place.
2 *Take statements*   An inspector can ask anyone questions relevant to the investigation and also require them to sign a declaration as to the truth of the answers.
3 *Check records*   All books, records and documents required by legislation must be made available for inspection and copying.
4 *Give information*   An inspector has a duty to give employees or their safety representative information about the safety of their workplace and details of any action he proposes to take. This information must also be given to the employer.

5 *Demand*   The inspector can demand the seizure, dismantling, neutralizing or destruction of any machinery, equipment, material or substance that is likely to cause immediate serious personal injury.
6 *Issue an improvement notice*   (Figure 6)   This requires the responsible person (employer or manufacturer etc.) to put right within a specified period of time any minor hazard or infringement of legislation.
7 *Issue a prohibition notice*   (Figure 7)   This requires the responsible person to immediately stop any activities which are likely to result in serious personal injury. This ban on activities continues until the situation is corrected. An appeal against an improvement or prohibition notice may be made to an industrial tribunal.
8 *Prosecute*   All persons, including employers, employees, the self-employed, designers, manufacturers and suppliers who fail to comply with their safety duty may be prosecuted in a magistrates court or in certain circumstances in the higher court system. Conviction can lead to unlimited fines, or a prison sentence, or both.

Safety documentation

In order to comply with the various safety legislation an employer is required to:

HEALTH AND SAFETY EXECUTIVE
Health and Safety at Work etc. Act 1974, Sections 21, 23, and 24

IMPROVEMENT NOTICE

Serial No. I

Name and address (See Section 46)

To ....

(a) Delete as necessary

(a) Trading as ....

(b) Inspector's full name

I (b) ....

one of (c)

(c) Inspector's official designation

of (d) .... Tel no. ....

(d) Official address

(e) ....

hereby give you notice that I am of the opinion that at

(e) Location of premises or place and activity

you, as (a) (a) an employer/a self employed person/a person wholly or partly in control of the premises,

(f) ....

(f) Other specified capacity

(a) .... are contravening/have contravened in circumstances that make it likely that the
contravention will continue or be repeated

(g) Provisions contravened

(g) ....

The reasons for my said opinion are:—

and I hereby require you to remedy the said contraventions or, as the case may be, the matters
occasioning them by

(h) ....

(h) Date

(a) in the manner stated in the attached schedule which forms part of the notice.

Signature .... Date ....

Being an inspector appointed by an instrument in writing made pursuant to Section 19 of the said
Act and entitled to issue this notice.

(a) An improvement notice is also being served on ....

LP 1

of ....
related to the matters contained in this notice.

Dd 347139 5000 Pads 2/75 COH

NOTES

1 Failure to comply with an Improvement Notice is an offence as provided by Section 33 of this
Act and renders the offender liable to a fine not exceeding £400 on summary conviction or to an
unlimited fine on conviction on indictment and a further fine of not exceeding £50 per day if the
offence is continued.

2 An Inspector has power to withdraw a notice or to extend the period specified in the notice,
before the end of the period specified in it. You should apply to the inspector who has issued the
notice if you wish him to consider this, but you must do so before the end of the period given in it.
(Such an application is not an appeal against this notice.)

3 The issue of this notice does not relieve you of any legal liability resting upon you for failure to
comply with any provision of this or any other enactment, before or after the issue of this notice.

4 Your attention is drawn to the provision for appeal against this notice to an Industrial Tribunal.
Details of the method of making an appeal are given below *(see also Section 24 of the Health and
Safety at Work etc. Act 1974).*

(a) Appeal can be entered against this notice to an Industrial Tribunal. The appeal should be
sent to:—

(for England and Wales) The Secretary of the Tribunals
Central Office of the Industrial Tribunals
93 Ebury Bridge Road LONDON SW1W 8RE

(for Scotland) The Secretary of the Tribunals
Central Office of the Industrial Tribunals
Saint Andrew House
141 West Nile Street GLASGOW G1 2RU

(b) The appeal must be commenced by sending in writing to the Secretary of the Tribunals a
notice containing the following particulars:—

(1) The name of the appellant and his address for the service of documents.

(2) The date of the notice or notices appealed against; and the address of the premises or
place concerned.

(3) The name and address *(as shown on the notice)* of the respondent.

(4) Particulars of the requirements or directions appealed against.

(5) The grounds of the appeal.

and A form which may be used for appeal is attached.

(c) Time limit for appeal

A notice of appeal must be sent to the Secretary of the Tribunals within 21 days from the
date of service on the appellant of the notice or notices appealed against, or within such
further period as the tribunal considers reasonable in a case where it is satisfied that it was
not reasonably practicable for the notice of appeal to be presented within the period of
21 days. If posted, the appeal should be sent by recorded delivery.

(d) The entering of an appeal suspends the improvement Notice until the appeal has been
determined, but does not automatically after the date given in this notice by which it must be
determined, but does not automatically after the date given in this notice by which it must be
remedied.

(e) The rules for the hearing of an appeal are given in:

The Industrial Tribunals (Improvement and Prohibition Notices Appeals) (S) 1974
No. 1925) for England and Wales.

and The Industrial Tribunals (Improvement and Prohibition Notices Appeals) (S) 1974
No. 1926) for Scotland.

Figure 6 *Improvement notice*

HEALTH AND SAFETY EXECUTIVE
Health and Safety at Work etc. Act 1974, Sections 22—24

PROHIBITION NOTICE

Serial No. **P** ....

Name and address (See Section 46)

To ....

(a) Delete as necessary   *(a) Trading as* ....

(b) Inspector's full name   **I** *(b)* ....

one of *(c)* ....

(c) Inspector's official designation   of *(d)* .... tel no. ....

(d) Official address   hereby give you notice that I am of the opinion that the following activities,

namely:— ....

....

which are *(a)* being carried on by you/about to be carried on by you/under your control

(e) Location of activity   at *(e)* ....

involve, or will involve *(a)* a risk/an imminent risk of serious personal injury the following statutory

I am further of the opinion that the said matters involve contravention of the following statutory provisions:—

....

....

because ....

....

and I hereby direct that the said activities shall not be carried on by you or under your control *(a)* immediately/after ....

unless the said contraventions and matters included in the schedule, which forms part of this notice, have been remedied.

(f) Date   Signature .... Date ....

being an inspector appointed by an instrument in writing made pursuant to Section 19 of the said Act and entitled to issue this notice.

LP 2
Dd 347139 5000 Pads 2/75 COH

NOTES

1 Failure to comply with a Prohibition Notice is an offence as provided by Section 33 of this Act and renders the offender liable to a fine not exceeding £400 on summary conviction or to an unlimited fine or to imprisonment for a term not exceeding two years or both on conviction on indictment fine and a further fine of not exceeding £50 per day if the offence is continued.

2 An inspector has power to withdraw a notice or to extend the period specified in the notice, before the end of the period specified in it. You should apply to the inspector who has issued the notice if you wish him to consider this, but you must do so before the end of the period given in it. *(Such an application is not an appeal against this notice.)*

3 The issue of this Notice does not relieve you of any legal liability resting upon you for failure to comply with any provision of this or any other enactment, before or after the issue of this notice.

4 Your attention is drawn to the provision for appeal against the notice to an Industrial Tribunal. Details of the method of making an appeal are given below *(see also Section 24 of the Health and Safety at Work etc. Act 1974).*

(a) Appeal can be entered against this notice to an Industrial Tribunal. The appeal should be sent to —

(for England and Wales)   The Secretary of the Tribunals
Central Office of the Industrial Tribunals
93 Ebury Bridge Road LONDON SW1W 8RE

(for Scotland)   The Secretary of the Tribunals
Central Office of the Industrial Tribunals
Saint Andrew House,
141 West Nile Street GLASGOW G1 2RU

(b) The appeal must be commenced by sending in writing to the Secretary of the Tribunals a notice containing the following particulars:—
(1) The name of the appellant and his address for the service of documents.
(2) The date of the notice or notices appealed against and the address of the premises or place concerned.
(3) The name and address *(as shown on the notice)* of the respondent.
(4) Particulars of the requirements or directions appealed against.
(5) The grounds of the appeal.
and   A form which may be used for appeal is attached.

(c) Time limit for appeal

A notice of appeal must be sent to the Secretary of the Tribunals within 21 days from the date of service on the appellant of the notice or notices appealed against, or within such further period as the tribunal considers reasonable in a case where it is satisfied that it was not reasonably practicable for the notice of appeal to be presented within the period of 21 days. If posted the appeal should be sent by recorded delivery.

(d) The entering of an appeal does not have the effect of suspending this notice. Application can be made for the suspension of the notice to the Secretary of the Tribunals, but the notice continues in force until a Tribunal otherwise direct. An application for suspension of the notice must be in writing and must set out —
(a) The case number of the appeal, if known, or particulars sufficient to identify it and
(b) The grounds on which the application is made, it may accompany the appeal.

(e) The rules for the hearing of an appeal are given in —

The Industrial Tribunals (Improvement and Prohibition Notices Appeals) Regulations 1974 (SI 1974 No. 1925) for England and Wales.
and   The Industrial Tribunals (Improvement and Prohibition Notices Appeals) (Scotland) Regulations 1974 (SI 1974 No. 1926) for Scotland.

SPECIMEN

Figure 7   *Prohibition notice*

Health and Safety Executive

F 10
Reprinted December 1979

For official use
Registered..................................
Visited......................................

FACTORIES ACT 1961

Notice of building operations or works of engineering construction*

1	Name of person, firm, or company undertaking the operations or works.	
2	State whether main contractor or sub-contractor.	
3	Trade of the person, firm or company undertaking the operations or works.	
4	Address of registered office (in case of company) or of principal place of business (in other cases).	
5	Address to which communications should be sent (if different from above).	
6	Place where the operations or works are carried on.	
7	Name of Local Government District Council (in Scotland, County Council or Burgh Town Council) within whose district the operations or works are situated.	
8	Telephone No. (if any) of the site.	
9	How many workers are you likely to employ on the site?	
10	Approximate date of commencement.	
11	Probable duration of work.	
12	Is mechanical power being, or to be, used? If so, what is its nature (e.g. electric, steam, gas or oil)?	
13	Nature of operations or works carried on:	

(a) Building operations *(tick items which apply)*

Construction ....
Maintenance ....
Demolition ....

of

Industrial building ....
Commercial or public building ....
Dwellings over 3 storeys ....
Dwellings of 3 storeys or less ....
Others ....

(b) Works of engineering construction *(specify type)*

I hereby give notice that I am undertaking the building operations or works of engineering construction specified above.

Signature Date

NOTE

* Any person undertaking any building operations or works of engineering construction to which the Act applies is required by the Act, not later than seven days after the beginning of any such operations or works, to serve on the Inspector for the district a written notice giving particulars specified in section 127(6) unless (a) they are operations or works which the person undertaking them has reasonable grounds for believing will be completed in less than six weeks, or (b) notice has already been given to the Inspector in respect of building operations or works of engineering construction already in progress at the same place. This form should be filled up and sent to HM Inspector of Factories for the district in which the operations or works are carried on.

572 8033375 200M 12/79 HGW 752

Figure 8 *Notice of building operations*

Health and Safety Executive
Health and Safety at Work etc Act 1974
Reporting of Injuries, Diseases and Dangerous Occurrences Regulations 1985

Spaces below
are for office
use only

Report of an injury or dangerous occurrence

- Full notes to help you complete this form are attached.
- This form is to be used to make a report to the enforcing authority under the requirements of Regulations 3 or 6.
- Completing and signing this form does not constitute an admission of liability of any kind, either by the person making the report or any other person.
- If more than one person was injured as a result of an accident, please complete a separate form for each person.

A   Subject of report *(tick appropriate box or boxes) — see note 2*

Fatality	Specified major injury or condition	"Over three day" injury	Dangerous occurrence	Flammable gas incident (fatality or major injury or condition)	Dangerous gas fitting
1	2	3	4	5	6

B   Person or organisation making report (ie person obliged to report under the Regulations) — *see note 3*

Name and address —

Post code —

Name and telephone no. of person to contact —

Nature of trade, business or undertaking —

If in construction industry, state the total number of your employees —

and indicate the role of your company on site *(tick box)* —

Main site contractor	Sub contractor	Other
7	8	9

If in farming, are you reporting an injury to a member of your family? *(tick box)*

Yes   No

C   Date, time and place of accident, dangerous occurrence or flammable gas incident — *see note 4*

Date   19   Time —
day month year

Give the name and address if different from above —

ENV

Where on the premises or site —
and
Normal activity carried on there

Complete the following sections D, E, F & H if you have ticked boxes, 1, 2, 3 or 5 in Section A. Otherwise go straight to Sections G and H.

D   The injured person — *see note 5*

Full name and address —

Age	Sex	Status *(tick box)* —	Employee	Self employed	Trainee (YTS)
	(M or F)		10	11	12
			Trainee (other) 13	Any other person 14	

Trade, occupation or job title —

Nature of injury or condition and the part of the body affected —

F2508 (rev 1/86)   *continued overleaf*

Figure 9   *Report of accident*

E Kind of accident - *see note 6*

Indicate what kind of accident led to the injury or condition (*tick one box*) —

Contact with moving machinery or material being machined ☐ 1	Injured whilst handling lifting or carrying ☐ 5	Trapped by something collapsing or overturning ☐ 8	Exposure to an explosion ☐ 12
Struck by moving, including flying or falling, object. ☐ 2	Slip, trip or fall on same level ☐ 6	Drowning or asphyxiation ☐ 9	Contact with electricity or an electrical discharge ☐ 13
Struck by moving vehicle ☐ 3	Fall from a height* ☐ 7	Exposure to or contact with a harmful substance ☐ 10	Injured by an animal ☐ 14
Struck against something fixed or stationary ☐ 4	*Distance through which person fell ☐ (metres)	Exposure to fire ☐ 11	Other kind of accident (give details in Section H) ☐ 15

Spaces below are for office use only.

F Agent(s) involved — *see note 7*

Indicate which, if any, of the categories of agent or factor below were involved (*tick one or more of the boxes*) —

Machinery/equipment for lifting and conveying ☐ 1	Process plant, pipework or bulk storage ☐ 5	Live animal ☐ 9	Ladder or scaffolding ☐ 13
Portable power or hand tools ☐ 2	Any material, substance or product being handled, used or stored. ☐ 6	Moveable container or package of any kind ☐ 10	Construction formwork, shuttering and falsework ☐ 14
Any vehicle or associated equipment/machinery ☐ 3	Gas, vapour, dust, fume or oxygen deficient atmosphere ☐ 7	Floor, ground, stairs or any working surface ☐ 11	Electricity supply cable, wiring, apparatus or equipment ☐ 15
Other machinery ☐ 4	Pathogen or infected material ☐ 8	Building, engineering structure or excavation/underground working ☐ 12	Entertainment or sporting facilities or equipment ☐ 16
			Any other agent ☐ 17

Describe briefly the agents or factors you have indicated —

G Dangerous occurrence or dangerous gas fitting — *see notes 8 and 9*

Reference number of dangerous occurrence ☐   Reference number of dangerous gas fitting ☐

H Account of accident, dangerous occurrence or flammable gas incident - *see note 10*

Describe what happened and how. In the case of an accident state what the injured person was doing at the time —

Signature of person making report ☐   Date ☐

Display notices and certificates
Notify relevant authorities
Keep relevant records

Notices and Certificates

An employer must prominently display on site, in the workshop, or in an office where the employees attend, a number of notices and certificates, the main ones being (where applicable):

Copy of the certificate of insurance; this is required under the Employers Liability (Compulsory Insurance) Act 1969

Copy of fire certificate

Abstract of the Factories Act 1961 for building operations and works of engineering constructions (form F3)

Details of the area Health and Safety Executive Inspectorate; the employment medical adviser and the site safety supervisor should be indicated on this form

Abstract of the Offices Shops and Railway Premises Act 1963 (form OSR 9)

The Woodworking Machines Regulations 1974 (form F2470)

The Abrasive Wheels Regulations 1970 (form 2345) and cautionary notice (form 2347)

The Electricity (Factories Act) special regulation 1908 and 1944 (form F 954), electric shock (first aid) placard (form 731)

The Asbestos Regulations 1969 (form F2358)

The Highly Flammable Liquids and Liquified Petroleum Gases Regulations 1972 (form F2440)

Notifications

The following are the main notifications required. They are usually submitted on standard forms obtainable from the relevant authority.

The commencement of building operations or works of engineering construction that are likely to last more than six weeks. See Figure 8.

The employment of persons in an office or shop for more than 21 hours a week.

The employment or transfer of young persons (under 18 years of age) must be notified to the local careers office.

Accidents resulting in death or major injuries or notifiable dangerous occurrences or more than three days absence. See Figure 9. Major injuries can be defined as most fractures, amputations, loss of sight or any other injury involving a stay in a hospital. Many incidents can be defined as notifiable dangerous occurrences, but in general they include the collapse of a crane, hoist, scaffolding or building, an explosion or fire, or the escape of any substance that is liable to cause a health hazard or major injury to any person.

A poisoning or suffocation incident resulting in acute ill health requiring medical treatment.

An application for a fire certificate if required under the fire certificate (special premises regulations).

Records

Employers are required to keep various records. These should be kept ready for inspection on the site or at the place of work and should include:

The general register for building operations and works of engineering construction (form F36). This is used to record details of the site or workshop and the nature of work taking place, any cases of poisoning or disease and the employment and transfer of young persons.

An accident book (form B1 510) in which details of all accidents are recorded. See Figure 10.

A record of accidents, dangerous occurrences and ill-health enquiries (form F2509). Entries in the record must be made whenever the Health and Safety Executive is notified of an accident resulting in death, major injury or a notifiable dangerous occurrence and when enquiries are made by the Department of Health and Social Security concerning claims by employees for industrial diseases.

Register for the purposes of the Abrasive Wheels Regulations 1970 (form F2346). A register used to record details of persons appointed to mount abrasive wheels. See Figure 11.

See Instructions on pages 1 and 2					
ACCIDENT BOOK, as approved by the Secretary of State for Social Services for the purposes of the SOCIAL SECURITY ACT 1975					
Full name, address and occupation of person who suffered an accident	Signature of person making this entry (state address and occupation if different from column (1).)	Date when entry made	Date and time of accident	Room or place in which accident happened	Circumstances of the accident (State clearly the work or process being performed at the time of the accident, and full details of any injury suffered.)
(1)	(2)	(3)	(4)	(5)	(6)

Figure 10   *Accident book*

Records of inspections, examinations and special tests (form 91 part 1). This is a booklet of forms on which details of inspections etc. on scaffolding, excavations, earthworks and lifting appliances must be recorded. See Figure 12 for scaffold form.

Record of reports (form 91 part 11). This provides forms for recording the thorough examination of lifting appliances, hoists, chains, ropes and other lifting gear and also the heat treatment of chains and lifting gear.

Register and certificate of shared welfare arrangements (form F2202). To be completed where an employer, normally the main contractor, provides welfare facilities for another employer (subcontractor).

Certificates of test and examinations of various lifting appliances. These are records of the

PART 2

Appointment of persons to mount abrasive wheels (regulation 9)

APPOINTMENT				REVOCATION	
Name of person appointed	Class or description of abrasive wheels for which appointment is made *(See Note 7)*	Date of appointment	Signature of occupier or his agent	Date of revocation of appointment *(See Note 5)*	Signature of occupier or his agent
(1)	(2)	(3)	(4)	(5)	(6)

3

Figure 11   *Abrasive wheel register*

weekly, monthly or other periodic tests and examinations required by the construction regulations, as follows:

Cranes (form F96)
Hoists (form F75)
Other lifting appliances (form F80)
Wire ropes (form F87)
Chain slings and lifting gear (form F97)

Safety signs

Formerly there were many vastly different safety signs in use. BS 5378: Part 1: 1980: *Safety Signs and Colours* introduced a standard system for giving health and safety information with a minimum use of words. Its purpose is to establish an internationally understood system of safety signs and safety colours which draw attention to objects and situations that do or could affect health and safety. Details of these signs and typical examples of use are given in Table 2.

Accident prevention

It should be the aim of everyone to prevent accidents. Ask yourself the following questions and 'if in doubt find out'. Remember, you are required by law to be aware and fulfil your duties under the Health and Safety at Work etc. Act.

1 Do I know what safety legislation is relevant to my job?
2 Have I received, read and understood my employer's safety policy?

Name or title of employer or contractor	Factories Act 1961		
Address of site	Construction (Working Places) Regulations 1966		SECTION A

Work commenced—Date **SCAFFOLD INSPECTIONS**

Reports of results of inspections under Regulations 22 of scaffolds, including boatswain's chairs, cages, skips and similar plant or equipment (and plant or equipment used for the purposes thereof)

Location and description of scaffold, etc. and other plant or equipment inspected	Date of inspection	Result of inspection State whether in good order	Signature (or, in case where signature is not legally required, name) of person who made the inspection
(1)	(2)	(3)	(4)

NOTES TO SECTION A

(1) *Short check list—at each inspection check that your scaffolding does not have these faults:*

		Week 1 2 3 4			Week 1 2 3 4			Week 1 2 3 4
FOOTINGS	Soft and uneven / No base plates / No sole boards / Undermined		BRACING 'Facade and ledger'	Some missing / Loose / Wrong fittings		TIES	Some missing / Loose	
STANDARDS	Not plumb / Joined at same height / Wrong spacing / Damaged		PUTLOGS and TRANSOMS	Wrongly spaced / Loose / Wrongly supported		BOARDING	Bad boards / Trap boards / Incomplete / Insufficient supports	
			COUPLINGS	Wrong fitting / Loose / Damaged / No check couplers		GUARD RAILS & TOE BOARDS	Wrong height / Loose / Some missing	
LEDGERS	Not level / Joint in same bays / Loose / Damaged		BRIDLES	Wrong spacing / Wrong couplings / Weak support		LADDERS	Damaged / Insufficient length / Not tied	

(2) *This check list is not part of the report required by Regulation 22: see also para 5 of Notes and Regulation 22 on page (ii) of cover and Notes on page 13.*

Figure 12 *Scaffold form*

3 Have I been given all the training and information required to do my job safely?

4 Am I aware of the hazards involved in my particular job?

5 Am I aware of the hazards involved with using particular materials?

6 Do I know what protective equipment is required for a particular operation? Have I been issued with it and do I wear it?

7 Do I understand the meaning of the safety signs that I come into contact with?

8 Do I always work in the safest possible way?

Self-assessment questions

1 What information must be recorded in the general register?

2 List the main powers of the health and safety inspector.

3 Explain the meaning of:
(i) Outline planning permission
(ii) Full planning permission

4 Briefly define the need for planning controls.

5 List *four* building stages when the builder must forward inspection notices to the local authority.

6 Give examples of *two* situations where Building Regulations approval will be required.

Table 2   **Safety signs**

Purpose	Sign	Definition	Examples of use
Prohibition	white — red	A sign prohibiting certain behaviour	No smoking; Smoking and naked flames prohibited; Do not extinguish with water; Not drinking water; Pedestrians prohibited
Caution	yellow — black	A sign giving warning of certain hazards	Caution, risk of fire; Caution, toxic hazard; Caution, corrosive substance; General warning caution, risk of danger; Caution, risk of electric shock; Perimeter of hazard
Safe condition	green	A sign providing information about safe conditions	First aid; Indication of direction; Indication of direction

Mandatory

blue

A sign indicating that
a special course of
action is required

 Head protection
must be worn

 Eye protection
must be worn

 Hearing protection
must be worn

 Foot protection
must be worn

 Hand protection
must be worn

Respiratory protection
must be worn

Supplementary

white or colour of sign
it is supporting

A sign with text.
Can be used in con-
junction with a safety
sign to provide addi-
tional information.

IMPORTANT
REPORT ALL
ACCIDENTS
IMMEDIATELY

SCAFFOLDING
INCOMPLETE

SAFETY HELMETS
ARE PROVIDED FOR
YOUR SAFETY
AND MUST BE WORN

PETROLEUM MIXTURE
HIGHLY FLAMMABLE
NO SMOKING OR
NAKED LIGHTS

WARNING
HIGH VOLTAGE
CABLES
OVERHEAD

 EYE WASH
BOTTLE

7 Describe the purpose of a prohibition notice.

8 List *two* duties under the Health and Safety at Work etc. Act of each of the following:
(a) Employers
(b) Employees

9 Explain briefly what is meant by a notifiable dangerous occurrence and state to whom it should be reported.

10 Name the statutory document applicable to each of the following:
(a) Provision of site accommodation
(b) Machinery in a joiner's shop
(c) Scaffolding
(d) First-aid requirements

Building administration

After reading this chapter the student should be able to:

1 Specify the necessary procedures both prior to and during building operations.

2 Name, state the purpose of, and interpret various contract documents.

3 State the purpose of and describe the preparation of various site records and reports.

4 Outline the main employment conditions applicable to the industry.

Contract procedures

The first step in building projects is for a prospective building client to appoint an architect to act for him in the construction or alteration of a building. On being appointed the architect will obtain from the client a brief, consisting of full details of his requirements and the proposed site. Having inspected the site and assessed the feasibility of the client's requirements, the architect will prepare sketch designs and submit them to the client for approval and apply for outline planning permission.

When approval is obtained, a design team consisting of the architect, a structural engineer, a services engineer and a quantity surveyor is formed. This team will consider the brief and sketch designs and come up with proposals that will form the basis of the structure. Location drawings, outline specifications and preliminary details of costs are then produced and are submitted to the client for approval. If these details are acceptable, applications will be made for full planning permission and Building Regulations approval. When these approvals have been obtained, contract documents will be prepared and sent to a number of building contractors for them to produce and submit tenders. The returned tenders will be considered by the quantity surveyor who will advise the architect and client of the most suitable contractor. The client and contractor will then sign the contract.

Contract documents

These documents will vary depending on the nature of the work, but will normally consist of:

Working drawings
Specification
Schedules
Bill of quantities
Conditions of contract

Working drawings

These are scale drawings showing the plans, elevations, sections, details and locality of the proposed construction. These drawings can be divided into a number of main types:

Location drawings (Figure 13)
Block plans, scale 1:2500, 1:1250, identify the proposed site in relation to the surrounding area.
Site plans, scale 1:500, 1:200, give the position of the proposed building and the general layout of roads, services and drainage etc. on the site.
General location plans (Figure 14), scale 1:200, 1:100, 1:50, show the position occupied by the various areas within the building and identify the location of the principal elements and components.

Component drawings
Range drawings (Figure 15), scale 1:100, 1:50, 1:20, show the basic sizes and reference system of a standard range of components.

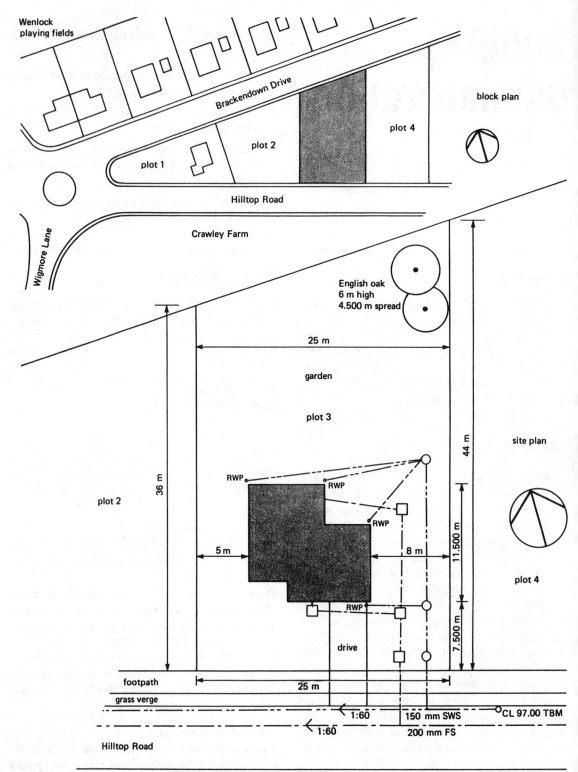

Figure 13   *Location drawings*

NOTES

end elevation

front elevation

rear elevation

section

bath | bed 1
garage | WC | hall | living

dining | kitchen

hall

living | WC | garage

ground floor plan

bed 2 | bed 3

bed 1 | cupbd | bath

first floor plan

BBS DESIGN

JOB TITLE
PLOT 3 HILLTOP ROAD
DRAWING TITLE
GENERAL LOCATION

JOB No.	DRAWING No.
41/83	3/41

SCALE	DATE	DRAWN	CHECK
1:100	20/7	P₃B	CAB

Figure 14 *General location plans*

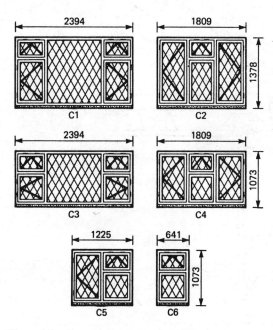

Figure 15 *Component range drawing*

Detail drawings (Figure 16), scale 1:10, 1:5, 1:1, show all the information that is required in order to manufacture a particular component.

Assembly drawings
Assembly details (Figure 17), scale 1:20, 1:10, 1:5, show in detail the junctions in and between the various elements and components of a building.

Note: All working drawings should be produced in accordance with the recommendations contained in BS 1192: *Construction Drawing Practice*.

Specification
Except in the case of very small building works the drawings cannot contain all the information required by the builder, particularly concerning the required standards of materials and workmanship. For this purpose the architect will prepare a document, called the specification, to supplement the working drawings. The speci-

Figure 16   *Component detail drawing*

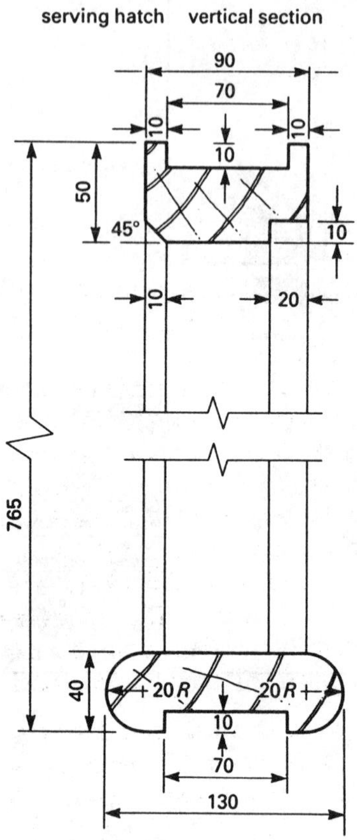

serving hatch   vertical section

fication is a precise description of all the essential information and job requirements that will affect the price of the work but cannot be shown on the drawings. Typical items included in specifications are:

1   Site description
2   Restrictions (limited access and working hours etc.)
3   Availability of services (water, electricity, gas, telephone)
4   Description of materials, quality, size, tolerance and finish
5   Description of workmanship, quality, fixing and jointing
6   Other requirements: site clearance, making good on completion, nominated suppliers and subcontractors, who passes the work etc.

Various clauses of a typical specification are shown in Figure 18.

Figure 17   *Assembly details*

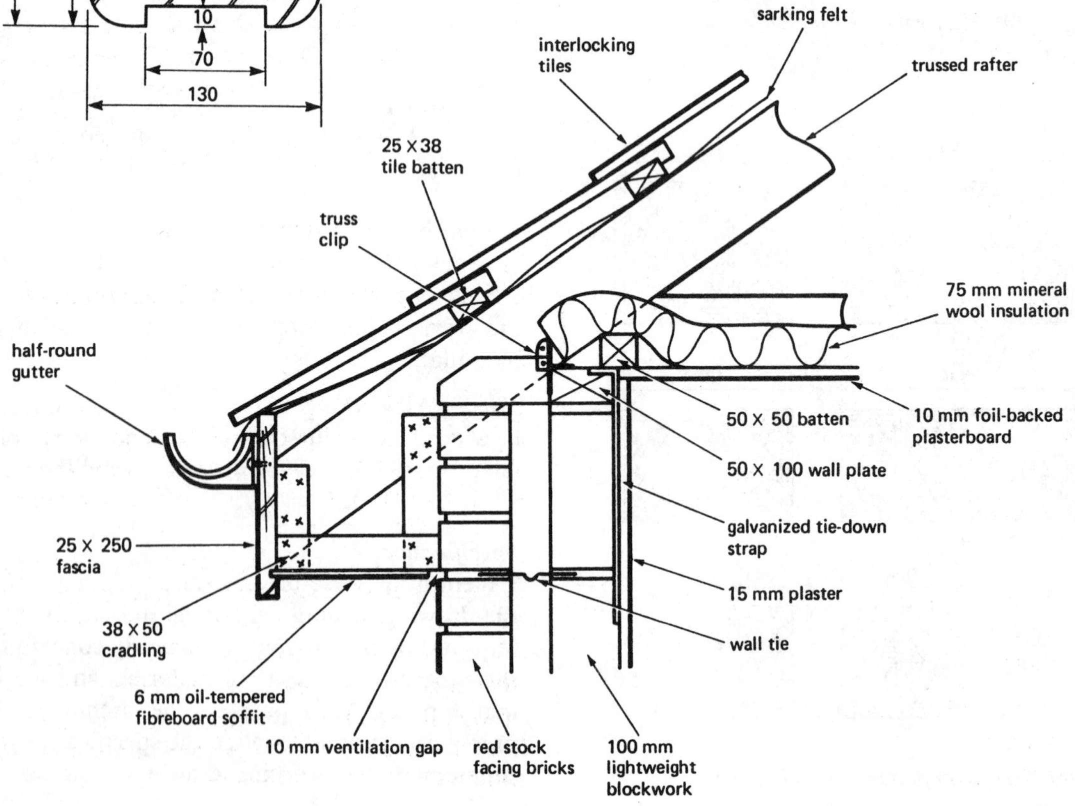

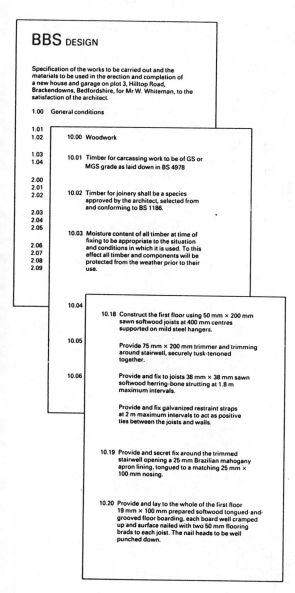

BBS DESIGN

Specification of the works to be carried out and the materials to be used in the erection and completion of a new house and garage on plot 3, Hilltop Road, Brackendowns, Bedfordshire, for Mr W. Whiteman, to the satisfaction of the architect.

1.00 General conditions

1.01
1.02
1.03
1.04

2.00
2.01
2.02
2.03
2.04
2.05
2.06
2.07
2.08
2.09

10.00 Woodwork

10.01 Timber for carcassing work to be of GS or MGS grade as laid down in BS 4978

10.02 Timber for joinery shall be a species approved by the architect, selected from and conforming to BS 1186.

10.03 Moisture content of all timber at time of fixing to be appropriate to the situation and conditions in which it is used. To this effect all timber and components will be protected from the weather prior to their use.

10.04
10.05
10.06

10.18 Construct the first floor using 50 mm × 200 mm sawn softwood joists at 400 mm centres supported on mild steel hangers.

Provide 75 mm × 200 mm trimmer and trimming around stairwell, securely tusk-tenoned together.

Provide and fix to joists 38 mm × 38 mm sawn softwood herring-bone strutting at 1.8 m maximum intervals.

Provide and fix galvanized restraint straps at 2 m maximum intervals to act as positive ties between the joists and walls.

10.19 Provide and secret fix around the trimmed stairwell opening a 25 mm Brazilian mahogany apron lining, tongued to a matching 25 mm × 100 mm nosing.

10.20 Provide and lay to the whole of the first floor 19 mm × 100 mm prepared softwood tongued-and-grooved floor boarding, each board well cramped up and surface nailed with two 50 mm flooring brads to each joist. The nail heads to be well punched down.

Figure 18 *Extracts from a specification*

Schedules

These are used to record repetitive design information about a range of similar components. The main areas where schedules are used includes:

1 Doors, frames, linings
2 Windows
3 Ironmongery
4 Joinery fitments
5 Sanitary ware, drainage
6 Heating units, radiators
7 Finishes, floor, wall, ceiling
8 Lintels
9 Steel reinforcement

The information that schedules contain is essential when preparing estimates and tenders. In addition, schedules are also extremely useful when measuring quantities, locating work and checking deliveries of materials and components.

Obtaining information from a schedule about any particular item is fairly straightforward. For example, the range drawing, floor plans and door schedules shown in Figures 19, 20 and 21 are consulted. Details relevant to a particular door opening are indicated in the schedules by a dot or cross; a figure is also included where more than one item is required. The following information concerning the WC door D2 has been extracted or 'taken off' from the schedules:

One polished plywood internal flush door type B2 762 mm × 1981 mm × 35 mm hung on 38 mm × 125 mm softwood lining with planted stops, transom and 6 mm obscure tempered safety glass fanlight infill, including the following ironmongery:

One pair of 75 mm brass butts
One mortise lock/latch
One brass mortise lock/latch furniture and
Two brass coat hooks

Bill of quantities

The bill of quantities (BoQ) is prepared by the quantity surveyor. This document gives a complete description and measure of the quantities of labour, material and other items required to carry out the work, based on drawings, specification and schedules. Its use ensures that all estimators prepare their tender on the same information. An added advantage is that as each individual item is priced in the tender they can be used for valuing the work in progress and also form the basis for valuing any variation to the contract.

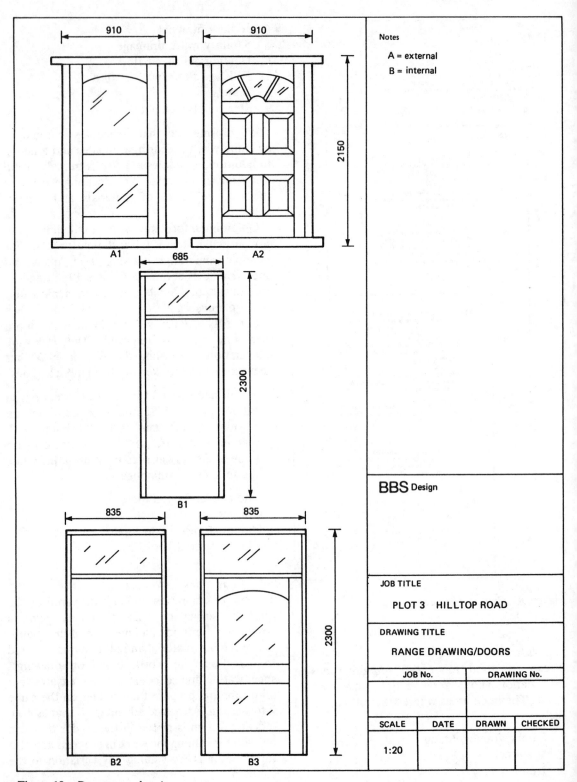

Figure 19   *Door range drawing*

Mandatory

blue

A sign indicating that a special course of action is required

 Head protection must be worn

 Eye protection must be worn

 Hearing protection must be worn

Foot protection must be worn

Hand protection must be worn

Respiratory protection must be worn

Supplementary

white or colour of sign it is supporting

A sign with text. Can be used in conjunction with a safety sign to provide additional information.

 IMPORTANT REPORT ALL ACCIDENTS IMMEDIATELY

SCAFFOLDING INCOMPLETE

 SAFETY HELMETS ARE PROVIDED FOR YOUR SAFETY AND MUST BE WORN

PETROLEUM MIXURE HIGHLY FLAMMABLE NO SMOKING OR NAKED LIGHTS

WARNING HIGH VOLTAGE CABLES OVERHEAD

 EYE WASH BOTTLE

  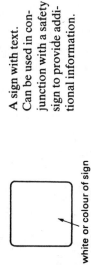

7 Describe the purpose of a prohibition notice.

8 List *two* duties under the Health and Safety at Work etc. Act of each of the following:
   (a) Employers
   (b) Employees

9 Explain briefly what is meant by a notifiable dangerous occurrence and state to whom it should be reported.

10 Name the statutory document applicable to each of the following:
    (a) Provision of site accommodation
    (b) Machinery in a joiner's shop
    (c) Scaffolding
    (d) First-aid requirements

chapter 3

Building administration

After reading this chapter the student should be able to:

1 Specify the necessary procedures both prior to and during building operations.

2 Name, state the purpose of, and interpret various contract documents.

3 State the purpose of and describe the preparation of various site records and reports.

4 Outline the main employment conditions applicable to the industry.

Contract procedures

The first step in building projects is for a prospective building client to appoint an architect to act for him in the construction or alteration of a building. On being appointed the architect will obtain from the client a brief, consisting of full details of his requirements and the proposed site. Having inspected the site and assessed the feasibility of the client's requirements, the architect will prepare sketch designs and submit them to the client for approval and apply for outline planning permission.

When approval is obtained, a design team consisting of the architect, a structural engineer, a services engineer and a quantity surveyor is formed. This team will consider the brief and sketch designs and come up with proposals that will form the basis of the structure. Location drawings, outline specifications and preliminary details of costs are then produced and are submitted to the client for approval. If these details are acceptable, applications will be made for full planning permission and Building Regulations approval. When these approvals have been obtained, contract documents will be prepared and sent to a number of building contractors for them to produce and submit tenders. The returned tenders will be considered by the quantity surveyor who will advise the architect and client of the most suitable contractor. The client and contractor will then sign the contract.

Contract documents

These documents will vary depending on the nature of the work, but will normally consist of:

Working drawings
Specification
Schedules
Bill of quantities
Conditions of contract

Working drawings

These are scale drawings showing the plans, elevations, sections, details and locality of the proposed construction. These drawings can be divided into a number of main types:

Location drawings (Figure 13)
Block plans, scale 1:2500, 1:1250, identify the proposed site in relation to the surrounding area.
Site plans, scale 1:500, 1:200, give the position of the proposed building and the general layout of roads, services and drainage etc. on the site.
General location plans (Figure 14), scale 1:200, 1:100, 1:50, show the position occupied by the various areas within the building and identify the location of the principal elements and components.

Component drawings
Range drawings (Figure 15), scale 1:100, 1:50, 1:20, show the basic sizes and reference system of a standard range of components.

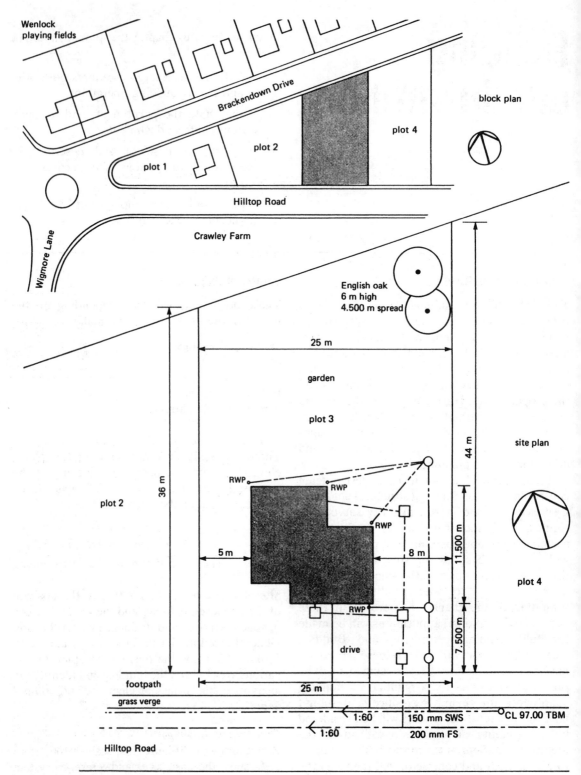

Figure 13   *Location drawings*

NOTES

BBS DESIGN

JOB TITLE
PLOT 3 HILLTOP ROAD

DRAWING TITLE
GENERAL LOCATION

JOB No.	DRAWING No.
41/83	3/41

SCALE	DATE	DRAWN	CHECK
1:100	20/7	PₒB	CAB

end elevation · front elevation · rear elevation · section · ground floor plan · first floor plan

Figure 14   *General location plans*

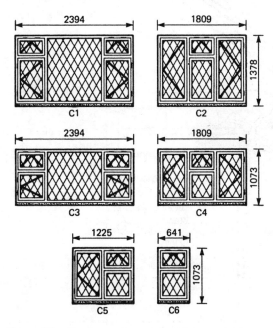

Figure 15   *Component range drawing*

Detail drawings (Figure 16), scale 1:10, 1:5, 1:1, show all the information that is required in order to manufacture a particular component.

Assembly drawings

Assembly details (Figure 17), scale 1:20, 1:10, 1:5, show in detail the junctions in and between the various elements and components of a building.

Note: All working drawings should be produced in accordance with the recommendations contained in BS 1192: *Construction Drawing Practice*.

Specification

Except in the case of very small building works the drawings cannot contain all the information required by the builder, particularly concerning the required standards of materials and workmanship. For this purpose the architect will prepare a document, called the specification, to supplement the working drawings. The speci-

Figure 16   *Component detail drawing*

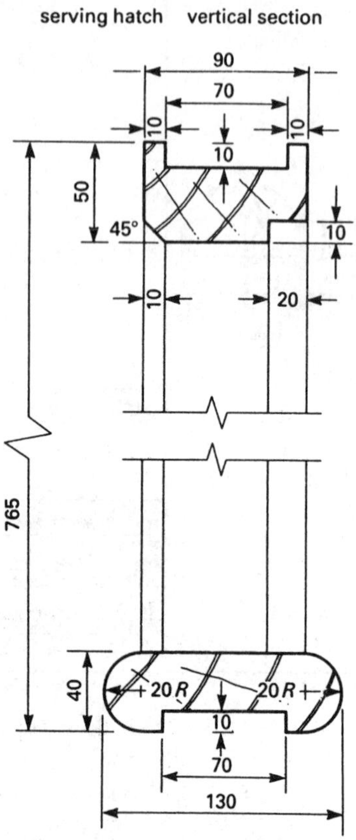

serving hatch   vertical section

fication is a precise description of all the essential information and job requirements that will affect the price of the work but cannot be shown on the drawings. Typical items included in specifications are:

1 Site description
2 Restrictions (limited access and working hours etc.)
3 Availability of services (water, electricity, gas, telephone)
4 Description of materials, quality, size, tolerance and finish
5 Description of workmanship, quality, fixing and jointing
6 Other requirements: site clearance, making good on completion, nominated suppliers and subcontractors, who passes the work etc.

Various clauses of a typical specification are shown in Figure 18.

Figure 17   *Assembly details*

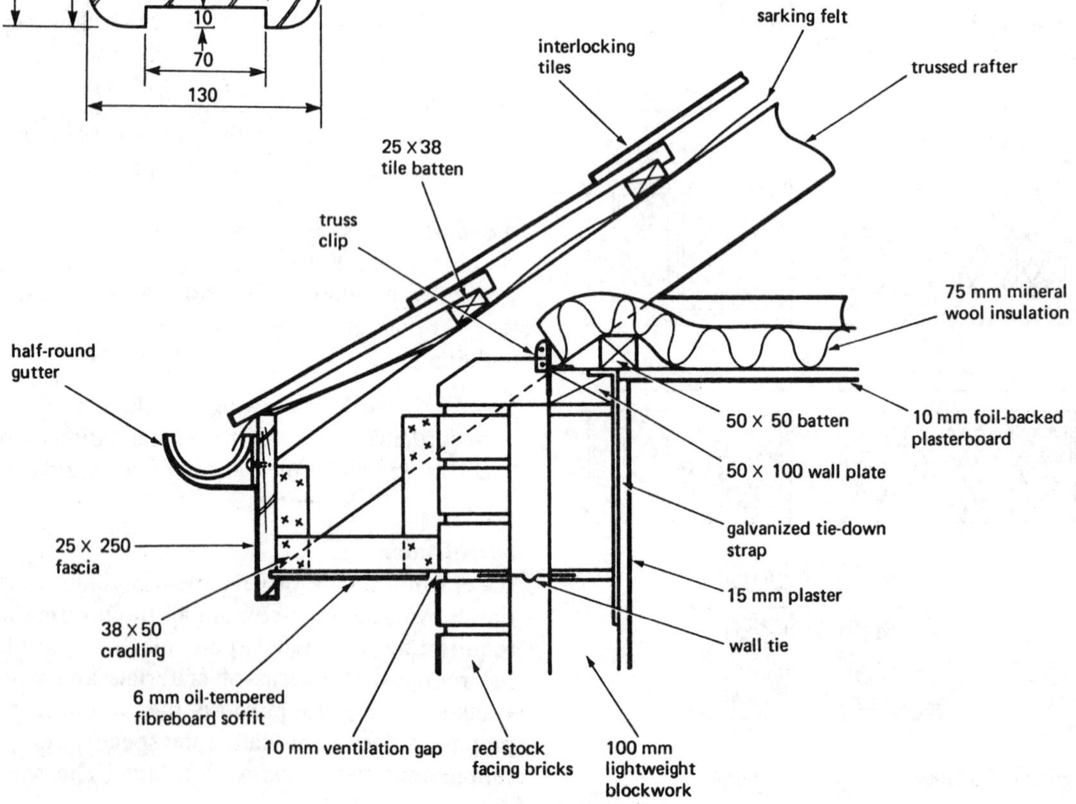

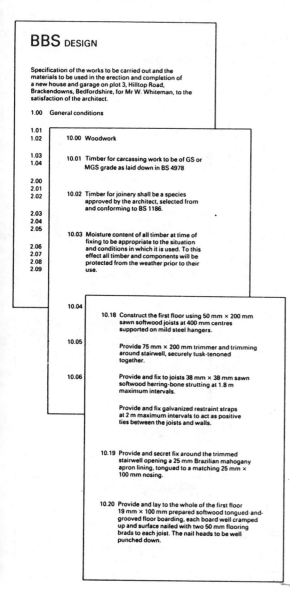

BBS DESIGN

Specification of the works to be carried out and the materials to be used in the erection and completion of a new house and garage on plot 3, Hilltop Road, Brackendowns, Bedfordshire, for Mr W. Whiteman, to the satisfaction of the architect.

1.00   General conditions

1.01
1.02

1.03
1.04

2.00
2.01
2.02

2.03
2.04
2.05

2.06
2.07
2.08
2.09

10.00 Woodwork

10.01 Timber for carcassing work to be of GS or MGS grade as laid down in BS 4978

10.02 Timber for joinery shall be a species approved by the architect, selected from and conforming to BS 1186.

10.03 Moisture content of all timber at time of fixing to be appropriate to the situation and conditions in which it is used. To this effect all timber and components will be protected from the weather prior to their use.

10.04

10.05

10.06

10.18 Construct the first floor using 50 mm × 200 mm sawn softwood joists at 400 mm centres supported on mild steel hangers.

Provide 75 mm × 200 mm trimmer and trimming around stairwell, securely tusk-tenoned together.

Provide and fix to joists 38 mm × 38 mm sawn softwood herring-bone strutting at 1.8 m maximum intervals.

Provide and fix galvanized restraint straps at 2 m maximum intervals to act as positive ties between the joists and walls.

10.19 Provide and secret fix around the trimmed stairwell opening a 25 mm Brazilian mahogany apron lining, tongued to a matching 25 mm × 100 mm nosing.

10.20 Provide and lay to the whole of the first floor 19 mm × 100 mm prepared softwood tongued-and-grooved floor boarding, each board well cramped up and surface nailed with two 50 mm flooring brads to each joist. The nail heads to be well punched down.

Figure 18   *Extracts from a specification*

Schedules

These are used to record repetitive design information about a range of similar components. The main areas where schedules are used includes:

1 Doors, frames, linings
2 Windows
3 Ironmongery
4 Joinery fitments
5 Sanitary ware, drainage
6 Heating units, radiators
7 Finishes, floor, wall, ceiling
8 Lintels
9 Steel reinforcement

The information that schedules contain is essential when preparing estimates and tenders. In addition, schedules are also extremely useful when measuring quantities, locating work and checking deliveries of materials and components.

Obtaining information from a schedule about any particular item is fairly straightforward. For example, the range drawing, floor plans and door schedules shown in Figures 19, 20 and 21 are consulted. Details relevant to a particular door opening are indicated in the schedules by a dot or cross; a figure is also included where more than one item is required. The following information concerning the WC door D2 has been extracted or 'taken off' from the schedules:

One polished plywood internal flush door type B2 762 mm × 1981 mm × 35 mm hung on 38 mm × 125 mm softwood lining with planted stops, transom and 6 mm obscure tempered safety glass fanlight infill, including the following ironmongery:

One pair of 75 mm brass butts
One mortise lock/latch
One brass mortise lock/latch furniture and
Two brass coat hooks

Bill of quantities

The bill of quantities (BoQ) is prepared by the quantity surveyor. This document gives a complete description and measure of the quantities of labour, material and other items required to carry out the work, based on drawings, specification and schedules. Its use ensures that all estimators prepare their tender on the same information. An added advantage is that as each individual item is priced in the tender they can be used for valuing the work in progress and also form the basis for valuing any variation to the contract.

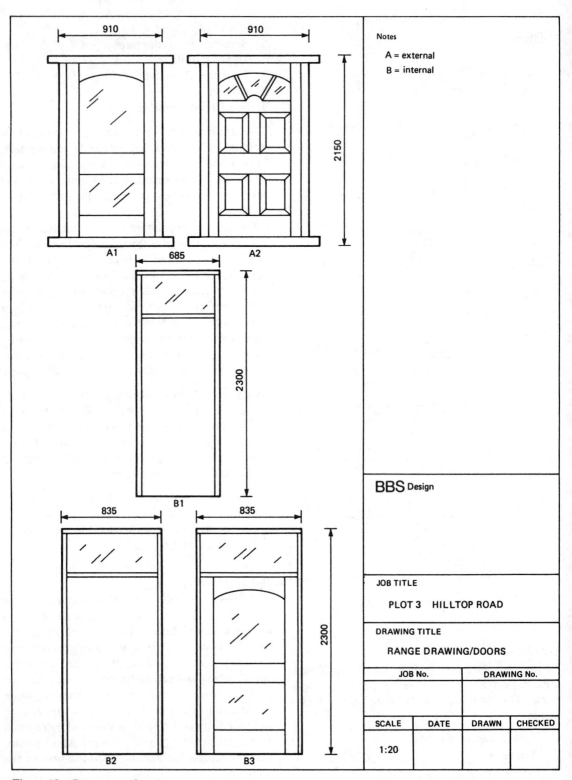

Notes

A = external

B = internal

BBS Design

JOB TITLE

PLOT 3   HILLTOP ROAD

DRAWING TITLE

RANGE DRAWING/DOORS

JOB No.		DRAWING No.	

SCALE	DATE	DRAWN	CHECKED
1:20			

Figure 19   *Door range drawing*

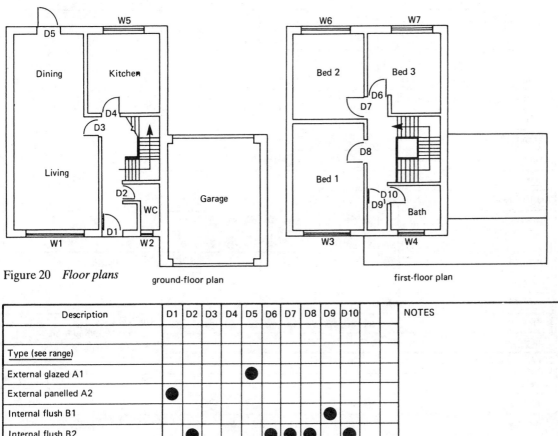

Figure 20   *Floor plans*   ground-floor plan   first-floor plan

Description	D1	D2	D3	D4	D5	D6	D7	D8	D9	D10		NOTES
Type (see range)												
External glazed A1					●							
External panelled A2	●											
Internal flush B1									●			
Internal flush B2		●				●	●	●		●		
Internal glazed B3			●	●								
Size												
813 mm × 2032 mm × 44 mm	●				●							
762 mm × 1981 mm × 35 mm		●	●	●		●	●	●		●		
610 mm × 1981 mm × 35 mm									●			
Material												BBS DESIGN
Hardwood	●											
Softwood			●	●	●							
Plywood/polished		●										
plywood/painted						●	●	●	●	●		JOB TITLE PLOT 3 Hilltop Road
												DRAWING TITLE Door Schedule/doors
Infill												JOB NO. DRAWING NO.
6 mm tempered safety glass												
clear			●	●	●							
obscured	●											SCALE DATE DRAWN CHECKED

Figure 21   *Door schedules*

continued over page

TURN TO PAGE 96

Description	D1	D2	D3	D4	D5	D6	D7	D8	D9	D10
Frames										
75 mm × 100 mm (outward opening)				●						
75 mm × 100 mm (inward opening)	●									
Linings										
38 mm × 125 mm		●	●	●						
38 mm × 100 mm						●	●	●	●	●
Shape										
Rebated stop	●				●					
Planted stop		●	●	●		●	●	●	●	●
Transom		●	●	●		●	●	●	●	●
Sill	●				●					
Material										
Hardwood	●									
Softwood		●	●	●	●	●	●	●	●	●
Fanlight infill										
6 mm tempered safety glass										
clear										
obscured		●							●	
6 mm plywood								●		

BBS DESIGN

JOB TITLE — PLOT 3 Hilltop Road
DRAWING TITLE — Door Schedule/frames/lining
JOB NO. | DRAWING NO.
SCALE | DATE | DRAWN | CHECKED

Figure 21 *Door schedules — continued*

All bills of quantities will contain the following information:

Preliminaries These deal with the general particulars of the work, such as the names of the parties involved, details of the works, description of the site and conditions of the contract etc.

Preambles These are introductory clauses to each trade covering descriptions of the material and workmanship similar to those stated in the specifications.

Measured quantities A description and measurement of an item of work, the measurement being given in metres run, metres square, kilograms etc. or just enumerated as appropriate.

Provisional quantities Where an item cannot be accurately measured, an approximate quantity to be allowed for can be stated. Adjustments will be made when the full extent of the work is known.

Prime cost sum (PC sum) This is an amount of money to be included in the tender for work services or materials provided by a nominated subcontractor, supplier or statutory body.

Provisional sum A sum of money to be included in the tender for work which has not yet been finally detailed or for a 'contingency sum' to cover the cost of any unforeseen work.

Extracts from a typical bill of quantities are shown in Figure 22.

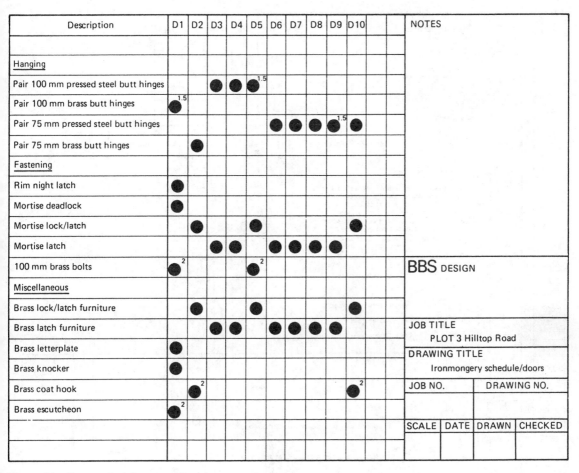

Description	D1	D2	D3	D4	D5	D6	D7	D8	D9	D10		
Hanging												
Pair 100 mm pressed steel butt hinges		●	●	●1.5								
Pair 100 mm brass butt hinges	●1.5											
Pair 75 mm pressed steel butt hinges						●	●	●	●1.5	●		
Pair 75 mm brass butt hinges		●										
Fastening												
Rim night latch	●											
Mortise deadlock	●											
Mortise lock/latch			●		●					●		
Mortise latch				●	●		●	●	●	●		
100 mm brass bolts	●2				●2							
Miscellaneous												
Brass lock/latch furniture			●		●					●		
Brass latch furniture				●	●		●	●	●			
Brass letterplate	●											
Brass knocker	●											
Brass coat hook		●2								●2		
Brass escutcheon	●2											

NOTES

BBS DESIGN

JOB TITLE — PLOT 3 Hilltop Road

DRAWING TITLE — Ironmongery schedule/doors

JOB NO. | DRAWING NO.

SCALE | DATE | DRAWN | CHECKED

Figure 21 *Door schedules – continued*

Standard method of measurement

In order to ensure that the bill of quantities is readily understood and interpreted in a consistent manner by all concerned, the various items should be described and measured in accordance with the latest edition of the *Standard Method of Measurement of Building Works* (SMM). This document, prepared by The Royal Institution of Chartered Surveyors and the Building Employers' Confederation, provides a uniform basis for measuring building work and it embodies the essentials of good practice.

The main requirements of the SMM as far as the carpenter and joiner is concerned are as follows:

Carcassing All carcassing timber, for example, joists, plates, studs, rafters and firrings etc. shall be given in metres run, stating the cross-section dimensions.

First fixing Boarding, sheeting and cladding shall be described, stating width, thickness, the method of jointing and fixing and given in square metres. Studs, plates and grounds etc. shall be given in metres run stating the cross-section dimensions.

Second fixing Unframed second-fixing items such as skirting, picture rails, dado rails, architraves, cover fillets, stops, glazing beads, window boards, shelves, worktops and handrails shall be given in metres run, stating the cross-section dimensions.

Composite items This means all items which

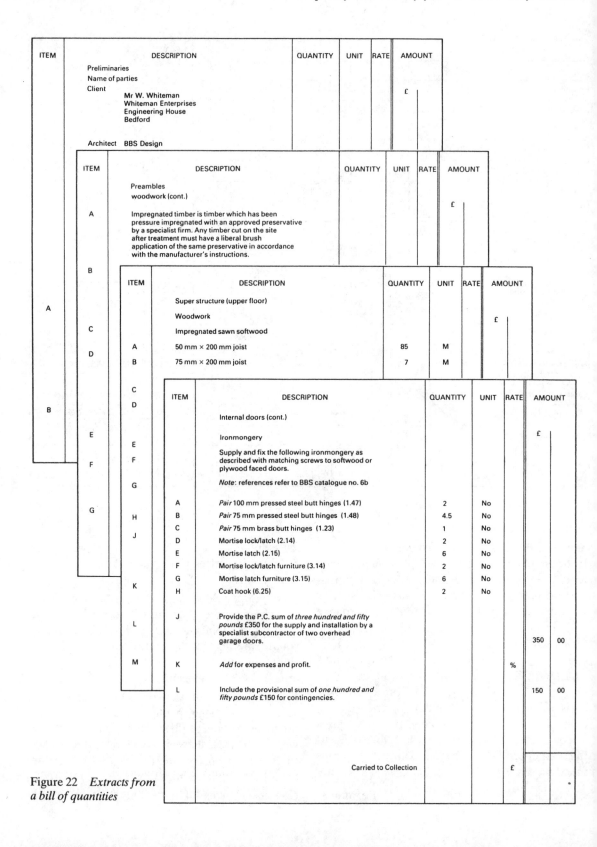

The bill of quantities consists of several overlapping sheets. The details are as follows:

Sheet 1

ITEM	DESCRIPTION	QUANTITY	UNIT	RATE	AMOUNT
	Preliminaries				£
	Name of parties				
	Client				
	Mr W. Whiteman				
	Whiteman Enterprises				
	Engineering House				
	Bedford				
	Architect BBS Design				
A					
B					

Sheet 2

ITEM	DESCRIPTION	QUANTITY	UNIT	RATE	AMOUNT
	Preambles				£
	woodwork (cont.)				
A	Impregnated timber is timber which has been pressure impregnated with an approved preservative by a specialist firm. Any timber cut on the site after treatment must have a liberal brush application of the same preservative in accordance with the manufacturer's instructions.				
B					
C					
D					
E					
F					
G					

Sheet 3

ITEM	DESCRIPTION	QUANTITY	UNIT	RATE	AMOUNT
	Super structure (upper floor)				£
	Woodwork				
	Impregnated sawn softwood				
A	50 mm × 200 mm joist	85	M		
B	75 mm × 200 mm joist	7	M		
C					
D					
E					
F					
G					
H					
J					
K					
L					
M					

Sheet 4

ITEM	DESCRIPTION	QUANTITY	UNIT	RATE	AMOUNT
	Internal doors (cont.)				£
	Ironmongery				
	Supply and fix the following ironmongery as described with matching screws to softwood or plywood faced doors.				
	Note: references refer to BBS catalogue no. 6b				
A	*Pair* 100 mm pressed steel butt hinges (1.47)	2	No		
B	*Pair* 75 mm pressed steel butt hinges (1.48)	4.5	No		
C	*Pair* 75 mm brass butt hinges (1.23)	1	No		
D	Mortise lock/latch (2.14)	2	No		
E	Mortise latch (2.15)	6	No		
F	Mortise lock/latch furniture (3.14)	2	No		
G	Mortise latch furniture (3.15)	6	No		
H	Coat hook (6.25)	2	No		
J	Provide the P.C. sum of *three hundred and fifty pounds* £350 for the supply and installation by a specialist subcontractor of two overhead garage doors.				350 00
K	*Add* for expenses and profit.			%	
L	Include the provisional sum of *one hundred and fifty pounds* £150 for contingencies.				150 00
	Carried to Collection			£	

Figure 22   *Extracts from a bill of quantities*

are fabricated or partly fabricated off-site. Where an item requires assembly or other works on-site this should be included in its description.

Trussed rafters and roof trusses These should be described, enumerated and accompanied by component details.

Doors Doors shall be described and enumerated, double or multileave doors being counted according to the number of leaves.

Door frames and linings Group these together, stating the number required. Numbers of jambs, heads, sills, mullions and transoms should be stated along with their description, metres run and cross-section dimensions.

Windows These should be described, enumerated and accompanied by component details.

Staircases and balustrades These should be described, enumerated and accompanied by component details.

Fittings Fittings should be described, enumerated and accompanied by component details.

Ironmongery Each unit or set should be enumerated separately. In all cases particulars of the following must be given:

Kind and quality
Surface finish
Constituent parts of a unit or set
Material to which item is to be fixed
Constraints in respect of fixing

Sundries All other items not mentioned should be described and enumerated and, where applicable, given in square metres or metres run and cross-section dimensions etc.

Conditions of contract

Most building work is carried out under a 'standard form of contract' such as the Joint Contractors Tribunal (JCT) forms of contract or the Building Employers' Confederation (BEC) form of contract. The actual standard form of contract used will depend on the following:

Type of client (local authority, public limited company or private individual)
Size and type of work (subcontract, small or major project, package deal)

Contract documents (with or without quantities or approximate quantities).

A building contract is basically a legal agreement between the parties involved in which the contractor agrees to carry out the building work and the client agrees to pay a sum of money for the work. The contract should also include the rights and obligations of all parties and details of procedures for variations, interim payments retention and the defects liability period.

These terms can be defined as follows:

Variations A modification of the specification by the client or architect. The contractor must be issued with a written variation order or architect's instruction. Any cost adjustment as a result of the variation must be agreed between the quantity surveyor and the contractor.

Interim payment A monthly or periodic payment made to the contractor by the client. It is based on the quantity surveyor's interim valuation of the work done and the materials purchased by the contractor. On agreeing the interim valuation the architect will issue an interim certificate which authorizes the client to make the payment.

Final account Final payment on completion. The architect will issue a certificate of practical completion when the building work is finished. The quantity surveyor and the contractor will then agree the final account less the retention.

Retention A sum of money which is retained by the client until the end of an agreed defects liability period.

Defects liability period A period of normally six months after practical completion to allow any defects to become apparent. The contractor will be entitled to the retention after any defects have been rectified to the architect's satisfaction.

Work programming

On obtaining a contract for a building project a contractor will prepare a programme which shows the sequence of work activities. In some cases an architect may stipulate that a programme of work is submitted by the contractor at the time of tendering; this gives the architect a measure of the contractor's organizing ability.

A programme will show the interrelationship between the different tasks and also when and for what duration resources such as materials, equipment and workforce are required. Once under way the progress of the actual work can be compared with the target times contained in a programme. If the target times are realistic, a programme can be a source of motivation for the site management who will make every effort to stick to the programme and retrieve lost ground when required. There are a number of factors, some outside the management's control, which could lead to a programme modification. These factors include: bad weather; labour shortages; strikes; late material deliveries; variations to contract; lack of specialist information; bad planning and bad site management etc. Therefore when determining the length of a contract the contractor will normally make an addition of about 10 per cent to the target completion date to allow for such eventualities.

Note: Contracts that run over the completion date involve extra costs, loss of profit and often time penalty payments.

There are a number of different ways in which a programme can be produced and displayed. These include:

Bar charts
Line of balance charts
Critical path diagrams
Procedure diagrams

The most widely used and popular as far as the building contractor is concerned are the bar or Gantt charts. These charts are probably the most simple to use and understand.

They are drawn up with the individual tasks listed in a vertical column on the left-hand side of the sheet and a horizontal time scale along the top. The target times of the individual tasks are shown by a horizontal bar. A second horizontal bar is shaded in to show the work progress and the actual time taken for each task. Plant and labour requirements are often included along the bottom of the sheet. A typical bar/Gantt chart is shown in Figure 23. In addition to their use as an overall contract programme, bar charts can be used for short-term, weekly and monthly plans.

Site layout

A building site can be seen as a temporary workshop and store from which the building contractor will erect the building. Site layouts can be planned on a pinboard using cardboard cutouts held with map pins to represent the various requirements. The cutouts can then be moved around until a satisfactory layout is achieved. See Figure 24 for a typical layout. A satisfactory layout is one which minimizes the movement of operatives, materials and plant during the course of construction while at the same time providing protection and security for materials.

Points to bear in mind when planning the layout are as follows:

1   Site accommodation must comply with the requirements of the HASAWA Construction Regulations (health and welfare) and the National Working Rules for the building industry.
2   Materials storage areas should be convenient to the site access and the building itself. Different materials have differing requirements. For example, timber in general should be stacked in 'stick' clear of the ground and covered with a tarpaulin; kiln-dried timber should be in a heated store; cement in a dry store; frames, pipes and drains etc. in a locked compound; and ironmongery, copper pipe, plumbing and electrical fittings in a locked secure store.
3   Consider phased deliveries of materials. It is often impossible to store on site the complete stock required. Delay delivery of joinery fitments etc. Use can be made of the new building for storage.
4   On larger sites, provide work areas for formwork, reinforcement and pipework fabrication etc.; provide through routes for material deliveries, to avoid any reversing of lorries and traffic congestion; locate site

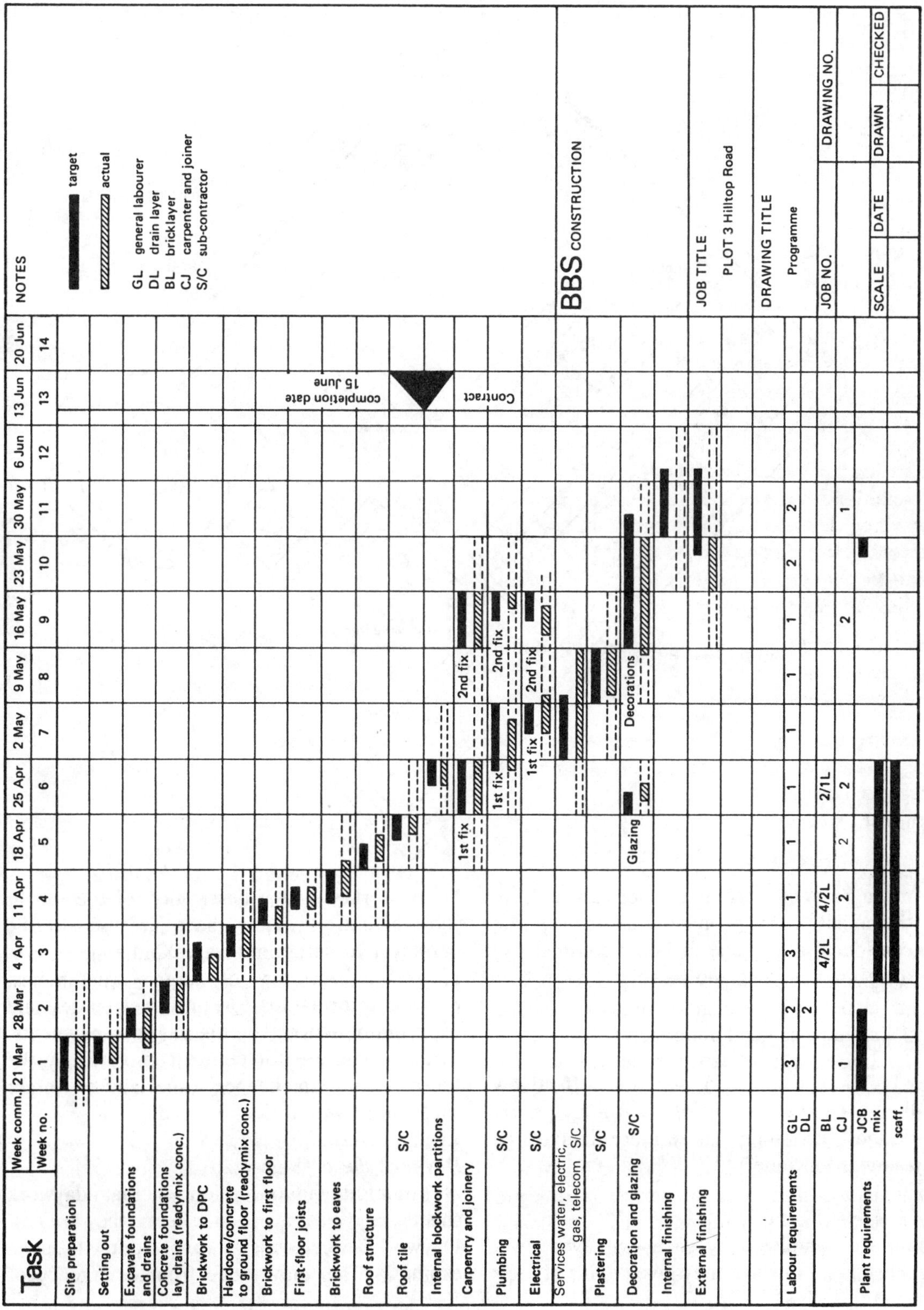

Figure 23 *Bar/Gantt chart*

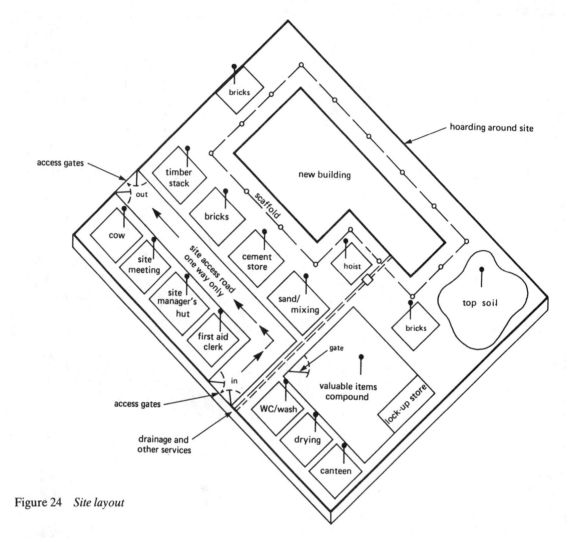

Figure 24   *Site layout*

management's accommodation away from the noise of the main building works; consider use of crane or hoist; consider use of security lighting and patrols.

General site paperwork

No building site could function effectively without a certain amount of day-to-day paperwork and form filling. Those more likely to be encountered include:

Time sheets (Figure 25)
These are completed by each employee on a weekly basis, on which they give details of their

hours worked and a description of the job or jobs carried out. Time sheets are used by the employer to determine wages and expenditure, gauge the accuracy of target programmes, provide information for future estimates and form the basis for claiming daywork payments. These sheets are sometimes completed by the foreman and timekeeper, especially on larger sites where a time clock is used.

Daywork sheets (Figure 26)
A common misconception is that daywork sheets are the same as time sheets; they are not. Daywork is work which is carried out without an estimate. This may range from emergency or

BBS CONSTRUCTION
WEEKLY TIME SHEET

Name _____

Craft _____

Week commencing _____

Registered office

	Job title	Description of work	Time: start/finish	total
MON				
TUE				
WED				
THUR				
FRI				
SAT				
SUN				

Details of expenses
(attach receipts)

Authorized by _____ Position _____

For office use only

Standard hours	_____	at	_____	=	_____
Overtime hours	_____	at	_____	=	_____
Overtime hours	_____	at	_____	=	_____
Overtime hours	_____	at	_____	=	_____

TOTAL = _____

Figure 25   *Time sheet*

BBS CONSTRUCTION
DAYWORK SHEET

Registered office

Sheet no. _____

Job title _____

Week commencing _____

Description of work

Labour	Name	Craft	Hours	Gross rate	Total
			Total labour		

Materials	Quantity	Rate	% Addition		
			Total materials		

Plant	Hours	Rate	% Addition		
			Total plant		

Note Gross labour rates include a percentage for overheads and profit as set out in the contract conditions.	Sub total		
	VAT (where applicable) _____ %		
	Total claim		

Site manager/foreman _____

Architect _____

Figure 26   *Daywork sheet*

repair work carried out by a jobbing builder to work that was unforeseen at the start of a major contract, for example, repairs, replacements, demolition, extra ground work, late alterations etc. Daywork sheets should be completed by the contractor, authorized by the clerk of works or architect and finally passed on to the quantity surveyor for inclusion in the next interim payment. This payment is made from the provisional contingency sum included in the bill of quantities for any unforeseen work. Details of daywork procedures should be included in the contract conditions. A written architect's instruction is normally required before any work commences.

Confirmation notice (Figure 27)
Where architects issue verbal instructions for daywork or variations, written confirmation of these instructions should be sought by the contractor from the architect before any work is carried out. This does away with any misunderstanding and prevents disputes over payment at a later date.

Note: Although clerk of works's instructions are of an advisory or informative nature and do not normally involve extra payment, written confirmation of these should be received from the architect.

Daily report/site diary (Figure 28)
This is used to convey information back to head office and also to provide a source for future reference, especially should a problem or dispute arise later in the contract regarding verbal instructions, telephone promises, site visitors, delays or stoppages due to late deliveries, late starts by subcontractors or bad weather conditions. Like all reports its purpose is to disclose or record facts; it should therefore be brief and to the point. Many contractors use a duplicate book for the combined daily report and site diary. After filling in, the top copy is sent to head office, the carbon copy being retained on site. Some firms use two separate documents to fulfil the same function.

Orders/requisitions (Figure 29)
The majority of building materials are obtained through the firm's buyer, who at the estimating stage would have sought quotes from the various suppliers or manufacturers in order to compare prices, qualities and discounts. It is the buyer's responsibility to order and arrange phased deliveries of the required materials to coincide with the contract programme. Each job would be issued with a duplicate order/requisition book for obtaining sundry items from the firm's central stores or, in the case of a smaller builder, direct from the supplier. Items of plant would be requisitioned from the plant manager or plant hirers using a similar order/requisition book.

Delivery notes (Figure 30)
When materials and plant are delivered to the site, the foreman is required to sign the driver's delivery note. A careful check should be made to ensure all the materials are there and undamaged. Any missing or damaged goods must be clearly indicated on the delivery note and followed up by a letter to the supplier. Many suppliers send out an advice note prior to delivery which states details of the materials and the expected delivery date. This enables the site management to make provision for its unloading and storage.

Delivery records (Figure 31)
This forms a complete record of all the materials received on site and should be filled in and sent to head office along with the delivery notes on a weekly basis. This record is used to check deliveries before paying suppliers' invoices and also when determining the interim valuation.

Memorandum (memo) (Figure 32)
This is a printed form on which internal communications can be carried out. It is normally a brief note about the requirements of a particular job or details of an incoming inquiry (representative/telephone call) while a person was unavailable.

BBS CONSTRUCTION
CONFIRMATION NOTICE

No._____ Date_____

Job title _____

From _____

To _____

Registered office

I confirm that today I have been issued with * verbal/written instructions from _____

Position _____

to carry out the following * daywork/variation to the contract

Additions

Omissions

Please issue your official * confirmation/variation order

Copies to head office   Signed _____
_____
_____   Position _____

* Delete as appropriate

Figure 27 *Confirmation notice*

BBS CONSTRUCTION
DAILY REPORT/SITE DIARY

Registered office

No. _____ Date _____

Job title _____

Labour force on site		Labour force required	
Our employ	Subcontract	Our employ	Subcontract

Materials	Information
Received (state delivery no.) Required by (state requisition no.)	Received Required by

Plant	Drawings
Received (state delivery no.) Required by (state requisition no.)	Received Required by

Telephone calls	Site visitors
To	
From	

Accidents	Stoppages

Weather conditions	Temperature
	a.m. p.m.

Brief report of progress and other items of importance

Site manager/foreman _____

Note Send top copy daily to head office and retain carbon copy as an on-site record.

Figure 28   *Daily report/site diary*

BBS CONSTRUCTION
ORDER/REQUISITION

Registered office

No. _____

Date _____

To _____   From _____

Address   Site address

_____   _____

_____   _____

Please supply or order for delivery to the above site the following:

Description	Quantity	Rate		Date required by

Site manager/foreman _____

Note Please advise site within 24 hours of request if order cannot be fulfilled by the date required

Figure 29   *Order/requisition*

BBS SUPPLIES
DELIVERY NOTE

Registered office

No. _____

Date _____

Delivered to

_____

_____

_____

Invoice to

_____

_____

_____

Please receive in good condition the undermentioned goods

Received by _____

Remarks _____

Note Claims for shortages and damage will not be considered unless recorded on this sheet.

Figure 30 *Delivery note*

BBS CONSTRUCTION
DELIVERIES RECORD

Registered office	

Week no. _____ Date _____

Job title _____

Delivery note no.	Date	Supplier	Description of delivery	For office use only		
				Rate	Value	
				Total		

Site manager/foreman _____

Note Send weekly to head office with delivery notes

Figure 31   *Deliveries record*

```
┌─────────────────────────────────────────────────────────────────┐
│                                                                   │
│  BBS CONSTRUCTION          MEMO                                    │
│                                                                   │
│  From _____   To _____ │
│                                                                   │
│  Subject _____   Date _____ │
│  ┌─────────────────────────────────────────────────────────────┐ │
│  │ Message                                                       │ │
│  │                                                               │ │
│  │                                                               │ │
│  │                                                               │ │
│  │                                                               │ │
│  │                                                               │ │
│  │                                                               │ │
│  │                                                               │ │
│  │                                                               │ │
│  └─────────────────────────────────────────────────────────────┘ │
└─────────────────────────────────────────────────────────────────┘
```

Figure 32   *Memorandum*

Employment conditions

The employment of any person is controlled by various Acts of Parliament. The main ones are:

Employment Protection (Consolidation) Act 1978

Sex Discrimination Act 1975 (this embodies the Equal Pay Act 1970)

Race Relations Act 1976

On engagement an employee record card as shown in Figure 33 should be completed and signed by the employee. This card should be kept up to date during the employment to form a permanent record. The employee should be given a copy of the company's safety policy and a statement of the company's terms of employment. In addition many companies issue their employees with a handbook containing details of general policy and procedures, safety policy and disciplinary rules.

Terms of employment

These terms of employment, a typical copy of which is shown in Figure 34, include details of commencement date; job title; hours of work; rates of pay; overtime; pay-day; holiday entitlement and pay; sick pay; pension scheme; disciplinary procedures; termination of employment; disputes procedure.

Disciplinary rules

This is a written statement outlining the company's disciplinary rules and dismissal procedures. It should be issued to all employees to ensure they are fully aware of the rules and procedures involved. They normally provide for verbal warnings of unsatisfactory conduct – for example, bad attendance, timekeeping or production, and the failure to comply with working instructions or safety rules – followed by a final written warning. Where this written warning is not heeded, dismissal may follow. Figure 35 shows a typical written final warning.

Note: Verbal and written warnings are not required in cases of gross misconduct where instant dismissal can result. These cases are defined as: theft from the company; falsification of records for personal gain; and acts placing persons or property in danger.

BBS CONSTRUCTION
EMPLOYEES
RECORD CARD

Registered office

Surname _____   Forenames _____

Permanent address _____   Temporary address _____

_____   _____

_____   _____

National Insurance number _____   Date of birth _____

Title of job _____

Commencement date _____

Other relevant details _____

_____

_____

_____

Documents received

P45 yes/no _____

Holiday card   yes/no   if yes state number and value of stamps

_____

_____

Documents issued

Statement of terms of employment   yes/no

The Company handbook   yes/no

(i) general policy and procedures
(ii) safety policy
(iii) disciplinary rules

I certify that the above details are correct and that I have been issued with the documents indicated.

Employees signature _____   Date _____

Personnel/training manager _____   Date _____

Full name	Title of job

QUALIFICATIONS

Title	School/college	Dates from to

COURSES ATTENDED

Title	Location	Dates from to

SITE TRANSFER

From	To	Date/signature

ABSENCES FROM WORK

From	To	Reason

CONDUCT WARNINGS

Type	Reason	Date/signature

EMPLOYMENT TERMINATED

Reason	Comments	Date/signature

BBS CONSTRUCTION
CONTRACT OF EMPLOYMENT

Registered office

STATEMENT OF MAIN TERMS OF EMPLOYMENT

Name of employer _____

Name of employee _____

Title of job _____

Statement issue date _____

Employment commencement date _____

Your hours of work, rates of pay, overtime, pay-day, holiday entitlement and payment, pension scheme, disciplinary procedures, notice and termination of employment and disputes procedure are in accordance with the following documents:

1 The National Working Rules for the Building Industry, approved by the National Joint Council for the Building Industry.

2 The Company wages register.

3 The Company handbook
  (i) general policy and procedures
  (ii) safety policy
  (iii) disciplinary rules

Copies of the above documents are available for your inspection on request at all site offices. Any future changes in the terms of employment will be made to these documents within one month of the change.

Figure 34   *Terms of employment*

National working rules

Most building operatives are employed using the wage rates, terms and conditions of employment as laid down in the National Working Rules for the building industry by the National Joint Council for the Building Industry (NJCBI). The main exceptions to this would be plumbing and mechanical services operatives whose terms of employment are negotiated by the Joint Industry Board (JIB), others who are employed under terms negotiated by the Building and Allied Trades Joint Industrial Council (BATJIC), and the self-employed.

National Joint Council for the Building Industry Rules

The main functions of the Council and their working rules are to:

1   Fix basic wage rates
2   Determine conditions of employment

```
┌─────────────────────────────────────────────────────────────────────┐
│  BBS CONSTRUCTION              ┌──────────────────────────────────┐   │
│  DISCIPLINARY NOTICE           │ Registered office                │   │
│                                │                                  │   │
│                                │                                  │   │
│                                │                                  │   │
│                                │                                  │   │
│                                └──────────────────────────────────┘   │
│                                                                       │
│                     FINAL WARNING                                     │
│                                                                       │
│  To _____  Date _____   │
│  Site _____   │
│                                                                       │
│  It is being brought to your attention that since the verbal warning  │
│  given to you on _____   │
│  _____ by _____   │
│  concerning _____   │
│                                                                       │
│  * No significant improvement has been made/this conduct has been     │
│  repeated.                                                            │
│                                                                       │
│  This is a final warning* failure to show improvement/repetition of   │
│  this conduct will result in your employment being terminated.        │
│                                                                       │
│                                                                       │
│  Personnel/training manager _____    │
│                                                                       │
│  * Delete as appropriate                                             │
└─────────────────────────────────────────────────────────────────────┘
```

Figure 35   *Final warning*

3   Settle disputes referred to them by both employers and operatives

The basic rates and main conditions of employment are determined on a national level by the National Joint Council, which consists of representatives on the employers' side from the Building Employers' Confederation (BEC) and other associated employers' organizations, and on the operatives side from the trade unions.

There are also local and regional committees that negotiate regional variations and additions to the National Working Rules. These rules are published in booklet form. They should be available for reference at your place of work and your college or they may be purchased through booksellers.

The main contents of this booklet are the twenty-seven National Working Rules which are grouped under the following headings:

Wages
Hours, conditions and holidays
Allowances
Retirement and death benefit
Apprentices/trainees
Scaffolders
Safety
General

In addition to these rules the booklet contains certain explanatory notes, additional regional rules and variations, and also details of the annual holidays with pay scheme which is operated by the Building and Civil Engineering Holidays Scheme Management Company.

Advisory, Conciliation and Arbitration Services (ACAS)

In the event of a dispute or grievance at work, the problem should first be taken to the foreman or site manager with the accompaniment of a union representative if required. Where the problem cannot be solved at this level it may be referred to a regional conciliation panel of the National Joint Council for settlement. If the outcome of this is unsatisfactory, individuals may refer their cases to the independent ACAS. Typical cases referred to ACAS include complaints in respect of: unfair dismissal; equal pay; sex or racial discrimination; suspension; redundancy; and trade union activities or membership.

To make a complaint an individual must complete a form which is obtainable from job centres. The completed form should be sent to the Central Office of Industrial Tribunals who will pass a copy to ACAS. An ACAS conciliation officer will contact both sides in the dispute. If both parties are willing to accept conciliation the officer will explain the views and legal position of each party to the other. In cases where parties cannot agree on a settlement the matter will be decided by the industrial tribunal.

Note: Both parties, for example, employers and employees, can also get advice from ACAS without an official complaint having been made, through the Central Office of Industrial Tribunals.

Self-assessment questions

1 List the main contract documents.

2 Define the term 'specification'.

3 State the purpose of the bill of quantities.

4 What is a door schedule?

5 State what is meant by the term 'defects liability period'.

6 What is the role of ACAS?

7 State the difference between a range and an assembly drawing.

8 Explain the difference between a daywork sheet and a time sheet.

9 Give *two* functions of the National Joint Council for the Building Industry.

10 Describe the purpose of the Standard Method of Measurement.

chapter 4

Applied calculations

After reading this chapter the student should be able to:

1 Identify the SI units of measurement.

2 Perform calculations using the basic processes.

3 Perform calculations on an electronic calculator.

4 Apply mathematical processes to solve work measurement and costing problems.

Calculations at advanced level consist mainly of applying the previously learned basic processes to the solution of more advanced practical problems. Although many readers will have mastered the main basic processes, they are briefly covered in this chapter to provide a source of reference and revision where required.

Units of measurement

The system of measurement employed by much of the world is the Système International d'Unités (SI) or metric system. For each quantity of measurement (length, mass, capacity etc.) there is a base unit, a multiple unit and a submultiple unit. The base unit of length is the metre (m). Its multiple unit the kilometre (km) is a thousand times larger: m × 1000 = km. The submultiple unit of the metre is the millimetre (mm), which is a thousand times smaller: m ÷ 1000 = mm. The units used most frequently by the carpenter and joiner are shown in Table 3.

Basic processes

Addition
It is most important that the decimal points in all numbers to be added are directly underneath one another.

Example
11.38 + 6.57 + 0.124

```
11.38
 6.57
 0.124
------
18.074
```

Answer 18.074

Subtraction
When subtracting one number from another it is also very important that the decimal points are underneath one another, as they were for addition.

Example
16.697 − 8.565

```
16.697
 8.565
------
 8.132
```

Answer 8.132

Multiplication
When multiplying, the decimal points can be forgotten until the two sets of numbers have been multiplyed together. The position of the decimal point can then be located by the following rule:

The number of figures to the right of the decimal point in the answer will always equal the number of figures to the right of the decimal point in the problem.

Example 11.6 × 4.5
      (1)   (2)

Two figures to the right of the decimal point

```
 116 ×
  45
------
 580
4640
------
5220
  ↑ ↑
 (2)(1)
```

Two figures to the right of the decimal point

Answer 52.20

Table 3   **Units for carpenters and joiners**

Quantity	Base unit	Multiple	Submultiple	Equivalents
Length				
	metre m	kilometre km m × 1000	millimetres mm m ÷ 1000	1 km = 1,000,000 mm
Area				
	square metre m^2	square kilometre km^2 m × 1,000,000 or hectare ha m × 10,000	square millimetres mm^2 m ÷ 1,000,000	
Volume				
	cubic metre m^3		cubic millimetres mm^3 m ÷ 1,000,000	$1\ m^3$ = $1,000,000,000\ mm^3$
Capacity				
	litre (no symbol)		millilitre ml litre ÷ 1000	$1\ m^3$ = 1000 litres
Mass				
	kilogram kg	tonne (no symbol) kg × 1000	gram g kg ÷ 1000	1 litre water = 1 kg

Quantity	Base unit	Multiple	Submultiple	Equivalents
Density	kilograms per cubic metre kg/m³			water = 1000 kg/m³
Force	newton N	kilonewton kN N × 1000		1 kg = 9.81 N
Pressure	bar 1000 kN/m² (no symbol)		millibar mb bar ÷ 1000 or pascal P mb ÷ 100	1 bar = atmospheric pressure (approximately)
Temperature	degree Celsius (centigrade) °C			100 °C = boiling point of water 0 °C = freezing point of water
Time	second s			60 s = 1 minute 1 hour = 60 minutes

continued

Table 3 continued

Quantity	Base unit	Multiple	Submultiple	Equivalents
Heat	joule J	kilojoule kJ J × 1000		
Heat flow	watt W	kilowatt kW W × 1000		

J/s

Division
When dividing we need to make the number we are dividing by a whole number. If it is not we can move its decimal point a number of places to the right until it is a whole number, but to compensate we must also move the decimal point in the number to be divided by the same number of places.

Example
164.6 ÷ 0.2 $164\overrightarrow{6}. ÷ 0\overrightarrow{2}.$

Move point to make the number you are dividing by a whole number

$$\begin{array}{r} 823 \\ 2\overline{)1646} \end{array}$$ *Answer* $\underline{823}$

Approximate answers
Common causes of incorrect answers to calculation problems are incomplete working out and incorrectly placed decimal points. Rough checks of the expected size of an answer and the position of the decimal point would overcome this problem. These rough checks can be carried out quickly using approximate numbers.

Example
$$\frac{4.65 \times 2.05}{3.85}$$

For a rough check, say
$$\frac{5 \times 2}{4} = 2.5$$
Correct answer $\underline{2.476}$

The rough checks and the correct answer are of the same order. This confirms that the answer is 2.476 and not 0.2476 or 24.76 etc.

Rough checks will be nearer to the correct answer if, when choosing approximate numbers, some are increased and some are decreased. In cases where the rough check and the correct answer are not of the same order the calculation should be reworked to find the cause of the error.

Note: This process of approximating answers should be carried out even when using an electronic calculator, as wrong answers are often the result of miskeying, even a slight hesitation on a key can cause a number to be entered twice.

Fractions
Parts of a whole number are represented in the metric system by decimals. The imperial system uses fractions. Where fractions are encountered they may be converted into decimals by dividing the bottom number into the top number.

Example
⅞ as a decimal

```
      0.875
   8 )7.000
      6 4
      ───
       60
       56
       ──
       40
       40
       ──
       00
       ──
```

Answer   0.875

Ratio and proportion

Ratios and proportions are ways of comparing or stating the relationship between two like quantities.

Example
If £72 is to be shared by two people in a ratio of 5:3, what will each receive?

number of shares = 5 + 3 = 8
one share = 72 ÷ 8 = £9
five shares = 5 × 9 = £45
three shares = 3 × 9 = £27

Answer   £45 and £27

Example
A 1:3 pitched roof has a span of 3.600 m: what is its rise?
This means that for every 3 m span the roof will rise 1 m or the rise is ⅓ of the span:

```
             1.200
rise =    ─────────        Answer   1.200 m
          3 )3.600
```

Percentages

This is another way of representing part of a quantity. Percentage means per hundred.
When finding a certain percentage of a given quantity, the first step is to turn the percentage into a decimal. This is done by dividing the percentage by 100. This can be done quickly by placing an imaginary point behind the percentage and then moving two places forward.

Example
10% becomes   0.10

There are three circumstances where percentages are used:

1 *Where a straightforward percentage of a number is required*

Turn percentage into decimal and multiply by it.

Example
12% of 55

```
      55
   × .12
   ────
     110
     550
   ────
     660
   ────
```

Answer   6.6

2 *Where a number plus a certain percentage (increase) is required*
Turn percentage into decimal, place a one in front of it (to include the original quantity) and multiply by it.

Example
55 plus 12%

```
       55
     1.12
   ─────
      110
      550
     5500
   ─────
     6160
   ─────
```

Answer   61.6

3 *Where a number minus a certain percentage (decrease) is required*
Take away percentage from 100, place a point in front and then multiply by it.

Example
55 minus 12%

```
      55
     .88
   ────
     440
    4400
   ────
    4840
   ────
```

Answer   48.4

Averages

An average is the mean value of several quantities. It is found by adding the quantities and dividing by the number of quantities.

Example
Find the average mark obtained for a number of college assessments.

48, 27, 49, 75, 84, 44, 65,
Total marks = 392.

```
                             56
divide by number of marks  7 )392
```

Answer   Average mark 56

Powers and roots

A simple way of writing repeated factors (multiplication) is to raise the number to a power or index.

Example

$10 \times 10 \qquad\qquad = \quad 100$ or 10^2
$10 \times 10 \times 10 \qquad = \quad 1000$ or 10^3
$10 \times 10 \times 10 \times 10 = 10000$ or 10^4
and so on.

Large numbers can be written in a standard form by the use of an index.

Example

$30000 = 3 \quad \times 10000$ or $3 \quad \times 10^4$
$\;\;6600 = 6.6 \times \quad 1000$ or 6.6×10^3
$\;\;\;\;990 = 9.9 \times \quad 100$ or 9.9×10^2

The index is the number of places that the decimal point will have to be moved to the right if the number is written in full.

Standard form can also be used for numbers less than one, by using a negative index.

Example

$0.036 \quad = 3.6 \times 10^{-2}$ or 36×10^{-3}
$0.0099 \; = 9.9 \times 10^{-3}$ or 99×10^{-4}
$0.00012 = 1.2 \times 10^{-4}$ or 12×10^{-5}

The negative index is the number of places that the decimal point will have to be moved to the left if the number is written in full.

It is sometimes necessary to find a particular root of a number. The square root is a number multiplied by itself to give the number in question.

Example

The square root of 25 is 5, since $5 \times 5 = 25$. The common way of writing this is to use the square root sign.
$\sqrt{25} = 5$

The cube root is a number multiplied by itself twice to give the number in question.

Example

The cube root of 125 is 5, since $5 \times 5 \times 5 = 125$. The common way of writing this is to use the root sign and an index.
$\sqrt[3]{125} = 5$

From this it can be seen that there is a connection between powers and roots, in fact they are opposite processes.

Example

$10^2 = \quad 100 \quad \sqrt{100} = 10$
$10^3 = 1000 \; \sqrt[3]{100} = 10$

Electronic calculators

All of the basic calculators will look similar. They consist of:

Ten numbered keys 0 1 2 3 4 5 6 7 8 9

Four operation keys $\quad +\quad -\quad \div\quad \times$

An equals key $\quad =$

A decimal point key $\quad \cdot$

A square root key $\quad \sqrt{}$

A percentage key $\quad \%$

A $\;$ C $\;$ key which clears everything in the machine and a CI or CE key to clear the last key pressed. This enables you to clear a wrongly pressed key without clearing the whole calculation.

The operation of your calculator will vary depending on the model; therefore consult the booklet supplied with it before use. After some practice you should be able to operate your calculator quickly and accurately.

Example

$55.335 \times 2.1 \div 3.52$

Press these keys

switch on	Display
C	0.
5 5 · 3 3 5	55.335
×	55.335
2 · 1	2.1
÷	116.2035
3 · 5 2	3.52
=	33.012357

Answer   33.012357

For most purposes calculations which show three decimal figures are considered accurate. These can therefore be rounded off to three decimal places. This entails looking at the fourth decimal figure; if it is a five or above add one to the third decimal figure. Where it is below five ignore it. For example:

33.012357   becomes   33.012
2.747642   becomes   2.748

Example
Twelve doors costing £15.55 each are to be purchased. What would be the total amount payable if a 10 per cent discount is allowed.

This means 12 × £15.55 − 10%

Press these keys	*Display*
switch on	
C	0.
1 2	12.
×	12.
1 5 . 5 5	15.55
−	186.6
1 0	10.
%	167.94
=	167.94

Answer   Total cost £167.94

Note: A decimal point is used to separate pounds and pence.

Formulae

Formulae are normally stated in algebraic terms. Algebra uses letters and symbols instead of numbers to simplify statements and enable general relations to be worked out.

Example
The area of a triangle can be found by using the formula:

Area = Base × Height ÷ 2

If we say A = area, B = base and H = height, then

$$A = B \times H \div 2$$

In algebra we can abbreviate by missing out the multiplication sign (×) and expressing a division in its fractional form:

$$A = \frac{BH}{2} \text{ means } A = B \times H \div 2$$

Plus and minus (+, −) signs cannot be abbreviated and must always be shown.

In general, multiplication and division must be done before addition and subtraction, except in formulae that contain brackets. These are used to show that the work inside the brackets must be done first.

Example
The perimeter of a rectangle can be found by using the formulae $P = 2(L + B)$. To obtain the correct answer L must be added to B before multiplying by 2.

Transposition of formulae
When solving a problem, sometimes formulae have to be rearranged in order to change the subject of the formulae before the calculation is carried out. Basically anything can be moved from one side of the equals sign to the other by changing its symbol. This means that on crossing the equals sign, plus changes to minus, multiplication changes to division, powers change to roots and vice versa.

Example
The formula for the perimeter or circumference of a circle is:

circumference = π × diameter

Suppose we were given the circumference as 7.855 m and asked to find the diameter:

$$C = \pi \times D$$
$$C \div \pi = D$$
$$7.855 \div 3.142 = D$$
$$2.5 = D$$

Answer   The diameter is 2.500 m.

Alternatively, where the multiplication and division signs have been abbreviated out of a formula, we can cross-multiply. This means that on crossing the equals sign anything on the top line moves to the bottom line, and conversely anything on the bottom line moves to the top line.

Example
If the area and base of a triangle were known, but we wanted to find out its height, the formula could be rearranged to make the height the subject. For example, to find the height if area = 4.500 m, base = 1.500 m:

$$\text{area} = \frac{\text{base} \times \text{height}}{2}$$

$$A = \frac{BH}{2}$$

$$2A = BH$$

$$\frac{2A}{B} = H$$

$$\frac{2 \times 4.5}{1.5} = H$$

$$\frac{9}{1.5} = H$$

$$6 = H$$

Answer   The height is 6 m.

Areas and perimeters

The areas and perimeters of common figures can be found by using the formulae given in Table 4. The area of a figure is the extent of its surface (square measurement, given in square metres (m^2)). The perimeter of a figure is the distance or length around its boundary (linear measurement, given in metres run).

Complex areas can be calculated by breaking them into a number of recognizable areas and solving each one in turn.

Example
The area of the room shown in Figure 36 is equal to area *A* plus area *B* minus area *C*. What is the area of the room?

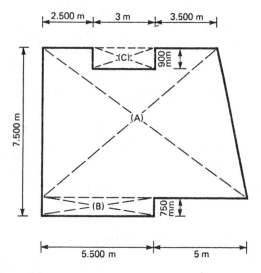

Figure 36

Table 4   **Areas and perimeter**

Name	Figure	Area equals	Perimeter equals
Square		*A A*	*4 A*

Name	Figure	Area equals	Perimeter equals
Rectangle		LB	$2(L+B)$
Parallelogram		BH	$2(A+B)$
Triangle		$\dfrac{BH}{2}$ or $S(S-A)(S-B)(S-C)$ where $S = \dfrac{A+B+C}{2}$	$A+B+C$
Trapezium		$\dfrac{A+B}{2}H$	$A+B+C+D$
Circle		πR^2	πD or $2\pi R$
Ellipse		πAB	$\pi(A+B)$
Sector		$\dfrac{\sigma^\circ}{360}\pi R_2$	(arc only) $\dfrac{\sigma^\circ}{360}2\pi R$

Note: π is the same for any circle. It is the number of times the diameter will divide into the circumference, circumference/diameter and is taken to be 3.142.

$$\text{area } A = \frac{9 + 10.5}{2} \times 6.75$$

$$= 65.813 \text{ m}^2$$
$$\text{area } B = 0.75 \times 5.5$$
$$= 4.125 \text{ m}^2$$
$$\text{area } C = 0.9 \times 3$$
$$= 2.7 \text{ m}^2$$
$$\text{total area} = 65.813 + 4.125 - 2.7$$
$$= 67.238 \text{ m}^2$$

Answer   The area of the room is 67.238 m².

Note: We can only multiply like terms. Where metres and millimetres are contained in the same problem, first convert the millimetres into a decimal part of a metre by dividing by 1000. Move the imaginary point behind the number three places forward.

Example
50 mm becomes 0.050 m

Volumes

The volume of an object can be defined as the space it takes up (cubic measurement, given in cubic metres (m³)).

Many solids have a uniform cross-section and parallel edges. The volume of these can be found by multiplying their base area by their height:

volume = base area × height

Example
A house contains forty-eight 50 mm × 225 mm softwood joists, 4.50 m long. How many cubic metres of timber are required?

$$\text{volume} = 48 \times 0.05 \times 0.225 \times 4.5$$
$$= 2.43 \text{ m}^3$$

Answer   2.43 m³ are required.

The lateral surface area of a solid with a uniform cross-section is found by multiplying its base perimeter by their height.

lateral surface area = base perimeter × height

The formulae for calculating the volume and lateral surface area of frequently used common

solids are given in Table 5. It can be seen from the table that the volume of any pyramid or cone will always be equal to one-third of its equivalent prism or cylinder.

Complex volumes are found by breaking them up into a number of recognizable volumes and solving for each one in turn. This is the same as the method used when solving for complex areas.

Example
The horizontal cross-section of a 2.400 m high concrete column is shown in Figure 37. What volume of concrete would be required to cast it?

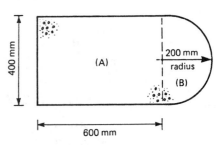

Figure 37

The column can be considered as a rectangular prism (A) and half a cylinder (B).

$$\text{volume } A = 0.4 \times 0.6 \times 2.4$$
$$= 0.576 \text{ m}^3$$
$$\text{volume } B = \frac{3.142 \times 0.2 \times 0.2 \times 2.4}{2}$$
$$= 0.151$$
$$\text{total volume} = 0.576 + 0.151$$
$$= 0.727 \text{ m}^3$$

Answer   0.727 m³ of concrete is required.

Where a solid tapers, its volume can be found by multiplying its average cross-section by its height.

volume = average cross-section × height

Example
How many cubic metres of concrete are required to cast the 4.500 m high tapered column shown in Figure 38?

Table 5 **Volume and surface areas of common solids**

Name	Solid	Volume	Lateral surface area
Rectangular prism		LBH	$2(L+B)H$
Rectangular pyramid		$\dfrac{LBH}{3}$	$S(L+B)$
Cylinder		$\pi R^2/H$	πDH
Cone		$\dfrac{\pi R^2 H}{3}$	πRL
Sphere		$\dfrac{4\pi R^3}{3}$	$4\pi R^2$

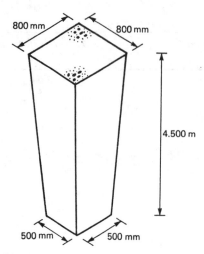

Figure 38

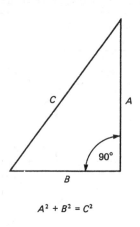

Figure 39   *Pythagoras's Theorem*

$$\text{volume} = \frac{(0.8 \times 0.8) + (0.5 \times 0.5)}{2} \times 4.5$$

$$= \frac{0.64 + 0.25}{2} \times 4.5$$

$$= 2.003 \ \text{m}^3$$

Answer   2.003 m³ of concrete are required.

Pythagoras's Theorem

The lengths of the sides in a right-angled triangle can be found using Pythagoras's Theorem. According to this theorem, in any right-angled triangle the square of the hypotenuse is equal to the sum of the square of the other two sides. This is illustrated in Figure 39.

A simple version of this is the 3:4:5 rule shown in Figure 40. This is often used for setting out and checking right angles, since a triangle whose sides equal 3 units, 4 units and 5 units must be a right-angled triangle because $5^2 = 3^2 + 4^2$. If we known the lengths of two sides of a right-angled triangle we can use Pythagoras's Theorem to find the length of the third side. In fact this theorem forms the basis of pitched roof calculations.

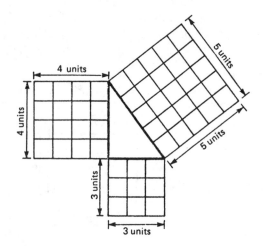

Figure 40   *3:4:5 rule*

Example
Figure 41 represents a line diagram of a pitch roof section. Calculate the length of the common rafter.

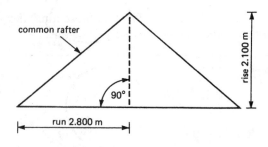

Figure 41

A = rise 2.100 m
B = run 2.800 m
C = common rafter
$C^2 = A^2 + B^2$
$C^2 = 2.1^2 + 2.8^2$
$C^2 = 4.41 + 7.84$
$C^2 = 12.25$
$C = \sqrt{12.25}$
$C = 3.5$ m

Answer The common rafter is <u>3.500 m</u> long.

Intersecting chords' rule

Where two chords intersect in a circle, the product (result of multiplication) of the two parts of one chord will always be equal to the product of the two parts of the other chord. This rule is shown in Figure 42. It is very useful for finding radius lengths.

Example
What radius would be used to set out the turning piece shown in Figure 43?

$A = 0.600$ m, $B = 0.600$ m, $C = 0.100$ m, $D = ?$

$$A \times B = C \times D$$
$$\frac{A \times B}{C} = D$$
$$\frac{0.6 \times 0.6}{0.1} = D$$
$$\frac{0.36}{0.1} = D$$
$$3.6 = D$$

Since $C + D$ is the chord representing the diameter, the radius must be half of this:

$$\text{radius} = \frac{C + D}{2}$$
$$R = \frac{0.1 + 3.6}{2}$$
$$R = 1.850 \text{ m}$$

Answer The radius would be <u>1.850 m</u>.

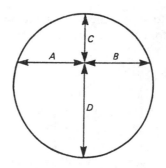

$A \times B = C \times D$

Figure 42 *Intersecting chords' rule*

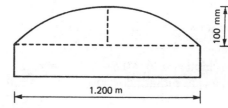

Figure 43

Problem solving

You should tackle any problem in a simple straightforward manner. Marks are awarded for each part of a calculation, not just for the final answer: therefore it is very important that you write down what you are doing at each stage, even when using a calculator.

Example
The following materials are required for a refurbishing contract:

Softwood
Sawn softwood at £158.50 per m³

Item	Number	Size
Joists	16	50 × 225 × 3600
Strutting	10	50 × 50 × 4200
Studwork	84	50 × 100 × 2400
Battening	50	25 × 50 × 4800

Flooring
18 mm flooring grade chipboard at £49 per 10 m²: 30 sheets 600 × 2400 mm

Calculate the total cost including an allowance of 10 per cent for cutting and wastage and 15 per cent for VAT.

Typical answer

Softwood
Joists $16 \times 0.05 \times 0.225 \times 3.600 = 0.648$ m³
Strutting $10 \times 0.05 \times 0.05 \times 4.200 = 0.105$ m³
Studwork $84 \times 0.05 \times 0.1 \times 2.400 = 1.008$ m³
Battening $50 \times 0.025 \times 0.05 \times 4.800 = 0.003$ m³

volume	2.061
+ 10 per cent cutting allowance	0.2061
total	2.2671 m³

Cost of softwood $2.2671 \times 158.5 = £359.33\frac{1}{2}$

Flooring
18 mm chipboard $30 \times 0.6 \times 2.4 = 43.200$ m²
+ 10 per cent cutting allowance   4.320

                                      47.520 m²

Cost of flooring $\dfrac{47.520 \times 49}{10} = £232.85$

Total cost $359.33\frac{1}{2} + 232.85 = £592.18\frac{1}{2}$
             + 15 per cent VAT   £ 88.83

                                 £681.01½

The total cost is £681.01½ inclusive.

Self-assessment questions

1 Calculate: $36.432 + 827.4 + 0.14 + 51.002 + 22.22$.

2 Calculate: $46.215 - 24.307$.

3 Calculate: 3.72×81.12.

4 Calculate: $35.948 - 1.75$.

5 Calculate: $\dfrac{55.335 \times 2.1}{3.52}$

6 What radius is required to set out a centre for a segmental arch having a rise of 550 mm and a span of 4.500 m?

7 What is the diameter of a circular rostrum if its perimeter measures 12 m?

8 A rectangular room 4.200 m × 6 m is to be floored using hardwood boarding costing £9.55 per square metre.
   (a) Allowing 12½ per cent for cutting and wastage, how many square metres are required?
   (b) What would be the total cost including 15 per cent VAT?

9 The hipped-end roof shown in Figure 44 has a pitch of 45°. Calculate:
   (a) Length of common rafter
   (b) Length of hip rafter

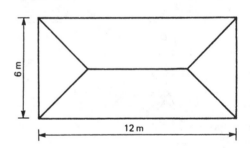

Figure 44

10 The roof shown in Figure 44 has 50 mm × 100 mm common rafters spaced at 400 mm c/c. Calculate:
    (a) Volume in m³ of the common rafters, including two crown rafters, allowing 20 per cent for eaves and cutting
    (b) Total cost of common rafters if 1 m³ of carcassing softwood is £123.50

chapter 5

Timber technology and design

After reading this chapter the student should be able to:

1 Identify commercial timbers and timber-based materials.

2 Describe the procedures involved in timber marketing.

3 Describe the various methods of grading timber and plywood.

4 Describe the various methods of timber conversion.

5 Describe the various methods and purpose of timber seasoning.

6 Describe the main causes of timber decay and procedures to be followed for their prevention and eradication.

7 State the various types and methods of application of timber preservatives.

8 List and state the main characteristics of woodworking adhesives.

9 State and use the mechanical principles of structural timber design.

Available forms of timber

The word 'timber' was traditionally taken to mean sawn or planed wood in its natural state. Today timber is available in many diverse forms, from the felled log right through to a wide range of timber panel products and reconstituted wood. Details of the main forms of timber available and their uses are given in Table 6.

Commercial timbers

All commercial timbers are botanically divided into two classes, softwoods and hardwoods. Softwoods (gymnosperms) are produced by coniferous trees which are in the main evergreen. Hardwoods (angiosperms) come from broadleaf trees. The temperate hardwoods are mostly deciduous whereas many tropical hardwoods are evergreen.

This classification has little to do with the relative hardness of the timber concerned, as the division is based on the cellular structure of the trees. Softwoods have a simple structure with only two types of cell, tracheids and parenchyma. Hardwoods have a more complex structure consisting of three types of cell, fibres, vessels or pores, and parenchyma.

Tracheids have a dual function. The thin-walled spring growth of cells (early wood) conduct raw sap up the tree from the roots to the leaves, and the thicker-walled summer growth of cells (late wood) provide most of the tree's mechanical strength.

In hardwoods the tracheids' dual function is carried out by two different cells. Fibres are the structural tissue giving the tree most of its mechanical strength, and the vessels or pores are the sap-conducting cells.

Parenchyma cells in both softwoods and hardwoods are food storage tissue.

Table 6 **Timber forms and uses**

Form		Main uses
Log		Hardwoods are often shipped in this form for conversion in United Kingdom sawmills Poles or posts for agricultural, garden, dock and harbour work
Baulk		Reconversion into smaller section Dock and harbour work, shoring hoarding, beams and posts in heavy structural work
Waney edge (*utskott*)		Slash sawn timber mainly hardwoods Reconversion into smaller section Cladding and rustic garden furniture
Sawn or planed sections		For general use in construction and joinery
Premachined sections		Floorboarding, cladding, skirting, architraves, cover mouldings, sash stock and other premachined mouldings
Glue-laminated timber		Structural use especially where large sections, long spans, shapes are required, for example, arches, columns, beams, portals etc. Furniture, shelving, counter and work tops

Form	Main uses

Plywoods

These consist of an odd number of thin layers of timber with their grains alternating across and along the panel or sheet. They are then glued together to form a strong board which will retain its shape and not have a tendency to shrink, expand or distort

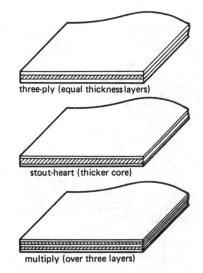

three-ply (equal thickness layers)

stout-heart (thicker core)

multiply (over three layers)

Stressed skin panels, flooring, decking, cladding, panelling, sheathing and formwork
Furniture, shelving and cabinet construction

Laminated boards

These consist of strips of wood which are laminated together and sandwiched between two veneers. The width of the strips varies with each type of board. Laminboard has strips which are up to 8 mm in width; in blockboard these are up to 25 mm and battenboard, which is now rarely available, has strips up to 75 mm

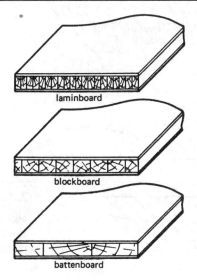

laminboard

blockboard

battenboard

Flooring, panelling, partitions, door blanks
Furniture, shelving and cabinet construction

Chipboard (particle board)

This is manufactured mostly from softwood forest thinnings and timber waste from sawmills or manufacturing processes.

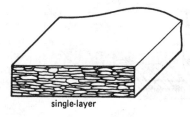

single-layer

Flooring, decking, cladding, panelling, sheathing, formwork, ceilings, partitions
Furniture, shelving and cabinet construction
Extruded boards are thicker for partitioning and door blanks. Also used as core stock for veneering

continued

Table 6 *continued*

Form	Main uses

(Chipboard continued)

It is made up of a mixture of
wood chips and wood flakes
which are impregnated with
resin. They are then pressed to
form a flat, smooth-surfaced
board. In general its strength
increases with its density

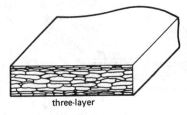

three-layer

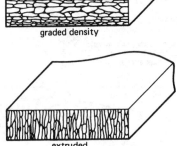

graded density

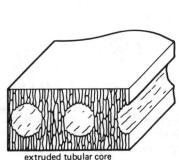

extruded tubular core

extruded

Fibreboards

These are manufactured from
pulped wood or other
vegetable fibre, which is mixed
with an adhesive and pressed
into sheets to the required
thickness. Use tempered
hardboard where extra
strength or moisture resistance
is required.
Bitumen-impregnated
insulating board is also used
where moisture resistance is
required and for expansion
strips to support mastic sealer

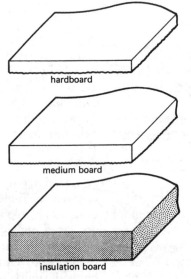

hardboard

medium board

insulation board

Stressed skin panels
Floor, wall, ceiling and formwork
linings
Cladding, sheathing, insulation,
display boards expansion strips

Form		Main uses
Woodwool slabs These are manufactured from long wood shavings, coated with a cement slurry and pressed into slabs between 25 mm and 100 mm thick	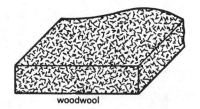 woodwool	Permanent formwork, roof decks, insulation, ceiling and wall linings
Decorative paper laminates (plastic laminate) These are thin synthetic plastic sheets, manufactured from about ten layers of kraft paper bonded and impregnated with a resin. A printed pattern paper is used for the top layer which is coated with a clear coat of melamine formaldehyde to provide a matt, satin or gloss finished surface	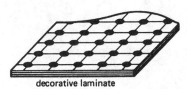 decorative laminate	Decorative, hygienic, hardwearing finish Applied to board material for use both on horizontal and vertical surfaces

Note: In addition to the boards mentioned there is also a wide range of composite boards and panels manufactured for certain specific purposes, but these are far too varied and numerous to be considered in this table.

Source of supply

Hundreds of different spieces of timber are used in Britain. Very few of these are in fact British grown; the vast majority have to be imported from various sources worldwide.

Table 7 gives the main sources of supply for a number of timbers that are most frequently used.

Properties of timber

The properties of different species of timber vary widely. There can even be a distinct difference between the same species of timber grown in different parts of the world.

The selection of a particular species of timber for a specific end use depends on a number of factors:

Availability (often varies widely from merchant to merchant)
Suitability
Density
Durability
Impregnability
Moisture movement
Price

As an aid to selection a summary of these factors is given in Table 7. The timbers are listed in descending colour order from light to dark and are listed under their common name; where a timber is also known by an alternative name this is indicated. Often different species of timber but with similar properties are grouped together and given one commercial name. Their geographical origin is sometimes given for further

Table 7 Properties of commercial timbers

Common name	Country of origin	Hardwood or softwood	Structural	Cladding	Flooring	External joinery	Internal joinery	Fitments/furniture	Density, kg/m³	Durability	Impregnability	Moisture movement	Price range	Remarks
Sycamore (plane)	Europe UK	Hardwood	*					*	625	P	P	M	££	Good turning properties
Birch European (silver birch white birch)	Europe UK	Hardwood			*			*	670	P	P	L	£	Works fairly easily
Whitewood (Norway spruce white deal)	N. Europe UK	Softwood	*		*			*	470	ND	R	S	£	Also suitable for external joinery if preservative treated
Maple (rock or hard)	Canada E. USA	Hardwood						*	740	ND	MR	M	££	Hard-wearing but can be difficult to work
Beech	Europe UK	Hardwood			*		*	*	740	P	P	L	££	Often steamed to produce a light pink colour
Jelutong	Malaysia Indonesia	Hardwood					*	*	470	MD	P	S	££	Also used for pattern-making
Redwood European (Scots pine, yellow deal, red pine)	N. Europe	Softwood	*	*	*	~	*	*	515	ND	MR	M	£	Should be preservative treated when used externally
Oak European	Europe UK	Hardwood	*		*	*	*	*	720	D	VR	M	£££	Hard-wearing; avoid damp contact with iron
Idigbo (emeri, framiré)	W. Africa	Hardwood		*	*	*	*	*	560	D	VR	S	££	Avoid damp contact with iron
Obeche	W. Africa	Hardwood					*	*	390	ND	R	S	£	Very stable. Often used as core stock for plywood
Ash	Europe UK	Hardwood	*					*	710	P	MR	M	££	Has good bending properties; also used for plywood and decorative veneer

Name	Origin	Type				Properties	Price	Notes
Ramin (ramin telur, malawis)	Sarawak Malaysia	Hardwood	*	*	*	670 P P L	££	Ideal for mouldings
Douglas fir (Columbian pine, Oregon pine, British Columbian pine)	Canada USA, UK	Softwood	*	*	*	530 MD R S	££	Avoid damp contact with iron
Western red cedar (red cedar, British Columbian red cedar)	Canada USA, UK	Softwood	*	*	*	390 D R S	££	Ideal cladding, weathers to silver-grey. Avoid damp contact with iron
Meranti	Malaysia	Hardwood	*	*	*	550/710 D VR S	££	Wide variation in properties. Varies in colour from light to dark red
Oak (red oak)	E. Canada USA	Hardwood	*	*		790 ND R M	£££	Good bending properties
Mahogany African	W. Africa E. Africa Central Africa	Hardwood	*	*	*	480/720 MD VR S	££	Variations in character, particularly in density
Keruing (gurjun, yang)	E. Asia, India, Burma, Thailand, Philippines	Hardwood	*	*	*	740 MD MR L	£	Often extrudes resin
Yew	Europe UK	Softwood	*	*	*	670 D R	£££	Can be difficult to work
Elm English	England Europe	Hardwood	*	*	*	560 ND MR M	££	Often used for boat construction
Parana pine	Brazil	Softwood	*	*	*	545 ND MR M	££	Straight grained, works easily and has attractive variations in colour
Afrormosia (kokrodua assamela)	W. Africa	Hardwood	*	*	*	710 VD VR S	£££	Avoid damp contact with ferrous metals. Often used as an alternative to teak
Mahogany American	Central America	Hardwood	*	*	*	560 D VR S	£££	Easy to work and finish. Often used in high-class furniture and cabinet-making
Hemlock Western (Pacific hemlock, British Columbian hemlock)	Canada USA	Softwood	*	*	*	500 ND R S	££	Requires preservative treatment for external use

continued

Table 7 continued

Common name	Country of origin	Hardwood or softwood	Structural	Cladding	Flooring	External joinery	Internal joinery	Fitments/furniture	Density, kg/m³	Durability	Impregnability	Moisture movement	Price range	
Greenheart	Guyana	Hardwood	*						1040	VD	VR	M	££	Mostly used for external construction and marine work
Agba (Tola)	W. Africa	Hardwood		*	*	*	*	*	510	D	R	S	££	A tendency to extrude resin
Walnut African	W. Africa	Hardwood		*	*	*	*	*	560	MD	VR	S	£££	Works well and produces a fine finish
Oak Japanese	Japan	Hardwood			*	*	*	*	670	MD	VR	M	£££	Lighter in colour than European oak
Lauan	Philippines	Hardwood	*	*	*	*	*	*	630	MD	R	S	££	Widely used for veneer
Utile	E. Africa W. Africa	Hardwood	*	*	*	*	*	*	660	D	VR	M	£££	Works well but tends to blunt cutting edges
Iroko	W. Africa E. Africa	Hardwood	*	*	*	*	*	*	660	VD	VR	S	££	Used as an alternative to teak
Teak	India, Burma Thailand	Hardwood	*	*	*	*	*	*	660	VD	VR	S	£££	Produces a good finish if the cutting edges are kept sharp. Extremely resistant to chemicals
Makore	W. Africa	Hardwood			.*	*	*	*	640	VD	VR	S	££	Requires tipped tools and dust extraction
Sapele	E. Africa W. Africa	Hardwood		*	*	*	*	*	640	MD	R	M	££	Has a tendency to distort
Rosewood	India S. America	Hardwood						*	870	VD		S	£££	Can be difficult to work, blunts cutting edges easily, can be oily but highly decorative
Ekki (eba)	W. Africa	Hardwood	*		*				1070	VD	VR	L	££	Can be very difficult to work but ideal for heavy construction

Note: See text for explanation of table

identification, for example, European oak, Japanese oak and American oak. To enable formal scientific identification every plant also has a botanical Latin name consisting of two parts, the first indicating its genus and the second its species. In addition trees with similar genera are grouped into families and related families are put together in orders. The botanical classification of trees is shown in Figure 47.

Note: Only a few examples of family, genus and species are shown although there are, of course, many more. In some cases it is not possible to give a commercial timber an individual botanical name because it can consist of more than one species. In these cases the generic name is followed by 'SPP', for example, oak in general can be referred to as *quercus SPP*.

The columns in Table 7 contain the following information:

Country of origin
This column lists the main areas of supply in the world for the most commonly used commercial timbers.

Suitability
This often depends on the timber's natural appearance, strength and durability etc. A general guide to the typical uses of each timber is given but the list is not comprehensive as many timbers, given the right conditions or treatment, are suitable for other uses; for example, European redwood requires preservative treatment when used in external joinery.

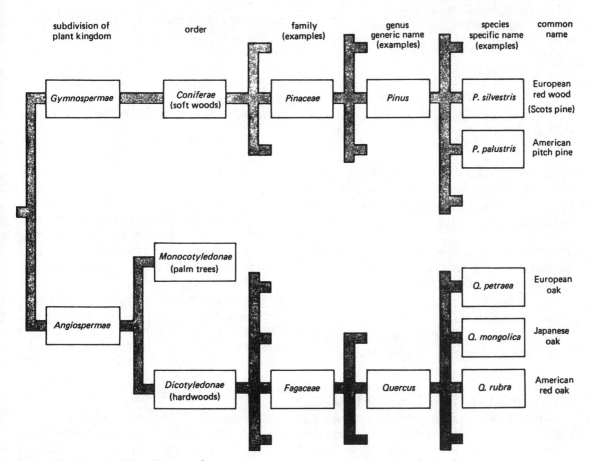

Figure 47 *Botanical classification of trees*

Density

Average density in kilograms per cubic metre (kg/m^3) is given for timbers with a moisture content of 15 per cent, although in many cases the density can vary by as much as 20 per cent or more.

Durability

This is the natural durability of the timber and refers to its resistance to fungal decay in use. Each timber is given a grade of durability based on the approximate life of a 50 mm × 50 mm heartwood section stake in contact with the ground.

	Grade
VD	very durable
D	durable
MD	moderately durable
ND	non-durable
P	perishable

	Life in ground contact
VD	more than 25 years
D	15–25 years
MD	10–15 years
ND	5–10 years
P	less than 5 years

Note: The sapwood of most timbers is graded as non-durable or perishable. External timbers not in contact with the ground can be expected to have a longer life than indicated.

The durability of timbers that are not naturally durable can be increased by treating with an appropriate preservative.

Impregnability

This is a measure of the permeability or treatability in relation to preservative penetration. Complete preservative penetration is easily obtained in permeable timbers, whereas it is difficult to achieve little more than a surface coating with timbers that are very resistant. The following grades are given for the timber's heartwood, sapwood normally being more permeable.

VR	very resistant
R	resistant
MR	moderately resistant
P	permeable

Moisture movement This refers to the dimensional changes that occur when seasoned timbers are exposed to changes in atmospheric conditions. All timbers are classified into one of three groups, according to the sum of their average radial and tangential percentage change in dimension occurring as a result of a 30 per cent change in the relative humidity of the atmosphere. In general radial shrinkage is about half that of tangential shrinkage.

L	more than 4.5 per cent
M	3.0 per cent to 4.5 per cent
S	less than 3.0 per cent

This proportion varies from timber to timber.

Price range

The price of timber is dependent on world market conditions, the method of purchase and the grade of timber required, but as a general guide prices are indicated as:

£££	high
££	medium
£	low

Colour

A description of colour is not given in the table as most timbers vary in colour to some extent and nearly all become either lighter or darker on exposure to the weather and also when finishing treatments are applied. Printed colour samples are available, at a small charge to non-members, from the Timber Research and Development Association. These samples can be used for comparing and identifying many readily available commercial timbers.

Marketing of timber

The marketing process for timber can be a complicated one. Most timber is purchased in its country of origin and shipped to the United Kingdom by an importer. Timber importers sell their supplies to timber merchants and major users (large joinery works). The larger timber merchants may also be importers and sometimes major users are both importers and merchants.

Imported timbers may be purchased at any stage of its travel from the forest to the port of entry in the United Kingdom. Typical methods of purchase are FAS, FOB and CIF.

FAS

When a buyer contracts to purchase timber FAS the purchase price will include the actual cost of the timber and its delivery alongside the vessel at the port of departure. FAS means 'free along side' or inclusive of all costs alongside the vessel. The buyer is responsible for chartering the ship, loading the timber and arranging insurance cover for the passage.

FOB

This is a similar method to FAS but in addition the purchase price includes the cost of loading the timber on the ship. FOB therefore means 'free on board' or inclusive of all costs on board the vessel. The buyer is still responsible for chartering the ship and arranging insurance cover.

CIF

This stands for 'cost, insurance, freight'. This means that the contract price includes the actual cost of the timber, the insurance cover and all transport, handling and shipping charges from the forest to its destination in the United Kingdom.

Grading of timber

Most imported timber and plywood is graded for quality at its source of origin by the exporting sawmill. Quality varies from country to country but in all cases it is the higher grades, which are practically defect free, that command the higher prices.

Shipping marks

The exporting mill marks every piece of timber with its own private trade or shipping mark. This

identifies its origin and quality. It may be stamped, stencilled or hammer branded on the end of each piece; different combinations of letters, symbols and colours are used for each grade. A typical shipping mark is illustrated in Figure 48.

As many hundreds of marks are in use they are of little significance to the end user, but details of the timber may be obtained by consulting a directory of timber shipping marks.

Softwood grading

A number of countries, using different gradings, export timber to the United Kingdom. Only a small percentage is British grown. Most softwoods are graded using a defects system which specifies the maximum amount or size of defect permissable for each grade of timber.

The North European countries – Sweden, Finland etc. – have a unified grading system. Their mill grading rules describe six basic qualities of redwood and whitewood, numbered I, II, III, IV, V, and VI (first, second, third, fourth, fifth and sixth). Figure 49 shows typical examples of 100 mm wide sawn boards graded to these rules.

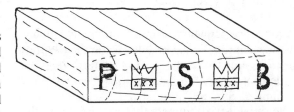

Figure 48   *Typical shipping mark*

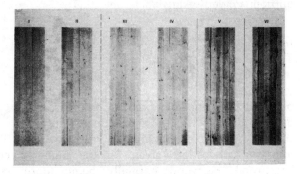

Figure 49   *Softwood grading*

Table 8   **Approximate comparison of softwood qualities**

Northern Europe and Eastern Canada	Russia	Canada and North America	Brazil	Common end use
		All clear qualities	No. 1	Joinery and high-class work
			No. 2	
I II III IV U/S (unsorted)	I II III U/S (unsorted)	Selected merchantable No. 1 merchantable		
V	IV	No. 2 merchantable		General construction and carcassing
VI	V	No. 3 common		Utility grade mainly for packaging

The basic qualities I, II, III, IV are rarely obtainable separately. The normal procedure employed by most sawmills is to group these together and sell them as one grade known as unsorted (U/S). This is also known as joinery quality.

The V quality is available separately and is used for general construction and carcassing work. The VI quality is a low-grade timber used mainly for packaging. It is available separately and often known as *utskott*, a term used to describe any edge boards.

Other parcels of timber may be described as saw felling quality. This is a mixed batch of qualities I to V sold without further sorting, but will consist mainly of IV and V qualities, percentages of I, II and III qualities being very limited. Saw felling quality is termed by some sawmills as V and better.

East Canadian timber for export to Europe is often graded using these Northern Europe qualities.

The Russian grading system is similar, but uses only five basic qualities; I – III are exported as unsorted, and this is approximately the same as the North European unsorted. The Russians basic qualities IV and V are similar or slightly better than the Swedish/Finnish V and VI.

Canadian and North American timber is often grown and marketed in mixed species groups such as hem/fir (Western hemlock and Amabilis fir) and spruce/pine/fir. The main grades are:

Selected merchantable and No. 1 merchantable; these are similar to the Swedish/Finnish unsorted qualities

No. 2 merchantable is general carcassing quality

No. 3 common is a utility grade, used mainly for packaging timber

Clear grades of virtually knot-free timber are available for high-quality work:

No. 2 clear and better (B and better) is the top grade of clear timber normally free of all imperfections

No. 3 clear (C clear) and No. 4 clear (D clear) are slightly lower qualities containing a number of imperfections.

Door stock and remanufacturing grades are also produced.

Parana pine from Brazil is graded into four basic qualities, but only No. 1 and No. 2 qualities are normally exported to Europe. Table 8 gives an approximate comparison of softwoods together with their stated common end uses.

British-grown softwood was previously graded to a British Standard which described five basic qualities: I clear, I, II, III and IV. This standard was rarely used. The common practice in most British sawmills is to produce what is known as 'run of the mill'; this is normally sorted into joinery and carcassing qualities by the timber merchants.

Hardwood grading

Hardwoods are obtained from a far wider range of sources than softwoods. This results in more varied grading systems. Often a grading system is not applied and the timber is sold for a specific end use, by mutual agreement between the buyer and seller.

Most hardwood grading is based on a 'cutting system' which estimates the percentage of clear defect-free timber, or timber with minimal acceptable defects that can be obtained from each plank.

The main system which is used by North America and West Africa contains five main export grades: first, seconds, selects, No. 1 common and No. 2 common. The top two qualities are often grouped together and sold as FAS quality ('first and seconds'). This quality consists of clear defect-free timber and is used for high-quality joinery work. Selects and No. 1 common qualities will contain minor defects. The No. 2 common quality often contains a high percentage of timber that is not suitable for joinery.

Round logs are also exported from West Africa and may be described as FAQ (fair average quality).

The Malaysian grading rules consist of four basic qualities: prime, select, standard, and serviceable. The serviceable grade is not exported.

British-grown hardwoods can be graded into four basic qualities: 1, 2, 3 and 4 under the cutting system, or A, B, C, and D qualities under the defects system. However, as for British-grown softwood, this grading system is rarely applied; most home-grown timbers are sold for a specific end use.

Timber for joinery work, both softwoods and hardwoods, may be specified in accordance with BS 1186 Part 1, *Quality of Timber*. This standard lists timbers that are suitable for joinery work and defines four classes for the exposed surfaces of joinery timber: class 1S, class 1, class 2, and class 3. Class 1S must be defect-free timber and is intended for clear finishings. The other classes can contain a limited number of permitted defects.

Plywood grading

Plywood is graded according to the appearance of its outer faces, each face being assessed separately. In common with timber, the grading rules for plywood vary widely from country to country. There are three basic qualities of face veneers from which plywood is manufactured:

Clear veneer quality This is the best-quality face veneer and is intended for clear finishing. Therefore it should be virtually blemish free. No manufacturing or natural defects are permitted and any permitted knots are restricted in both number and size. Where joints occur in the face veneer this must be grain and colour matched.

Repaired veneer quality Repaired or 'solid' veneer is a lower quality and will have a number of visible defects. These will be repaired by patching unsound knots and making good shakes either with shims or filler to present a flush, solid face. Mismatching and discolouration of veneer is to be expected.

Unrepaired veneer quality As its name suggests, no attempt is made to repair the veneer in this quality. A large number of manufacturing and natural defects is to be expected. Therefore unrepaired veneer is mainly used as a backing veneer or for industrial or structural uses where its visual appearance is not important.

Most plywood manufacturers base their grading rules on these three basic qualities, but it is normal to further subdivide them into five or six different board grades. Typical examples of the grades available are as follows:

Northern Europe/Russia

Grade mark	Permitted defects
A	practically defect free
B	a few small knots and minor defects
BB	several knots and well-made plugs
C or WG	all defects allowed, only guaranteed to be well glued

It is rarely necessary for the face and back veneer to be of the same grade; most manufacturers offer a wide combination of face and back veneer grades: A/B A/C B/BB B/C etc.

Canada/America

Plywood from these sources is available in the following grades, which are approximately equivalent to the Northern Europe and Russian grades shown.

Grade mark		Equivalent to
G2S	(good two sides)	A/A
G/S	(good one side/solid reverse)	A/B
G1S	(good one side)	A/C
Solid 2S	(solid two sides)	B/B
Solid 1S	(solid one side)	B/C
Sheathing		C/C

Note: In some cases the grade marks are followed by the letter X. This indicates boards of exterior quality.

Common abbreviations

On reading the previous sections and looking through timber price lists and catalogues it will be apparent that there is a vast selection of abbreviations used in the timber trade. Many of these are defined in Table 9.

Stress grading

The strength properties of timber vary widely between species and even between different pieces cut from the same tree. To be used as a structural material some method must be used to classify the stronger from the weaker pieces.

Stress or strength grading classifies timber for structural purposes and provides architects and structural designers with material of a known minimum strength. Stress grading is based upon

Table 9 Common abbreviations

a.d.	air dried	p.a.r.	planed all round
avge	average	p.e.	plain edged
bd	board	p.h.n.d.	pin-holes no defect (a grading term
bdl	bundle		indicating that pin-holes are not
Com. & Sels	common and selects		considered to be a defect)
Clr & Btr	clear and better	p.s.e.	planed and square edged
Com.	common	p.s.j.	planed and square jointed
d.b.b.	deals, battens, boards (sizes of	p.t.g.	planed, tongued and grooved
	timber)	qtd	quartered
FAS	first and seconds	sap	sapwood
f.s.p.	fibre saturation point	S/E	square edged
hdwd	hardwood	sftwd	softwood
h.g. or B.g.	home grown	sels	selects
k.d.	kiln dried	s.n.d.	sapwood no defect (a grading term
lgth	length		indicating that sapwood is not
m.c.	moisture content		considered to be a defect)
Merch.	merchantable	t. & g.	tongued and grooved
P1E or S1E	planed or surfaced one edge	t. & t.	through and through
P2E or S2E	planed or surfaced two edges	t.g.b.	tongued, grooved and beaded
P1S or S1S	planed or surfaced one side	t.g.v.	tongued, grooved and V-jointed
P2S or S2S	planed or surfaced two sides	U/E	unedged
P1S1E or	planed or surfaced one side and one	U/S	unsorted
S1S1E	edge	v.j.m.	V-jointed matching
P2S1E or	planed or surfaced two sides and one	W/E	waney edged
S2S1E	edge	w.h.n.d.	worm-holes no defect (a grading
P1S2E or	planed or surfaced one side and two		term indicating that worm-holes are
S1S2E	edges		not considered to be a defect)
P4S	planed four sides	wt	weight

the strength of clear defect-free timber. This strength, or basic stress as it is known, is the stress which can be permanently and safely sustained by a piece of timber. The basic stress does not make allowance for the inevitable inclusion in practice of strength-reducing defects (knots, rate of growth, slope of grain and distortions etc.). By measuring these defects it is possible to select timber that has a strength equal to a certain percentage of clear defect-free timber.

BS Code of Practice 112: Part 2: 1971, *The Structural Use of Timber*, defined four main grades, 40, 50, 65 and 75, meaning that the timbers were equivalent to 40, 50, 65 and 75 per cent, respectively, of the basic stress. The numbered grade system has been superseded by a visual grading method based on knot/area ratio (KAR), and a machine grading method which measures the amount of deflection or stiffness of the timber.

This method, introduced by BS 4978: 1973: *Timber Grades For Structural Use*, defined the following grades:

Visually graded: general structural (GS)
       special structural (SS)
Mechanically graded: machine general structural (MGS)
         machine special structural (MSS)

There is no direct relationship between the numbered grades and the grades defined in BS 4978, as the grading rules differ. However, in general the following are acceptable approximations:

GS = 30–35 per cent of basic stress
SS = 50–60 per cent of basic stress

The machine grades have the same grade stresses as the visual grades, thus allowing interchangeability:

MGS = GS
MSS = SS

In addition, numbered mechanical grades are available. Grading machines can be set to select timber of any strength up to the maximum basic stress for a particular species. Although in principle it is possible to obtain any numbered mechanical grades, the two almost exclusively specified are M50 and M75, having grade stresses of 50 per cent and 75 per cent. Therefore there is a range of six commercially available stress grades which in descending strength order are M75, MSS/SS, M50, MGS/GS.

The grading of tropical hardwoods for structural use is catered for by BS 5756: 1979: Graded Tropical Hardwoods for Structural Use. This specifies the visual characteristics of a single tropical hardwood, Structural Grade HS.

BS 5268: Part 2: 1984 Structural Use of Timber (which replaced CP 112) uses the grades defined in BS 4978 and BS 5756 and further classifies them by grade and species into new strength classes.

Grading rules

Visual
British Standard 4978 limits the size of permitted defects for visual grades in respect of knots, wane, slope of grain, rate of growth, fissures and other defects. A summary of these defects is given in Table 10.

Knots
These are measured by the knot/area ratio (KAR) at the worst cross-section. A distinction being made between knots near the edge (margin knots) and knots near the centre: the reason for this is that margin knots affect strength to a far greater extent than knots in the relatively unstressed central cross-section. No distinction is made betwen knot holes, live knots or dead knots. Knots less than 5 mm in diameter can be ignored.

The following definitions apply to knot assessment:

KAR This is the ratio of the sum of projected cross-sectional areas of all knots at any particular cross-section to the cross-sectional area of the piece being considered.
Margin area This is the area of a cross-section which adjoins an edge and occupies a quarter of the total cross-section; the top and bottom quarters of a piece, as shown in Figure 50.

Table 10 Stress grading rules

Defects	GS		MGS	SS		MSS	M50	M75
Knots Maximum permitted value of ratio projected area of knots total area of section	If margin condition applies 1/3	If no margin condition 1/2	No limit other than that automatically imposed by the machine as a result of reduction in strength 1/3	If margin condition applies 1/5	If no margin condition 1/3	No limit other than that automatically imposed by the machine as a result of reduction in strength		1/8
Wane	1/3 except that not nearer the end than 300 mm wane may be up to 1/2 within one continuous length not exceeding 300 mm		1/3	1/4		1/4	1/4	1/8
Slope of grain Slope of grain must not be greater than	1 in 6		No limit	1 in 10		No limit		
Rate of growth	Not less than 4 annual rings per 25 mm		No limit	Not less than 4 annual rings per 25 mm		No limit other than that automatically imposed by the machine as a result of reduction in strength		
Fissures Resin pockets are measures as fissures	If the size of the defect is less than or equal to 1/2 the thickness of the piece, then the fissures may be unlimited in number wherever they occur in the piece If the size of the defect is greater than 1/2 the thickness of the piece, but less than the thickness of the piece, then the length of the fissures shall not exceed 900 mm or 1/4 the length of the piece, whichever is the lesser If the size of the defect is equal to the thickness of the piece, then the length of the fissures shall not exceed 600 mm: if the fissures occur at the end of the piece their length shall not exceed 1 1/2 times the width of the piece		If the size of the defect is less than or equal to 1/2 the thickness of the piece, then the fissures may be unlimited in number wherever they occur in the piece If the size of the defect is greater than 1/2 the thickness of the piece, but less than the thickness of the piece, then the length of the fissures shall not exceed 600 mm or 1/4 the length of the piece, whichever is the lesser If the size of the defect is equal to the thickness of the piece, then the fissures shall be permitted only if they occur at the ends of the piece and their length shall not exceed the width of the piece	If the size of the defect is less than or equal to 1/2 the thickness of the piece, then the fissures may be unlimited in number wherever they occur in the piece If the size of the defect is greater than 1/2 the thickness of the piece, but less than the thickness of the piece, then the length of the fissures shall not exceed 600 mm or 1/4 the length of the piece, whichever is the lesser If the size of the defect is equal to the thickness of the piece, then the fissures shall be permitted only if they occur at the ends of the piece and their length shall not exceed the width of the piece				For defects less than, or equal to 1/2 the thickness of the piece, the length of the fissure shall not exceed 600 mm or 1/4 the length of the piece whichever is the lesser For defects greater than 1/2 the thickness of the piece, the fissures shall be permitted only if they occur at the ends of the piece and their length shall not exceed the width of the

Sap stain	Sap stain is not a structural defect and may be permitted to a limited extent
Worm-holes	Pin-holes and worm-holes are permitted to a slight extent in a small number of pieces provided there is no active infestation of the material. Wood wasp-holes are not permitted
Distortion	Any piece which is bowed, twisted, cupped or sprung to an excessive extent, having regard to the end use, shall be rejected BS4978 does not give precise limits for distortion but, for guidance, states that the following limits of bow, spring, twist and cup may be applied to parcels of graded timber: Bow should not exceed ½ of the thickness in any 3 m length Spring should not exceed 15 mm in any 3 m length Twist should not exceed 1 mm per 25 mm of width in any 3 m length Cup should not exceed 1/25 of the width
Abnormal defects	All pieces showing fungal decay, brittle heart and other abnormal defects affecting strength shall be excluded Pieces may be accepted, however, where the reduction in strength caused by the abnormal defect is obviously less than that caused by the defects admitted by the grade of timber, subject to the provision that these abnormal defects are of a type which will not progress after conversion and seasoning (for example, white pocket rot derived from the standing tree)

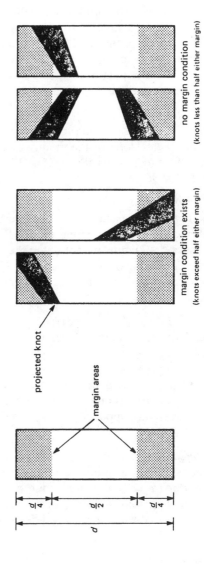

Figure 50   *Margin areas and margin condition*

Margin condition This exists when more than half of either margin area is occupied by the projected area of knots. Figure 50 shows the method used to determine whether or not a margin condition exists.

Wane
The amount of wane in proportion to the face or edge of a piece is limited to one-third when within 300 mm of either end or up to one-half when further away and not exceeding 300 mm in any one continuous length. Figure 51 shows how to measure the proportion of wane.

Slope of grain
Surface checks when present can give an indication of the slope of the grain. A slope to the edge of up to 1 in 6 is allowed for GS and up to 1 in 10 for SS.

Rate of growth
This is measured on one end of a piece and is taken to be the average number of growth rings per 25 mm on a 75 mm line normal to the curve. On smaller sections the average per 25 mm should be measured over the longest normal line possible.

Fissures
A fissure can be defined as a separation of the wood tissue appearing on the face, side or end of a piece of timber, and so includes all checks, shakes, splits and resin pockets etc. Figure 52 shows how fissures should be measured; adjacent fissures on opposite faces should be measured as one.

Other defects
Distortions, sap stain and worm-holes are all permitted to a limited extent, but pieces of timber showing fungal decay, brittle heart or other abnormal strength reducing defects will be rejected.

Machine grading
Mechanical grading is based on the relationship between the timber's stiffness and its breaking strength. Each piece of timber is passed through the grading machine where a constant load is applied by rollers. A small computer measures the amount of deflection and quickly determines

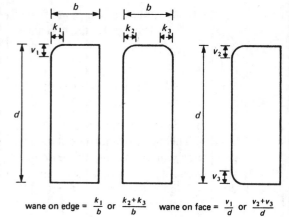

wane on edge = $\frac{k_1}{b}$ or $\frac{k_2+k_3}{b}$ wane on face = $\frac{v_1}{d}$ or $\frac{v_2+v_3}{d}$

Figure 51   *Measurement of wane*

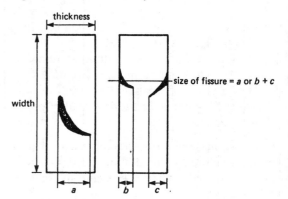

Figure 52   *Measurement of fissures*

the grade, which it marks on the timber in the same operation by splashes of coloured dyes towards one end of the piece or at intervals throughout its length. The standard colour coding recommended for the machine stress grades is:

M75	red
MSS	purple
M50	blue
MGS	green

Although machine-graded timber is not inspected for knots, slope of grain or rate of growth, it does have to comply with the other limitations set out for the visual grades. See Table 10 for details.

Marking
In accordance with BS 4978 each piece of

visually stress-graded timber or component must be clearly marked at least once on one face, edge or end, with:

1 Its grade mark GS or SS
2 A mark to indicate the grader or the company responsible for the grading.

The timber may also be stamped with the TRADA mark. This means that the grader and the company supplying the timber are members of TRADA's quality assurance scheme for visually stress-graded softwood (see Figure 53).

Machine-graded timber must be marked at least once on each piece, normally on its face, with:

1 The licence number of the grading machine
2 The grade mark MGS, M50, MSS or M75
3 The British Standards Institution kitemark
4 The British Standard number BS 4978
5 The species of timber (required by the British Standards Institution quality assurance scheme)

A typical machine stress-grading mark is illustrated in Figure 54. In addition the timber may also be marked with the relevant splashes of coloured dye.

Remarking

Where a company removes the grade mark during processing (regularizing or planing) it should remark the timber with its original grade and their own identification mark. The original grade mark should be prefixed by the letter R to denote that the timber has been remarked. The resawing of timber into smaller sections invalidates its original grade. Each resulting piece requires regrading and marking.

Overseas stress grading

Timber may be imported not stress graded, ready for grading in the United Kingdom, or it may have been stress graded at source.

Stress-graded timber that is imported from Europe can be visually or mechanically graded at source in accordance with British Standard 4978, and is marked in the same way. It will also contain a mark to identify its country of origin,

Figure 53   *Visual stress-grading mark*

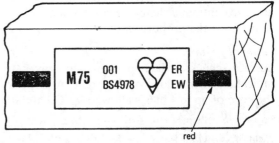

Figure 54   *Machine stress-grading mark*

for example, S for Sweden, the axe outline $\triangledown$ for Finland and L 'eagle' P for Poland.

Timber imported from Canada is stress graded under the NLGA (National Lumber Grades Authority) rules. The timber is grouped into sizes according to its end use. Three basic end-use groups are mainly imported to the United Kingdom. These basic groups are subdivided into a number of grades and marked accordingly, as follows:

Size group	Grade
Light framing	
38 mm thick by 38 mm to 100 mm wide	Construction standard utility
Stud	
38 mm to 89 mm thick by 38 mm to 140 mm wide	One grade only, not subdivided
Structural joists and planks	
38 mm to 100 mm thick by 114 mm and wider	Select structural
	No. 1 structural
	No. 2 structural
	No. 3 structural

Often the grades within each end-use groups are shipped in mixed packages, the higher grades being selected in the United Kingdom for more critical structural applications before use.

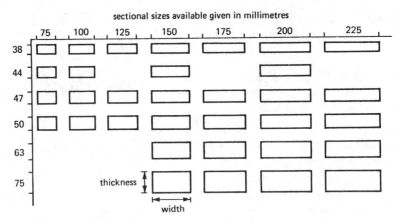

Figure 55 *Common sawn stress-graded sizes*

Commercial sizes

Stress-graded timber is available either sawn or processed. The basic range of sawn sizes commonly available is shown in Figure 55. Other sizes may be made available by special arrangement with the grading company. Any sawn size may be processed by regularizing or planing.

Regularizing of structural timber ensures a uniform width, which is most useful for floor joists and wall studs. It may be carried out by machining one or both edges. A reduction in width of 3 mm is allowed for timbers up to 150 mm and 5 mm over this width, for example, 50 mm × 200 mm joist may be regularized to 50 mm × 195 mm.

Planed all round (PAR) structural timber is easier to handle and has the advantage of being uniform in width. Certain sawmills, notably the Canadian ones, often supply PAR structural timber with its four arrises eased or pencil rounded. The normal reductions from the basic sawn size, for planing two opposite faces or edges is 3 mm for dimensions up to 100 mm, 5 mm for dimensions between 100 mm and 150 mm, and 6 mm for dimensions over 150 mm.

Size tolerance

It is recognized that the moisture content of timber affects its actual size. The basic sizes refer to timber with a 20 per cent moisture content. Certain size tolerances are permissible, but any minus tolerances are restricted to not more than 10 per cent of the pieces in any one parcel of sawn softwood.

For sawn wood, a tolerance of minus 1 mm plus 3 mm for dimensions up to 100 mm is allowed, and for dimensions over 100 mm it is increased to minus 2 mm plus 6 mm. For regularized, a tolerance on the width of plus or minus 1 mm is given and for PAR a tolerance of plus or minus 0.5 mm.

Standard lengths start at 1.800 m and rise by 300 mm increments. European timber is rarely available over 5.700 m but lengths of up to 12 m are available from Canadian sources. Longer lengths can be obtained from most sources by using structurally finger-jointed timber.

Strength Class A comparison of the various grades is made possible through BS 5268: Part 2: 1984 Structural Use of Timber. This classifies different species and stress grades of timber into one of the nine strength classes as shown on p. 97.

Conversion of timber

The conversion of timber is the sawing up or breaking down of the tree trunk into variously sized pieces of timber for a specific purpose. Theoretically a tree trunk can be sawn to the required size in one of two ways: by sawing in a tangential direction (see Figure 56); and by sawing in a radial direction.

Species	Strength class (SC) and grade								
	1	2	3	4	5	6	7	8	9
Imported softwood									
Parana Pine			GS	SS					
Redwood			GS/M50	SS	M75				
Whitewood			GS/M50	SS	M75				
Western Red Cedar	GS	SS							
Douglas Fir	No.3		GS	SS					
			No.1 No.2	Sels					
Hem-Fir	No.3		GS/M50	SS	M75				
			No.1 No.2	Sels					
Spruce-Pine-Fir	No.3		GS/M50	SS/M75					
			No.1 No.2	Sels					
British grown softwood									
Douglas Fir		GS	M50/SS		M75				
Larch			GS	SS					
Scots Pine			GS/M50	SS	M75				
Spruce	GS	M50/SS	M75						
Tropical hardwood									
Ekki								HS	
Greenheart									HS
Iroko					HS				
Keruing							HS		
Teak					HS				

The terms 'radial' and 'tangential' refer to the cut surfaces of the timber in relation to the growth rings of the tree. Both methods have their advantages and disadvantages. In practice very little timber is cut either truly tangentially or truly radially because there would be too much wastage in both timber and manpower.

To be classified as either a tangential or a radial cut, the timber must conform to the following standards:

Tangential Timber converted so that the annual rings meet the wider surface of the timber over at least half its width, at an angle of less than 45°. See Figure 57.

Radial Timber converted so that the annual rings meet the wider surface of the timber throughout its width at an angle of 45° or more. See Figure 58.

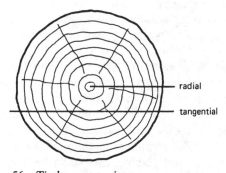

Figure 56 *Timber conversion*

Figure 57 *Tangential cut, annual rings at less than 45°*

Figure 58 *Radial cut, annual rings at 45° or more*

There are four main methods of conversion to produce timber to these standards:

Through and through
Tangential
Quarter
Boxed heart

Through and through (Figure 59)

This method is also known as slash or slab sawing. It is the simplest and cheapest way to convert timber, with very little wastage.

Note: Approximately two-thirds of the boards will be tangential and one-third (the middle boards) will be radial.

The majority of boards produced in this way are prone to a large amount of shrinkage and distortion.

Tangential (Figure 60)

This method is used when converting timber for floor joists and beams, since it produces the strongest timber. It is also used for decorative purposes on timbers which have distinctive annual rings, for example, pitch pine and Douglas fir, because it produces 'flame figuring' or 'fiery grain'.

Quarter (Figure 61)

This is the most expensive method of conversion, although it produces the best quality timber which is ideal for joinery purposes. This is because the boards have very little tendency to shrink or distort. In timber where the medullary rays are prominent, the boards will have a figured finish, for example, figured or silver-grained oak. See Figure 62.

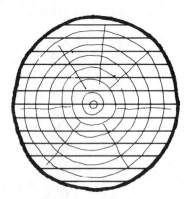

Figure 59   *Through-and-through conversion*

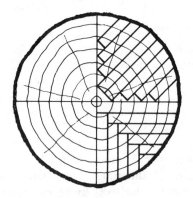

Figure 61   *Quarter conversion*

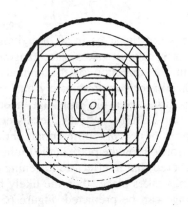

Figure 60   *Tangential conversion*

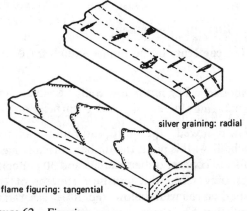

silver graining: radial

flame figuring: tangential

Figure 62   *Figuring*

Boxed heart (Figure 63)

This is a type of radial sawing and is done when the heart of a tree is rotten or badly shaken. It is also known as floorboard sawing as the boards produced are ideal for this purpose because they wear well and do not distort. The waste pieces of timber are of an inferior quality but are often used for fencing etc.

Types of machine

There are three main types of machine used to convert round tree trunks into square-section timber.

The circular sawmill

This is also known as a rack saw bench. It consists of a circular saw blade of up to 2.1 m in diameter and a travelling table on to which the tree trunk is fastened.

The log band mill

This can be of either horizontal or vertical type. Both types consist of a continuous band saw blade, up to 250 mm in width, mounted on two large-diameter pulleys and a travelling carriage on to which the tree trunk is fastened. The carriage runs on a track and feeds the tree trunk through the saw.

The log frame saw

This consists of a number of vertically mounted saw blades which move up and down in a frame. The tree trunk is fed through the saw by large feed rollers.

Moisture and movement

Moisture occurs in the timber in two forms:

As free water in the cell cavities
As bound water in the cell walls

When all of the free water in the cell cavities has been removed, the fibre saturation point is reached. At this point the timber normally has a moisture content of between 25 and 30 per cent. It is only when the moisture content of the timber is reduced below the fibre saturation point that shrinkage occurs. The amount of

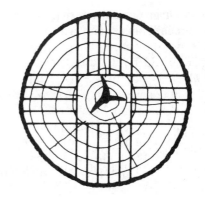

Figure 63   *Boxed heart conversion*

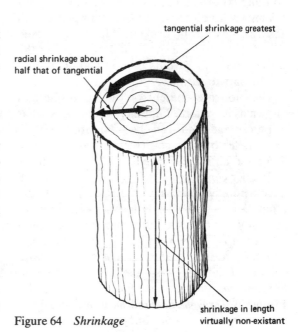

tangential shrinkage greatest

radial shrinkage about
half that of tangential

shrinkage in length
virtually non-existant

Figure 64   *Shrinkage*

shrinkage is not the same in all directions. The majority of shrinkage takes place tangentially, that is, in the direction of the annual rings. Radial shrinkage is approximately half that of tangential shrinkage, while shrinkage in length is virtually non-existent and can be disregarded (see Figure 64). This differential shrinkage causes distortion to take place in the timber. If it is remembered that in effect a shortening of the annual rings takes place, then the likely results of shrinkage can be predicted. Figure 65 gives typical results of shrinkage for different sections.

Timber is a hygroscopic material; this is to say that it will readily absorb or give off moisture depending on the surrounding environment. The timber should be dried out to a moisture content which is approximately equal to the surrounding atmosphere in which it will be used. This moisture content is known as the equilibrium moisture content and, providing the moisture content and temperature of the air remains constant, the timber will remain stable and not shrink or expand. But in most situations the moisture content of the atmosphere will vary to some extent and sometimes this variation can be quite considerable.

Timber fixed in a moist atmosphere will absorb moisture and expand. If it was then fixed in a dry atmosphere the bound moisture in the cells of the timber would dry out and the timber would start to shrink.

The moisture content of the atmosphere is known as its relative humidity. It is expressed as a percentage and can be measured with a hygrometer or wet-and-dry bulb thermometers. Saturated air is said to have a relative humidity of 100 per cent and air that is half saturated will have a relative humidity of 50 per cent. If the temperature of the air is increased its relative humidity will fall; this is because warm air has a greater capacity than cold air for absorbing and holding moisture. The equilibrium moisture content of the timber is therefore dependent on the relative humidity of the air. Externally, equilibrium will be reached at about 18–20 per cent moisture content. Internally, the relative humidity of the air is generally much lower, particularly near sources of heat, where equilibrium might be reached as low as 7–10 per cent moisture content.

The moisture content of timber is expressed as a percentage. This refers to the weight of the water in the timber compared to the dry weight of the timber. In order to determine the average moisture content of a stack of timber, select a board from the centre of the stack, cut off the end 300 mm and discard it, as this will normally be dryer than sections nearer the centre. Cut off a further 25 mm sample and immediately weigh it. This is the wet weight of the sample. Place

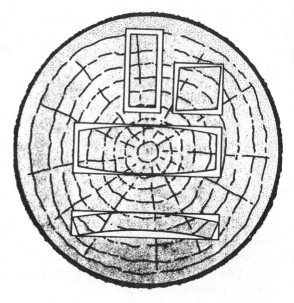

Figure 65   *Results of shrinkage*

this sample in a small drying oven and remove it periodically to check its weight. When no further loss of weight is recorded, assume this to be the dry weight of the sample.

The moisture content of a piece of timber can now be found by using the following formula:

$$\text{moisture content (per cent)} = \frac{\text{wet weight} - \text{dry weight}}{\text{dry weight}} \times 100$$

Example
Wet weight of sample 50 g
Dry weight of sample 40 g

$$\text{moisture content} = \frac{50 - 40}{40} \times 100 = 25 \text{ per cent}$$

An alternative way of finding the moisture content of timber is to use an electric moisture meter. Although not as accurate, it has the advantage of giving an on-the-spot reading and it can even be used for determining the moisture content of timber already fixed in position. The moisture meter measures the electrical resistance between the two points of a twin electrode which is pushed into the surface of the timber.

Figure 66   *Moisture meter*

Its moisture content can then easily be read off a calibrated dial (see Figure 66).

Figure 67 consists of two charts that show the average range of relative humidity that will be encountered both internally and externally throughout the year. From these charts the relationship between relative humidity of the air and moisture content of timber can be seen. These moisture contents must be taken as average values. This is because different species of timber have different hygroscopic values which cause them to achieve equilibrium at slightly higher or lower moisture contents.

As it is almost impossible to maintain a constant relative humidity, timber is all the time absorbing and giving off moisture in an attempt to maintain equilibrium. This inevitably causes a certain amount of moisture movement that the carpenter and joiner must make allowances for. The following are typical points of consideration.

Figure 67   *Relative humidity and moisture content*

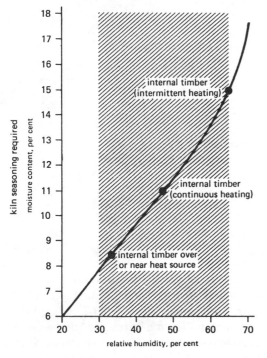

average range of relative humidity (internal)

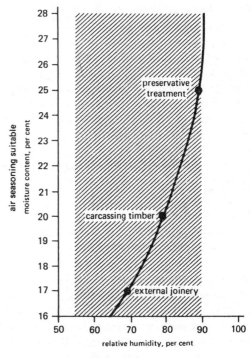

average range of relative humidity (external)

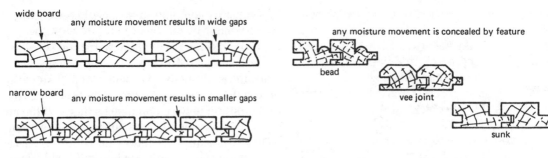

Figure 68   *Moisture movement*

Figure 69   *Use of features*

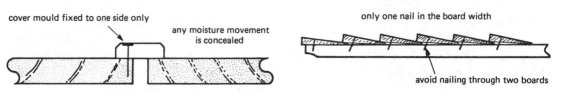

Figure 70   *Use of cover mould*

Figure 71   *Nailing*

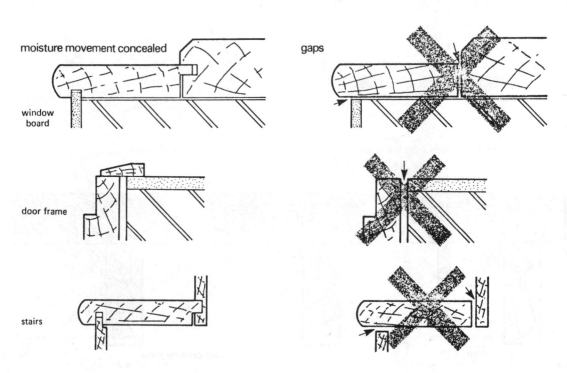

Figure 72   *Concealing effects of movement*

Figure 68 illustrates that wide boards show a bigger open joint as a result of moisture movement than do narrow boards. This open joint might be acceptable for floorboards etc. but for panelling and cladding etc. it is preferable to incorporate a decorative feature that conceals the movement. Typical examples are shown in Figure 69.

Figure 70 shows how a cover mould can be used to conceal movement.

Note: It is only fixed to one side; this prevents it splitting.

Care must be taken when fixing fencing and cladding not to double nail in the board width as this would restrict movement and result in the board splitting. This is shown in Figure 71.

Tongued joints and cover moulds are often used to mask the effects of moisture movement. Typical details are illustrated in Figure 72.

Wide tangentially sawn boards always cup away from the heart. Greater stability can be achieved by using narrower boards or ripping wider boards and joining up with alternative heart side up, heart side down, as shown in Figure 73.

Made-up wide boards, such as solid table and countertops, act as one board, with any movement taking place over the total width. The use of slot-screwed battens on the underside is desirable to prevent distortion while still allowing movement. Slotted steel washers may be used in conjunction with the battens (see Figure 74). When fixing solid timber tops, differential

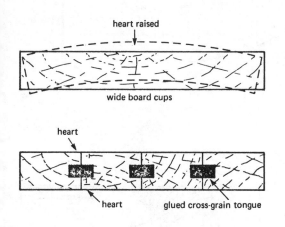

Figure 73 *Greater stability with narrow board*

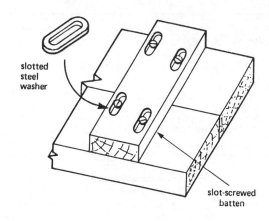

Figure 74 *Slot-screwed batten*

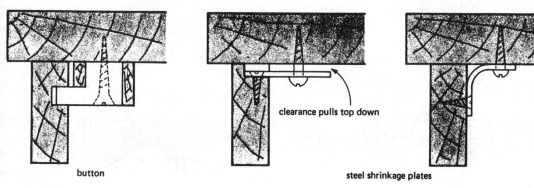

Figure 75 *Allowing for movement*

Figure 76 *Cabinet construction*

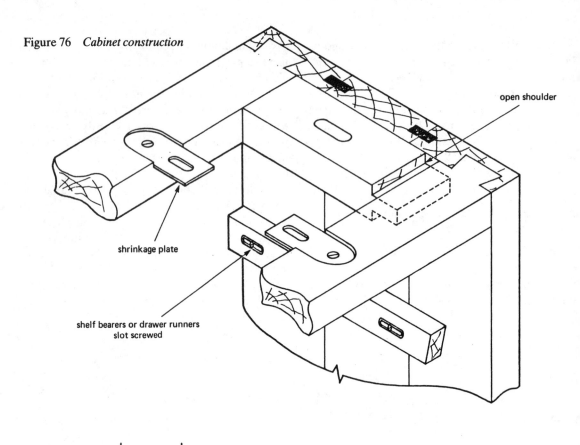

open shoulder

shrinkage plate

shelf bearers or drawer runners
slot screwed

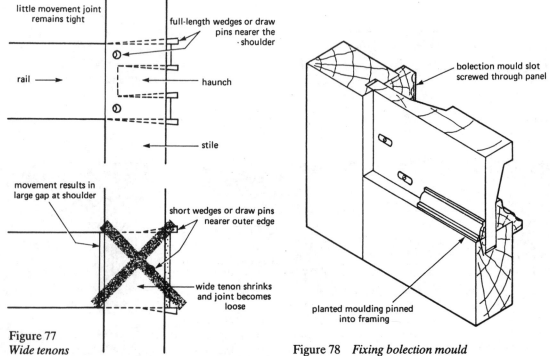

little movement joint
remains tight

full-length wedges or draw
pins nearer the
·shoulder

rail →

haunch

stile

movement results in
large gap at shoulder

short wedges or draw pins
nearer outer edge

wide tenon shrinks
and joint becomes
loose

Figure 77
Wide tenons

bolection mould slot
screwed through panel

planted moulding pinned
into framing

Figure 78 *Fixing bolection mould*

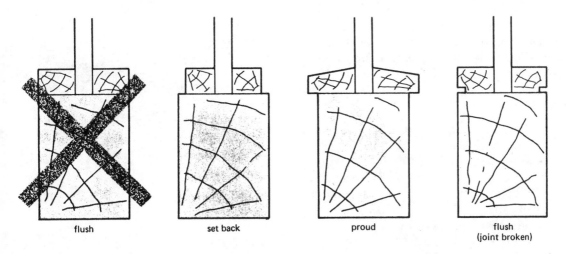

| flush | set back | proud | flush (joint broken) |

Figure 79   *Planted mouldings*

movement between the top and frame or carcass is allowed for by using buttons or shrinkage plates as shown in Figure 75.

Cabinet construction in solid timber involves a number of considerations. These are illustrated in Figure 76.

The width of tenons in framed joinery should be restricted to a maximum of five times their thickness. Wide tenons should be avoided as these are prone to a large amount of movement. The use of a haunch reduces their effective width, thus minimizing movement. Movement at shoulders is avoided by using full-length wedges or draw pinning near the shoulder. See Figure 77.

Figure 78 shows how bolection mouldings should be slot screwed through the panel in order to prevent the panel splitting. The planted moulding used to cover the screw holes should be fixed to the framing and not the panel. When planted mouldings are used such as glazing or panel beads they should never finish flush with the framing as an unsightly gap will result. Always either set them back, make them proud or break the joint by incorporating a decorative feature. See Figure 79.

Seasoning of timber

The term seasoning refers to the controlled drying by natural or artificial means of converted timber. There are many reasons why seasoning is necessary, the main ones being:

To ensure the moisture content of the timber is below the dry rot safety line of 20 per cent

To ensure that any shrinkage takes place before the timber is used

Dry timber is easier to work with than wet timber

Using seasoned timber, the finished article will be more reliable and less likely to split or distort (in general, dry timber is stronger and stiffer than wet timber)

Wet timber will not readily accept glue, paint or polish

Timber may be seasoned in one of two ways:

By natural means (air seasoning)
By artificial means (kiln seasoning)

Air seasoning

In this method the timber is stacked in open-sided covered sheds which protect the timber from rain while still allowing a free circulation of air. In Britain a moisture content of between 18 per cent and 20 per cent can be achieved in a period of two to twelve months, depending on the size and type of timber. Figure 80 shows an ideal timber stack for the air seasoning of softwoods. The following points should be noted:

1 Brick piers and timber joists keep the bottom of the stack well clear of the ground and ensure good air circulation underneath.
2 The boards are laid horizontally, largest at the bottom, smallest at the top, one piece above the other. This reduces the risk of the timber distorting as it dries out.
3 The boards on each layer are spaced approximately 25 mm apart.
4 Piling sticks or stickers are introduced between each layer of timber at approximately 600 mm distances, to support the boards and allow a free air circulation around them.

    Note: The piling sticks should be the same type of timber as that being seasoned otherwise staining may occur.

5 The ends of the boards should be painted or covered with strips of timber to prevent them from drying out too quickly and splitting.

Hardwood can be seasoned in the same air seasoning sheds, but when the boards have been converted using the through-and-through method they should be stacked in the same order as they were cut from the log. Figure 81 shows a slash sawn hardwood log stacked in stick, air seasoning prior to kilning.

Kiln seasoning

Most timber for internal use is kiln seasoned as this method, if carried out correctly, is able to safely reduce the moisture content of timber to any required level without any danger of degrading (causing defects). Although timber can be completely kiln seasoned, sometimes when a sawmill has a low kiln capacity the timber is air seasoned before being placed in the kiln for final seasoning. The length of time the

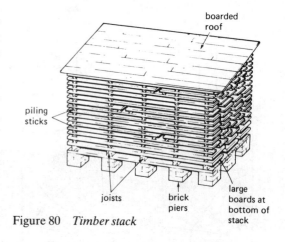

Figure 80   *Timber stack*

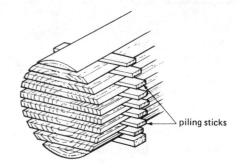

Figure 81   *Hardwood stacked for seasoning*

timber needs to stay in the kiln normally varies between two days and six weeks according to the type and size of timber being seasoned.

There are two main types of kiln in general use:

Compartment kiln
Progressive kiln

Compartment kiln

This is normally a brick or concrete building in which the timber is stacked. The timber will remain stationary during the drying process, while the conditions of the air are adjusted to the correct levels as the drying progresses.

Note: The timber should be stacked in the same way as that used for air seasoning. Figure 82 shows a battery of 20 kilns installed by a large timber merchant. Each kiln has a capacity ranging from 28 m^3 to 56 m^3 per load.

Figure 82   *Compartment kiln battery*

Figure 83 shows a section through a compartment kiln, in which the drying of the timber
depends on three factors:

1 Air circulation, which is supplied by fans
2 Heat, which is normally supplied by heating
   coils through which steam flows
3 Humidity (moisture content of the air).
   Steam sprays are used for raising the
   humidity

Progressive kiln
This can be thought of as a tunnel full of open
trucks containing timber which are progressively
moved forward from the loading end to the
discharge end. The drying conditions in the kiln
become progressively more severe so that loads
at different distances from the loading end are at
different stages of drying.

Progressive kilns are mainly used in situations

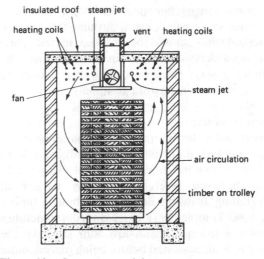

Figure 83   *Compartment kiln*

where there is a need for a continuous supply of timber which is of the same species and dimensions.

Drying schedules

These are available for the kiln drying of different types of timbers. They set out the drying conditions required for a given size and type of timber. Although all types of timber require different conditions for varying lengths of time, the drying process in general involves three stages:

1 Wet timber inserted; controls set to high steam, low heat
2 Timber drying; controls set to reduce steam, increase heat
3 Timber almost dry; controls set to low steam, high heat. The seasoned timber can then be removed from the kiln.

Developments in seasoning

Other innovatory methods of seasoning are in limited use or are being developed. These include the following.

In chemical or salt seasoning the timber is treated with hygroscopic salts before air or kiln seasoning. This encourages the moisture in the inner core to move outward while at the same time preventing the surface layers drying prematurely.

Press drying has been used for the rapid seasoning of very permeable timber. It involves pressing the timber between two metal plates across which an electric potential is applied. This raises the temperature of the moisture up to boiling, when it escapes as steam.

Microwave energy has ben used to season timber. The centre core of the timber is excited by the microwave energy; at the same time cool air is circulated over its surface. This creates a temperature difference which causes the moisture in the warmer centre core to move to the cooler surfaces.

Seasoning has been carried out in kilns using dehumidifying equipment. Basically this involves forcing completely dried air through timber stacked in a drying chamber. This absorbs a great deal of moisture from the timber. The wet air is then dehumidified by a refrigeration and heating technique before being recirculated through the chamber. This process is repeated until the required moisture content is achieved.

Second seasoning

This is rarely carried out nowadays, but refers to a further drying of high-class joinery work after it has been machined and loosely framed up but not glued or wedged. The framed joinery is stacked in a store which has a similar moisture content to the building where it will be finally fixed. Should any defects occur during this second seasoning, which can last up to three months, the defective component can easily be replaced.

Water seasoning

This is not seasoning as we understand it at all. It refers to timber logs which are kept under water before conversion in order to protect them from timber decay. This process is also sometimes used to wash out the sap of some hardwoods that are particularly susceptible to attack by the Lyctus beetle.

Conditioning

This is a form of reverse seasoning. It refers to the practice of brushing up to one litre of water on the back of hardboard twenty-four to forty-eight hours before fixing. This is so that the board will tighten on its fixings as it dries out and shrinks. If this were not done, expansion could take place which would result in the board bowing or buckling.

Seasoning defects

Incorrect or haphazard seasoning can be very costly as it causes a number of defects in timber which may lead to the excessive waste of material. Some defects, if undetected, can present a potential source of danger to the woodworking machinist.

Distortions (Figure 84)

These may be the result of an inherent weakness

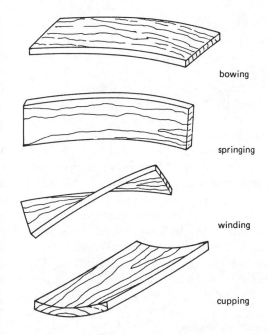

bowing

springing

winding

cupping

Figure 84   *Distortions*

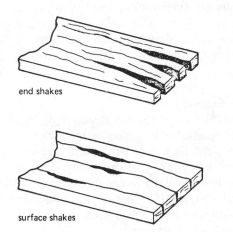

end shakes

surface shakes

Figure 85   *Shaking*

in the timber or bad conversion, but often they develop during seasoning through poor stacking or uneven air circulation. Returning the timber to the kiln and subjecting it to a high humidity followed by restacking, placing heavy weights on top of the load and then reseasoning to a suitable drying schedule may straighten the timber out. Often the results of this reversal are of a temporary nature, the distortion soon returning.

Shaking (Figure 85)

These are splits or checks which develop along the grain of a piece of timber, particularly at its ends. They are the result of the surface or ends of the timber drying out too fast during seasoning, or possibly the result of high-humidity reversal treatment. Small surface checks often close up or, if shallow may be removed completely by planing.

Collapse (Figure 86)

This is also known as wash boarding and is caused by the cells collapsing through being kiln dried too rapidly. This can rarely be reversed but in certain circumstances prolonged high-humidity treatment is successful.

Case hardening (Figure 87)

This is also the result of too rapid kiln drying. In this case the outside of the board is dry but moisture is trapped in the centre cells of the timber. This defect is not apparent until the board is resawn, when it will tend to twist and distort. The kerf will close in and bind on the saw. See Figure 88. Case hardening can be remedied if the timber is quickly returned to the

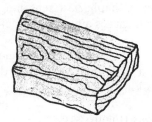

Figure 86   *Collapse*

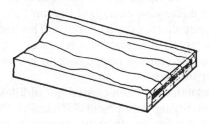

Figure 87   *Case hardening*

kiln and given a high-humidity treatment followed by reseasoning.

Honeycombing (Figure 89)
This is internal shaking or splitting and may occur when the inner core of case-hardened timber subsequently dries out. No reversal of this defect is possible.

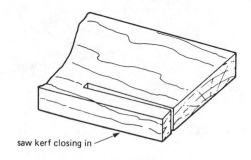

Figure 88   *Result of case hardening*

Protection of seasoned timber and joinery components

The seasoning of timber is a reversible process. As stated previously, timber will readily absorb or lose moisture in order to achieve an equilibrium moisture content. Care must therefore be taken to ensure the stability of the required moisture content during transit and storage.

Conditions during transit and storage are rarely perfect, but by observing the points in the following checklist, materials wastage, damage and subsequent drying-out defects can be reduced to a minimum.

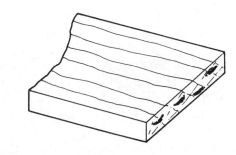

Figure 89   *Honeycombing*

Transit and storage checklist

1 *Plan all deliveries* of timber and joinery to coincide with the work programme, in order to prevent unnecessarily long periods of site storage.

2 *Prepare suitable storage areas in advance of deliveries* Carcassing timber and external joinery should be stacked on bearers clear of the ground using piling sticks between each layer or item, and covered with waterproof tarpaulins as shown in Figure 90.

Note: The stack is covered to provide protection from rainwater, snow and direct sunlight etc. Care must be taken to allow a free air circulation through the stack thereby preventing problems from condensation that would form under the covering.

Trussed rafters can be racked upright and covered with a waterproof tarpaulin as shown in Figure 91. Alternatively they could be laid flat on bearers.

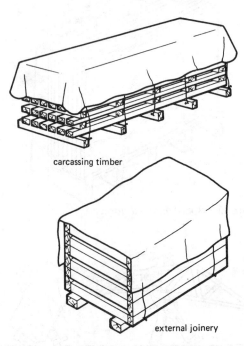

Figure 90   *Storage of carcassing timber and external joinery*

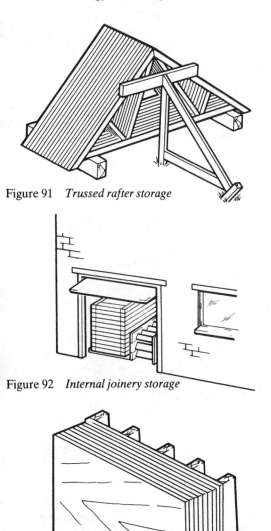

Figure 91 *Trussed rafter storage*

Figure 92 *Internal joinery storage*

Figure 93 *Board material storage*

Internal joinery items are stacked in a dry, preferably heated, store using piling sticks where required (Figure 92).

Note: As far as practically possible the conditions in the store (humidity, temperature etc.) should be equal to those in which the material is to be used.

Where the materials are stored in the building under construction it should be fully glazed, heated and ventilated. The ventilation of the building is essential to prevent the build-up of high humidities, which could increase the moisture content of the timber.

All types of board material must be kept flat and dry. Ideally they should be stacked flat, in conditions similar to internal joinery. Piling sticks can be used to provide air circulation between each sheet. Alternatively where space is limited board material can be racked on edge (see Figure 93).

3 *Ensure timber and joinery items are protected during transit* The supplier should make deliveries in closed or tarpaulin-covered lorries. Priming or sealing should preferably be carried out before delivery to the site or, where this is not possible, promptly thereafter. Many joinery suppliers now protect their products by vacuum sealing them in plastic coverings directly after manufacture.

4 *Build to the work programme* Do not allow carcassing work to stand exposed to the weather for any longer than necessary. Ensure glazing and roof tiling is complete before laying the flooring.

Note: It is advisable to protect the floor after laying by completely covering with polythene sheet or building paper.

Prevent moisture absorption from 'wet trades' by drying out the building before introducing kiln-dried timber and joinery components.

5 *Handle with care* Careless or unnecessary, repeated handling can cause extra costs through damaged material and even personal injury. Both can be avoided by a little planning and care. (See Figure 94).

Figure 94 *Bad handling*

Decay of timber

In general, decay in building timbers can be attributed to two main causes or a combination of both. These are:

An attack by wood-destroying fungi
An attack by wood-boring insects

Wood-destroying fungi (Table 11)

Dry rot

The most common type of wood-destroying fungus is *Merulius lacrymans*. Its common name is dry rot or weeping fungus. As well as being the most common, it is also more serious and more difficult to eradicate than any other fungus.

Dry rot attacks the cellulose found mainly in sapwood and causes the affected timber to:

Lose strength and weight
Develop cracks, both with and across the grain
Become so dry and powdery that it can be easily
   crumbled in the hand

The appearance of a piece of timber after an attack of dry rot is shown in Figure 95. Note the deep cracking of the timber into a brick-shaped pattern.

Two initial factors for an attack of dry rot in timber are:

1 Damp timber (i.e. timber with a moisture content above 20 per cent)

Note: 20 per cent is known as the dry rot safety line.

Table 11   **Wood-destroying fungi**

Type	Location and timber attacked	External appearance	Fruit bodies	Effect on wood
Dry rot *Merulius lacrymans*	Houses and buildings internally Attacks mainly softwoods but occasionally hardwoods	White mat of cotton-wool-like threads later turning to a matted grey skin often tinged yellow or lilac	Large fleshy pancake with a white border and a red-brown centre	Rotted wood shrinks becomes dry and powdery. Develops cracks in a brick like pattern
Wet rot Cellar rot *Coniophora-cerebella*	Very damp buildings External joinery, fences and sheds Attacks both softwood and hardwoods	Very often no external signs of growth. When apparent the fine yellowish thread-like strands quickly turn dark brown or black	Rarely found in buildings, but are thin, irregular, plate shaped, olive-green in colour with a pimpled surface	Darkened and brittle with longitudinal cracks and often cubical cracking below a thin skin of sound timber
Mine rot *Poria vaillantii* and other *poria*	Very damp buildings Attacks mainly softwoods	Fan shaped spread of white branching strings forming into white or cream sheets	Flat, white, plate shaped covered with fine pores	Similar to dry rot but cracking is less severe
Polystictus versicolor	Timber in ground contact External joinery Attacks mainly hardwoods but sometimes painted softwoods	Rarely shows any external growth, sometimes forms a whitish sheet	Rarely seen, when apparent are thin brackets grey and brown on top with a cream pore surface underneath	Rotted wood turns light in colour and becomes much weaker

Figure 95　*Timber after dry rot attack*

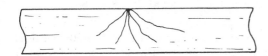

Figure 96　*Dry rot attack stage 1: spores land on damp timber and send out hyphae*

Figure 97　*Dry rot attack stage 2: hyphae branch out and form mycelium, and a fruiting body starts to grow*

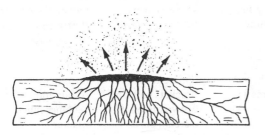

Figure 98　*Dry rot attack stage 3: fruiting body ripens and starts to eject millions of spores into the air*

2　Bad or non-existent ventilation (for example, no circulation of air)

Given these two conditions and a temperature above freezing, an attack by dry rot is practically certain.

Stages of attack
An attack of dry rot occurs in three stages:

Stage 1　The microscopic spores (seeds) of the fungus are blown about in the wind and are already present in most timbers. Given the right conditions, these spores will germinate and send out hyphae (fine hair-like rootlets) which bore into the timber surface. See Figure 96.

Stage 2　The hyphae branch out and spread through and over the surface of the timber forming a mat of cotton-wool-like threads called mycelium. It is at this stage that the hyphae can start to penetrate plaster and brickwork in search of new timber to attack. The hyphae are also able to conduct water and this enables them to adjust the water content of the new timber to the required level for their continued growth. Once the mycelium becomes sufficiently prolific a fruiting body will start to form. See Figure 97.

Stage 3　The fruiting body, which is like a large

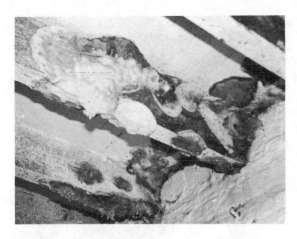

Figure 99   *Advanced dry rot*

fleshy pancake, with a white border and an orange-brown centre, starts to ripen. When fully ripe, the fruiting body starts to discharge into the air millions of rust-red spores which begin the process elsewhere (see Figure 98). Figure 99 shows an attack of dry rot in an advanced stage. The hanging sheets of mycelium can be clearly seen.

Prevention
As the two main factors for the growth of dry rot are damp timber and bad ventilation, by paying attention to the following points an attack of dry rot can be prevented:

Always keep all timber dry (even before fixing into the building)
Always ensure good ventilation

Note: All constructional timbers should be placed so as to allow a free circulation of air around them.

Always use well-seasoned timber
Always use preservative-treated timbers in unfavourable or vulnerable positions.

Recognition
Very often in the early stages there is little evidence of a dry rot attack on the surface of the timber. It is not until panelling, skirting boards or floorboards, etc. are removed that the full effect of an attack is realized.

When dry rot is suspected a simple test is to probe the surface of the timber with a small penknife blade. If there is little resistance when the blade is inserted there is a good possibility that dry rot is present. In addition to the other results of dry rot previously mentioned, a damp musty smell can also be taken as an indication of the presence of some form of fungal attack.

Eradication
By following the stages in the order given, an attack of dry rot can be successfully eradicated:

Stage 1   Increase the ventilation and cure the cause of the dampness which may be one or a combination of any of the following:

Cracked or missing tiles
Defective flashings to parapet walls and chimneys etc.
Defective drains and gulleys
Defective, bridged or non-existent damp-proof course
Defective plumbing, including leaking gutters, downpipes, radiators, sinks, basins or WC etc.
Blocked, or an insufficient number of, air bricks

Stage 2   Remove all traces of the rot. This involves cutting away all the infected timber and at least 600 mm of apparently sound wood beyond the last signs of attack, since this may also have been penetrated by the hyphae.
Stage 3   Burn immediately, on site, all the infected timber, and all materials which are likely to contain traces of the fungus, including dust, dirt, old shavings, sawdust and insulating material etc.
Stage 4   Strip the plaster from the walls at least 600 mm beyond the last signs of hyphae growth.
Stage 5   Clean off all brickwork with a wire brush and sterilize the walls by playing a blowlamp flame over them until the bricks are too hot to touch. While still warm brush or spray the walls with a dry rot fungicide. Apply a second coat when the first is dry.
Stage 6   Treat all existing sound timber with three coats of a dry rot preservative. This can be applied with brush or spray.
Stage 7   Replace all timber which has been taken out with properly seasoned timber, which

has also been treated with three coats of dry rot preservative, or timber which has been pressure impregnated with a preservative.

Note: All fresh surfaces which have been exposed by cutting or drilling must also be treated with a preservative.

Wet rot

This is another common type of wood-destroying fungus which is also known as cellar rot. Its name is *Coniophora cerebella*.

Wet rot is mainly found in wet rather than damp conditions such as:

Cellars
Neglected external joinery
Ends of rafters
Under leaking sinks or baths
Under impervious (waterproof) floor coverings

Note: *Coniophora cerebella* is the main wet rot but others are listed in Table 11.

Recognition

The timber becomes considerably darker in colour and has longitudinal cracks (along the grain). Very often the timber decays internally with a fairly thin skin of apparently sound timber remaining on the surface. The hyphae of wet rot, when apparent, are yellowish but quickly turn to dark brown or black. Fruiting bodies, which are rarely found, are thin, irregular in shape and olive-green in colour. The spores are also olive-green. Figure 100 shows the results of wet rot in the rafters of a roof.

Identification

The chart shown in Table 11 gives a concise list of the main wood-destroying fungi stating their principal characteristics and the location and type of timber likely to be attacked.

Eradication

Wet rot does not normally involve such drastic treatment as dry rot, as wet rot does not spread to adjoining dry timber. All that is normally required to eradicate an attack of wet rot is to cure the source of wetness. Where the decay has become extensive, or where structural timber is affected, some replacement will be necessary.

Figure 100   *Wet rot in rafters*

Weathering

In addition, exterior timber is subject to the effects of the weather (weathering). Exposure to sunlight can cause bleaching, colour fading and movement. Exposure to rainwater will cause swelling and distortion. Exposure to freezing causes moisture in the timber to expand, thus assisting in the break-up of the surface layers. Weathering results in repeated swelling and shrinkage of the timber or joinery item, often causing distortion, surface splitting and joint movement, leading to a breakdown in the paint or other finish. Water will penetrate into the splits and open joints. As the main paint finish is intact there will be little ventilation to the actual surface of the timber to evaporate this moisture: the timber will therefore remain damp, almost inevitably leading to an attack by a wet rot fungi.

Wood-boring insects (Table 12)

The majority of damage done to building timber in the British Isles can be attributed to five

Table 12   **Characteristics of wood-boring insects**

Species	Actual size	Bore dust	Location and timber attacked
Furniture beetle (*Anobium punctatum*) This is the most common wood-boring insect in the British Isles. Its life cycle is usually 2–3 years, with adult beetles emerging during the period between May and September. After mating the females usually lay between 20 and 40 eggs each	beetle / flight holes	Small gritty pellets which are egg shaped under magnification	Attacks both hardwoods and softwoods, although heartwood is often immune. Commonly causes a considerable amount of damage in structural timber floorboards, joists, rafters and furniture
Death-watch beetle (*Xestobium rufovillosum*) Rarely found in modern houses, its attack being mainly restricted to old damp buildings, normally of several hundred years old, e.g. old churches and historic buildings. Named the death-watch because of its association with churches and its characteristic hammering noise that the adults make by hitting their heads against the timber. This hammering is in fact the adults' mating call. Its life cycle is between 4 and 10 years with adult beetles emerging during the period between March and June. Females normally lay between 40 and 70 eggs each		Coarse gritty bun-shaped pellets	Attacks old oak and other hardwoods. Can occasionally be found in softwoods near infested hardwoods. Mainly found in large-sectioned structural timber in association with a fungal attack.
Lyctus or powder-dust beetle In the British Isles there are four beetles in this species which attack timber. The most common is: *Lyctus brunneus* This species is rarely found in buildings, as it attacks mainly recently felled timber before it has been seasoned. Therefore it is only usually found in timber yards and storage sheds. Its life cycle is between 1 and 2 years, but is often less in hot surroundings. Adult beetles emerge during the period between May and September. Females normally lay between 70 and 220 eggs each		Very fine and powdery	Attacks the sapwood of certain hardwoods, oak, ash, elm, walnut etc., normally before seasoning, but has been known to attack recently seasoned timber. An attack is considered unlikely in timber over 10–15 years old

Species	Actual size	Bore dust	Location and timber attacked
House longhorn beetle (*Hylotrupes bajulus*) This is by far the largest wood-boring insect found in the British Isles. It is also known as the Camberley beetle, for its attacks are mainly concentrated around Camberley and the surrounding Surrey and Hampshire areas. Its life cycle is normally between 3 and 10 years, but can be longer. The adult beetles emerge during the period between July and September, with females laying up to 200 eggs each.	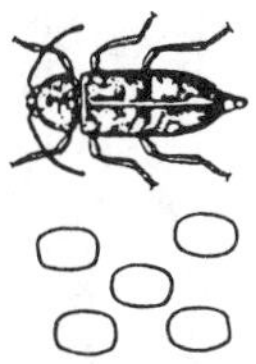	Barrel-shaped pellets mixed with fine dust	Attacks the sapwood of softwood, mainly in the roof spaces e.g. rafters, joists and wall plates etc. Owing to its size and long life cycle, very often complete collapse is the first sign of an attack by this species. Therefore complete replacement of timber is normally required
Weevils (*Euophryum confine* and *Pentarthrum huttoni*) These are mainly found in timber which is damp or subjected to a fungal attack. Unlike other wood-boring insects the adult weevils as well as the larvae bore into the timber and cause damage. Its life cycle is very short, between 6 and 9 months. Two life cycles in one year are not uncommon. Adult beetles can be seen for most of the year. Females lay about 25 eggs each		Small gritty egg-shaped pellets. Similar to bore dust of furniture beetle but smaller	Attacks both damp or decayed hardwoods and softwoods. Often found around sinks, baths, WCs and in cellars.

species of insect or woodworm, as they are commonly called. See Figure 101.

In addition to these five main types of wood-boring insects, several other species such as the bark borer, the pinhole borer and the wharf borer may occasionally be found in forests or timber yards and, in the case of the wharf borer, in waterlogged timber.

Recognition
It is easy to distinguish an attack of wood-boring insects and other forms of timber decay by the presence of their characteristic flight holes which appear on the surface. Also, when a thorough inspection is made below the surface of the timber, the tunnels or galleries bored by the

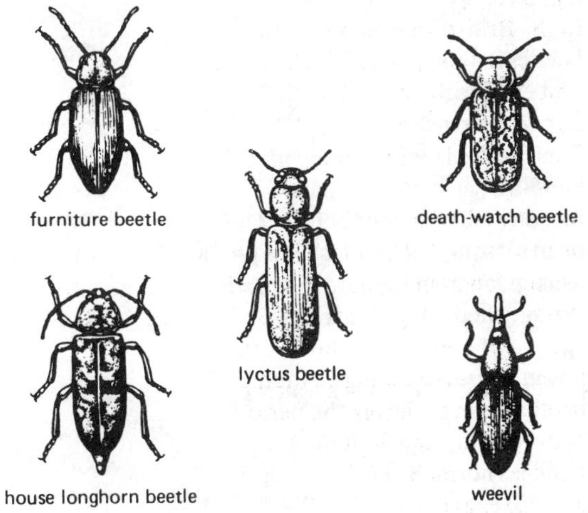

Figure 101   *Common species of wood-boring insects*

larvae will be found. The adult beetles of the different species can be readily identified but, as these only live for a short period in the summer, the identification of the species is generally carried out by a diagnosis of the flight holes, bore dust and the type and location of the timber attacked.

Life cycle

The life cycle of all the wood-boring insects is a fairly complex process, but it can be divided up into four distinct stages:

Stage 1: Eggs (Figure 102) The female insect lays eggs during the summer months, usually on the end grain or in the cracks and shakes of the timber which afford the eggs a certain amount of protection until they hatch.

Stage 2: Larvae (Figure 103) The eggs hatch into larvae, or woodworm, between two and eight weeks after being laid. It is at this stage that damage to the timber is done. The larvae immediately start to bore into and eat the timber. The insects, while boring, digest the wood and excrete it in variously shaped pellets or bore dust, which is often used to identify the particular species of insect that is attacking the timber. The destructive stage can last between six months and ten years, according to the species.

Stage 3: Pupae (Figure 104) During the early spring, the larva hollows out a pupal chamber near the surface of the timber, in which it can change into a pupa or chrysalis. The pupa remains inactive for a short period of time in a mummified state. It is during this period that it undergoes the transformation into an adult insect.

Stage 4: Adult insects (Figure 105) Once the transformation is complete, the insect bites its way out of the timber, leaving its characteristic flight hole. This is often the first external sign of an attack.

Once the insect has emerged from the timber, it is an adult and capable of flying. The adult insect's sole purpose is to mate. This usually takes place within twenty-four hours. Very soon after mating, the male insect will die, while the

stage 1 — female lays eggs in shakes, etc.

Figure 102   *Eggs*

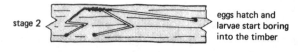

stage 2 — eggs hatch and larvae start boring into the timber

Figure 103   *Larvae*

stage 3 — larvae change into pupae near the surface of the timber

Figure 104   *Pupae*

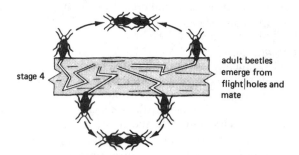

stage 4 — adult beetles emerge from flight holes and mate

Figure 105   *Adult insects*

Figure 106   *Adult furniture beetles*

female will search for a suitable place in which to lay her eggs, thus completing one life cycle and starting another. The female insect will also die, normally within fourteen days.

Figure 106 shows adult furniture beetles on the surface of the timber after emerging from the flight holes.

Identification
The chart shown in Table 12 outlines the main identifying characteristics of the various species of wood-boring insects and also gives the location and type of timber mainly attacked.

Prevention
The wood-boring insects feed on the cellulose and starch which is contained in all timber, both heartwood and sapwood, although sapwood is usually more susceptible to insect attacks. The only sure way of preventing an attack is to poison the food supply by pressure-treating the timber, before it is installed in the building, with a suitable preservative.

Eradication
By following the stages in the order given, an attack of wood-boring insects can be successfully eradicated:

Stage 1 Open up affected area, for example, take up floorboards or remove panelling. Carefully examine all structural timber.
Stage 2 Remove and burn all badly affected timber.
Stage 3 Strip off any surface coating or finish on the timber, for example, paint, polish or varnish.

Note: This is because the fluid used to eradicate the woodworm will not penetrate the surface coating.

Stage 4 Thoroughly brush the timber in order to remove from its surface all dirt and dust.
Stage 5 Replace all timber which has been taken out with properly seasoned timber that has been treated with two or three coats of woodworm preservative or, alternatively, with timber that has been pressure-impregnated with a preservative.

Note: All fresh surfaces which have been exposed by cutting or drilling must also be treated with a preservative.

Stage 6 Apply a proprietary woodworm killer, by brush or spray, to all timber, even that which is apparently unaffected. Pay particular attention to joints, end grain and flight holes. Apply a second coat of the fluid as soon as the first has been absorbed.

Note: Floorboards must be taken up at intervals to allow thorough coverage of the joists and the underside of the floorboards. Care must be taken to avoid the staining of plaster, particularly when treating the ceiling joists and rafters in the loft.

Stage 7 In most cases it is possible to completely eradicate an attack by one thorough treatment as outlined in stages 1 to 6, but to be completely sure inspections for fresh flight holes should be made for several successive summers. If fresh holes are found, retreat timber with a woodworm killer.

Large-section timber
To eradicate an attack of wood-boring insects in large-section structural timber, deeper preservative penetration is required. A timber injection system is available. This involves drilling holes into the timber at intervals, inserting a nozzle and then pumping preservative under pressure into the timber. This method is also suitable for the *in situ* treatment of external joinery etc.

Alternatively, a paste preservative can be used for structural timbers. The paste, like thick creamy butter, is spread on all the exposed surfaces of the affected timber. Over a period of time the paste releases toxic chemicals which penetrate deep into the timber.

Note: Neither of these methods impart structural strength to timber, therefore replacement of badly affected timbers is still required.

Furniture
When timbers inside a building have been attacked by a wood-boring insect, it is almost certain that the furniture will also be affected. Therefore, to successfully eradicate the attack,

the furniture must also be treated. This can be done by following the stages in the order given.

Stage 1 Remove all dirt and dust, then inject a proprietary woodworm killer into the flight holes. A special aerosol can with tube, or nozzled injector bottles, are available for this purpose.

Stage 2 Apply two coats of a proprietary woodworm killer to all unfinished surfaces, that is, all surfaces which are not painted, polished or varnished.

Stage 3 Make inspections for fresh flight holes for several successive summers. Repeat if required.

Preservation of timber

All timbers, especially their sapwood, contain food on which fungi and insects live. The idea behind timber preservation is to poison the food supply by applying a toxic liquid to the timber. The ideal requirements of a timber preservative are as follows:

It must be toxic to the fungi and insects, but safe to animals and humans.

It should be permanent and not liable to be bleached out by sunshine or leached out by rain.

It should be economical and easy to obtain.

It should not corrode or affect metal in any way.

It should be easy to handle and apply.

It should, as far as possible, be odourless.

It should not affect the subsequent finishing of the timber, for example, painting or polishing.

It should be non-flammable.

Note: Although these are the ideal requirements of a preservative, bear in mind that most preservatives will not embody all these points. Care should be taken therefore to select the best type of preservative for the work in hand.

There are three main types of timber preservative available:

Tar oils
Water-soluble preservatives
Organic solvent preservatives

Tar oils

These are derived from coal and are dark brown or black in colour. They are fairly permanent, cheap, effective and easy to apply. However, they should not be used internally, as they are flammable and possess a strong lingering odour. They should never be used near foodstuffs as the odour will contaminate the food. The timber, once treated, will not accept any further finish; that is, it cannot be painted. Its main uses are for the treatment of external timber such as fences, sheds, telegraph poles etc.

Water-soluble preservatives

These are toxic chemicals which are mixed with water. They are suitable for use in both internal and external situations. The wood can be painted subsequently. They are odourless and non-flammable.

Note: As the toxic chemicals are water soluble, some of the types available are prone to leaching out when used in wet or damp conditions.

Organic solvent preservatives

These consist of toxic chemicals which are mixed with a spirit that evaporates after the preservative has been applied. This is an advantage because the moisture content of the timber is not increased. The use and characteristics of these types of preservatives are similar to those of water-soluble preservatives, but with certain exceptions. Some of the solvents used are flammable, so care must be taken when applying or storing them. Some types also have a strong odour. In general, organic solvent preservatives are the most expensive type to use but are normally considered to be superior because of their excellent preservation properties.

Methods of application

To a large extent it is the method of application rather than the preservative that governs the degree of protection obtained. This is because each method of application gives a different depth of preservative penetration. The greater the depth of penetration the higher the degree of protection. Preservatives can be applied using a number of methods but all of these can be classed in two groups:

Non-pressure treatment, for example, brushing, spraying, dipping and steeping
Pressure treatment, for example, empty-cell process and full-cell process

Non-pressure treatment

Brushing
In this method the preservative is brushed on. It can be used for all types but the effect is very limited as only a surface coating is achieved (very little penetration of the preservative into the timber).

Spraying
The preservative is sprayed on, but the effect is similar to brushing, that is, little penetration is achieved.

Dipping
In this method the timber is immersed in a container full of preservative. After a certain length of time the timber is taken out and allowed to drain. The depth of penetration depends upon the length of time that the timber is immersed. Although better than brushing or spraying, penetration may still be very limited.

Steeping
This is known as the hot and cold method. The timber is immersed in large tanks containing the preservative. The preservative is then heated for about two hours, the heat is then removed and the preservative allowed to cool. As the preservative is heated, the air in the cells of the timber expands and escapes as bubbles to the surface. On cooling the preservative is sucked into the spaces left by the air. Fairly good penetration can be achieved, making this by far the best non-pressure method.

Pressure treatment
This is the most effective form of timber preservation, as almost full penetration of the cells can be achieved.

Empty-cell process
The timber is placed in a sealed cylinder. The air in the cylinder is then subjected to pressure which causes the air in the timber cells to compress. At this stage preservative is run into the cylinder and the pressure increased further. This forces the preservative into the timber. The pressure is maintained at this high level until the required amount of penetration is achieved. The pressure is then released and the surplus preservative is pumped back into a storage container. As the air pressure is reduced, the compressed air in the cells expands and forces out most of the preservative, leaving only the cell walls coated.

Full-cell process
The timber is placed into the sealed cylinder as before but this time, instead of compressing the air, it is drawn out. This creates a vacuum in the cylinder, as well as a partial one in the cells of the timber. At this stage the preservative is introduced into the cylinder. When the cylinder is full, the vacuum is released and the preservative is sucked into the timber cells by their partial vacuum. This method is ideal for timbers which are to be used in wet locations, for example, marine work, docks, piers, jetties, etc. as water cannot penetrate into the timbers cells because they are already full of preservative.

A variation of these pressure treatments which is often used is the double-vacuum method. The timber is placed in a sealed cylinder as before and a vacuum is applied. An organic solvent preservative is introduced into the cylinder. With the cylinder full the vacuum is released and a positive air pressure applied. This causes the preservative to be sucked and forced into the timber. Finally the vacuum is once again applied to remove the excess preservative. No further seasoning or drying of the timber is required before use. See Figure 107.

Diffusion
This method of application can only be used with green unseasoned timber and is mainly carried out in the country of origin before being shipped. Immediately after conversion a water-soluble preservative is applied to the timber, preferably by dipping. The timber is then close

Figure 107   *Double-vacuum pressure treatment*

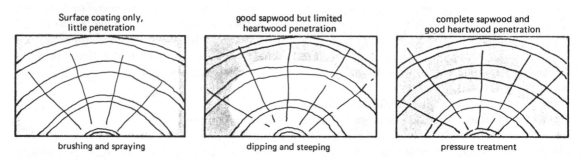

Figure 108   *Preservative penetration*

stacked and covered for several weeks to prevent drying. After this time the preservative will have diffused through the timber, giving fairly deep penetration even in timbers which prove difficult to treat by other methods. The main disadvantage of this method is that it is prone to leaching.

Preservative penetration
The depth of preservative penetration will depend on the permeability of the timber

concerned, the method of application and the amount of heartwood present. Figure 108 shows typical depths of preservative penetration when using different methods of application.
Note: In each case sapwood penetration is greater than heartwood penetration.

Preservative safety
Preservatives contain chemicals which can be harmful to your health. They must therefore always be handled and used with care.

1 Always follow the manufacturer's instructions with regard to use and storage.
2 Avoid contact with skin, eyes or clothing.
3 Avoid breathing in the fumes, particularly when spraying.
4 Keep away from foodstuffs, to avoid contamination.
5 Always wear protective clothing:
   (a) Barrier cream or disposable protective gloves
   (b) A respirator when spraying.
6 Do not smoke or use near a source of ignition.
7 Ensure adequate ventilation when used internally.
8 Thoroughly wash your hands before eating and after work with soap and water or an appropriate hand cleanser.
9 In the case of accidental inhalation, swallowing or contact with the eyes, medical advice should be sought immediately.

Adhesives

Primarily an adhesive must be capable of sticking or adhering to timber. Adhesion results from the formation of a large number of very small chemical bonds between the adhesive and the timber when these are brought into contact. In addition, for the formation of a strong glued joint, it is essential that the adhesive penetrates the timber surface and keys into the porous layers below. This is known as mechanical adhesion. The most important factors affecting the depth of penetration when gluing are as follows:

The amount of pressure applied to the joint (this forces the adhesive into the timber surface)
The viscosity (thickness) of the adhesive (thinner adhesives penetrate more easily than thicker adhesives)

Apart from penetrating and adhering to the timber an adhesive must also have strength within itself (cohesion). Only solids have a high cohesive strength; therefore every adhesive after application must be able to change from its liquid state to a solid state. This change takes place during the setting and curing of the adhesive in one of the following ways:

By loss of solvent   This takes place either by the evaporation of the solvent as with contact adhesives or by its absorption into the timber, as with emulsion adhesives.

By cooling   Some adhesives are applied in a molten condition and subsequently solidify on cooling. This method has the advantage that a very fast set is achieved, as with animal and hot melt.

By chemical reaction   This is brought about by the addition of a hardener or catalyst or by the application of heat, as with synthetic resin adhesives.

Note: Many adhesives set by using a combination of the previous processes.

Factors affecting strength

Timber preparation
The timber should be seasoned, preferably to the equilibrium moisture content it will obtain in use. The timber should be planed to a smooth even surface and all dust must be removed before gluing. The gluability of a timber surface deteriorates with exposure; therefore the time between preparation and gluing should be as short as possible.

Adhesive preparation
Adhesives that consist of two or more components must be mixed accurately in accordance with the manufacturer's instructions. It is normally advisable to batch the component parts by weight rather than volume.

Application of adhesive
Adhesives may be applied either by brush, roller, spray, spatula or mechanical spreader. For maximum strength a uniform thickness of adhesive should be applied to both sides of the joint. Adhesives that set by chemical reaction begin to react as soon as the components are mixed. This reaction rate is dependent mainly on the temperatures of the adhesive, the timber and the surrounding room or workshop. These

factors must be taken into account to ensure that the pot life of the adhesive is not exceeded, otherwise the strength of the joint will be affected.

Assembly time

This is the elapsed time between the application of the adhesive and the application of pressure. Some adhesives benefit in strength if they are allowed to partly set before the surfaces are brought into contact (open assembly time). Other adhesives require a period to thicken while the surfaces are in contact but before pressure is applied (closed assembly time). These times will be specified by the manufacturer and must be carefully controlled to ensure that the adhesive is not too thick to spread out into a uniform layer or too thin that all the adhesive is squeezed out when the pressure is applied.

Pressure

Pressure should be applied to the glued joint in order to:

1 Spread the adhesive uniformly
2 Squeeze out excess adhesive and pockets of air
3 Ensure close contact between the two adjoining surfaces

This pressure must be sustained until the joint has developed sufficient strength (cramping period). The application of heat will speed the development of strength and therefore reduce the cramping period.

Curing

This is the process that leads to the development of full strength and resistance to moisture. It starts during the cramping period and is completed while the components are in storage prior to use (conditioning period). Curing is also dependent on temperature and can be speeded up by heating.

Radiofrequency heating

In order to gain the maximum possible output from jigs, cramps and presses etc., cramping periods should be kept to a minimum. A shorter cramping period can be achieved by raising the temperature of the glue line. There are two main ways of doing this:

By applying heat externally However, because of timber's low thermal conductivity the outside has to be raised to a much higher temperature than the centre and the heat is required for a long period of time.

By generating heat internally using radio or high-frequency heating This involves sandwiching the timber component between two metal plates (electrodes) that are connected to a source of radiofrequency (RF) energy. When a positive voltage is applied to one electrode and a negative voltage to the other the timber molecules (minute particles) which all have a positive and negative end will tend to turn so that their charged ends face their like-charged electrodes. On reversing the voltage the molecules will tend to turn back immediately, causing internal friction and thus heat. The amount of heat is dependent on the frequency of the voltage reversals.

quicker reversals = higher temperatures

Glue lines can be cured in a matter of minutes or even seconds using this process.

Classification of adhesives

Timber adhesives are made from either naturally occurring animal or vegetable products or from synthetic resins.

Adhesives made from synthetic resins fall into two classes:

1 *Thermoplastic* This class of adhesive sets by either loss of solvent or cooling and will soften again if solvent is added or it is reheated.
2 *Thermosetting* This class of adhesive undergoes a chemical reaction which causes the adhesive to solidify and set. This is an irreversible change, and the adhesive cannot be melted or dissolved.

Adhesives that will set at room temperature are known as cold setting. Those that require heating to a temperature of around 100 °C are known as hot setting. In addition some adhesives require heating between these two ranges and are called intermediate temperature setting adhesives.

The durability of an adhesive is important as it must retain its strength under the conditions it will be subjected to during its service. Durability can be tested by exposure tests over long periods, or by quick tests made over a few days, that subject the adhesive to heating, soaking, boiling and micro-organisms. Timber adhesives can be classified into one of the following durability classes.

Weather and boil-proof (WBP) These adhesives have a very high resistance to all weather conditions. They are also highly resistant to cold and boiling water, steam and dry heat, and micro-organisms.

Boil resistant (BR) These adhesives have a good resistance to boiling water and a fairly good resistance to weather conditions, and are highly resistant to cold water and micro-organisms, but they will fail on prolonged exposure to the weather.

Moisture resistant (MR) These adhesives are moderately weather resistant and will withstand prolonged exposure to cold water but very little to hot water. They are also resistant to micro-organisms.

Internal (INT) These adhesives are only suitable for use in dry internal locations. They will fail on exposure to weather or in damp conditions, and are not normally resistant to micro-organisms.

Types of adhesive

Animal glue (INT)

Animal glue is made from the bones and hides of animals. It is light brown in colour and sold in solid form which has to be dissolved before application. It sets by cooling as well as by the loss of water and will resoften on exposure to moisture. Although it was used extensively in the past in cabinet-making and joinery, it has now been largely replaced by synthetic adhesives.

Casein (INT)

Casein is derived from soured, skimmed milk curds which are dried and crushed into a powder. An alkali and certain fillers are added to the powder to make it soluble in water and give it its gap-filling properties. Its main use is for general joinery although it is inclined to stain some hardwoods, particularly oak. Little preparation is required as the powder is simply mixed in a non-metal container with a measured quantity of cold water and stirred until a smooth creamy consistency is achieved. It sets by a chemical reaction accompanied by the loss of water. Prolonged exposure will soften casein, causing a loss in strength.

Polyvinyl acetate (INT)

This is a thermoplastic adhesive supplied as a white ready-mixed creamy emulsion which sets by the loss of water to form a clear glue line. It requires no preparation and sets rapidly at room temperature, although it will resoften on exposure to high temperature or moisture.

Contact adhesives (INT)

These consist of a rubber solution in a volatile solvent ready for use. When the adhesive has been applied to both surfaces, a ten to thirty minute open assembly time must elapse to enable the solvent to evaporate. After this the two surfaces can be brought together, forming an immediate contact bond. Little or no adjustment is possible except with the thixotropic types which have a certain amount of manoeuvrability. Care must be taken to use contact adhesives in a well-ventilated area, where no smoking or naked lights are allowed.

Hot melts (INT)

These are made from ethylene vinyl acetate and are obtained in a solid form. They become molten at very high temperatures and set immediately on cooling. Small hand-held electric glue guns and automatic edging machines normally use this type of adhesive.

Phenol formaldehyde (WBP)

Phenol formaldehyde resin is a dark brown

thermosetting adhesive that sets at either high temperatures or upon the addition of an acid catalyst.

Resorcinol formaldehyde (WBP)

Resorcinol formaldehyde resin is a dark purplish-brown thermosetting adhesive that is classified as cold setting and sets by the addition of a hardener. As the resorcinol is very expensive it is often mixed with the cheaper phenol, making a phenol/resorcinol formaldehyde adhesive. This has the same properties as the pure resorcinol adhesive, although a higher setting temperature is required.

Melamine formaldehyde (BR)

Melamine formaldehyde resin is a colourless thermosetting adhesive that sets at high temperatures and is suitable for use where the dark colour of the phenol and resorcinol adhesives are unacceptable.

Urea formaldehyde (MR)

Urea formaldehyde is also a colourless thermosetting adhesive that will set at either high or low temperatures. Urea is often mixed with the more expensive melamine or resorcinol resin to form a fortified urea formaldehyde adhesive that has an increased (BR) durability.

General characteristics

A summary of the main characteristics, properties and uses of woodworking adhesives is given in Table 13.

Adhesive safety

Adhesives can be harmful to your health. Many adhesives have an irritant effect on contact with the skin and may result in dermatitis. Some are poisonous if swallowed, while others can result in narcosis if the vapour or powder is inhaled. These and other harmful effects can be avoided if proper precautions are taken:

1 Always follow the manufacturer's instructions
2 Always use a barrier cream or disposable protective gloves.

3 Do not use those with a flammable vapour near sources of ignition.
4 Always provide adequate ventilation.
5 Avoid inhaling any toxic fumes or powders.
6 Thoroughly wash your hands, before eating or smoking and after work, with soap and water or an appropriate hand cleanser.
7 In the case of accidental inhalation, swallowing or contact with eyes, medical advice should be sought immediately.

Mechanics

Mechanics can be defined as the study of the effect of forces on materials. Remember forces are measured in newtons (N); owing to the earth's gravitational pull, every mass will exert a force. The force will vary slightly from place to place on the earth's surface, but on average the force of gravity on a mass of 1 kg is 9.81 N; therefore the 'weight' of 1 kg is 9.81 N. For most practical purposes it is sufficiently accurate to take the weight of 1 kg to be 10 N, thus simplifying any calculations and at the same time erring on the safe side.

A 50 kg box of nails placed on the ground will exert a force of almost 500 N; the earth in turn will push back with an equal and opposite reaction of 500 N (see Figure 109).

The force that supports a force is called a reaction. Where no movement is taking place as a result of these forces, they are said to be in equilibrium or balanced. A force that is not in direct line with its reaction will have a turning

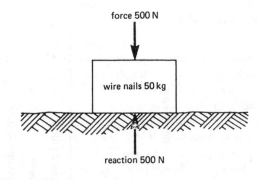

Figure 109 *Force and reaction*

Table 13 Characteristics of woodworking adhesives

Type of adhesive	Suitable service conditions						Classification				Gap filling — Capable of filling 1.3 mm without loss of strength		Available form — one part			Available form — two parts		Life expectancy in fully exposed external conditions
	Fully exposed external use	Protected external use	Internal or external use in chemically polluted areas	Internal use in high-heat or high-humidity areas	Internal use in dry normal heat conditions	Internal use in dry normal heat conditions. Non-structural	INT	WBP	BR	MR	Yes	No	Solid	Powder	Liquid	Powder/liquid	Liquid/liquid	
Animal glue						*	*				*		*					3–4 months
Casein					*	*	*				*			*				1–2 years
Polyvinyl acetate						*	*					*			*			—
Contact adhesive						*	*					*	*		*			
Hot melts					*	*	*				*		*					
Phenol formaldehyde	*		*	*	*	*		*				*				*		25 + years
Resorcinol formaldehyde	*	*	*	*	*	*		*			*					*	*	25 + years
Melamine formaldehyde		*		*	*	*			*		* can be						*	5–10 + years
Urea formaldehyde					*	*				*	* can be			*		*	*	2–5 + years

effect. This turning effect is known as the moment of a force. It is equal to the product of the force and its distance from the point of support or fulcrum:

moment = force × distance

Consider the see-saw arrangement shown in Figure 110. This consists of a beam loaded at either end, the reaction being provided by the fulcrum (pivot point). The two forces can be seen as having either a clockwise or an anticlockwise moment. For the beam to be in equilibrium (balanced), force A multiplied by distance A must be equal to force B multiplied by distance B:

$$F_A \times D_A = F_B \times D_B$$

This can be summed up by the statement known as the *principle of moments*. For a body to exist in a state of equilibrium the sum of the anticlockwise moments must equal the sum of the clockwise moments:

anticlockwise moments (ACWM)
           = clockwise moments (CWM)

Example
The see-saw arrangement shown in Figure 111 balances when the three forces are placed in the positions illustrated. Find distance Z.

Taking moments about the fulcrum:

$$
\begin{aligned}
\text{ACWM} &= \text{CWM} \\
3 \times 500 + 1 \times 250 &= Z \times 350 \\
1750 &= Z \times 350 \\
\frac{1750}{350} &= Z \\
5 &= Z
\end{aligned}
$$

Answer Distance Z must be 5 m.

Levers
A lever is a simple machine that can turn about a pivot. It operates on the principle of moments. When using a lever a force (effort) is applied at one position on the lever to overcome a resisting force (load) acting at another position on the lever. The positions of the effort and load will

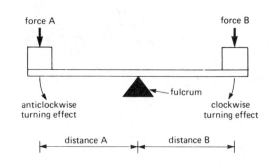

Figure 110 *Moments*

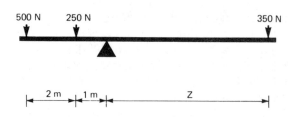

Figure 111 *Moments*

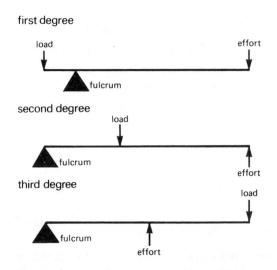

Figure 112 *Levers*

vary depending on which of the three orders or degrees of lever is being used. These three degrees of lever are illustrated in Figure 112. In the first-degree lever the distance between the load and the fulcrum is normally less than the distance between the effort and the fulcrum. This in effect magnifies the effort, enabling a bigger load to be moved than the effort applied, but the effort has to move further than the load. This magnification of the effort is called the mechanical advantage of the machine and can be expressed as:

$$\text{mechanical advantage} = \frac{\text{load}}{\text{effort}}$$

The second-degree lever has a similar mechanical advantage in that the effort is less than the load. In the third-degree lever, where the effort is positioned between the load and the fulcrum, the effort will always be greater than the load, but the load will move further than the effort. Typical examples of levers in use are shown in Figure 113. These can be seen in daily use on any building site.

To find the effort required in each of these examples involves a simple calculation.

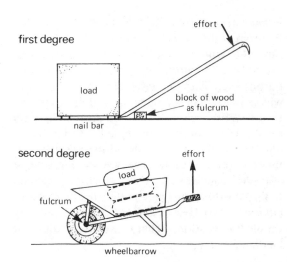

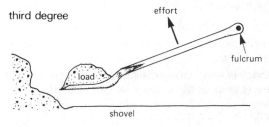

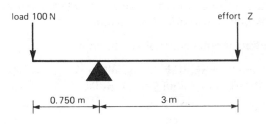

Figure 113 *Levers in use*

Example
What effort is required at Z to lift the load of 100 N shown in Figure 114? What is the mechanical advantage of the arrangement?

Taking moments about the fulcrum:

$$\text{ACWM} = \text{CWM}$$

$$0.750 \times 100 = 3 \times Z$$

$$75 = 3 \times Z$$

$$\frac{75}{3} = Z$$

$$25 = Z$$

Answer Effort just greater than 25 N.

Note: With an effort of 25 N the forces will be in equilibrium; therefore an effort just greater than this will be required to lift the load.

Figure 114 *Levers*

The mechanical advantage (MA) of the set-up shown in Figure 114 is

$$\text{MA} = \frac{\text{load}}{\text{effort}}$$

$$\text{MA} = \frac{100}{25}$$

$$\text{MA} = 4$$

Answer The mechanical advantage is 4.

Beam reactions

A beam is the general name given to a wide range of structural members within a building. These include lintels, joists, binders, rafters and purlins etc. They all have the same purpose, which is to span an opening and transfer any loads imposed upon them back to the supports (wall columns etc.). If the beam is to remain in equilibrium, and in a building it obviously must, these supports must provide an equal and opposite reaction.

To determine the support reaction required to bear a known load system normally involves a simple calculation. There are two ways of loading a beam:

Point loads
Uniformly distributed loads

Point loads

If a load is placed in the centre of a beam the reaction at each support will be half the load. When the load is not central or where there is more than one load the reactions will have to be calculated. This means taking moments about each end in turn. An easy way of doing this is to consider the beam to be a second-degree lever, one of the reactions being considered as the fulcrum and the other the effort required.

Example

A simply supported beam with a point load of 16 kN is illustrated in Figure 115. Find both support reactions.

Taking moments about R_L:

$$ACWM = CWM$$
$$8 \times R_R = 3 \times 16$$
$$8 \times R_R = 48$$
$$R_R = \frac{48}{8}$$
$$R_R = 6 \text{ kN}$$

If R_R is 6 kN then R_L must be 10 kN since the sum of the reactions must be equal to the total applied load. But the calculation should always be checked by taking moments about the other reaction.

Taking moments about R_R:

$$ACWM = CWM$$
$$5 \times 16 = 8 \times R_L$$
$$80 = 8 \times R_L$$
$$\frac{80}{8} = R_L$$
$$10 \text{ kN} = R_L$$

Answer

Left-hand reaction equals 10 kN.
Right-hand reaction equals 6 kN.

Example

Where there is more than one point load, as in the beam shown in Figure 116, the method used to find the support reactions will be similar.

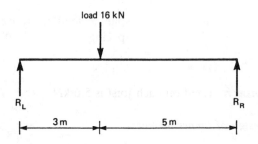

Figure 115 *Beam reactions, one point load*

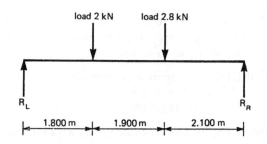

Figure 116 *Beam reactions, two point loads*

Taking moments about R_L:

$$\begin{aligned} \text{ACWM} &= \text{CWM} \\ 5.8 \times R_R &= 1.8 \times 2 + 3.7 \times 2.8 \\ 5.8 \times R_R &= 3.6 + 10.26 \\ R_R &= \frac{13.96}{5.8} \\ R_R &= 2.407 \text{ kN} \end{aligned}$$

Therefore R_L must be 2.393 kN since $4.8 - 2.407 = 2.393$.

Check by taking moments about R_R.

$$\begin{aligned} \text{ACWM} &= \text{CWM} \\ 2.1 \times 2.8 + 4 \times 2 &= 5.8 \times R_L \\ 5.88 + 8 &= 5.8 \times R_L \\ 13.88 &= 5.8 \times R_L \\ \frac{13.88}{5.8} &= R_L \\ 2.393 \text{ kN} &= R_L \end{aligned}$$

Answer
Left-hand reaction equals 2.393 kN.
Right-hand reaction equals 2.407 kN.

Uniformly distributed loads

When a load is evenly dispersed along the whole or part of a beam it is said to be a uniformly distributed load (UDL). The self-weight of a beam is a uniformly distributed load and must be taken into account when it forms a significant proportion of the total load.

The total UDL on a beam must be calculated and it can then be considered as a point load acting through its centre of gravity.

Example
The beam shown in Figure 117 has a UDL of 2.5 kN/m run and a point load of 3 kN. Determine the support reactions.

$$\begin{aligned} \text{total UDL} &= \text{span} \times \text{load/m run} \\ &= 5 \times 2.5 \\ &= 12.5 \text{ kN} \end{aligned}$$

This UDL is now considered as a point load acting through the centre of gravity (centre of the UDL). The beam diagram now has two

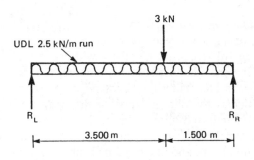

Figure 117   *UDL and one point load*

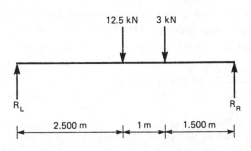

Figure 118

point loads as shown in Figure 118. The support reactions can now be calculated using the same procedure as before. In the case of a floor or roof a UDL or imposed load will be stated in kN/m^2 and not as the load carried by one joist or rafter. It will be necessary to find the load carried by one member before the support reactions can be determined.

Example
Floor joists spanning 3.500 m and spaced at 400 mm centres carry a UDL of kN/m^2. Find the load carried by one joist.

$$\begin{aligned} \text{load on one joist} &= \text{span} \times \text{load/m}^2 \times \text{c/c spacing} \\ &= 3.5 \times 4 \times 0.4 \\ &= 5.6 \text{ kN} \end{aligned}$$

Answer   Load on each joist is 5.6 kN.

Design of timber members

Stress
When a body is subjected to a force it is said to

be in a state of stress. There are three types of stress:

Tensile stress (Figure 119)   This tends to pull or stretch a material; it has a lengthening effect.
Compressive stress (Figure 120)   This causes squeezing, pushing and crushing; it has a shortening effect.
Shear stress (Figure 121)   This occurs when one part of a member tends to slip or slide over another part; it has a slicing effect.

When a beam is subjected to a load, bending occurs, causing an internal combination of these stresses (see Figure 122). The centre line of the beam is subjected to neither compression or tension and is known as the neutral stress line, although maximum horizontal shear occurs along this line as the two halves of the beam tend to slide over each other. The amount of compression or tension increases with the distance from the neutral stress line. This is represented in the section by the shaded areas. The maximum stresses therefore occur at the top and bottom edges of the beam, the upper part being in a state of compression and the lower part in a state of tension. This stress along the beam varies and is related to the amount of bending. The larger the bending the larger the stress. In the case of a centre point load the maximum bending and therefore the maximum stress will occur at the centre of the beam. This will diminish towards the supports where vertical shear occurs. When a beam has an additional central support the position of the stresses in this area will be reversed (see Figure 123).

Strength tests
The strength of timber varies according to the type of stress and whether it is applied with or at right angles to the grain (see Figure 124). Strength tests on timber form the basis for determining permissible stress values used in structural timber design calculations. Various types of stress are now considered.

Ultimate stress
Small clear defect-free samples of timber are tested to destruction to obtain their breaking or ultimate stress value.

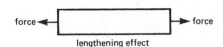

Figure 119   *Tensile stress*

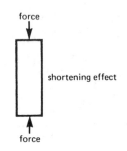

Figure 120   *Compressive stress*

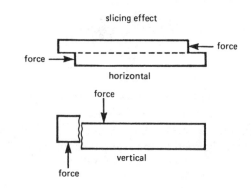

Figure 121   *Shear stress*

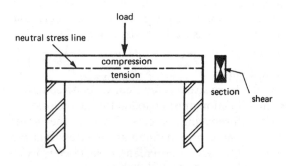

Figure 122   *Beam under stress*

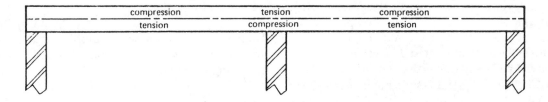

Figure 123 *Stress reversal in centrally supported beam*

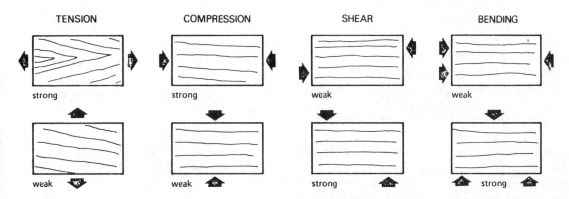

Figure 124 *Relative strength of timber*

Characteristic stress
The ultimate stress value will vary between different samples of the species. Therefore a characteristic stress value is determined and is normally defined as the stress below which only 1 per cent of the samples will fail.

Basic stress
The characteristic stress makes no allowance for accidental overloading of the timber in use; therefore it must be divided by an appropriate factor of safety to obtain the basic stress. This is defined as the stress that can be safely and permanently sustained by clear defect-free timber.

Grade stress
As the basic stress is for clear defect-free timber a modification must be made for the inclusion of strength-reducing defects. This is the grade stress, and can be defined as the stress that can be safely and permanently sustained by a particular grade of timber.

Permissible stress
Grade stresses are used for conditions where the timber may have to support a load throughout its useful life, which could be in excess of 50 to 60 years. This is known as long-term loading conditions. Clearly some adjustment can be made where the loading is for a short period. In addition grade stresses are for dry timber (below 18 per cent moisture content (MC)); where green timber (above 18 per cent (MC)) is used another adjustment must be made.

The stress value after making these adjustments is known as the permissible stress, and is defined as the stress that can be safely sustained after allowing for the duration of load and moisture content.

Beam design
In general the strength of a beam varies in direct proportion to changes in its breadth and in proportion to the square of its depth. For example, doubling the breadth of a section

doubles its strength, whereas doubling the depth of the section increases its strength by four times. Thus less material is required for the same strength when the greatest dimension of a beam is placed vertically rather than horizontally.

The size of a timber beam depends on its loading, span and spacing. It is most important that these factors are taken into consideration when determining what sectional size to use. The Building Regulations Approved Documents (AD) A Tables B contains various tables of suitable sectional sizes for use in different situations, although some situations do not fall within the scope of these tables.

Sectional sizes can be determined by the rule of thumb method:

$$\frac{\text{span of joists in millimetres}}{20} + 20$$

$$= \text{depth of 50 mm wide joist}$$

While this may be suitable for a one-off situation it is not very accurate or cost effective as it usually results in sectional sizes far bigger than is really necessary. It is therefore desirable that a carpenter and joiner has a basic understanding of the principles of beam design.

A beam has to be designed so that the permissible bending and shear stresses for the grade of timber being used are not exceeded. At this level beam design is restricted to simply supported beams with centre point or uniformly distributed loads.

Bending
The equation that is used for determining the sectional size is:

maximum bending moment (BM$_{max}$) = moment of resistance (MR)

Maximum bending moment
This is the total sum of forces acting on the beam which are tending to bend or even break it. Although the maximum bending moment will vary according to the beam's loading and support, Table 14 contains the formulae for use in standard situations.

Moment of resistance
This is the resistance to bending offered by the beam section. For timber beams of a rectangular section the moment of resistance is given by the following formula:

$$MR = \frac{fbd^2}{6}$$

where f is the permissible bending stress (N/mm^2), b is the breadth of the beam (mm), and d is the depth of the beam (mm).

Example
A timber beam spanning 3 m is required to carry a centre point load of 4 kN. Determine a suitable commercially available section, assuming that the permissible bending stress of the timber is 8 N/mm^2.

Note: All measurements must be stated in the same units; for example, change m to mm and kN to N by multiplying by 1000.

$$BM_{max} = MR$$
$$\frac{WL}{4} = \frac{fbd^2}{6}$$

transpose formula to get bd^2 on its own:

$$\frac{WL6}{4f} = bd^2$$
$$\frac{4000 \times 3000}{4 \times 8} \times = bd^2$$
$$\frac{72,000,000}{32} = bd^2$$
$$2,250,000 = bd^2$$

say $b = 75$: therefore

$$\frac{2,250,000}{75} = d^2$$
$$\sqrt{\left(\frac{2,250,000}{75}\right)} = d$$
$$173 = d$$

Answer Nearest commercial size (NCS) is 75 mm × 175 mm.

As an alternative to this section we could say b = 50 mm; therefore

Table 14 **Beam design formulae**

System	Diagram	Bending moment BM_{max}	Shear S_{max}
Simply supported beam with a centre point load		$\dfrac{WL}{4}$	$\dfrac{3W}{4bd}$
Simply supported beam with a uniformly distributed load		$\dfrac{WL}{8}$	$\dfrac{3W}{4bd}$

W = weight (load) L = length (span) b = breadth of beam d = depth of beam

$$\sqrt{\left(\frac{2,250,000}{50}\right)} = d$$

$$212 = d$$

In this case the NCS would be 50 mm × 225 mm.

Example
Floor joists spanning 3.500 m and spaced at 450 mm centres carry a uniformly distributed load of 2.5 kN/m^2. Using the formula $WL/8 = fbd^2/6$, calculate the depth of a 50 mm wide joist when $f = 6.8$ N/mm^2.

$$\text{total load per joist} = 3.5 \times 2.5 \times 0.45$$
$$= 3.938 \text{ kN}$$
$$BM_{max} = MR$$
$$\frac{WL}{8} = \frac{fbd^2}{6}$$
$$\frac{WL6}{f8} = bd^2$$
$$\frac{3938 \times 3500 \times 6}{8 \times 6.8} = bd^2$$
$$\frac{82,698,000}{54.4} = bd^2$$
$$1,520,183.8 = bd^2$$

$b = 50$ mm; therefore

$$\frac{1,520,183.8}{50} = d^2$$

$$\sqrt{\left(\frac{1,615,195.3}{50}\right)} = d$$

$$174.366 = d$$

Answer   NCS is 50 mm × 175 mm.

Shear
In general a timber beam that is designed to resist bending stresses will be more than strong enough to resist shear, but it can be checked by using the formulae shown in Table 14.

Example
Calculate the maximum shear stress for a 50 mm × 200 mm simply supported timber beam carrying a centre point load of 4.8 kN.

Answer

$$\text{maximum shear} \quad S(max) = \frac{3W}{4bd}$$

$$S(max) = \frac{3 \times 4800}{4 \times 50 \times 200}$$

$$S(max) = \frac{14,400}{40,000}$$

$$S(max) = 0.36 \text{ N/mm}^2$$

This is less than the typical value of 0.86 N/mm^2 for structural softwood and is therefore satisfactory for shear strength.

Note: In addition to the previous calculations a structural engineer will also check the following:

The minimum amount of end bearing required to avoid crushing

The amount of deflection or sag under load; deflection is normally limited to 0.003 of the span or 3 mm in every metre.

These calculations are not within the scope of your course.

Note: Tables of permissible stress values for bending and shear of various species, grades and strength classes are given in BS 5268.

Glue-laminated timber

Structural timber members which are of a large cross-section, long in length, or shaped, can be fabricated by the process of glue lamination (glulam). Examples of this are shown in Figure 125.

A glulam member comprises boards of small cross-section, glued and layered up either horizontally or vertically. The boards are layered with a parallel grain direction and cramped up in special jigs which are set up to provide the straight or curved profile of the finished member. Specifications for glulam members are given in BS 4169: *Glue-Laminated Timber for Structural Members*.

A reduction in sectional size or greater span over solid beams of the same section is possible when using glue-laminated sections. This is because higher stress values may be used in design calculations. There are a number of reasons for this, in addition to the grade of timber used, the main ones being:

1 The strength of timber is variable, but by joining a number of timbers together to act as one beam, the average strength of each layer (laminate) will be greater than the strength of the weakest laminate.
2 Strength-reducing defects, such as large knots or shakes, are restricted in size to the thickness of one laminate.

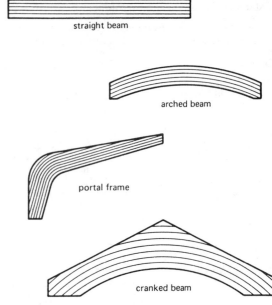

Figure 125   *Examples of glulam*

3 Higher-quality timber can be used in critical areas.
4 Members can be precambered to offset any deflection under loaded conditions.
5 Because of the relatively small cross-section of each laminate, a tightly controlled moisture content can be achieved, resulting in a dimensionally stable finished member.

Laminate thickness

In straight glulam members the thickness of each laminate is dependent upon the depth of the member, although no laminate should be in excess of 50 mm thick. When curved members are laminated the timber must be flexible enough to enable it to be bent easily without breaking. The timber must be bent in a dry state, as steam treatment or soaking of the laminate prior to bending is not permissible. The maximum thickness of the laminations that can be used will therefore depend on the radius of the curve, but in any case this should not exceed 50 mm. For practical purposes the following maximum laminate thicknesses may be used:

When bending softwood: radius (mm)/100

When bending hardwood: radius (mm)/150.

Example

What would be the maximum laminate thickness for a softwood arched beam having a radius of 2 m?

$$\text{maximum laminate thickness} = \frac{\text{radius}}{100}$$

$$= \frac{2000}{100}$$

Answer Maximum laminate thickness would be 20 mm.

Timber grade

In use, structural glulam members in common with other beams will be subjected to stress – the outer laminates to tension and compression and the middle ones to shear.

A glulam member may be manufactured using one grade of timber, but to reduce costs it is usual to employ a lower grade in the middle layers of a member. BS 4978 specifies three grades for laminating based on the knot/area ratio. These are LA, LB and LC, and are based on grade stresses of approximately 95, 75 and 50 per cent, respectively, of the basic stress of clear defect-free timber. A typical beam cross-section, shown in Figure 126, might consist of LA or LB timber in the outer layers and LB or LC in the middle layers. This lower-grade centre section, comprising one-third to one-half of the total depth, is possible because the shear strength of timber is not significantly affected by the drop in grade.

Jointing

Laminates can be jointed in various ways to produce full-length or -width laminations. End jointing is normally carried out using a scarf joint; ideally, for maximum strength, these should have a slope of 1:6 for laminates in the compression area and 1:12 for laminates in the tension area (see Figure 127). Scarfs with a slope outside this range will have an adverse affect on strength.

As an alternative, structural finger joints may be used (see Figure 128). These may vary in length but 50 mm is common in the United Kingdom. Finger joints are more economical in

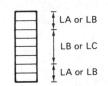

Figure 126   *Timber grades*

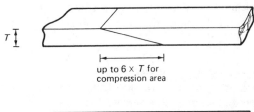

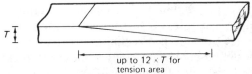

Figure 127   *Scarf joints*

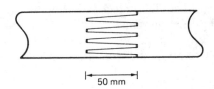

Figure 128   *Finger joints*

Figure 129   *Edge joints*

terms of timber wastage than scarf joints. The end joints of laminates should preferably be glued, preassembled, cured and flushed off before final assembly of the member, particularly where curved sections are involved. During final assembly all end joints should be evenly distributed throughout the member so that grouping in any one section is avoided.

Edge jointing of inside laminates to form the full width of a member is possible, but should be separated in adjacent laminates by about 25 mm or the thickness of the laminate if this is greater (see Figure 129).

Preparation of laminates

Each individual laminate must be carefully prepared to fine tolerances. Planing should be carried out within forty-eight hours prior to gluing. The use of sharp planer knives and suitable pressure is essential in order to ensure that the timber is cut cleanly without compressing or damaging the timber in any way.

At the time of gluing the moisture content of the timber should be either 12 per cent to 15 per cent or within plus or minus 3 per cent of its expected equilibrium. In addition the surface of each laminate must be free from oil, dust, excessive natural resin or any other substance likely to affect the strength of the glue line.

Assembly

Before gluing and cramping the laminates should be assembled dry (dry assembly) to determine the position of the different grades of laminate and stagger the end joints. Any laminates that show cupping, outside the permitted range shown in Table 15, at this stage must be rejected.

Table 15   Maximum permitted depth of cupping

Laminate thickness	For laminate widths	
	up to 150 mm	over 150 mm
Up to 16 mm	1.5 mm	1.5 mm
17 mm to 29 mm	1 mm	1.5 mm
30 mm to 47 mm	0.5 mm	1.0 mm

Wet assembly of the member follows. To achieve a controlled spread of glue, each laminate is passed in turn through a mechanical glue spreader. They are then placed into the cramping jig in their previously determined positions. The type of jig used will vary widely depending on the nature of the work in hand and the type of firm, from the occasional assembly of small glulam members in a joiner's shop to large-scale specialist timber engineering plants using complex machinery. A small cramping jig suitable for a limited number of members is shown in Figure 130.

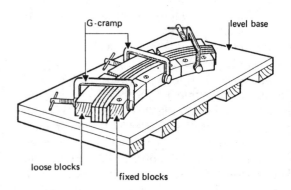

Figure 130   *Small cramping jig*

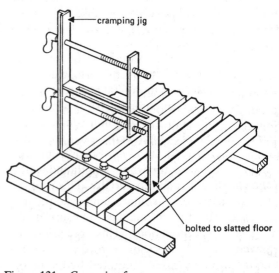

Figure 131   *Cramping frame*

Figure 132 *Cramping set-up for curved member*

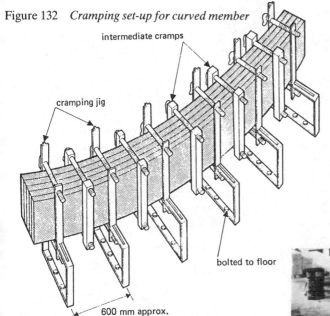

Where glulam assembly is carried out fairly frequently or large numbers of members are required, the vertical cramping frame shown in Figure 131 is often used. A number of these are bolted to a grillage or slots in the floor, so that the vertical uprights conform to the shape of the finished member. For most curved shapes this is achieved by setting up the jigs to the required shape, with the aid of a template. Figure 132 shows the cramping set-up for a curved member. Although the cramping jigs incorporate cramps, additional intermediate cramps and caulboards (outer pressure-distributing boards) are required to ensure the continuity of pressure necessary to achieve a thin uniform glue line. Cramps are spaced at up to 400 mm centres for straight work, but on curved work this must be reduced in some cases to 100 mm centres. The centre cramps are tightened first, gradually working outwards to the ends. Precise uniform clamp pressure over the whole length and width of the glue line is required initially. This is to be not less than 0.7 N/mm², and should be rechecked after fifteen minutes to ensure there has been no reduction. This precision is achieved with the use of a torque wrench, although in many cases calibrated hydraulic or pneumatic cramps are used.

Figure 133 *Finishing glulam member using wide-panel planer*

The type of adhesive used will depend on the intended use of the member. Casein or urea formaldehyde is specified for use in low-heat, low-humidity, internal conditions. Phenol and/or resorcinol formaldehyde is specified for use in any other conditions where there is no restriction on temperature or humidity levels.

Finish
After curing and conditioning, the member is finished to the required standard by planing,

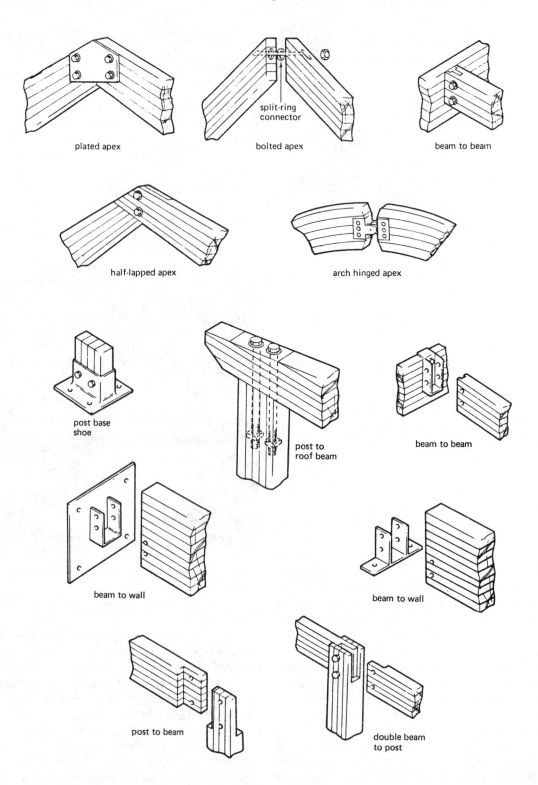

plated apex   bolted apex   beam to beam

split-ring
connector

half-lapped apex   arch hinged apex

post base
shoe

post to
roof beam

beam to beam

beam to wall   beam to wall

post to beam   double beam
to post

Figure 134   *Glulam joint and fixing details*

sanding, patching and filling. Figure 133 shows a large glulam member being finished using a wide-panel planer. Glulam members are normally finished to one of the following surface grades:

Regularized This must be at least 50 per cent sawn or planed to remove protruding laminations, mainly for industrial use where its surface is concealed or its appearance is not of prime importance.

Planed This has a fully planed surface free from glue stains; any significant defects (knot holes and fissures) will have to be filled or patched. Suitable for most applications except where a varnish or other clear finish is required.

Sanded This has a fully planed and sanded surface, any significant defects being filled or patched. End joints in the laminates or patching will, as far as possible, be matched for grain direction and colour. Suitable for all applications where a high-quality clear finish is required.

Marking

On completion each glulam member should be marked with the following information:

The manufacturer's name or trade mark
The type of adhesive used
The British Standard number BS 4169.

Protection and treatment

Glulam members, in common with other timber components, must be suitably protected during treatment, transit, storage and erection. Where preservative or fire-retardant treatments are used, these must be compatible with both the timber and the adhesive. It is preferable to carry out these treatments on the finished member, although in some cases treatment before lamination may be required, in which case water-repellent preservatives must be avoided.

Site erection

Glulam members are often delivered on site shrink-wrapped in a plastic or waterproof covering. This should be left in place after erection to protect the member from the effects of weather and subsequent wet and finishing trades. Where members are to be jointed or fitted into metal shoes etc. the protective covering can be temporarily pulled back.

The site work for glulam members normally involves jointing, erection, plumbing and fixing. In order to prevent accidental collapse, temporary ties and braces must be used until the structure is stable. Care must be taken to avoid distortions when lifting the members. For large structures manufacturers will provide or specify lifting points in certain positions, to ensure that any stresses in erection do not exceed the permissible stresses in any member.

A range of typical joint and fixing details are illustrated in Figure 134. The main method of securing a member is with bolts and metal plates. The feet of arched or portable frames and posts are fixed to the base by the use of a metal shoe. This method has the added advantage of preventing moisture rising up the timber.

Mechanical fasteners for structural work

This section covers some of the common types of mechanical fasteners that are used for structural work. Table 16 summarizes their main characteristics.

Nailed and screwed joints

Most nailed joints have good resistance to lateral or sideways movement, but little resistance when loaded in tension (withdrawal). See Figure 136.

Care must be taken when spacing the nails to avoid splitting the timber. In general this is related to the diameter of the nail. The minimum spacing distances for 2.5 mm diameter wire nails are shown in Table 17 and illustrated in Figure 137. These distances may be reduced if the timber being fixed is pre-bored or the points of the nails are blunted.

When compared to plain wire nails, screws have a better resistance to withdrawal but a reduced lateral resistance. The minimum spacing distances for screws is similar to those used for nailing.

Table 16 **Mechanical Fasteners**

Type		Material and finish	Notes
Nails			
Round plain wire		Mild steel with either bright galvanized or sherardized finishes	Used for the securing of all structural timbers
Lost-head wire			Machine driven nails are packed in strips or coils for use in various forms of pneumatic gun
Clout nail			
Machine driven nails		Copper and aluminium also available	Duplex nails have a double head, the lower one being driven home for maximum holding power while the upper head projects enabling easy withdrawal
Duplex nail			
Improved nails			
Twisted-shank nail		Mild steel with either a bright galvanized or sherardized finish	Used for all construction work where extra holding power is required. Especially good for fixing sheet materials and attaching proprietary metal nail plates, joist hangers and framing anchors
Annular ring shanked nail			
Staples		Steel coated in either zinc or resin	Used as an alternative to pneumatically driven nails for fixing plywood, fibreboard and insulation etc., particularly in the factory assembly of timber frame housing units
Screws			
Countersunk head		Steel with either a bright zinc sherardized enamelled or plated finish Stainless steel, brass and aluminium also available	Limited use in structural work because of their increased cost and assembly time when compared with nails
Round head			
Raised countersunk head			
Recessed head			
Coach screws		Steel usually finished in black, sometimes zinc	Used in heavy-duty constructional work for both timber to timber or metal to timber joints

Type		Material and finish	Notes
Bolts			
Hexagonal head		Steel usually finished in black	Used in heavy-duty constructional work for both timber to timber or metal to timber joints. Used in conjunction with connectors where extra strength is required
Square head			
Coach bolts			
Cartridge fasteners			
Nail		Zinc-plated steel	Available in a varied range for fixings to brickwork concrete and structural steel
Stud			
Eyelet			
Connectors			
Double-toothed plate		Steel, either zinc plated or galvanized	Used to increase the resistance to shear of bolted joints. Double and split-ring connectors are used for timber to timber joints, whereas single and shear-plate connectors are used for timber to metal, timber to other components or demountable timber to timber joints using two connectors back to back. Split-ring and shear-plate connectors are for heavy-duty structural joints; they require the use of special grooving and housing tools before assembly (see Figure 135). The teeth of the double- and single-toothed plate connectors are embedded into the timber by using a special high-tensile threaded steel rod, nuts and a ballbearing washer to draw up the joint prior to inserting the ordinary bolt
Single-toothed plate			
Split ring			
Shear plate			

continued

Table 16 *continued*

Type		Material and finish	Notes
Nail plates. Punched plate		Steel, either zinc plated or galvanized	Used for the manufacture of trussed rafters, trussed purlins and beams Punched plates are only suitable for factory installation where specialist machinery is available Gusset plates are suitable for on-site fabrication using hand or pneumatic driven nails
Gusset plate			
Joist hangers		Steel with a galvanized finish	Available in a wide range for either timber to timber or timber to wall connections
Framing anchors		Steel with a galvanized finish	Suitable for a wide range of applications including studwork, rafter to wall plate connections, and other uses where timbers run at right angles to one another

Type		Material and finish	Notes
Truss clip	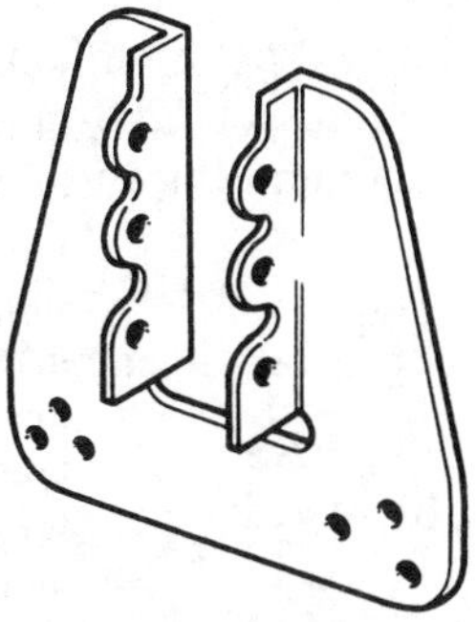	Steel with a galvanized finish	Used for ensuring a positive fixing between trussec
teel straps		Galvanized or stainless steel	Used for anchoring wall plates and roof joists and as lateral restraint straps to anchor floors and roofs. Normally required at 2 m centres where floors and roof meet the walls

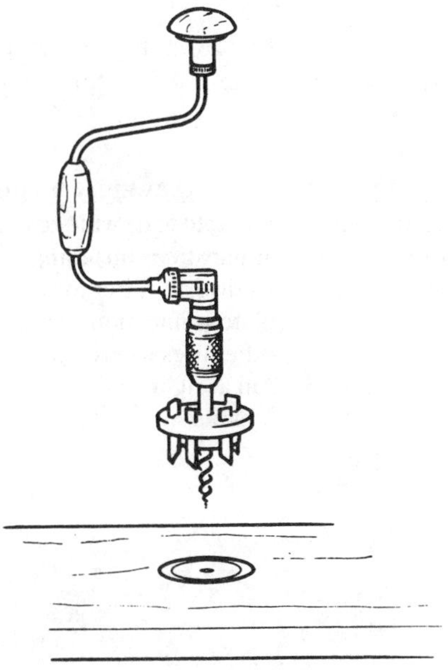

Figure 135   *Cutting the groove for a split-ring connector*

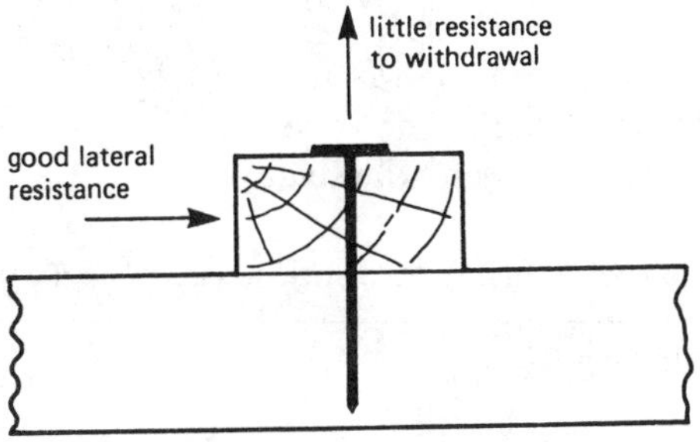

Figure 136   *Strength of a nailed joint*

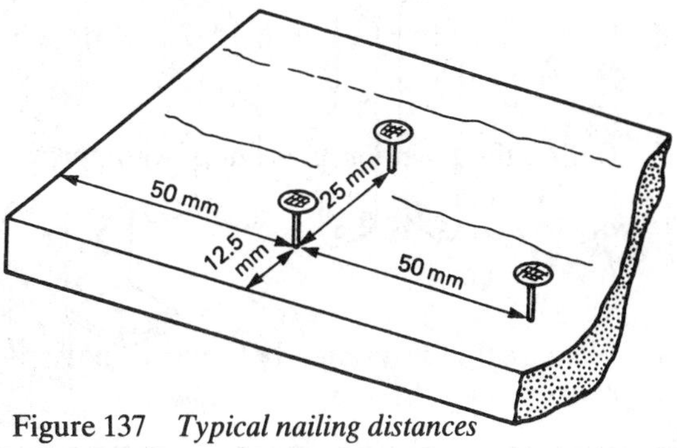

Figure 137   *Typical nailing distances*

Table 17   **Nailing distances**

Minimum spacing for	End distance	Edge distance	Side spacing between nails	Spacing between adjacent nails along the grain
Normal nailing	50 mm	1.25 mm	25 mm	50 mm
Nailing in pre-bored holes or nails with blunted points	25 mm	12.5 mm	7.5 mm	25 mm

Self-assessment questions

1 Describe what is meant by stress grading.

2 Describe with the aid of sketches *four* defects resulting from incorrect kiln seasoning.

3 List the safety precautions that should be observed by the operative when using synthetic resin adhesives.

4 Write a brief description of the following sheet materials:
(a) Plywood
(b) Chipboard
(c) Plastic laminate

5 Name and describe *two* methods of timber seasoning.

6 Define the meaning of the following terms:
(a) Compression
(b) Tension
(c) Shear

7 What is the difference between a thermoplastic and a thermosetting adhesive?

8 Briefly describe how the moisture content of timber can be found using a small drying oven.

9 In the manufacture of a glulam portal frame, softwood laminates have to be bent a radius of 1200 mm. What would be the maximum thickness of each laminate?

10 What do the following timber grading abbreviations mean?
(a) FAS
(b) FAQ
(c) US
(d) KAR

11 Floor joists spanning 4.8 m carry a uniformly distributed load of 2.1 kN/m². What is the load carried by one joist if they are spaced at 400 mm centres?

12 What is the difference between GS and MGS timber?

13 State a suitable procedure for the eradication of a dry rot attack in the suspended ground floor of a domestic house.

14 List the safety precautions to be observed by the operative when using timber preservatives.

15 Explain the precautions that must be taken during the transit and storage prior to fixing of kiln seasoned joinery components.

chapter 6

Principles of insulation

After reading this chapter the student should be able to:

1 State the principles involved in the following:
   (a) Fire-resistant construction
   (b) Thermal insulation
   (c) Sound insulation.
2 Prepare sketches to show insulation details suitable to a given situation.
3 State the Building Regulations that are applicable to fire, thermal and sound insulation.

Fire-resistant construction

In order to have an understanding of fire-resistant construction it is necessary to have a knowledge of the nature of fire and its related terminology.

Fire or combustion is burning. This is a chemical reaction between a substance and oxygen, during which heat is produced and the original form of the substance is destroyed. All substances or materials both solid and liquid can be classified into the two following groups:

Those that are capable of burning: solid materials are known as combustible and liquids as flammable.
Those that are incapable of burning: solid materials are known as non-combustible and liquids as non-flammable.

It is not the actual combustible or flammable material that combines with the oxygen when they burn. In both cases it is the vapour that they give off when they are heated that actually burns. The lowest temperature at which a material will give off a flammable vapour is known as the ignition temperature of combustible materials and the flashpoint of flammable materials. This ignition temperature or flashpoint of materials will vary widely. Combustible solids require preheating to fairly high temperatures before their flammable vapours are given off, for example, timber to about 300 °C, whereas many flammable liquids give off a flammable vapour at well below normal room

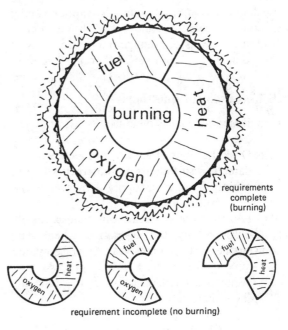

Figure 138 *Requirements for burning*

temperatures, for example, petroleum spirit at −43 °C.

Figure 138 shows the essential requirements for burning. These are:

Fuel A combustible or flammable material to burn.
Oxygen Normally from the air to combine with the flammable vapour given off by the material.
Heat Initial heat to bring a material up to its ignition temperature or flashpoint.

Burning takes place when all of the requirements are met. If one of the requirements is removed or is not available then burning cannot occur.

Growth of a building fire

Most building fires are started from a relatively small source of heat, for example, a lighted match, a cigarette end or an overloaded electric circuit. Any of these can supply the initial heat required to ignite a small fuel source, such as an armchair or waste paper in a rubbish bin etc. These heat sources in turn preheat other materials. This cycle of events will continue to escalate, with more flammable vapours being given off as each different material in a room is heated above its ignition temperature. It is at this point that a 'flashover' will occur. The term 'flashover' is used to describe the simultaneous ignition of the flammable vapours, causing an intense fire involving all the contents of a room or building.

The rate of burning depends upon the supply of oxygen. It is possible for a fire in a room or small building to burn itself out owing to the depletion of the oxygen supply. However, if the hot gases produced as a result of the fire are allowed to escape, then a fresh oxygen supply will be drawn in causing a rapid fire growth. The transference of heat in a fire takes place by one or a combination of the following processes.

Conduction
Convection
Radiation

Conduction

This is the transfer of heat within a material from hotter to cooler areas. Non-combustible materials such as brickwork and steel have been known to conduct heat sufficient to cause temperatures high enough to ignite combustible materials such as timber etc. in locations remote from the fire.

Convection

This is the transfer of heat within liquids and gases. The heated particles expand and become less dense; this causes them to rise, and their place is taken by colder and therefore denser particles. Convection currents can cause a rapid spread of fire within a building, especially in vertical shafts, for example, lift shafts, stairwells, cavities and ventilation ducts etc. Hot gases from a ground-floor fire can travel rapidly up a stairwell causing ignition in the upper floors and roof structure.

Radiation

Heat rays are given off by any hot object. This is known as radiated heat. These heat rays are transmitted through the air or even a vacuum in the same way as we receive heat from the sun. When the rays come into contact with a material most of them are absorbed, causing the material's temperature to rise. The remainder of the rays will be reflected. Radiant heat can raise the temperature of materials at great distances from the fire itself. Fire can even spread to adjacent buildings by this process.

Surface spread of flame

Some materials will ignite more readily and burn faster than others. In general the speed at which a flame will travel across the surface of a combustible material depends upon its density and the amount of surface exposed to the air. Low density means rapid flame spread. Porous materials burn quickly because of the oxygen supply inside them. Large surface area means rapid flame spread. A solid piece of timber will take longer to burn than the same piece of timber cut into a number of thin strips. This is because the thin strips expose a larger surface area to the fire.

Note: Wood dust and other fine combustible dusts expose a very large surface area. These are therefore highly combustible, and even a small spark can cause them to explode.

BS 476: Part 7: 1971: *Surface Spread of Flame Tests for Materials* sets out a method of test to establish the behaviour of the surface of a material during the early stages of a fire. The test equipment is illustrated in Figure 139. The results of this test grade combustible materials into the following four classes according to how rapidly the flame spreads across their surface:

Class 1   surfaces of very low flame spread
Class 2   surfaces of low flame spread
Class 3   surfaces of medium flame spread
Class 4   surfaces of rapid flame spread

The Building Regulations (surface spread of flame)

The Building Regulations AD: B Fire Spread, which exerts control over the types of material that can be used in various situations, introduces an additional class 0 surface. This is non-combustible material or class 1 material with a surface that has spread of flame characteristics similar to non-combustible material. Table 18 gives typical surface spread of flame classifications for a number of common materials used as wall and ceiling linings.

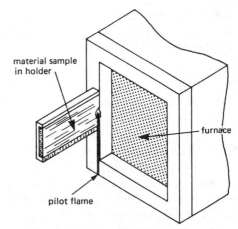

Figure 139   *Surface spread of flame test equipment*

partment's intended purpose. These are shown in Table 19.

The internal surfaces of walls and ceilings are controlled by the regulations and, apart from certain exceptions, the materials used to line walls and ceilings must have the minimum surface spread of flame classification shown in Table 20.

Table 18 **Surface spread of flame classification**

Material	Class of surface (untreated)
Brickwork	0
Blockwork	0
Concrete	0
Ceramic tiles	0
Asbestos boards and other proprietary non-asbestos substitutes	0
Plasterboard	0
Woodwool slabs	0
Hardboard	3
Particle board	3
Plywood	3
Timber	3

Note: Timber and other timber based materials with a density below 400 kg/m³ have a class 4 surface. Those with a class 3 surface may be brought up to class 1 with proprietary treatments.

The Building Regulations AD: B also classifies building into two main divisions, those with sleeping accommodation are called residential and those without are called non-residential. These divisions are further sub-divided into nine purpose groups according to the building's or com-

Table 19 **Purpose groups**

Main category	Purpose groups	Intended use
Residential		
	Dwelling house	Private dwelling house (not a flat or maisonette)
	Flat (including a maisonette)	Self-contained dwelling not being a house
	Institutional	Hospitals, schools and homes used as living accommodation for persons suffering from disabilities due to illness, old age, physical or mental disorders and those under five years old, where these persons sleep on the premises
	Other residential	Residential accommodation not included in previous groups, e.g. hotels, boarding houses, and hostels, etc.

Table 19   Purpose groups – *cont*

Main category	Purpose groups	Intended use
Non-residential		
	Assembly	Public building or assembly building where people meet for social, recreational, or business activities (not office, shop or industrial)
	Office	All premises used for administration procedures, e.g. clerical, drawing, publishing and banking, etc.
	Shop	All premises used for the retail sale of goods or services, including restaurants, public houses, cafes, hairdressers and hire or repair outlets
	Industrial	All premises defined as a factory in section 175 of the factories act 1961, not including slaughter houses, etc.
	Other non-residential	All places used for the deposit or storage of goods, the parking of vehicles and other premises not covered in the previous non-residential groups

Any part of the wall surface in rooms may be of a lower class provided it is not less than class 3 and does not exceed:

half the floor area of the room, 20 m² in any residential building.

60 m² in any non-residential building.

Note: fire surrounds, fitted furniture, frames, architraves, skirting, other trim and unglazed parts of doors are excluded from the surface spread of flame requirements

Small room   A totally enclosed room with a floor area not exceeding 4 m² for residential buildings and 30 m² in non-residential ones.

Circulation spaces   A hall, corridor, landing or lobby etc. used as an access between rooms or protected shafts, or as an access between rooms or protected shafts and an exist.

Protected shafts   A stairway, lift shaft, escalator or service duct opening that permits the passage of items and/or persons from one compartment to another.

Fire resistance

Unlike surface spread of flame, fire resistance is a property of an element of building construction (walls, floors and roofs etc.) and not an individual material. Fire resistance is defined as the ability of an element of building construction to satisfy stated criteria, when subjected to a standard fire test as defined in BS 476 Part 8. The fire resistance of an element can be defined by reference to the following criteria:

Stability   The ability of an element to resist collapse.

Integrity   The ability of an element to resist the passage of flames or hot gases, from its exposed to its unexposed face.

Insulation   The ability of an element to resist the passage of heat which would increase the surface temperature of the unexposed face to an unacceptable level.

Note: The unexposed face means the side of an element remote from the fire.

The results of a typical test might be expressed as 30/20/15, which means that the insulation of the element failed after 15 minutes, the integrity after 20 minutes and the stability either failed after 30 minutes or the test was terminated at this time.

Building Regulations (fire resistance)

The Building Regulations AD: B set out the periods of stability, integrity and insulation that are required for an element of building construction. These periods vary up to four hours depending on the buildings, purpose group, height, floor area, cubic capacity and its position in relation to the site boundary. The Approved Document contains a table of common construction giving notional periods of fire resistance for them. These constructions will be accepted as satisfying

Table 20 **Surface spread of flame requirements**

Purpose group	Location of surface	Class of surface		
		small room (max. 4 m²)	other room	circulation spaces and protected shaft
Dwelling house				
1 or 2 storey (not counting basements)	Walls	3	1	1
	Ceiling	3	3	3
3 or more storeys	Walls	3	1	0
	Ceiling	3	1	0
Flat	Walls	3	1	0
	Ceiling	3	1	0
Institutional	Walls	1	0	0
	Ceiling	1	1	0
Other residential	Walls	3	1	0
	Ceilings	3	1	0
Assembly		(max 30 m²)		
	Walls	3	1	0
	Ceilings	3	1	0
Offices Shops Industrial Other non-residential	Walls	3	1	0
	Ceilings	3	1	0

the relevant requirements of the regulations without the need of further proof or test.

Fire resistance of structural timber
The main purpose of structural fire precautions is public health and safety. A building should be constructed so that in the event of a fire it will in the early stages retain most of structural strength, thus enabling the safe evacuation of its occupants and the safe working of fire-fighting teams, without the fear of structural collapse.

Timber, although a combustible material, has a number of qualities that give an advantage over some structural materials:

High insulation
Low conductivity
Low thermal expansion
Known rate of charring
Charred layer provides further insulation
Mechanical strength not affected by high temperatures
Difficult to ignite
High spontaneous ignition temperature

Timber fire resistance will also depend on its density, sectional size and moisture content.

Timber in fire
On exposure to a flame or heat source, timber will not burn until the moisture in the outer layers has evaporated. This will temporarily hold the temperature at about 100 °C, thus causing a check to the fire. Little chemical change takes place until the temperature reaches

about 300 °C, when the exposed surface layers of timber begin to disintegrate and flammable vapours are released which can ignite if there is a flame present. Where there is a heat source but no flame, timber will not spontaneously ignite until it reaches a temperature of about 500 °C.

Note: At these temperatures aluminium and steel are rapidly losing their strength.

The process of heating and drying out the timber has little effect on its dimensions. The very minimal expansion on heating is balanced out by the slight shrinkage due to a reduction of its moisture content. As timber burns the disintegrating outer layers form into charcoal; this insulates the inner core from the effects of the fire, by preventing heat build-up and restricting the oxygen supply. The effect of this insulation is illustrated in Figure 140(a), which shows a temperature plot through a structural timber beam that has been subjected to a furnace temperature of almost 1000 °C. The unaffected

edges of the core at a temperature of around 200 °C are still well below their ignition temperature, while the centre of the beam is still less than 100 °C. The insulating charcoal layer will not burn below 500 °C; above this temperature a glowing combustion starts, gradually consuming the outer layers of charcoal as the charring area advances into the unburnt timber core at a steady rate. See Figure 140(b).

Note: During fire exposure the arrises will become progressively rounded; their radius of rounding will be equal to the total depth of charring.

The steady rate of charring varies with the type and density of the timber. Table 21 shows the charring rates for common structural timbers. Research has proved that the charring rate is little affected by the intensity of the fire, thus enabling the strength carrying capacity of a structural timber member to be calculated after a known period of exposure to a fire. Structural timber members can be designed oversize with a

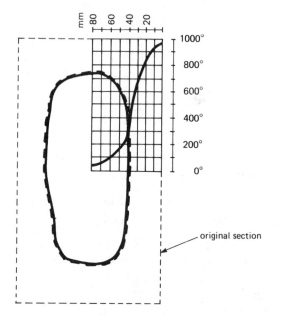

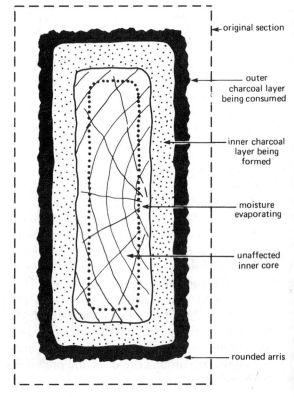

Figure 140   (a)   *Temperature plot*
(b)   *Timber burning*

layer of (sacrificial) timber to allow for the expected loss in dimensions after a particular period of fire.

When a timber member is exposed on all four faces it is normal to multiply the depth of charr by 1.25. This allows for the more rapid temperature rise experienced under such conditions. Glue-laminated members (glulam) can be considered to charr in a manner similar to solid timber providing that thermo-setting, resorcinol, phenol or urea formaldehyde adhesive has been used.

Where bolts, nails or screws are not totally enclosed in the unaffected core, rapid conduction of heat will cause localized charring around the fastener leading to a loss of anchorage.

Note: Where other adhesives are used for glulam members or mechanical fasteners are not fully enclosed within the unaffected core, charring must be assumed on all four faces of each laminate of the component to the depth shown in Table 21.

Fire treatments and seals

No amount of treatment can make timber completely fireproof, but treatment can be given to increase the timber's resistance to ignition and, to a large extent, stop its active participation in a fire. This treatment is known as a fire-resisting or fire-retarding treatment. It consists of treating the timber with a fire-resisting chemical. The main fire-resisting chemicals are: diammonium phosphate; monammonium phosphate; or a mixture of one of these with ammonium sulphate; ammonium chloride; zinc chloride; and boric acid. They work by giving off a vapour that will not burn. Alternatively there are intumescent paints available that when heated bubble and expand forming an insulating layer that cuts off the fire's oxygen supply. Intumescent material is also used for fire strips around door openings etc. (see Figure 141). These strips are activated by heat. In the early stages of a fire they will expand to up to 50 times their original thickness, thus efficiently sealing the gap around the door and prolonging its integrity.

Table 21   Rate of charring

Timber	Depth of charring after 30 minutes	Depth of charring after 60 minutes
Western red cedar and other timbers with a density below 420 kg/m^3	25 mm	50 mm
European redwood, douglas fir, Western hemlock, parana pine, spruce, larch, mahogany, ash and beech	20 mm	40 mm
Oak, utile, keruing, teak, green heart and jarrah	15 mm	30 mm

Note: Charring depths for periods between 15 minutes and 90 minutes can be found from this table, for example European redwood – charring depth after 15 minutes 10 mm, 90 minutes 60 mm.

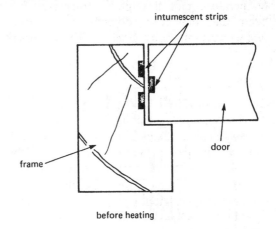

before heating

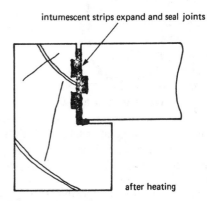

after heating

Figure 141   *Intumescent seals*

Thermal insulation

Thermal insulation can be seen as an attempt to isolate heat within a building. No thermal insulation system can be 100 per cent effective, because there is no known material that will completely isolate heat. Providing there is a difference in the temperature between the two sides of the material or structure, heat will transfer through the material from the warm to the cold side. Therefore the purpose of thermal insulation is to restrict heat transfer, thus preventing heat loss from the building in cold weather conditions and heat gain by the building in warm weather conditions.

Heat transfer

Remember there are three processes by which heat may be transferred:

Conduction The transfer of heat within a material from hotter to cooler areas
Convection The transfer of heat within liquids and gases
Radiation The transfer of heat from one object to another in the form of heat rays.

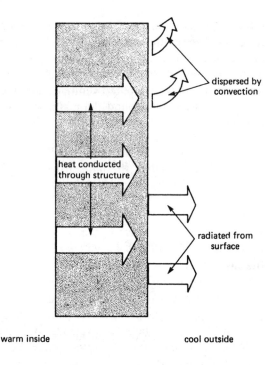

warm inside   cool outside

Figure 142   *Heat transfer through element of construction*

Heat is transferred through an element of construction by a combination of all three processes. This is shown in Figure 142. Warmth from the inside is conducted through the structure. The heated structure then radiates heat which is dispersed into the air with the assistance of convection currents.

The three main factors that influence the rate of heat transfer are:

Type of material
Temperature difference
Rate of air change

Type of material

Heat travels through a material by conduction. A material that is a poor conductor will therefore be a good insulator. Still air is a very good insulator as it is a poor conductor. In fact the majority of thermal insulators available are basically air traps.

Note: In order to be effective, thermal insula-

tors must be kept dry. This is because if they are allowed to become saturated, water, which is a better conductor, takes the place of the air.

Temperature difference

The rate of heat transfer from the warm to the cold side of the structure is dependent on the temperature difference. A small difference in temperature will result in a low rate of heat transfer, whereas a large difference in temperature will result in a high rate of heat transfer. For example, an unheated house in cold weather conditions will have almost no heat transfer as the inside and outside temperatures will be approximately equal, but when heat is switched on the rate of heat transfer will rise rapidly.

Rate of air change

This is the rate at which the warm air on one side of the structure is displaced by the cold air from the other side. Many buildings, especially those with badly fitting doors and windows, open fires and air vents, can have three to four complete air changes every hour. A rate of air change of between one-half and one every hour is considered suitable for most purposes. Much can be done to restrict this unwanted ventilation by the use of weather seals around door and window openings.

Note: Although ventilation increases the rate of air change and heat transfer, it is a necessary requirement for the physical comfort of the occupants of a building. Also, condensation can be attributed to poor ventilation.

k, *R* and *U* values (Figure 143)

k values

Some building materials are better for thermal insulation purposes than others. By looking at their *k* value (thermal conductivity) a comparison can be made between various options available. Thermal conductivity *k* value is a measure of a material's ability to conduct heat. It is expressed as the flow of heat, in watts, through a square metre of material, 1 metre thick, with a temperature difference of 1 °C between its inside and outside surfaces:

k has units W/M °C

The *k* value of many common building materials is given in Table 22. The *k* value for specific building materials can be obtained from the relevant manufacturer.

R value

Building materials are not of course used in 1 metre thicknesses; therefore their *R* value (thermal resistance) is required. The *R* value is a measure of a material's resistance to the flow of heat per square metre for any given thickness. It can be found by dividing the material's thickness in metres by its *k* value:

$$R = \frac{\text{material thickness in metres}}{k}$$

U value

The structure of a building is rarely a single material; it is commonly a combination of materials, possibly with cavities (air spaces) between them. To compare the thermal insulation values of various composite structures the *U* value (thermal transmittance) is used. Thermal transmittance is the rate of heat flow through an element of building construction. The *U* value is the reciprocal of the sum of the resistances of the component parts of the structure; the internal and external surfaces, and any cavity within the structure:

$$U = \frac{1}{\text{sum of resistances}}$$

Note: The internal and external surfaces of a structure have a certain resistance to heat flow owing to the thin layer of air clinging to the surface.

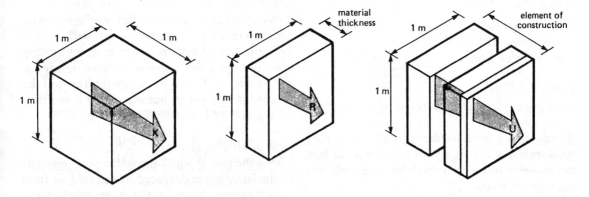

Figure 143   *Definition of terms*

Table 22 **K values of common materials**

Material	Thermal conductivity k value
Asbestos cement sheet	0.40
Asphalt	0.50
Brickwork (1700 kg/m³)	
outer leaf	0.84
inner leaf	0.62
Blockwork (1100 kg/m³)	
outer leaf	0.38
inner leaf	0.34
Blockwork (600 kg/m³)	
outer leaf	0.20
inner leaf	0.19
Cavity foams	
polyurethane	0.026
phenolic	0.031
urea formaldehyde	0.035
Concrete (2100 kg/m³)	
exposed	1.40
protected	1.28
Expanded polystyrene	0.037
Fibreglass	0.04
Glass	1.02
Plasterboard	0.16
Plastering/rendering	
gypsum	0.40
vermiculite	0.20
sand and cement	0.53
Rock fibre (mineral wool)	0.04
Roofing felt	0.20
Slate	1.80
Steel sheeting	48.00
Tiles (burnt clay)	0.83
Timber	
chipboard	0.11
fibreboard	
soft	0.057
medium	0.08
hard	0.13
hardwood	0.16
plywood	0.14
softwood	0.14
woodwool	0.09
Vermiculite	0.04

Note: The *k* value of brickwork and concrete will vary according to their density and whether they are in an exposed or protected situation.

The surface resistances of a structure will vary according to the type of material used and the height, location and exposure of the building. For comparison of the thermal insulation values of alternative materials and structures, the standard values given in Table 23 can be used.

Table 24 gives standard values for ventilated and unventilated cavities of thickness between 20 mm and 75 mm. For cavities outside this range these values would be reduced.

U value calculation

When calculating the *U* value of a particular element of construction, the following basic procedure can be adopted using Tables 22, 23 and 24 for *k* values and resistances:

- 1 Using a *U* value worksheet, shown in Figure 144, sketch in column 1 the element of construction being considered.
- 2 List in column 2 the materials and cavities that form each layer of the construction.
- 3 Select the *k* value for each material and enter in column 3.
- 4 Enter in column 4 the thickness in metres of each material (*t*).
- 5 Divide in turn each material's *t* by *k* to find resistance and enter in column 5.

Table 23 **Surface resistances**

Surface	Internal resistance	External resistance
Walls	0.12	0.05
Roof	0.11	0.04
Exposed floor	0.15	0.09

Table 24 **Cavity resistances**

Cavity	Resistance
Unventilated	0.18
Ventilated	0.11

Note: The surface and cavity values stated are for most normal building materials, but for corrugated materials these values are decreased and for shiny metallic surfaces they are increased.

U value worksheet no.	Job title		Date	Ref.
1	2	3	4	5
Element of construction	Component	Conductivity k value	Thickness t metres	Resistance $R = \dfrac{t}{k}$
	External surface resistance			
	Internal surface resistance			
BBS DESIGN		Total resistance		
		U value $\dfrac{1}{R}$		

Figure 144   *U value worksheet*

6 Select the internal, external and cavity resistances and enter in column 5.
7 Add up column 5 and enter the total resistance.
8 Divide total resistance into 1 to find the *U* value; enter this in the space provided.

An example of a *U* value calculation is given in Figure 145, which shows a completed *U* value worksheet for a typical cavity wall construction.

Building Regulations (thermal insulation)
The need to conserve heat within buildings is becoming increasingly more important. This has been brought about by the so-called 'energy crisis' resulting in the constant acceleration in fuel prices and the improved levels of comfort that people expect. These two points stress the need for buildings to be effectively insulated against heat loss.

The Building Regulations Part L lay down minimum standards of thermal insulation for the main enclosing elements (roof, walls, and exposed floors) of building construction. These regulations state the maximum U values permitted for each purpose group. These maximum U values are given in Table 25.

The area of glazing in windows and rooflights is also controlled by Part L. Table 26 gives the maximum area of single glazing permitted for each purpose group. For dwellings this is a percentage of the perimeter (external) wall area which is measured internally between the

U value worksheet no.		Job title		Date	Ref.
1		2	3	4	5
Element of construction		Component	Conductivity k value	Thickness t metres	Resistance $R = \dfrac{t}{k}$
fibreglass insulation gypsum plaster brickwork brickwork		External surface resistance			0·05
		BRICKWORK (OUTER LEAF)	0·84	0·105	0·125
		FIBREGLASS	0·04	0·075	1·875
		BLOCKWORK (LIGHTWEIGHT)	0·19	0·100	0·526
		GYPSUM PLASTER	0·40	0·015	0·038
		Internal surface resistance			0·12

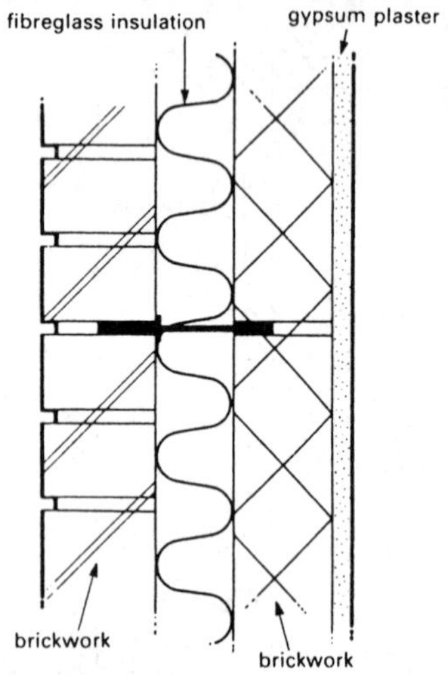

BBS DESIGN

Total resistance	2·734
U value $\dfrac{1}{R}$	0·366

Figure 145 *U value calculation*

Table 25 Maximum U values

Purpose group	Exposed wall	Roof	Exposed floor
Dwelling house Flat	0.6	0.35	0.6
Other residential Institutional	0.6	0.6	0.6
Assembly Office Shop	0.6	0.6	0.6
Industrial Other non-residential	0.7	0.7	0.7

Table 26 Maximum area of single glazing

Purpose group	Windows	Rooflights
Dwelling house Flat	12% of the perimeter wall area for both combined	
Other residential Institutional	25% of exposed wall area	20% of roof
Assembly Office Shop	35% of exposed wall area	20% of roof
Industrial Other non-residential	15% of exposed wall area	20% of roof

Note: This requirement does not include display windows in shops.

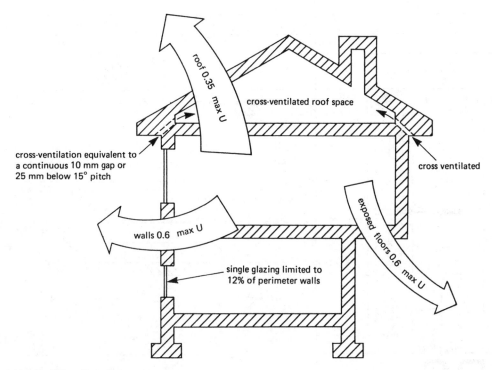

Figure 146   *Building Regulations requirements*

finished floor and ceiling. Whilst for other purpose groups it is a percentage of the exposed wall area. Exposed walls are those which are either external or separate a heated area from an unheated area (providing the unheated area itself contains an external wall).

Windows and roof lights which are double glazed may be up to twice the size of single glazed ones; whereas those which are triple glazed or are double glazed and have a low emissivity coating (low ability to radiate energy) may be up to three times the size of single glazing.

As an alternative to carrying out U value calculations AD: L states minimum acceptable thicknesses of insulation for enclosing elements of construction, depending on the buildings, purpose group and the material's K value.

Thermal insulation of existing buildings

Prior to 1974 only very modest standards of thermal insulation were required for new buildings; consequently houses built before 1974 have a very high rate of heat transfer. Approximately 75 per cent of the heat input in an uninsulated building can be lost to the outside. Improved thermal insulation in these buildings will reduce the rate of heat transfer and reduce the amount of energy used and/or increase the standards of comfort for the occupants.

Figure 147 shows the percentage of heat lost from the various elements of an uninsulated building.

When carrying out thermal insulation improvements the aim is to achieve the greatest benefit from the start with the least cost. The

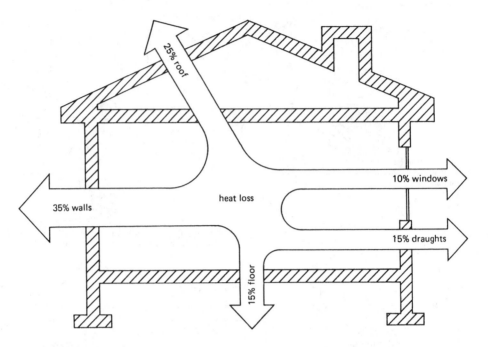

Figure 147   *Heat loss*

suggested order for carrying out these improvements is:

1   Weather seals around doors and windows; Figure 148 illustrates typical details.
2   Roof insulation, normally in the form of mineral/fibreglass between the ceiling joists.
3   Wall insulation, normally either by an injection of cavity wall foam/fibre or in the case of solid walls the external or internal application of an insulating material.
4   Double or triple glazing, preferably sealed units and not in the form of secondary glazing, as convection currents can be set up when the air space increases in width above about 25 mm.

Condensation

The atmosphere contains a certain amount of water vapour in the form of a invisible gas. The amount of water vapour that the air can hold is dependent on the air temperature. Warm air can hold more water vapour than cold air. The maximum amount of water vapour that the air can hold is known as its saturation point; the temperature at this point is known as its dew point. If air at its saturation point is cooled it can no longer hold all of its water vapour, and the excess will revert to water. This process is known as condensation. There are two main condensation problems:

Surface condensation (Figure 149)

Whenever warm moist air meets a cool surface, condensation will occur, possibly causing structural damage, mould growth and damp unhealthy living conditions.

Interstitial condensation (Figure 150)

This means condensation within a structure. Warm air has a higher vapour pressure than cool air; water vapour is therefore driven through most building materials. As this water vapour cools on its passage through the structure condensation can occur, even where there is no surface condensation, causing in many cases severe structural damage.

Over the last twenty years there have been a number of changes in new and modernized

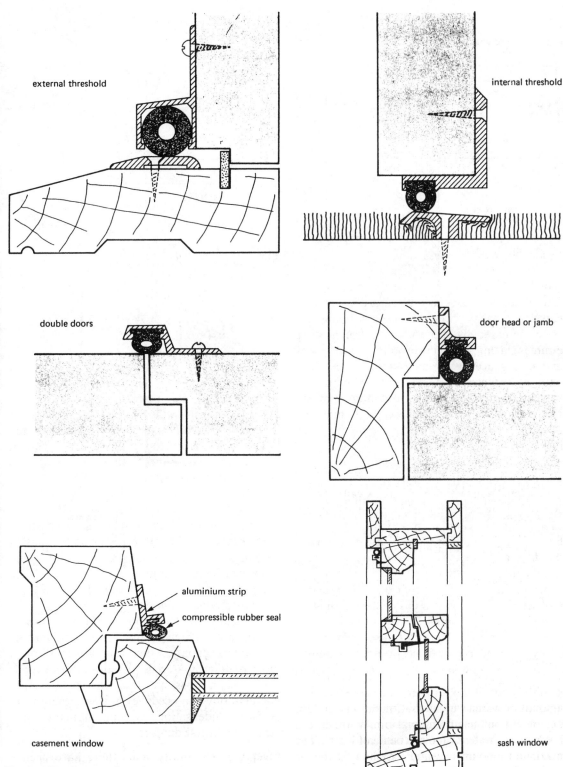

external threshold

internal threshold

double doors

door head or jamb

aluminium strip

compressible rubber seal

casement window

sash window

Figure 148 *Door and window seals*

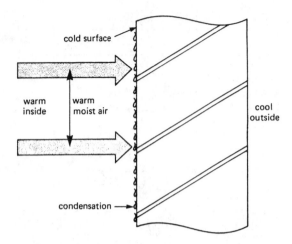

Figure 149   *Surface condensation*

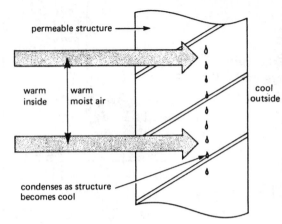

Figure 150   *Interstitial condensation*

buildings to reduce their energy consumption. The air temperature and therefore its vapour-carrying capacity within domestic buildings has been increased by the use of central heating, double glazing, draught-proofing, cavity wall and roof space insulation. At the same time, natural ventilation has been reduced by double glazing, draught-proofing, insulation and the virtual elimination of fireplaces and chimneys. Also the production of water vapour has been increased by the wider use of flueless gas and oil heaters, baths, showers, washing machines, dishwashers and tumble dryers.

Condensation within a building can only be controlled by achieving a proper balance between heating, ventilation and insulation. The two main vapour producing areas within a building are kitchens and bathrooms. These should be well ventilated, possibly by mechanical means, in order to prevent excessive spread of moisture into the living areas of the building. A small amount of natural ventilation in living rooms can make a big difference. This can be easily achieved using various proprietary adjustable window ventilators, one type of which is shown in Figure 151.

The risk of surface condensation can be reduced by the use of insulating wall lining materials. Interstitial condensation can be dealt with in two ways. One is to use a vapour check or barrier on the inside of a building, for example, polythene

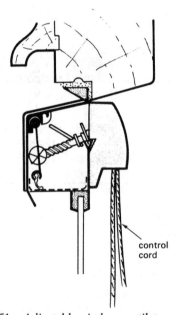

Figure 151   *Adjustable window ventilator*

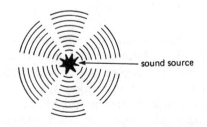

Figure 152   *Sound wave moving outwards from source*

sheet or foil-backed plasterboard etc. In the second, where the structure contains a ventilated cavity, the vapour can be allowed to enter the cavity where it will be dispersed by the ventilation.

Note: As it is almost impossible to provide a perfect vapour barrier because of leaks at joints and fixings etc., a combination of these methods is often used.

Building Regulations (condensation)

In order to limit the risk of condensation in roof spaces above insulated ceilings, the Building Regulations Part F states that a reasonable provision shall be made to prevent excessive condensation in the roof space of dwellings. AD: F sets out the conditions to satisfy the requirements. Roof spaces should have ventilation openings in opposite eaves or at the eaves and opposite high level in the case of a lean-to roof. The area of the opening along each side should be equivalent to a continuous gap of 10 mm for pitched roofs or 25 mm for flat roofs and those of less than 15 degrees pitch (see Figure 146). The AD allows these to be either continuous or distributed along the length of the roof. In addition it also suggests that provision should be made to ensure that the insulation does not obstruct the air flow where the insulation and roof slope meet.

Sound insulation

Nature of sound

Sound is a vibration. The sound we hear is a vibration of the air, which causes a sensation in the ear mechanism, which in turn sends a message to the brain where it is interpreted as sound. Anything that vibrates, normally causes a sound. Vibrations from a source of sound cause the air to move, resulting in a series of waves or ripples moving spherically outwards from the original source (see Figure 152), much like the ripple produced when a stone is thrown in a pond. The sound energy – its intensity or loudness – is progressively spread as the waves move outwards from the sound source until eventually the motion stops and the sound dies away. In addition to travelling through the air,

Table 27 **Common sound levels**

Sound source	Sound level dB(A)
Jet engine	140
Pneumatic drill	110
Machine shop	100
Busy traffic	80
Shouting	80
Car	70
Conversation	60
A whisper	30
Quiet house	20

sound waves can also travel through other media such as liquids and solids. When sound waves meet a hard surface most of their energy is reflected, much like light rays in a mirror. Soft surfaces reflect very little of the energy as most of it is absorbed. The number of vibrations or waves that occur in one second is known as the frequency. Something vibrating 200 times a second will produce a sound that has a frequency of 200 cycles per second or 200 Hz (hertz). It is the frequency of sound that determines its pitch; sound sources of high frequency produce high-pitch notes and sound sources of low frequency produce low-pitch notes.

Human hearing responds to a wide range of frequencies; anything between 20 and 20,000 Hz produces an audible sound. Decibels (dB) are the units which are used to define the loudness of a sound. The decibel scale ranges from 0 dB (threshold of hearing), which is virtually silence, to about 130 dB (threshold of feeling), which is painful sound. The approximate sound levels of common sources are given in Table 27.

Note: The suffix A after dB is a weighted decibel in which simple meter measurements can be made.

Sound control

In the building design process, architects and planners will consider sound control. In general the three essential considerations are:

1 To keep noisy areas and quiet areas as far apart as possible or erect a screen between

them to reflect or absorb the sound waves. See Figure 153.

2 Structural design, to reduce sound penetration and avoid sound transfer through the structure (sound insulation).

3 The acoustics of a room (sound absorption).

Sound insulation and sound absorption are two terms often taken to mean the same thing. To be specific, sound insulation is concerned with the transfer of sound energy through barriers from one area or space to another, whereas sound absorption is concerned with the reflection or absorption of sound energy by the surfaces within the area or space.

Sound insulation

There are two main types of sound insulation: airborne sound insulation and impact sound insulation.

Airborne sound

The transmission of airborne sound through the walls, roof, and floors of a building is dependent on their mass. Transmission occurs when a sound wave meets a building element, causing it to vibrate, which in turn sets up a new sound wave on the other side. Sound transmission through the building element is known as direct transmission. The vibrating building element will also cause its adjoining elements to vibrate, resulting in indirect or flanking transmission. Figure 154 illustrates the transmission of sound from one room to another.

Clearly, the greater the mass of the building elements the harder it is to set them into vibration, and therefore the better their sound insulation value. This value can be severely reduced by a lack of uniform resistance to sound, lightweight construction or air passages such as partially filled mortar joints, gaps around windows, doors and keyholes etc.

Impact sound

This results from an impact or vibration communicated directly to the building element, such as footsteps or vibrating machinery. Mass is of little advantage; the solution is to isolate

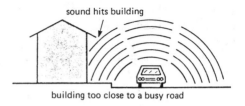

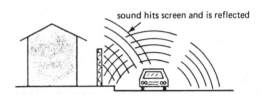

Figure 153   *Position of building in relation to sound source*

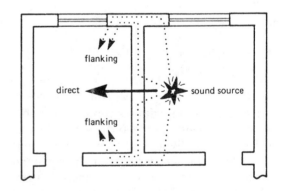

Figure 154   *Direct and flanking sound transmission*

elements or create a discontinuous structure so that vibrations are not allowed to pass through. Soft finishes such as thick carpet, rubber underlay and cork can significantly reduce the amount of vibrations generated.

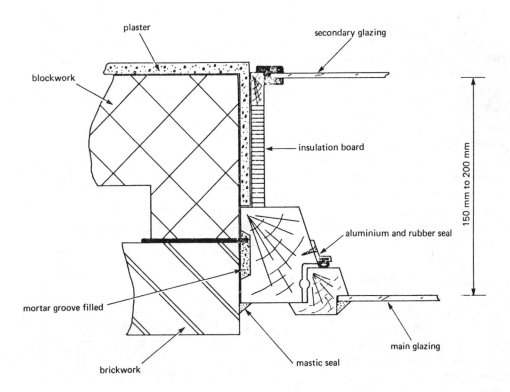

Figure 155   *Secondary double glazing*

Sound absorption

Sound within a room is made up of two parts: direct sound, which travels straight from its source to the ear, and reverberant sound, which is the sum of all the sound reflected back from the room surfaces. Much of this reverberant sound is absorbed by the soft furnishings, carpets and curtains within a room. In factories and offices sound absorption materials can be used to line walls and ceilings. Noisy sound sources, can be enclosed with free-standing sound absorption screens or panels hanging from the ceiling. The most commonly used absorbent materials are fibre insulation boards or mineral/glassfibre faced with perforated metal or hardboard. Basically, all soft materials and lightweight porous materials are good sound absorbers. They work by soaking up the sound and reflecting it to and fro between their particles or fibres until all the sound energy has been used up.

Practical sound insulation

Windows
The most effective form of sound insulation for windows is secondary double glazing. Air tightness of the existing window is extremely important. A typical detail is shown in Figure 155.

Note: Sealed unit double glazing with an air space of up to 20 mm is for thermal insulation. It gives only a minimal reduction in sound.

Floors
The need for sound insulation in the floors of a domestic house occupied by one family is fairly limited, but it is considered essential for buildings in multiple occupancy.

Figure 156 illustrates typical details for suspended timber floors. Detail A would be effective against airborne sound, but detail B incorporates a floating floor and would be

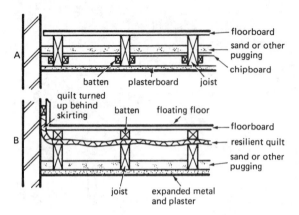

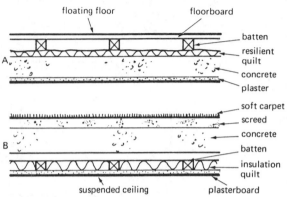

Figure 156 *Suspended floor details to reduce sound transmission*

Figure 157 *Concrete floor details to reduce sound transmission*

effective against both airborne and impact sound.

Figure 157 illustrates typical sound insulation details for concrete floors. Detail A shows a floating timber raft on top of the concrete floor. Detail B has a soft floor finish and a suspended ceiling.

Partition walls

Stud partition walls can be given a reasonable amount of airborne sound insulation by filling the spaces between the studs and noggins with mineral/fibreglass quilt. For a greater degree of insulation, especially from impact sound, some form of separation is required. Details A and B illustrated in Figure 158 show alternative horizontal sections through discontinuous partitions. Strips of insulation board are fixed to the back of the head, sole and wall studs to isolate the partition from any vibrations in the structure. The backs of any door linings should also receive the same treatment. Door openings or borrowed lights in a partition are often the weak link. Insulation of doors can be improved by the use of a solid-core door, proprietary sealing strips and thresholds. In extreme cases two doors are used, one on each face of the partition.

Borrowed lights in sound insulating partitions should be double glazed. A typical detail is shown in Figure 159. A packet of silica gel can be placed in the air space to keep it dry and prevent condensation.

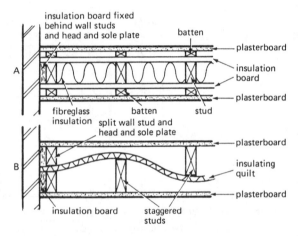

Figure 158 *Partition details to reduce sound transmission*

Building Regulations (sound insulation)

The Building Regulations Part E states that walls which separate one dwelling from another or that separate a dwelling from another part of a building used for a different purpose must have a reasonable resistance to the passage of airborne sound; whereas floors which separate one dwelling from another, or from another part of the same building used for a different purpose, must have a reasonable resistance to both airborne and impact sound.

AD: E gives details of typical constructions that satisfy these requirements.

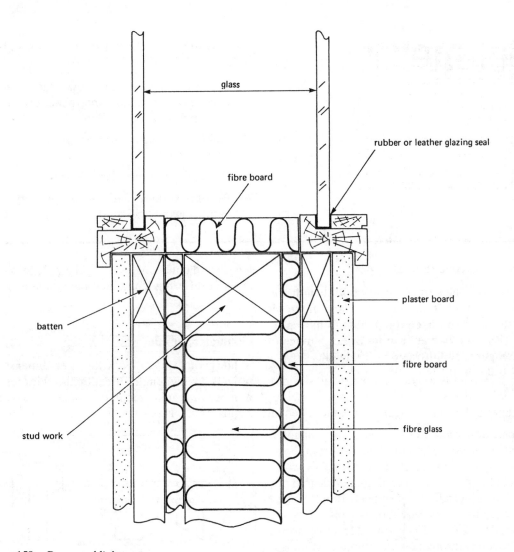

Figure 159 *Borrowed light*

Self-assessment questions

1 Briefly explain the process by which timber burns.

2 State the *three* requirements needed for burning.

3 Define what is meant by *k*, *R* and *U* values.

4 Briefly name the *three* processes by which heat may be transferred.

5 Describe the difference between sound insulation and sound absorption.

6 Briefly explain the principles of insulating against
   (a) Airborne sound
   (b) Impact sound

7 Explain why thermal insulation materials must be kept dry.

chapter 7

Geometry

After reading this chapter the student should be able to:

1 Produce drawings to show true sections, developments and interpenetrations of geometrical solids.

2 Apply geometrical principles to solve practical problems.

3 Recognize various plane figures.

4 Recognize and define the properties of various geometric solids.

Plane geometric figures

A plane is a flat surface; it has both length and breadth but no thickness. A plane figure is therefore a two-dimensional surface having an area bounded by one or more lines. A range of plane figures is illustrated in Table 28.

Note: When the bounding lines are all straight, the plane figure is said to be rectilineal or rectilinear. Regular polygons have sides of equal length and equal angles. Irregular polygons have sides of differing length and unequal angles.

Geometric solids

Solid geometry deals with three-dimensional objects having length, breadth and thickness. A number of regular geometric solids are shown in Figure 160. These include:

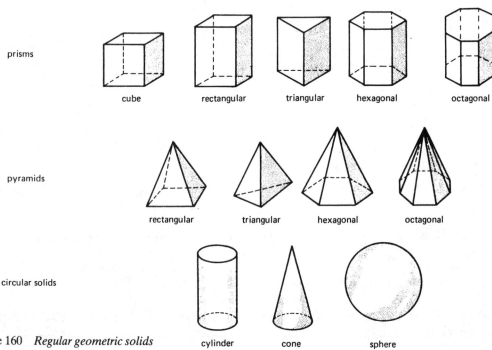

prisms

cube   rectangular   triangular   hexagonal   octagonal

pyramids

rectangular   triangular   hexagonal   octagonal

circular solids

Figure 160   *Regular geometric solids*   cylinder   cone   sphere

Table 28 **Plane figures**

Bounded by	Name of figure	Shape		Bounded by	Name of figure	Shape
1 line	circle				trapezium	
	ellipse				trapezoid	
2 lines	semicircle/segment				*polygons* (regular or irregular)	
3 lines	sector			5 lines	pentagon	
	triangle			6 lines	hexagon	
	quadrilaterals			7 lines	hectagon	
4 lines	square			8 lines	octagon	
	rectangle			9 lines	nonagon	
	rhombus			10 lines	decagon	
	parallelogram					

Cube This is a solid figure formed by six faces, all of which are squares.

Prism A solid figure formed by plane surfaces which are parallel to each other, named according to the shape of its base.

Pyramid This is also named according to its base shape, and is a solid figure formed by its base and triangular sloping sides.

Circular solids These include cylinders, cones and spheres.

Cylinder A solid figure described by the revolution of a rectangle about one of its sides, which remains fixed and is called its axis. The base or ends of a cylinder are circular in shape.

Cone A cone is a solid figure described by the revolution of a right-angled triangle about one of its sides, which remains fixed and is called its axis. The base of a cone is circular in shape.

Sphere A sphere is a solid figure described by the revolution of a semi-circle about its diameter, which remains fixed and is called its axis.

Solids may be described as being either right or oblique. The central axis of right solids is vertical, while oblique solids have a central axis that is inclined. Examples of right and oblique solids are shown in Figure 161.

Sections of solids

When a solid is cut through the cut surface is a section. A solid that has had its top cut off is called a truncated solid. The remaining portion is called the frustum of a solid. The problem usually encountered at a practical level is to determine the true shape of the cut section. This involves drawing the plan and elevation of the solid. The true shape of the cut section is determined by projecting lines at right angles to the cutting plane and drawing in the auxiliary view. Examples of this procedure are shown in Figures 162–167.

Development of solids

The development of a solid is a drawing of the shape of all its faces laid out flat in one plane. This can be done by unfolding or unrolling as illustrated by Figure 168. Examples of the procedures involved when developing solids, with pictorial sketches, are shown in Figures 169–173.

Interpenetration

When two surfaces intersect there will be a line of intersection common to both of them. The shape of these lines will depend upon the shape of the contacting surfaces. The lines of intersection of two plane surfaces will be straight, whereas the lines of intersection will be curved when one or both of the intersecting surfaces are curved. The geometry concerned with intersections is closely related to developments and true shapes. At least two views of the intersecting solids, normally a plan and elevation, will need to be drawn in order to determine the required line of intersection, the development and the true shapes. Examples of the geometry involved when solids intersect, along with a pictorial sketch of the intersecting solids, are shown in Figures 174–177.

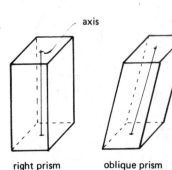

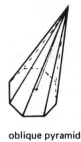

right prism   oblique prism   right pyramid   oblique pyramid   right cone   oblique cone

Figure 161 *Right and oblique solids*

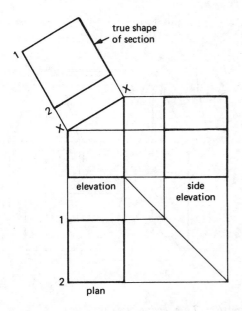

Figure 162 *True section of the frustum of a rectangular prism*

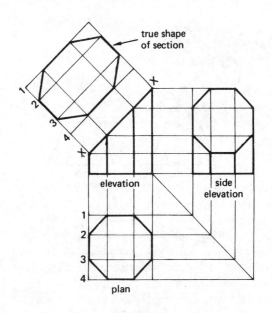

Figure 163 *True section of the frustum of an octagonal prism*

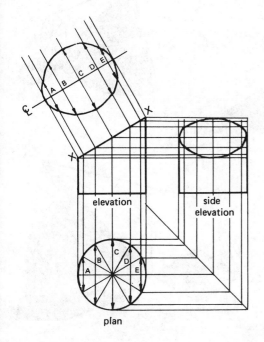

Figure 164 *True section of the frustum of a cylinder*

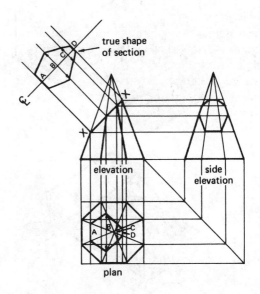

Figure 165 *True section of the frustum of an octagonal pyramid*

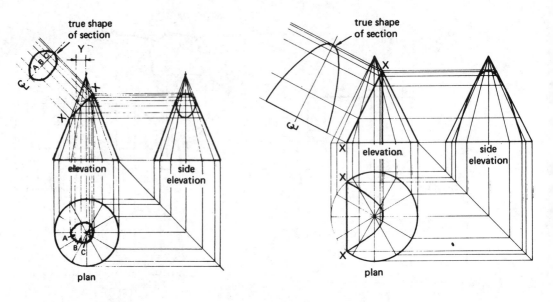

Figure 166   *True section of the frustum of a cone*   Figure 167   *True section of a cone*

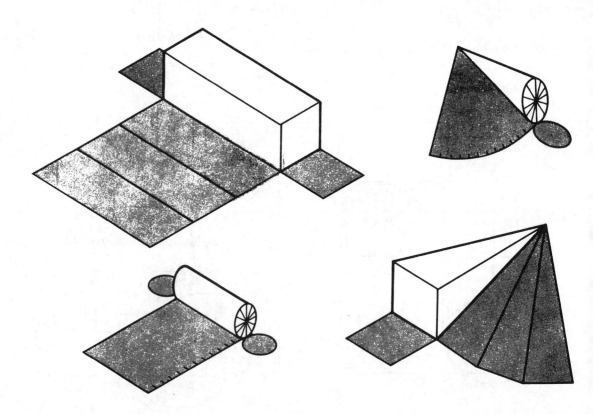

Figure 168   *Surface developments*

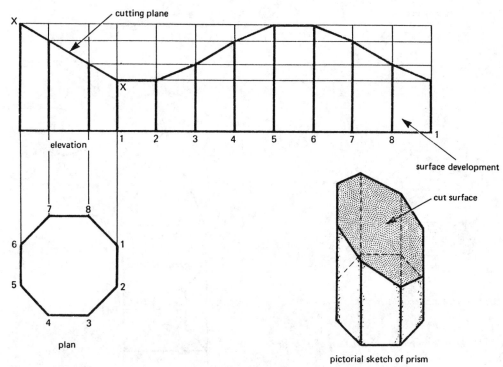

Figure 169 *Development of the frustum of an octagonal prism*

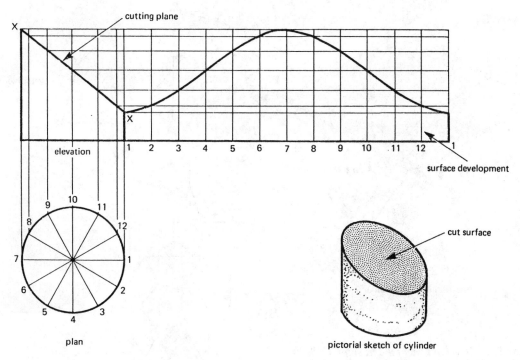

Figure 170 *Development of the frustum of a cylinder*

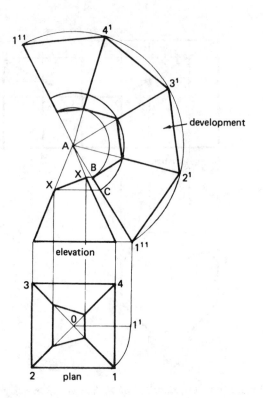

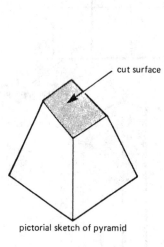

cut surface

pictorial sketch of pyramid

Figure 171   *Development of the frustum of a square pyramid*

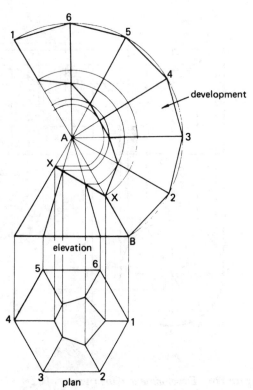

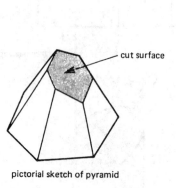

cut surface

pictorial sketch of pyramid

Figure 172   *Development of the frustum of a hex-agonal pyramid*

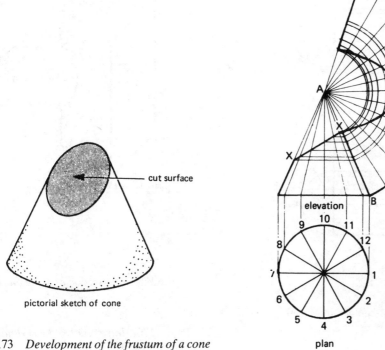

cut surface

pictorial sketch of cone

development

A

X

X

B

elevation

plan

Figure 173   *Development of the frustum of a cone*

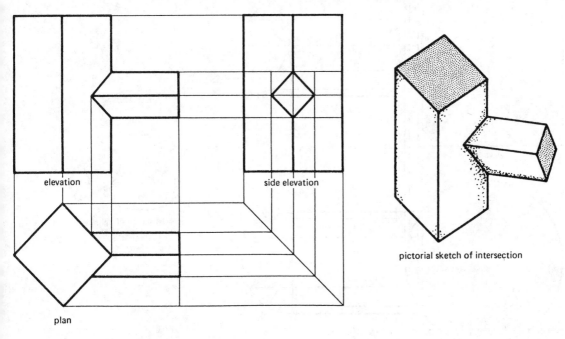

elevation

side elevation

plan

pictorial sketch of intersection

Figure 174   *Intersection of two prisms*

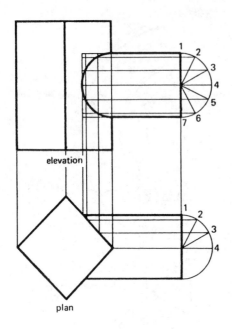

elevation

plan

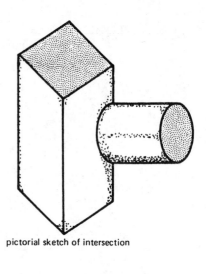

pictorial sketch of intersection

Figure 175   *Intersection of prism and cylinder*

Figure 176   *Intersection of two cylinders: perpendicular*

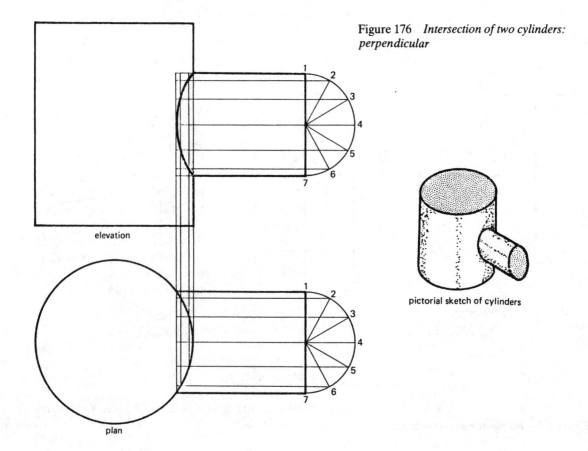

elevation

plan

pictorial sketch of cylinders

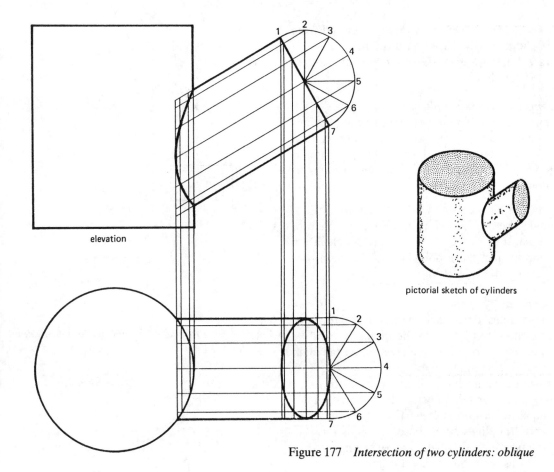

elevation

pictorial sketch of cylinders

Figure 177   *Intersection of two cylinders: oblique*

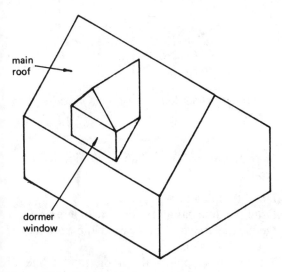

main
roof

dormer
window

Figure 178   *House with dormer window*

Practical examples

Dormer window in pitched roof
Figure 178 shows a sketch of a house with a dormer window in a pitched roof. The problem is to find the true shape of the opening in the main roof and the development of the dormer roof. The solution to this problem is shown in Figure 179. The method used is as follows:

Draw the plan and elevations.
Project up points A, B and C.
Mark points 1^1, 2^1 and 3^1 equal to distances 1, 2 and 3 taken from the elevation.
Draw lines to complete the true shape of the opening.
With centre E and radius ED, draw arc to give point F.

From F, project vertically down to G and from
G horizontally across on to plan.
Draw lines to give development of half of
dormer roof.

Segmental dormer in pitched roof

Figure 180 is a similar problem to the previous
example except in this case the dormer window
has a segmental-shaped roof. The solution is
shown in Figure 181. The method used is as
follows:

Draw the elevation and side elevation.
Divide the segmental roof into a number of
equal divisions 1, 2, 3, 4, 5 on the elevation
and project these points on to the main roof
line on the side elevation.

True shape of opening

Project lines down and across from the two
elevations and draw in the plan.
Project up the points of intersection on the main
roof line at right angles.
Draw in a centre line, which will carry 5^1.
Mark on either side of centre line points 1^1 to 4^1
equal to distances 1^1 to 4^1 on the elevation,
and draw lines from these points to form an
intersecting grid, with the right-angled projections from the main roof line.
Draw a smooth curve through the intersecting
grid to give the shape of the opening in the
main roof.

Development of dormer roof surface

Project points down from the plan and draw in
the centre line, which will carry point 5.
Mark on either side of the centre line points 1 to
4 equal to distances 1 to 4 on the elevation
and draw lines from these points to form an
intersecting grid with the projections from the
main roof line.
Draw a smooth curve through the intersecting
grid to give the development of the dormer
roof surface.

Intersection of two semicircular vaults

Figure 182 shows a pictorial sketch of two
intersecting semicircular vaults and the geometry required to determine the true shape of

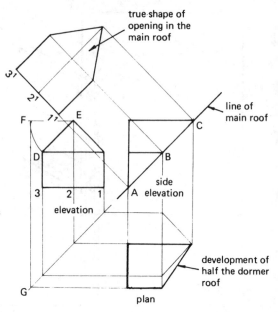

Figure 179   *Practical development (dormer window)*

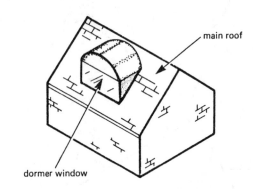

Figure 180   *House with dormer window with segmental roof*

intersection. This true shape is also known as the
groin.

Draw the plan and elevation.
Draw XY line parallel to the line of intersection.
Divide the arch in the elevation into a number of
equal divisions.
Project these points down on to the line of
intersection and then on past the XY line.

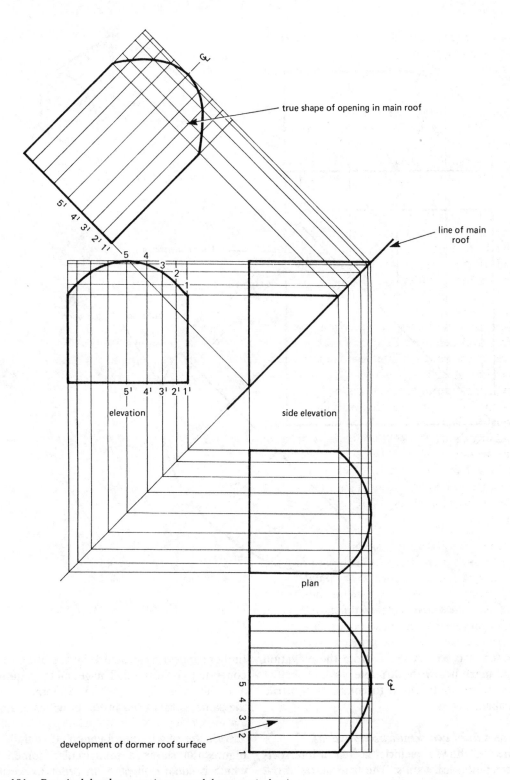

true shape of opening in main roof

line of main roof

5¹ 4¹ 3¹ 2¹ 1¹

5 4 3 2 1

5¹ 4¹ 3¹ 2¹ 1¹

elevation

side elevation

plan

5 4 3 2 1

development of dormer roof surface

Figure 181 *Practical development (segmental dormer window)*

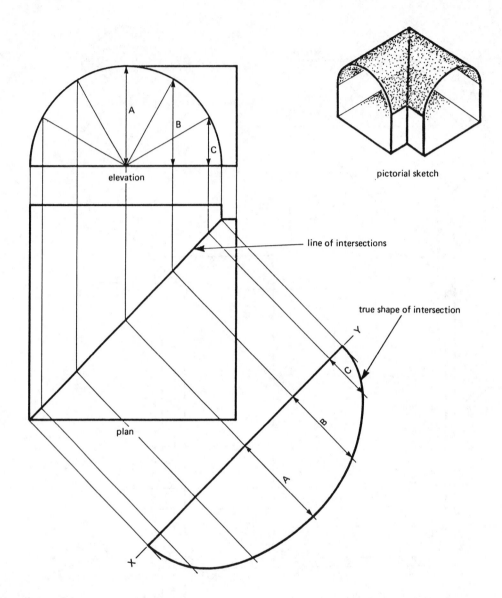

Figure 182   *Intersecting vaults: semicircular*

Transfer distances A, B, C from the elevation and mark below the XY line.

Draw in a smooth curve to complete the true shape.

Intersection of two semi-elliptical vaults

Figure 183 shows a pictorial sketch of intersecting semi-elliptical vaults. The true shape of the groin or intersection is required to enable the timber supporting structure for the brickwork or concrete to be formed. The geometry required is also shown in Figure 183. The method used is the same as that used in the previous example.

Domed roof with square plan

Figure 184 shows a semicircular domed roof which is square on plan. In order to construct the roof it is necessary to develop the true shape

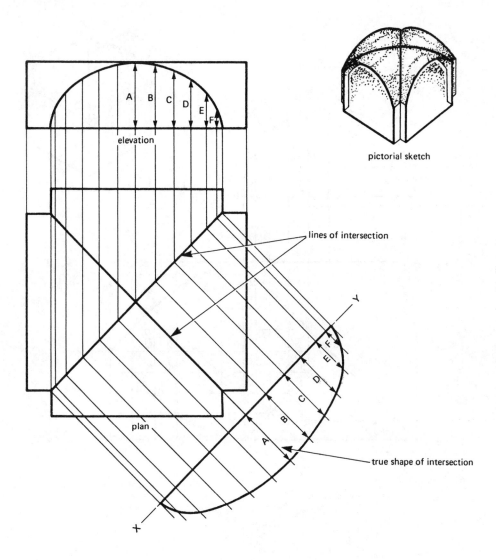

elevation

pictorial sketch

lines of intersection

true shape of intersection

plan

Figure 183 *Intersecting vaults: semi-elliptical*

of one surface of the roof, to determine the outine of the hip rib and backing bevel. The method used is as follows:

Development of surface

Draw plan and elevation of the roof.

Divide half the elevation into a number of equal divisions 1, 2, 3, 4, 5, 6, 7.

Project lines down from these points on to the plan to give a series of points on the hips.

Draw a horizontal line from each point on the hips.

Mark on the centre line points 1^1 to 7^1 equal to distances 1 to 7 on the elevation and draw lines through these points to form an intersecting grid with the horizontal lines.

Draw smooth curves through the intersecting grid to give the development of the roof surface.

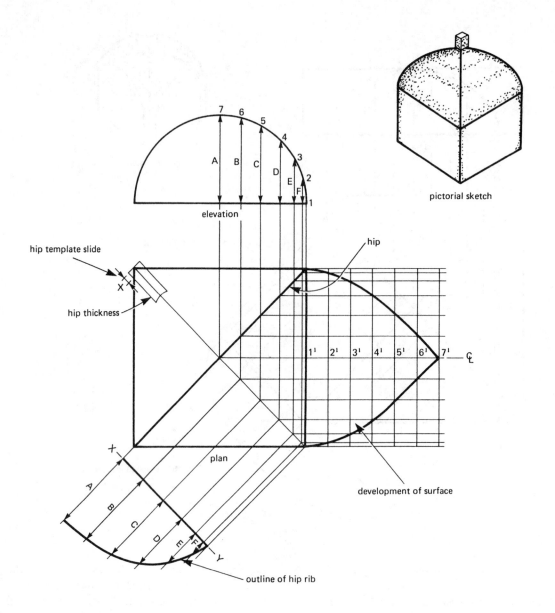

Figure 184 *Domed roof with square plan*

Outline of hip

Draw XY line parallel to one hip.

Project points from the hip at right angles through the XY line.

Transfer distances A, B, C, D, E, F from the elevation and mark below the XY line.

Draw in a smooth curve to give the outline of the hip rib (used to make hip template).

To form backing bevel

When the hip rib is cut to shape it will still require a backing bevel. This can be found by placing the hip template on the hip and sliding it sideways equal to distance X marked on the plan.

Mark around the template and repeat on the other side.

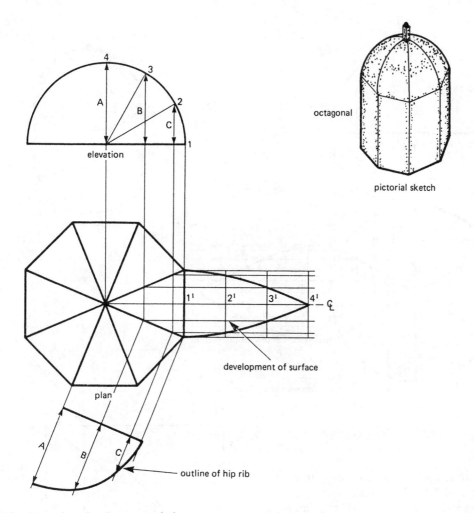

octagonal

pictorial sketch

elevation

development of surface

plan

outline of hip rib

Figure 185   *Domed roof with octagonal plan*

Mark the centre line on the top edge of the hip. Chamfer the edge to these lines to form the backing bevel.

Domed roof with octagonal plan
Figure 185 shows another example of a domed roof which in this case has an octagonal plan. The geometry involved is the same as that used in the previous example.

Hemispherical domed roof
Figure 186 shows a hemispherical domed roof. All that is required in this example is a development of one portion of the surface. The

outline of the hips will be the same as the elevation. It is not possible to develop accurately the surfaces of a hemisphere, but for practical purposes the method shown will give a close approximation. The method used is as follows:

Draw the plan and elevation.
Divide half of the elevation into a number of equal divisions 1, 2, 3, 4, 5, 6, 7.
Project lines down from these points on to the plan to give a series of points on the hips.
Draw a horizontal line from each point on the hips.
Mark on the centre line points 1^1 to 7^1 equal to distances 1 to 7 on the elevation and draw a

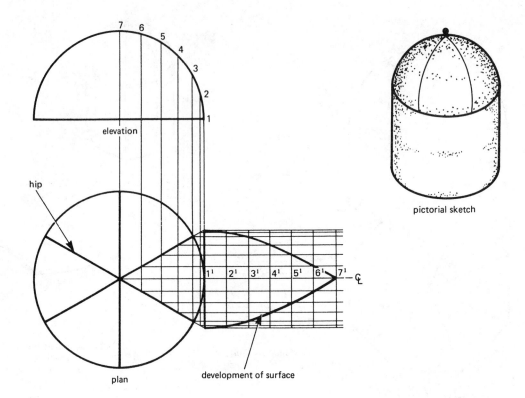

Figure 186   *Hemispherical domed roof*

line through these points to form an intersecting grid with the horizontal lines.

Draw smooth curves through the intersecting grid to give the approximate development of the roof surface.

Splayed linings

Figure 187 shows a part plan and elevation of a splayed timber reveal lining to a door or window opening. In order to construct the lining, two of three angles are required. If the corners of the lining are to be mitred, the face bevel and the edge bevel are required. If the corners of the lining are to be housed or butt jointed then the face bevel and shoulder bevel are required.

To obtain the side or face bevel (Figure 187)
Draw the plan and elevation.
With centre A and radius AB draw an arc to give B' on the line drawn horizontally from A.

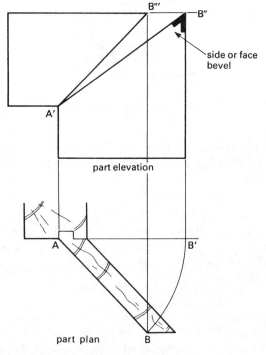

Figure 187   *Splayed lining face bevel*

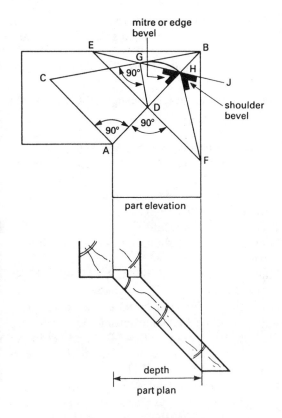

part elevation

depth

part plan

Figure 188   *Splayed lining edge and shoulder bevels*

Figure 189   *Bead cuts for a pivot hung sash*

Project B′ vertically upwards to give B″ on the line drawn horizontally from B‴.

Join A′ to B′ to give the required side or face bevel.

To obtain the edge and shoulder bevel (Figure 188)

Draw the plan and elevation.

At right angles to mitre line AB, draw line AC and mark on it the depth of the lining taken from the plan.

Join C to B.

Draw a line at right angles to AB at D (this can be anywhere along AB) to touch the edges of the lining at E and F.

Draw a line at right angles to CB at G to touch point D.

With centre D and radius DG, draw an arc to touch AB at H.

Join point E to H and extend on to J. Angle EHD is the required edge bevel.

Join point H to F. Angle FHJ is the required shoulder bevel.

Pivot hung sash

Figure 189 shows the method used to set out the bead cuts of a pivot hung sash window, where it must be possible to remove the sash from its frame without removing any beads.

Draw full size a part vertical section of the window showing the sash in its maximum open position.

Mark the centre of the pivot pin O.

Draw line OA and mark AB at right angles to it. This gives the cut for the inside frame bead.

With centre O and radii OA and OB draw arcs to give points A′ and B′.

Join A' to B' to give the cut for inside sash bead.

Draw a line parallel to the outside sash bead to give point C at a distance D equal to half the sash thickness, plus half the pin diameter.

Draw line OC and mark CE at right angles to line OC. This gives the cut for the outside frame bead.

With centre O and radii OC and OE draw arcs to give points C' and E'.

Join C' to E' to give the cut for the outside sash bead.

This method permits the sash to be removed by lifting it back and up a distance square to its face.

Ventilators

Figure 190 shows the geometry required in order to make a triangular ventilator. The method used is as follows:

Draw the elevation and vertical section of the ventilator.

Draw a rectangle to represent the development of inside surface of frame by projecting points on frame side over at right angles to the slope, the width of the rectangle equals the width of the frame.

To obtain bevels for housing

Project points A,B,C and D across from the vertical section on to the development of inside surface of frame to give A', B', C' and D'.

Draw lines BC and AD to give width and bevel for housing.

The edge bevel for the housing is the same as the slope of the frame.

To obtain true shape and side bevel of blade

Project lines across from points E and F in the vertical section.

Draw centre line at same angle as the slope of the blades (45°).

This gives points E and F.

Draw base line at right angles to centre line to pass through F'.

Make base line equal to length of bottom blade in elevation.

Draw lines from end of base line to E'. This gives outline for blade setting out template.

Project lines from points A, B, G and H in the vertical section across to the centre line to give points A', B', G' and H'.

Draw lines at right angles to the centre line from points A', B', G' and H' across width template to give the true shape of blade and side bevel.

Figure 191 shows the geometry required in order to make a circular louvre ventilator. The method

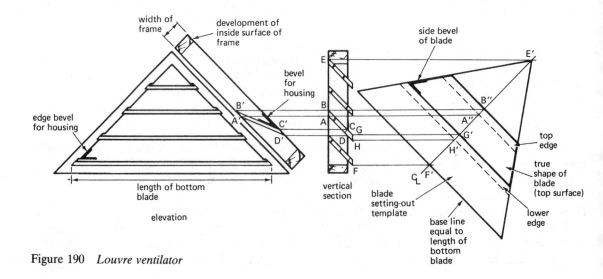

Figure 190   *Louvre ventilator*

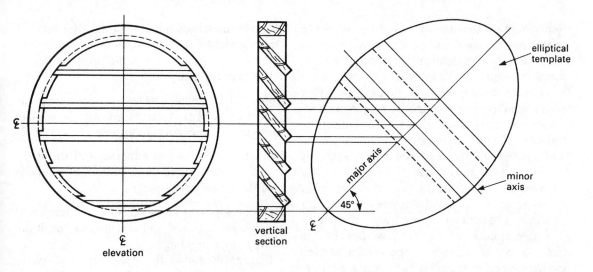

Figure 191 *Circular louvre ventilator*

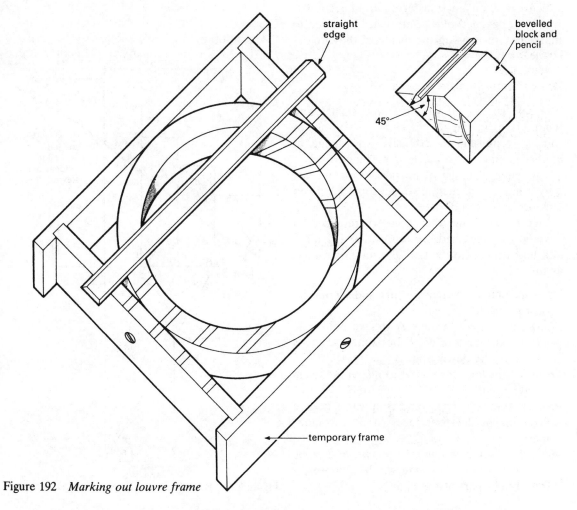

Figure 192 *Marking out louvre frame*

used to obtain the true shape of the blades is similar to that used in the previous example, except that the template will be elliptical with its minor axis equal to the internal diameter of the frame, plus the depth of the housing on either side. The major axis is found by projecting lines across from the elevation on to the centre line, drawn at the same angle as the slope of the blades (45°). The ellipse can be drawn using any of the true methods previously covered.

Figure 192 shows the method of marking out the housings in the circular frame. This entails the use of a temporary square frame made to fit over the circular one. The positions of the housings can be taken from the vertical section and marked on to the sides of the square frame. A straight edge is placed over these marks, which can then be transferred to the circular frame. A bevelled block and pencil are used to mark the housings on the inside of the circular frame.

Geometrical stairs

The construction of wreath stairs, strings and handrails is a highly specialized section of joinery, requiring an extensive knowledge of applied geometry. As much of it is inappropriate to the general range of purpose-made joinery only a basic introduction to the topic has been included in this book.

Figure 193 shows the geometry required to develop the wreathed portion of a string for a quarter-turn geometric stair. The method used is as follows:

Draw the plan of the quarter turn and set out the riser positions.

Draw a line at 60° through A to give points A′ and C on lines projected horizontally across and vertically down from B.

From C draw lines through the ends of the risers to give points D and E on line A′B.

Project points A′, D, E, and B upwards to give positions of the riser faces in the development.

Mark the riser positions of the two end steps (make the tread the same width as those on the straight part of the flight).

Draw in the treads making all the rises equal. Draw straight lines to join the lower corners of the stops. Draw lines parallel to these to give the required margin.

Note: The sharp corners produced at the intersections should be eased with a smooth curve to give one continuous line.

Draw the joint lines at either end of the string 'stretch-out'. Make these 90° to the underside of the string development.

This development gives the shape of the board or laminate required and also the set out of the string before bending.

Figure 194 shows the geometry required to develop the wreathed portion of a string for a

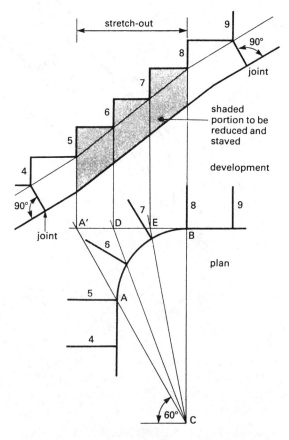

Figure 193 *Wreathed string geometry (quarter turn)*

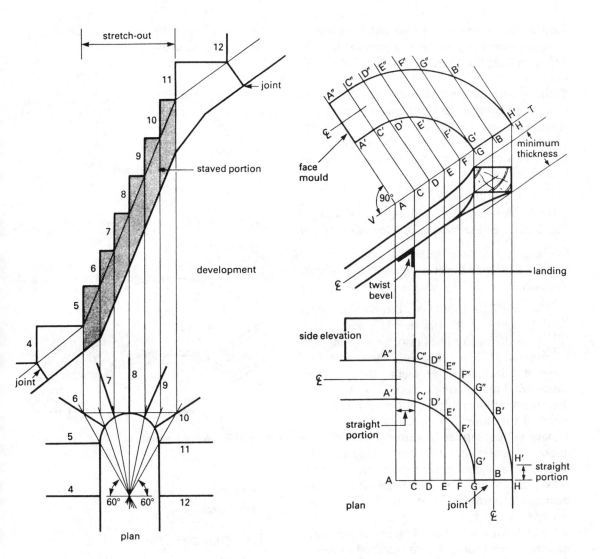

Figure 194   *Wreathed string geometry (half turn)*

Figure 195   *Wreathed handrail geometry*

half-turn stair. The method used is similar to the quarter stair, except that two 60° lines are required to give the 'stretch-out' of the steps.

Figure 195 shows the geometry required to obtain the face moulds and bevels for a simple quarter turn rake to a level wreath, as required between a straight flight and landing. The method used is as follows:

Draw the plan and side elevation of the handrail and top two steps.

Note: The joint lines have been positioned a short distance past the curve to ease their jointing.

Draw in the rectangular section of the level landing rail where the side elevation and plan centre lines intersect. This gives the minimum thickness of material required to form the wreath.

Draw VT line above the side elevation parallel to the pitch of the stair.

Project line vertically down and horizontally across from the joint lines in plan to give AB.

Mark on line AB a series of points C, D, E, F, G, H.

Project these points and AB vertically on the line and continue at right angles beyond.

Transfer distances A, A', A", C, C', C", etc. from plan and mark above the VT line.

Draw in a smooth curve to complete the face mould.

Figure 196 illustrates how the plywood face mould is applied to the timber blank and the rectangular end sections of the handrail marked out.

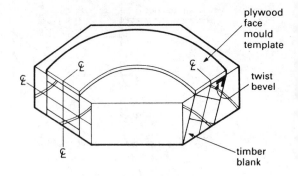

Figure 196   *Wreath blank and face mould template*

Note: The twist bevel is equal to the pitch of the stairs.

The joint faces should be accurately prepared at right angles to the timber's face and at right angles to the centre lines prior to marking out.

Figure 197 illustrates the blank after the perpendicular cuts have been made (slabbed wreath). This is often carried out on the bandsaw with the blank pitched at the same angle as the stairs.

The falling top and bottom face lines are marked on as a smooth curve, taking care that they start at right angles to the joint surfaces. This determines the final shaping of the rectangular wreath; the surplus timber is normally removed by hand.

Prior to the hand moulding of the wreath, it should be end jointed with handrail bolts and dowels to the moulded straight sections. This eases the moulding operation and ensures its smooth, proper continuity.

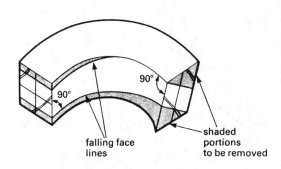

Figure 197   *Slabbed wreath*

2   Define the following:
   (a)   Prism
   (b)   Cone
   (c)   Truncated solid

3   Produce a scale drawing to show the face bevel and mitre required to mark out a set of splayed window linings with a splay of 45° and a depth of 200 mm.

4   Draw the development 'stretch out' of the wreathed portion of a 300 mm deep string for a quarter turn geometric stair to suit the following conditions:
Three tapered treads
Going 240 mm
Minimum going 100 mm
Step rise 160 mm
Wreath radius 200 mm

Self-assessment questions

1   The underside of a sloping canopy supported by 450 mm diameter concrete columns is to be covered with veneered plywood. Develop the true shape of the cut out required in the plywood sheeting if the canopy is inclined at 10° to the horizontal.

chapter 8

Job planning and design

After reading this chapter the student should be able to:

1 Explain the principles of joinery design.
2 Prepare a survey of an existing building.
3 Prepare setting out rods and cutting lists.
4 Mark out an item of joinery from a setting out rod.

Design

A large proportion of the joinery used in the building industry today is mass produced by large firms who specialize in the manufacture of a range of items (doors, windows, stairs, units) to standard designs and specifications. However, there is still a great need for independent joinery works to produce purpose-made joinery for high quality work, repair and replacement and one-off items to individual designs.

The design of purpose-made joinery is normally the responsibility of the architect, who should supply the joinery works with scaled working drawings, full size details and a written specification. However, architects' joinery details are often little more than a brief outline, leaving the construction details to the joinery works.

Often the best joinery is produced when the architect discusses his design at an early stage with the joinery manufacturer, so that each can appreciate the requirements and difficulties of the other, and amend the design accordingly. This communication between the two parties enables the work to be carried out efficiently and therefore have a noticeable effect on the finished joinery item. In addition the joinery manufacturer may also be involved in the joinery design for small works directly with the customer when an architect or designer has not been employed.

When designing and detailing joinery four main aspects must be taken into account. These are:

Function   Aesthetics
Production   Anthropometry.

All of these design aspects are important, although, depending on the nature of the work in hand, more or less priority may be given to any aspect in order to achieve a satisfactory design.

Function

This aspect is the first to be considered and concerns the general efficiency of an item. The designer will consider this by asking himself/herself a series of questions, such as:

What are the main functions of the item e.g., access, security, ventilation, seating etc.?
In what environment will it be used e.g., temperature, humidity, weather, likelihood of vandalism, harsh treatment etc.?
What statutory regulations might affect the design e.g. of stairs, fire doors etc.?

An analysis of the answers to these questions will point to suitable materials, construction details and finishes etc., resulting in a good functional design.

Note: The functional design may require amendment after considering the production, aesthetic and anthropometry aspects.

Production

This consideration is vital to the economic production of joinery. Construction details should be designed not only to avoid unnecessary handwork, enabling the maximum possible use of machinery and power tools, but also to utilize the minimum amount of material to the best possible effect.

The size and profile of a section will be

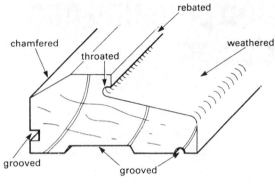

Figure 199   *Application of standard profiles*

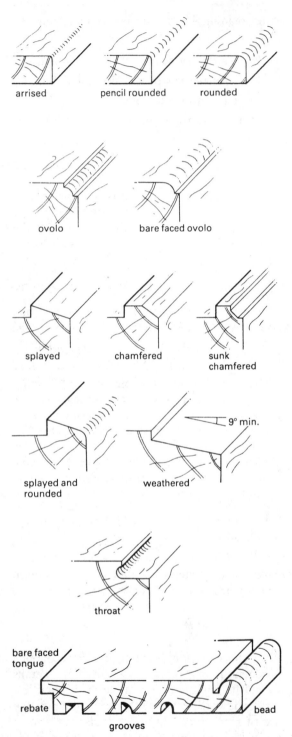

Figure 198   *Standard joinery profiles*

determined by the functional considerations and the desired finished appearance. Figure 198 illustrates a range of standard joinery profiles which can be economically produced by machine.

Figure 199 illustrates the typical application of various standard profiles to produce one section. This may be described in a specification as a three-times grooved, once chamfered, rebated, throated, weathered and pencil-rounded sill section.

The design and proportions of the profile should also take into account the type of joint to be used at intersections, as additional handwork can be involved at joints. Figure 200 illustrates a number of profiles and their suitability for machine scribed joints.

Pencil-rounded and steeply chamfered profiles are best hand mitred, as the razor edge produced by scribing them is difficult to machine cleanly and is easily damaged during assembly. These problems are avoided by the use of a sunk chamfer or ovolo profile. It is impossible to scribe bead or other undercut profiles, so hand mitring is the only option. An alternative to both scribing or hand mitring is the technique of routed profiles – see Figure 201 where rectangular sections are framed up and assembled, prior to being worked with a router.

Stopped rebates (see Figure 202) should be avoided whenever possible, as they are expensive to produce. This is because they require a

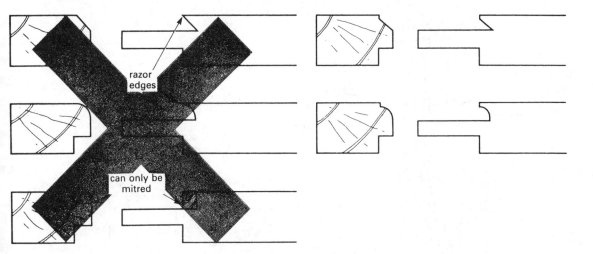

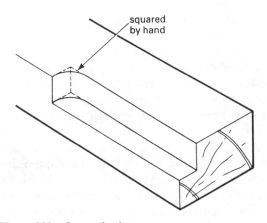

Figure 200 Machine scribing of joints

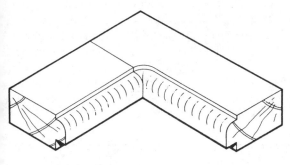

Figure 201 Routed profile

Figure 202 Stopped rebate

separate machine operation, and also the curve left by the cutter on exit has to be squared by hand.

Aesthetics

This is concerned with the appearance or 'beauty' of an item and is thus an individual opinion. What is in good taste or acceptable to one person may be the complete opposite to another.

The aesthetics of joinery is the province of the architect and designer who has a sensitive trained eye and can consider the complexities of proportion, shape, harmony, finish and compatibility, to produce a design that will have the desired effect.

In addition the aesthetic effect can be considerably enhanced or marred by the degree of enthusiasm and craftmanship exercised by the machinist and joiner during each stage of manufacture and installation.

Anthropometry

This is concerned with the measurement of the human body. If an item of joinery is to satisfactorily fulfil its function, it is essential that its shape and size is related to the bodily characteristics of the intended users.

In normal circumstances it is rarely practical to produce an item of joinery to one specific individual's bodily characteristics. Instead standard anthropometric data is used to suit as wide

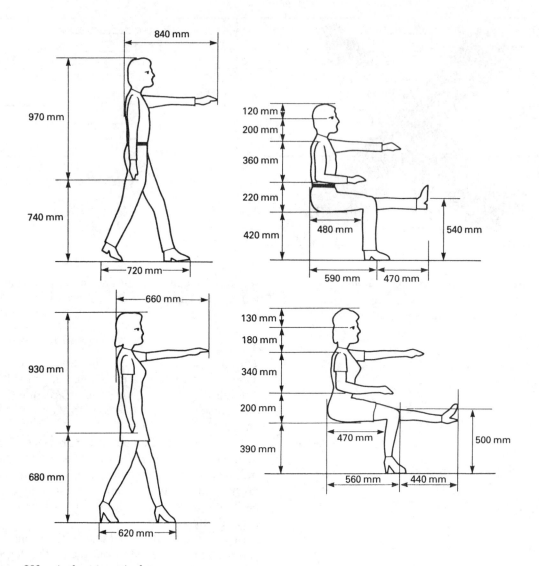

Figure 203 *Anthropometric data*

a range of people as possible. Figure 203 illustrates the more important, average body characteristics of adult males and females. Although the average data can be used for many circumstances, in certain situations allowances must be made to cater for people who fall either side of the average. For example, where headroom is concerned the design should accommodate tall people (above average measurement), since short people, in these circumstances, are insignificant. On the other hand, where reach is concerned, short-armed people should be accommodated (below average measurement). Average and long-armed people are insignificant, as they will achieve the smaller reach with ease.

Apart from the obvious need for doors and stairs the main items of joinery that require the application of anthropometric data are: work-tops, tables, seating, shelving and counters. In addition, other fixed dimensions must be consi-dered, particularly for storage compartments.

For example, the space between the shelves of a bar back fitting must allow for the upright storage and easy removal of bottles, etc.

Examples of typical joinery items along with suitable dimensions are illustrated in Figure 204.

Site measurement

Before a workshop rod can be set out, it is often necessary to make a site survey to check the actual measurements. It is preferable for this to be carried out by the joinery manufacturer's setter-out, since it is he who will later use the information when setting out the rod and deciding the allowances to be made for fitting and fixing.

Joinery items for existing buildings and rehabilitation work will always require a site survey, whereas the need for a site survey for joinery in new buildings will depend on the specification.

The two main methods of specifying joinery items are:

Built-in joinery
Fixed-in joinery

Built-in joinery

Where the joinery item is specified as 'built-in' or positioned during the main construction process, the work can normally be carried out directly from the architect's drawings and specifications without any need to take site dimensions. In many cases these may not even exist at the time.

Fixed-in joinery

In cases where the joinery item is specified as 'fixed-in' or inserted in position after the main construction process, it is the joinery manufacturer's responsibility to take all measurements required for the item from the building and not the architect's drawings.

The extent of the measurements and details taken during the site survey will depend on the nature of the work in hand. It can clearly be seen that the requirements of a survey for a small reception desk in a new building will be completely different to those of a survey for the complete refurbishment of an existing office block. The details taken may range from a single dimensioned sketch to a full external and internal survey of the whole building.

Procedure

Each survey is considered separately, and sufficient measurements and details are taken in order to fulfil the survey's specific requirements. However a methodical approach is always required to avoid later confusion. The following survey procedures can be used to advantage in most circumstances.

Drawings

The floor plans and details supplied by the architect for joinery items in a new building will form the basis of the survey. The relevant measurements etc. are taken and recorded on these.

Where the work is in existing buildings, make inquiries to the building's owner and the local authority before surveying to determine whether there are any drawings available concerning the property. If so these can simplify the task by forming the basis of the survey sketches.

Equipment

This will vary considerably depending on the survey requirements but a list of the basic equipment suitable for most tasks is as follows:

A4 or A3 sketch pad
Pens, pencils
30 m tape
2 m tape
2 m sectional measuring rod
1 m folding rule
Spirit level
2 m straight edge
Plumb-bob

In addition certain of the following items may be required for more detailed or specialist surveys.

Step ladder
Extension ladder
High power torch

Figure 204   *Typical joinery dimensions*

offices

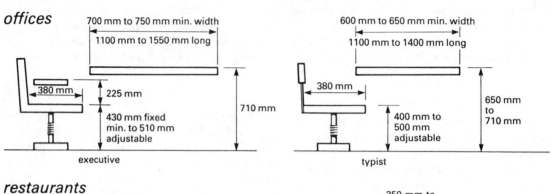

700 mm to 750 mm min. width
1100 mm to 1550 mm long
380 mm
225 mm
710 mm
430 mm fixed
min. to 510 mm
adjustable

executive

600 mm to 650 mm min. width
1100 mm to 1400 mm long
380 mm
650 mm
to
710 mm
400 mm to
500 mm
adjustable

typist

restaurants

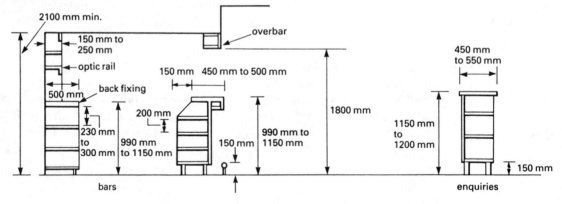

380 mm to
420 mm
95° to
100°
440 mm   460 mm   760 mm

meals

350 mm to
500 mm
300 mm
410
mm
800 mm

snacks

counters

2100 mm min.
150 mm to
250 mm
optic rail
back fixing
500 mm
230 mm
to
300 mm
990 mm
to 1150 mm
overbar
150 mm   450 mm to 500 mm
200 mm
150 mm
990 mm to
1150 mm
1800 mm
450 mm
to 550 mm
1150 mm
to
1200 mm
150 mm

bars   enquiries

public seating

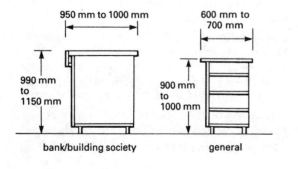

950 mm to 1000 mm
990 mm
to
1150 mm

bank/building society

600 mm to
700 mm
900 mm
to
1000 mm

general

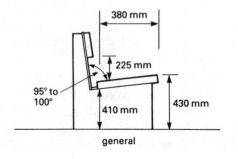

380 mm
225 mm
95° to
100°
410 mm   430 mm

general

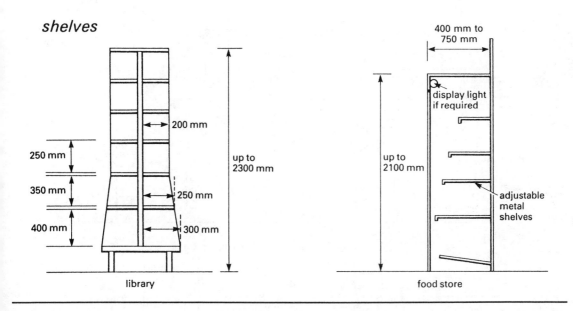

shelves

library

food store

Moisture meter
Penknife
Camera
Binoculars
Moulding template
Hammer, bolster and floorboard saw

Reconnaissance
Before the actual survey, the building should be looked over, both internally and externally to determine its general layout and any likely difficulties.

External survey
Sketch an outline plan and elevations of the building and then add the measurements. Wherever possible running dimensions are preferred to separate dimensions for plans, since an error made in recording one separate dimension will throw all succeeding dimensions out of place and also make the total length incorrect (see Figure 205). Running dimensions are recorded at right angles to the line, an arrow head indicates each cumulative point. To avoid confusing the position of the decimal point an oblique stroke is used to separate metres and

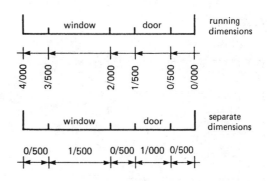

Figure 205   *Outline dimensions*

millimetres. Separate dimensions are recorded on the line, its extent being indicated by arrow heads at either end.

It is important that this distinction between the two methods is observed, because in certain situations it may be necessary to use both on the same sketch. Typical external survey sketches are shown in Figure 206.

Running dimensions are taken in a clockwise direction around the building. Vertical dimensions on the elevations are taken from a level

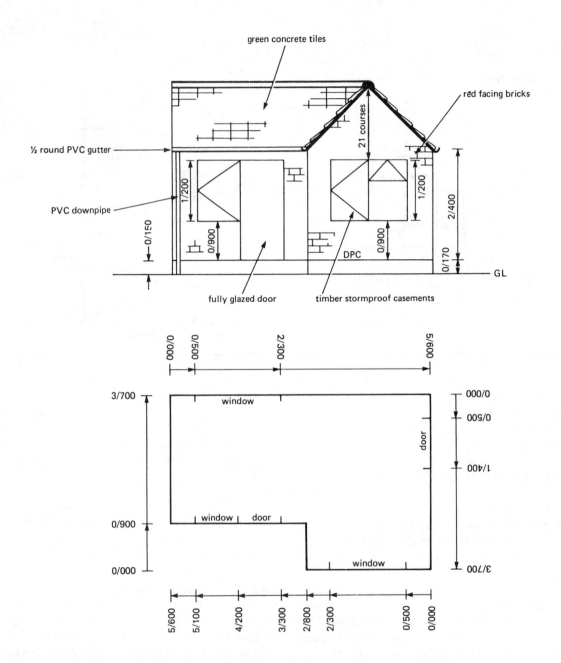

Figure 206   *Typical external survey sketches*

datum, often the damp proof course. Where measurements cannot be taken because they are inaccessible, they can be estimated by counting the brick courses and relating this to brickwork lower down that can be accurately measured.

All external details of materials and finishes etc. should be recorded on the elevation sketches.

Where the survey is for a shop front or similar, accurate dimensions of the opening will be required. Vertical measurements should be taken at either end and at a number of intermediate positions. Horizontal measurements at the top and bottom are required. The diagonals should be taken to check the squareness and accuracy of the opening. Also the reveals should be checked for plumb and straightness (see Figure 207). In addition the head of the opening should also be checked for level and the slope of the pavement or exterior surface measured. The slope can be determined by means of a long straight edge, spirit level and rule as shown in Figure 208. Where the opening is too wide the slope can be measured in several stages using the same method.

Photographs of the elevations are often taken as a back up to the sketches, especially for fine or intricate details.

Internal survey

Dimensioned sketches are made of each floor or room starting at ground level. All rooms should be named or numbered and corridors lettered. These sketches are traced from the external outline plan of the building, measuring through door or window openings to determine the thickness of the walls. Each floor plan should show a horizontal section through the building, about 1 metre above floor level. Measurements should be taken and recorded on the sketches in a clockwise direction around each room. Diagonal measurements from corner to corner check the shape of the room and enable one to redraw it later. Floor to ceiling heights are circled in the centre of each room. Floor construction and partition wall details are also shown on the floor plans. The floorboards run at right angles to the span of floor joists. The lines of nails indicate joist spacings (see Figure 209). Pattern staining on walls and ceilings indicate positions of grounds or battening and ceiling joists.

Walls can be identified by sounding them. When tapped with the fist, brick walls sound solid, thin blockwork walls tend to vibrate, stud walls sound solid over the studs and hollow between them. Walls should also be checked for straightness and plumb and any irregularities noted.

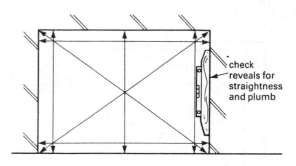

Figure 207 *Measuring an external opening*

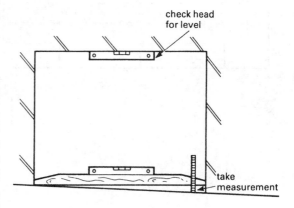

Figure 208 *Checking slope of ground across an opening*

Where joinery items are to be repaired or replaced, full-size details of the sections and mouldings must be made to allow them to be matched later at the workshop. This task can be eased considerably by the use of a moulding template (see Figure 210). The pins of the template are pressed into the contours of the moulding. It is then placed on the sketch pad and drawn around. The exact location from which the moulding is taken should be noted as this may vary from room to room.

Sketches of internal elevations or photographs may be required especially where intricate details are concerned.

Sketches of the vertical sections taken at right angles to the building's external walls complete

Figure 209 *Floor plans*

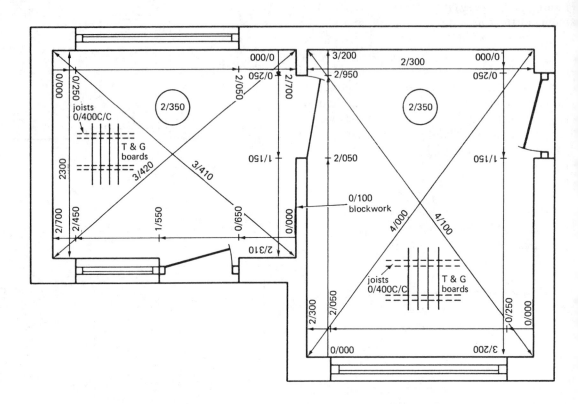

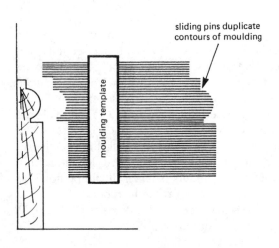

Figure 210 *Moulding templates*

the main sketches. A typical section is shown in Figure 211. Sections should include door and window heights, as well as the internal height of the roof. The thickness of upper floors and ceilings can be measured at the stairwell or loft trap door opening.

Note: Only details that can be seen and measured are sketched. No attempt should be made to guess details, so foundations, floor construction and lintels etc. are not shown.

It is often advantageous, particularly in large areas, to establish a datum line around the interior at this stage. They should be indicated thus ⼏. The datum line is established at a convenient height (about 1 m above the finished floor level) from this position all height measurements may then be taken, up or down as required. This reveals any differences in the floor to ceiling heights, any slope in the floor or

Figure 211 *Section through building*

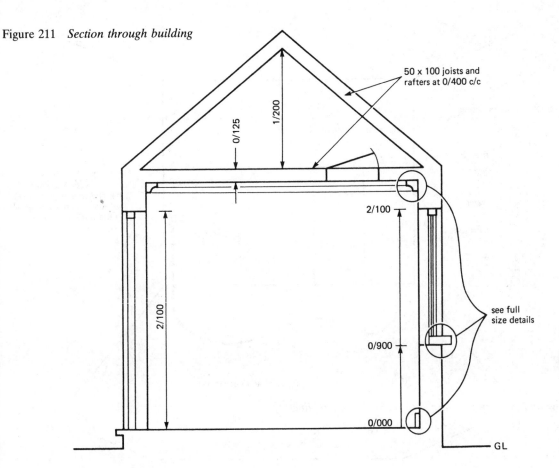

50 x 100 joists and
rafters at 0/400 c/c

1/200

0/125

2/100

2/100

see full
size details

0/900

0/000

GL

ceiling, as well as the heights of the openings and beams etc. as shown in Figure 212.

To establish the datum line transfer a level position to each corner of the room using either a water level as shown in Figure 213 or an optical instrument as shown in Figure 214. Having established the corner positions, stretch a chalk line between each of the two marks in turn and spring it in the middle, leaving a horizontal chalk dust line on the wall.

Note: A water level must be prepared well in advance of using it. This is done by filling it from one end with water, taking care not to trap any air bubbles. Check by holding up the two glass tubes side by side. The levels of the water should settle at the same height.

Cowley automatic level (Figure 215)
This simple levelling instrument is set up using the following procedure. Set up tripod, checking

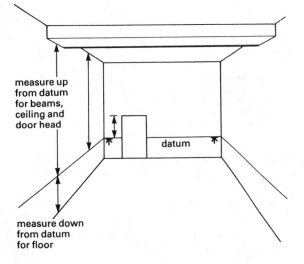

measure up
from datum
for beams,
ceiling and
door head

datum

measure down
from datum
for floor

Figure 212 *Datum line*

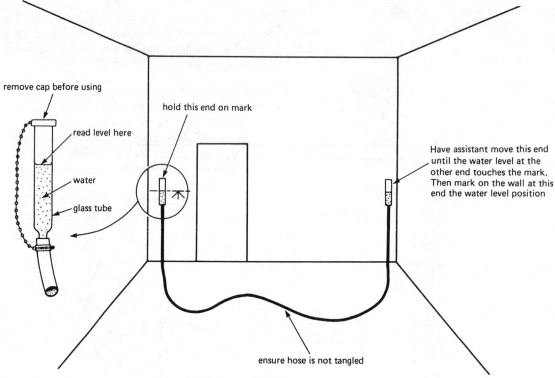

Figure 213 *Using a water level to establish datum line*

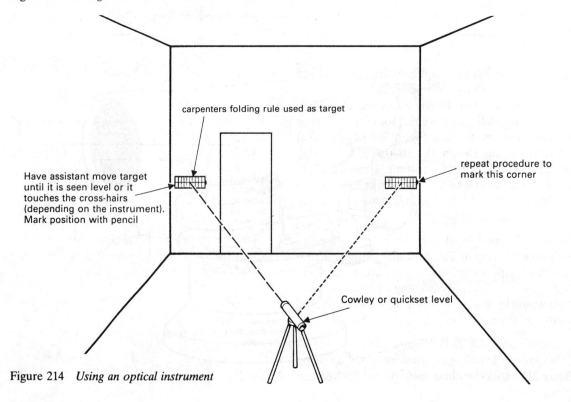

Figure 214 *Using an optical instrument*

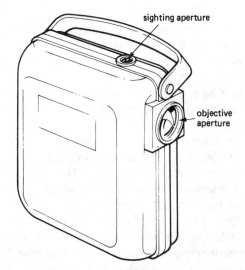

Figure 215 *Cowley automatic level head*

that the pin is fully inserted. Sight through the sighting aperture in the top of the level and adjust the tripod so that the two mirrors are seen to form an approximate circle.

Quickset tilting level (Figure 216)
The method of setting up is as follows:

Open up the tripod and extend the legs; ensure all the nuts, bolts and screws are tight. Place the instrument on the tripod, locate the screw thread and tighten when the circular bubble is central.

Adjust the eyepiece to focus cross-hairs. This is done by placing the palm of one hand just in front of the telescope. Then, sighting through the eyepiece, rotate it until the cross-hairs appear as black and as sharp as possible.

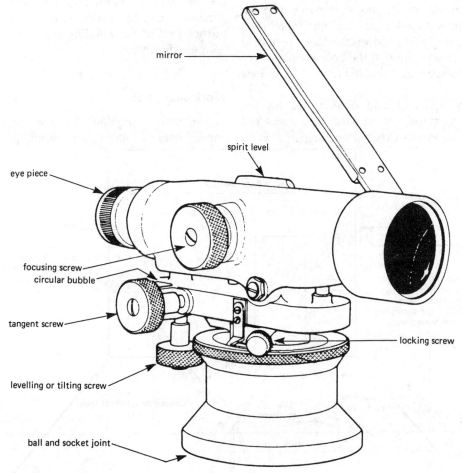

Figure 216 *Quickset tilting level*

Adjust the focusing screw to focus the telescope. This is done by sighting the target through the telescope and then slowly rotating the focusing screw until the target is seen clearly and sharply.

Adjust the spirit level by rotating the tilting screw so that the bubble is central when viewed in the mirror. It is most important that the bubble is centralized each time a sighting is made. Failure to do this results in inaccuracies, as the line of the sight is not truly horizontal.

Where a new flight of stairs is required the total rise and total going should be measured. The total rise is the vertical distance from the finished floor level at the bottom of the flight to the finished floor level at the top. The total going is the overall horizontal distance of travel from the nosing of the bottom step to the nosing of the upper floor or landing. Other items to check are the length and width of the opening in the floor, the position of the doorways at either end of the stairs and finally the floor level (see Figure 217).

Internal openings, and areas or recesses for screens, partitions or fitments are measured in the same way as external openings.

Depending on the nature of the survey, service details such as outlets, sockets and switches for gas, water, electricity, television, telephone etc., may be shown, although these are often recorded on separate 'service plans' to avoid overloading and confusing the main floor plans.

In addition brief notes should be taken, recording details of structural defects and signs of decay and deterioration. This may entail lifting several floorboards and the partial removal of panelling or casings.

On returning to the workshop or office the sketches can be drawn up to produce a set of scale drawings and the brief notes used to form the basis of the survey report. It is at this stage that the necessity of taking all the dimensions and details is realized. One vital missing dimension can be costly, as it will result in a further visit to the building at a later stage to take the dimension.

Workshop rods

Before making anything but the most simple one-off item of joinery, it is normal practice to

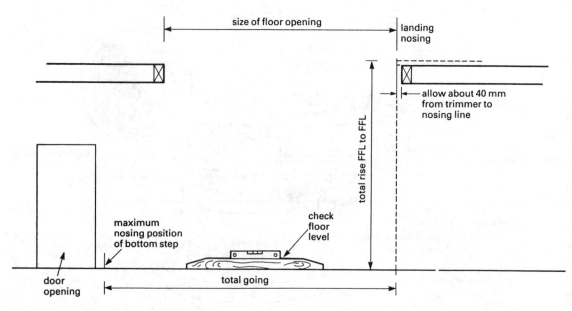

Figure 217   *Site measurement for stairs*

set out a workshop rod. This is done by the 'setter-out' who translates the architect's scale details and specification into full-size vertical and horizontal sections of the item. In addition, particularly where shaped work is concerned, elevations may also be required. Rods are usually drawn on either thin board, thin plywood, white painted hardboard or rolls of decorator's lining paper.

When the job with which they are concerned is complete and they are no longer required for reference, boards may be planed or sanded off and used again. Plywood and hardboard rods may be painted over with white emulsion. Although paper rods are often considered more convenient, because of their ease in handling and strorage, they are less accurate in use. This is because paper is more susceptible to dimen-sion changes as a result of humidity and also changes due to the inevitable creasing and folding of the paper. In order to avoid mistakes, the critical dimensions shown in Figure 218 should be included where paper rods are used. Sight size is the dimension between the inner-most edges of the components, also known as daylight size as this is the height and width of a glazed opening which admits light. Shoulder size is the length of the member (rail or muntin) between shoulders. Overall size (O/A) is the extreme length or width of an item.

Note: Where figured dimensions are different from the rod, always work to the stated size.

A typical rod for a casement window is shown in Figure 219. The drawings on the rod show the sections and positions of the various window components on a height and width rod. All of the component parts of the window can then be marked accurately from the rod. The rod should also contain the following information:

Rod number
Date drawn
Contract number and location
The scale drawing from which the rod was
    produced
The number of jobs required

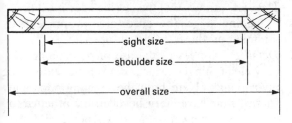

Figure 218   *Critical dimensions*

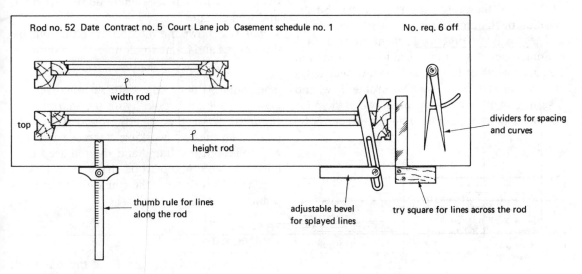

Figure 219   *Rod for a casement window*

Rod no. 64   Date   Contract no. 5   Court Lane Job   Door schedule no. 1B   No. req. 4 off

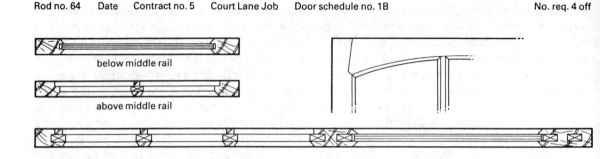

below middle rail

above middle rail

Figure 220   *Rod for half-glazed door*

The drawing equipment the setter-out will use to produce the rod is also shown in Figure 219.

1 A thumb rule for lines along the rod
2 An adjustable bevel for splayed lines
3 A try square for lines across the rod
4 Dividers for spacing and curves

It is standard practice to set out the height rod first, keeping the head or top of the item on the left of the rod and the face of the item nearest the setter-out.

Illustrated in Figure 220 is a workshop rod for a glazed door with diminished stiles and a shaped top rail. As the stiles section is different above and below the middle rail, two width rods are required. Also included on the rod is a half elevation of the curved top rail. In this rod the position of the mortises have been indicated by crosses, as is the practice in many workshops.

Sometimes it is not practical to set out the full height or width of very large items. In such cases the section may be reduced by broken lines and inserting an add-on dimension between them for use when marking out as shown in Figure 221.

When determining details for doors and windows the setter-out must take into account their opening radius. A number of applicable door and window sections are illustrated in Figure 222.

Detail A shows that the closing edge must have a leading edge (bevelled off) to prevent it jamming on the frame when opened.

Detail B applies to the use of parliament and easy-clean hinges which both have extended pivot points. Here both the opening edge and frame jamb have been bevelled off at 90° to a line drawn between the pivot point and the opposite inner closing edge.

Detail C shows how splayed rebates are determined for narrow double doors, bar doors and wicket gates etc.

Detail D shows the method of setting out the door edges and frame for double action doors on floor springs and top centre.

The radiused door edges are set out from the centre of the pivot point, with the sharp arrises removed from the slightly rounded meeting edges. To allow a working clearance between the hollow in the frame and the radiused door edge, the hollow should be struck from a point 3 mm to 6 mm nearer the frame than the pivot point.

Cutting lists

When a rod has been completed the setter-out will prepare a cutting list of all material required

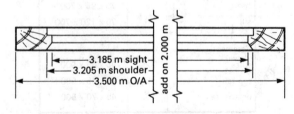

3.185 m sight
3.205 m shoulder
3.500 m O/A

add on 2.000 m

Figure 221   *Add-on dimensions*

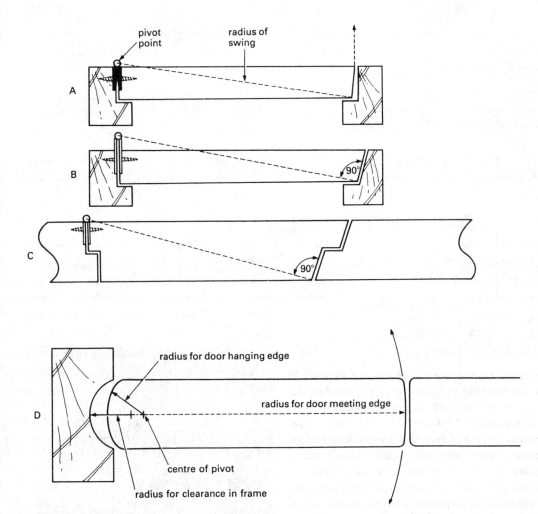

pivot point

radius of swing

A

B

90°

C

90°

D

radius for door hanging edge

radius for door meeting edge

centre of pivot

radius for clearance in frame

Figure 222 *Opening details (doors and windows)*

for the job. The list will accompany the rod throughout the manufacturing operations. It is used by the machinists to select and prepare the required materials with the minimum amount of waste. The cutting list or a duplicate copy will finally be passed on to the office for job costing purposes.

There is no standard layout for cutting lists; their format varies widely between firms. However, it is important that the list contains details of the job, rod and contract in addition to a description of each item, the number required (No. off) and its finished size. Figure 223 shows a typical cutting list for six casement windows.

The length of each item shown on the cutting

Cutting list		
Rod no. 52	Date	Contract no. 5
Job title	Casement window	
Item	No. off	Finished size (mm)
Frame:		
jambs	12	70 x 95 x 1000
head	6	70 x 95 x 700
sill	6	70 x 120 x 700
Casement:		
stiles	12	45 x 45 x 900
top rail	6	45 x 45 x 500
bottom rail	6	45 x 70 x 500

Figure 223 *Cutting list*

Cutting list					
Rod no. 52		Date			Contract no. 5
Job title		Casement window			
Item no.	Item	No. off	Finished size	Sawn size	Material
	Frame:				
1	Jambs	12	70 × 95 × 1000	75 × 100 × 1000	Redwood
2	Head	6	70 × 95 × 700	75 × 100 × 700	Redwood
3	Sill	6	70 × 120 × 700	75 × 125 × 700	Oak
	Casement:				
4	Stiles	12	45 × 45 × 500	50 × 50 × 500	Redwood
5	Top rail	6	45 × 45 × 900	50 × 50 × 900	Redwood
6	Bottom rail	6	45 × 70 × 500	50 × 75 × 500	Redwood

Figure 224   *Detailed cutting list*

list should be the precise length to be cut. It must include an allowance over the lengths indicated on the rod for manufacturing purposes. Between 50 mm and 75 mm is the normal allowance for each horn on heads and sills to take the thrust of wedging up and to facilitate its 'building-in'. A horn of at least 25 mm is required at each end of stiles for both wedging and protection purposes, and an allowance of 10 mm in length for rails that are to be wedged.

An alternative more detailed cutting list for the same six casement windows is shown in Figure 224. In addition to the previous one it contains the following information.

An item number that can be crayoned on each item to allow its easy identification during manufacture.

The sawn sectional sizes of the items to simplify the timber selection, sawing and final costing of the job.

The type of material to be used for each item e.g. softwood, hardwood or plywood etc.

Marking out

After the timber has been prepared and faces marked, the actual marking out of the item can be done. This is the process of transferring the lengths, shoulder lines and mortises from the rod to the machined material.

A workshop rod for a glazed door is illustrated in Figure 225. It shows how a stile and rail are laid on the rod and the sight, shoulder and mortise position lines squared up with the aid of a set square. The mortises and rebates etc. are set out as shown in the completed stile Figure 226. In many joiners' shops it is standard practice to sketch the section on a member to enable all who handle it to instantly see what it should finish at. Where a paired or handed member is required (stiles and jambs) the two pieces can be placed together on a bench with their face sides apart and the points squared over on to the second piece.

Whenever more than one joinery item of a particular design is required, the first to be marked out becomes a pattern for the rest of the job. After checking the patterns against the rod for accuracy, they can be used to mark out all the other pieces, and set up the machines. The positions of the mortises are normally marked out on all members, as it is not economical to spend time setting up chisel or chain mortising machines to work to stops, except where very

Figure 225 *Marking out from rod*

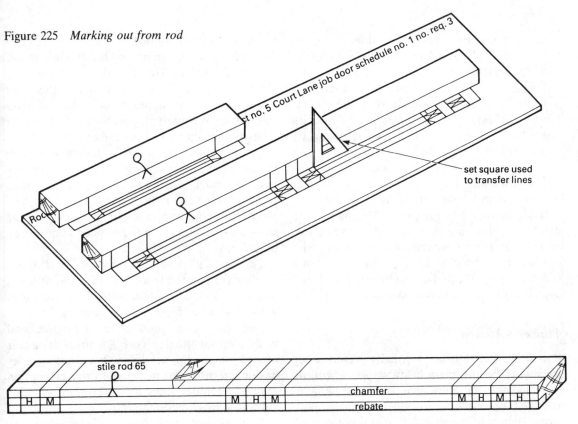

set square used
to transfer lines

Figure 226 *Marked out stile*

Figure 227 *Marking out paired stiles from pattern*

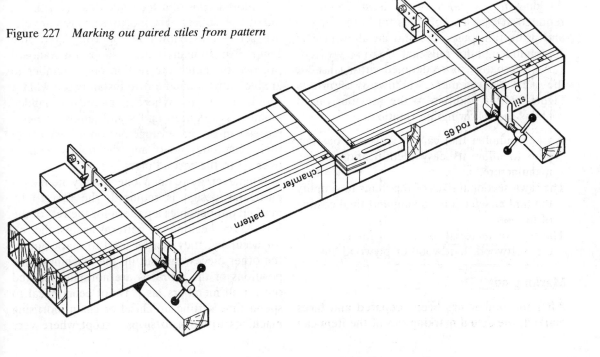

long runs are concerned. Shoulder lines for tenons are only required on the pattern as tenoning machines are easily set up to stops enabling all similar members with tenons in a batch to be accurately machined to one setting. Figure 227 shows a pattern being used to mark out a batch of paired stiles. As any distortion of the timber could result in inaccuracies they must be firmly cramped together.

The use of this method ensures greater accuracy than if each piece were to be individually marked from the rod. Alternatively, a batch of stiles can be cramped between two patterns and the positions marked across with the aid of a short straight edge. At the end of a run the pattern can be machined, fitted and assembled to produce the final item.

Timber selection

Radial sawn sections are normally preferred for joinery as these remain fairly stable, with little tendency to shrink or distort. However, for clear finished work this factor may take second place, as the important consideration will then be which face of a particular timber is the most decorative. For example, radial face oak gives figured or silver grain, tangential face douglas fir gives flame figuring. The timber's grain direction and defects must also be considered when marking out and machining. Careful positioning of a 'face mark' may allow defects such as knots, pith and wane etc. to be machined out later by a rebate or moulding. Knots and short graining should be avoided, especially near joints or on mouldings.

The visual effect of grain direction and colour shading for painted work is of little importance, but careful consideration is required for hardwood and other clear finished joinery.

The aim is to produce a decorative and well-balanced effect. Figure 228 illustrates a pair of well-matched panel doors. The meeting stiles have been cut from one board so that their grain

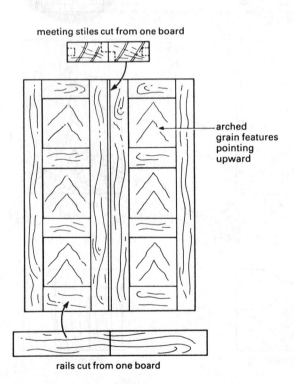

Figure 228   *Grain matching*

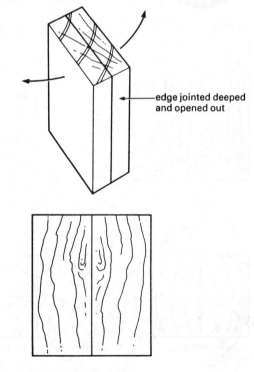

Figure 229   *Book matching*

matches. Likewise, adjacent rails have been cut from one continuous board to provide continuity of grain. Any heavily grained, or darker shaded timber is best kept to the bottom of an item for an impression of balance and stability. If these were placed at the top, the item would appear to be about to topple over. Panels have been matched and their arched top grain features all placed upwards. Edge jointed members are best matched by deeping a thicker section and opening out, just as the pages of this book are opened, as shown in Figure 229. This method of timber matching is termed 'book matching'.

Plywoods are mostly manufactured using rotary cut veneers which produce a widely varying grain pattern that is not usually considered very decorative. Therefore, when plywoods and other sheet materials are used for clear finished work their surface should be veneered with a radially or tangentially sliced veneer. See Figure 230. In addition, Figure 230 illustrates a number of different ways in which veneers may be matched, to create various decorative effects.

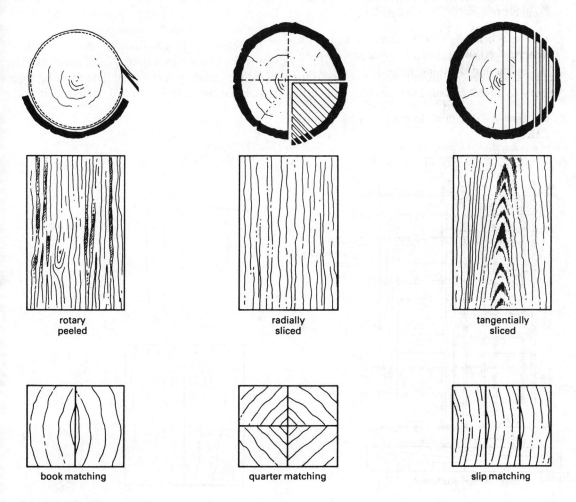

Figure 230 *Veneer matching*

Self-assessment questions

1 What is a datum?

2 Explain the reason for using patterns when marking out framed joinery.

3 What is the purpose of the eyepiece adjustment on a quickset level?

4 State the differences between joinery specified as:
   (i) 'built-in'
   (ii) 'fixed-in'

5 What is the difference between running and separate dimensions?

6 List and briefly describe *three* of the main general considerations applicable when designing and detailing joinery items.

7 Prepare a cutting list for the 762 mm × 1981 mm door shown in Figure 231.

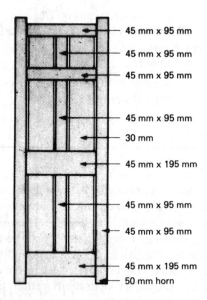

Figure 231 *A typical panelled door*

chapter 9

Machine utilization and workshop organization

After reading this chapter the student should be able to:

1 List general and individual safety precautions to be observed while using the following woodworking machines and portable power tools:
   Circular saws (cross, rip, dimension)
   Band saw
   Jig saw
   Planing machines (surfacer, thicknesser, combination)
   Mortisers (chisel, chain)
   Tenoner
   Spindle moulder
   Drill
   Screwdriver
   Orbital sander
   Belt sander
   Planer
   Router
   Automatic drivers
   Ballistic tool (cartridge-operated).

2 State the requirements of The Woodworking Machines Regulations 1974, applicable to each machine.

3 State the main requirements of The Abrasive Wheels Regulations 1970 and The Protection of Eyes Regulations 1974 applicable to the work of a joiner.

4 Name in sequence the machines used to produce a typical item of joinery.

5 Explain the cutting principles of each machine.

The extent to which joiners are expected to use woodworking machines and portable power tools varies widely from firm to firm. There are many where the operation of any machine is exclusively the province of the machinist, others where joiners are in fact joiners-cum-machinist and as such carry out all the machining. Also there are the firms that fall between these two extremes, where bulk work is carried out by machinists, but the joiners have at their disposal a limited range of machines for the occasional one-off job or replacement member.

However, the use joiners make of portable power tools is considerably more extensive. They are a useful aid to economic production in both the joiner's shop for drilling, trimming, moulding, shaping, recessing and finishing etc. and on site for the fixing of joinery. In addition it is often more convenient to use them for carrying out secondary operations rather than passing the job back to the machinist.

Whatever the provision and use of woodworking machines and portable power tools is, it is essential that the appropriate legislation is fully complied with at all times. This includes in particular:

The Woodworking Machines Regulations 1974
The Abrasive Wheels Regulations 1970
The Protection of Eyes Regulations 1974

It is the duty of every employer and employee in places where woodworking machines are used, to ensure that they are aware of these regulations and that they are carried out in their entirety. It is therefore essential that every user of woodworking machines, including students, has a thorough knowledge of the relevant regulations and it is in his/her own interest fully to implement them.

It is not possible to gain skills in the use of woodworking machines and powered hand tools by reading alone. Therefore all this section sets out to do is to identify the various machines and powered tools, their safe working procedures and cutting principles.

It is essential to receive the relevant practical training by a competent person before using any machine or power tool.

Safety

When using any woodworking machine it is essential that the following basic 'common sense' rules are observed at all times.

Before use:
1 Do not use any machine unless you have been fully instructed in its operation and you are capable of operating it.
2 Check that the machine is isolated from the power supply before setting it up.
3 Ensure that the machine and the working area around it are clean and free from obstruction, off-cuts, shavings etc.
4 Check that the cutters are in good condition and suitable for the work in hand.
5 Ensure that all the guards, guides and fences are correctly set up and held securely in place.
6 Make sure that push sticks and or a push block are close to hand.

During use:
7 Never feed timber into a machine until the cutters have reached maximum speed.
8 Never make any adjustment to a machine while the cutter is moving.

   Note: Even after switching off, many machines take a considerable time to stop.

9 Never leave a machine until its cutters have stopped moving.
10 Never allow yourself to become distracted while operating a machine.
11 Never pass your hands over the cutters, even on top of the timber being machined.
12 Always isolate the machine and clean it down after use.

General safety requirements

The safety requirements of the Woodworking Machines Regulations 1974 which are imposed wherever woodworking machines are in use may be summarized as follows:

1 The cutters of every machine must be enclosed by a substantial guard to the maximum possible extent.
2 In general no adjustment should be made to the guards or any other part of the machine while the cutters are in motion.
3 Every machine must have an efficient starting and stopping device. This should be located so that it is easily used by the operator, especially in the case of an emergency.
4 The working area around a machine must be kept free from obstruction, off-cuts, shavings etc.
5 The floor surface of the work area must be level, non-slip and maintained in good condition.
6 A reasonable temperature must be maintained in the work place and in any case must not fall below 13 °C or 10 °C in a saw mill. Where this is not possible because the machine is situated in the open air, radiant heaters must be provided near or adjacent to the work area, to enable operators to warm themselves periodically.

7 No person must use any woodworking machine unless he/she has been properly trained for the work being carried out or he/she is under close supervision as part of the training.
8 Machine operators must:
   (a) Use correctly all guards and safety devices required by the regulations.
   (b) Report to the supervisor or employer any faults or contraventions of the regulations.
9 Any person who sells or hires a woodworking machine must ensure it complies with the regulations.

Specific safety requirements
The safety requirements of the Woodworking Machine Regulations 1974 which are applicable to specific types of machines are illustrated and briefly described in the following section.

Circular saws (Figure 232)
1 The part of the saw blade which is below the saw table must be enclosed to the maximum possible extent.
2 A strong, adjustable riving knife must be fitted directly behind the saw blade. Its purpose is to part the timber as it proceeds through the saw and thus prevent it jamming on the blade and being thrown back towards the operator.
3 The upper part of the saw blade must be fitted with a strong adjustable crown guard which has flanges that cover the full depth of the saw teeth. The adjustable extension piece should be positioned to within 12 mm of the surface of the material being cut.
4 The diameter of the saw blade must never be less than 6/10 (60 per cent) of the largest saw blade for which the machine is designed. In the case of a multi-speed machine the diameter of the saw blade must never be less than 60 per cent of the largest saw blade which can be properly used at the highest speed. A notice must always be fixed to each machine clearly stating the minimum diameter of the saw blade that may be used.

5 Circular saws must not:
   (a) Be used for cutting tenons, grooves, rebates or moulding unless effectively guarded. These normally take the form of shaw 'tunnel type' guards which, in addition to enclosing the blade, apply pressure to the work piece, keeping it in place.
   (b) Be used for ripping unless the saw teeth project above the timber, i.e. deeping large sectioned material in two cuts is not permissible.
6 A suitable push stick must be provided and kept readily available at all times. They must be used for:
   (a) Feeding material where the cut is 300 mm or less.
   (b) Feeding material over the last 300 mm of the cut.
   (c) Removing cut pieces from between the saw blade and fence.
7 Anyone working at the machine, except the operator, must stand at the delivery end. A full-width table extension must be fitted so that the distance between the nearest part of the saw blade and the end of the table is at least 1200 mm (except in the case of a portable saw bench having a saw blade of 450 mm or less in diameter).

Band saw (Figure 233)
1 All moving parts must be totally enclosed with the exception of the cutting section.
2 The part of the blade between the top wheel and thrust wheel must be guarded at the front and one side. The front must be as close as practicable to the blade and the side extending beyond the back of the saw blade.
3 In use the thrust wheel and therefore the guard must be kept adjusted as closely as possible to the machine table.

Planing machines

Surfacing (Figure 234)
1 The cutter block must be cylindrical.
2 The gap between the cutting circle and the outfeed table (delivery table) must not

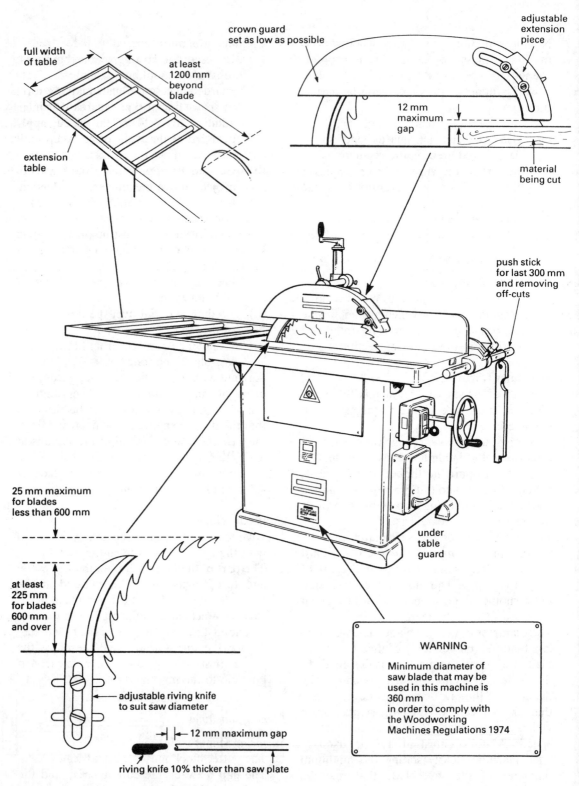

Figure 232 *Circular saw safety requirements*

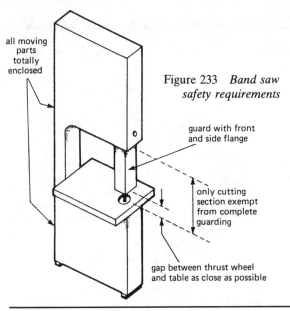

all moving parts totally enclosed

Figure 233 *Band saw safety requirements*

guard with front and side flange

only cutting section exempt from complete guarding

gap between thrust wheel and table as close as possible

exceed 6 mm measured radially from the block's centre. The gap between the two tables must be kept to a minimum.

3 Every machine must be equipped with an easily adjustable bridge guard fitted centrally over the cutter block. This guard must be long enough to cover the cutter block and be at least as wide as the diameter of the cutter block.

4 In use the bridge guard must be adjusted so that:

(a) When *surfacing*, the gap between itself and the fence does not exceed 10 mm

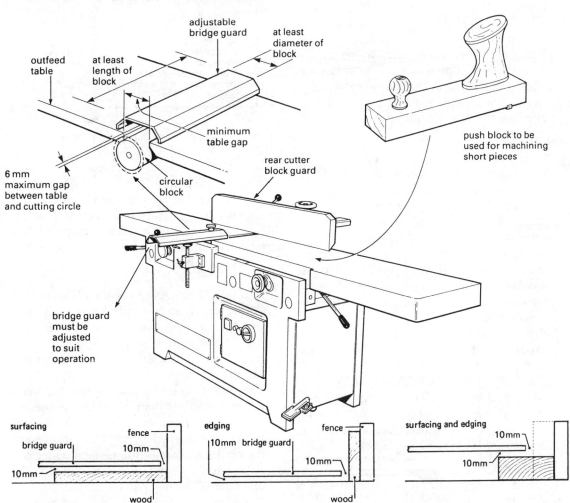

Figure 234 *Surface planer safety requirements*

and the gap between itself and the timber does not exceed 10 mm

(b) When *edging*, the gap between itself and the table does not exceed 10 mm and the gap between itself and the timber does not exceed 10 mm

(c) When *surfacing and edging* in operations one after the other, the gap between itself and the timber when it is being surfaced does not exceed 10 mm and the gap between itself and the timber when it is being edged does not exceed 10 mm.

5   An easily adjustable guard must be fitted to cover the exposed table gap behind the fence.

6   A push block should be used when machining timber less than about 450 mm in length.

7   Rebating or moulding etc. must not be carried out on a planing machine unless it is effectively guarded, normally by a shaw guard. The bridge guard is not considered effective for these operations.

Thicknessing (Figure 235)

1   Every machine used for thicknessing (including combination machines) must be fitted with a sectional feed roller or other anti-kickback device to prevent a piece of timber being violently forced back out of the machine by the action of the cutters.

2   Machines made before 1974 are exempt from the previous requirement provided that not more than one piece of timber at a time is fed through, and a notice to this effect is fixed to the machine.

3   When a combination machine is used, the exposed part of the cutter block in the surfacing table must be adequately guarded. The bridge guard is suitable for this purpose, although it has a tendency to trap the waste material. Therefore, although not compulsory, the use of a waste extraction hood is to be preferred.

Mortising machines

No specific requirements for mortising machines are contained in the regulations, although they must still comply with all general requirements.

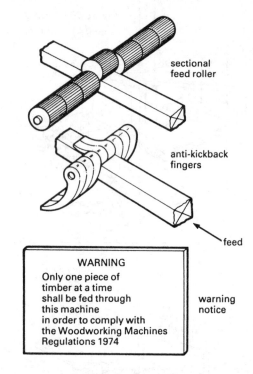

WARNING

Only one piece of timber at a time shall be fed through this machine in order to comply with the Woodworking Machines Regulations 1974

sectional feed roller

anti-kickback fingers

feed

warning notice

Figure 235   *Thicknessing safety requirements*

Tenoning machines

Again the regulations contain no specific requirements for tenoning machines, except for the provision and maintenance of chip and dust extraction equipment, where used for more than six hours a week.

Vertical spindle moulding machines (Figure 236)

1   All cutters must be of the correct thickness for the block or spindle in which they are used (thin cutters may become detached from their block in use with disastrous results).

2   The cutters must be enclosed to the maximum possible extent in order to contain them or other parts in the event of their becoming detached in use (also to prevent the operator's hands dropping on cutters).

3   A false fence should be used to minimize the exposure of moving parts.

4   Jigs with suitable hand holds must be used when the work in hand makes it impractic-

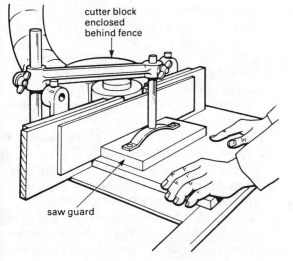

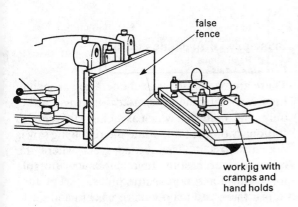

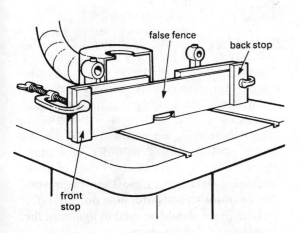

Figure 236 *Vertical spindle moulder safety requirements*

able to fully enclose the cutters (e.g. curved, tapered, short or small members).

5 Where the cut does not extend the full length of the material (stopped work), stops are required to prevent the cutters snatching and throwing back the work as they make contact.

6 Stopped work where the material is fed in the same direction as the cutters (backfeeding) is not permitted without the use of a jig with suitable hand holds.

7 Push sticks should be available for use where they would further reduce any element of risk.

8 Two-speed machines must be controlled so that they always start at the lower speed.

Extraction equipment

An effective chip and dust extraction and collection system must be fitted to the following machines:

(a) Thicknesser (panel planer)
(b) Vertical spindle moulder (if used for more than six hours per week)
(c) Multi-cutter machine
(d) Automatic lathe
(e) Tenoning machine (if used for more than six hours per week)
(f) High speed router

Maintenance

All machines must be maintained in good condition and where practicable be securely anchored.

Lighting

An efficient lighting system should be provided in any machine shop. Direct rays or artificial light must be shaded to prevent glare and so avoid dazzling the machine operator.

Noise

Suitable ear protectors must be readily available and used where any person is likely to be exposed to noise levels of 90 dB (A) for eight hours or more per day.

Eye protection

The Protection of Eyes Regulations 1974 as amended in 1975 makes provision for the protection of eyes of employees in several areas of work.

The following areas of work applicable to the carpenter and joiner require the use of eye protectors.

1 Striking masonry nails by hand tool or powered hand tool.
2 Any work with a hand-held cartridge-operated tool including loading and unloading.
3 Any high-speed metal-cutting saw or abrasive cutting-off wheel.
4 Dry grinding of materials or articles where fragments may be thrown off.
5 Drilling into brick, tiles, blocks or concrete with a portable power tool.
6 Using compressed air to remove dust or other particles.

In addition it is advisable to use eye protectors when carrying out any operation that is likely to produce dust, chips, sparks etc.

Suitable eye protectors must be supplied to employees where their use is specified in the regulations. All employees for their part must:

Take reasonable care of them
Report immediately any loss or damage
Use them to protect their eyes

Abrasive wheels

The mounting and use of abrasive wheels must comply with the Abrasive Wheels Regulations 1970. The following points summarize these regulations:

1 'Abrasive wheels' include any cones, cylinders, discs or wheels with abrasive particles and intended to be power driven for cutting various materials.
2 All abrasive wheels must be clearly marked to indicate their maximum permissible (RPM) speed as specified by its manufacturer. Those less than 55 mm in diameter must have their maximum permissible speed clearly indicated on an adjacent notice.

3 Every machine which uses an abrasive wheel must be clearly marked with its spindle speed.
4 Only fully trained competent persons appointed in writing by their employers may mount (set up for use) abrasive wheels.
5 Substantial guards must enclose abrasive wheels to the maximum possible extent. These should be capable of containing a wheel in the event of a fracture.
6 Where work or tool rests are used they must be of substantial construction and adjusted as closely as practicable to the wheel.
7 All persons who use an abrasive wheel have an obligation to do so in a safe and proper manner. All guards, rests and eye protection (goggles) must be used.

Principles of machine cutting

Circular saws

There are two basic types of operation as seen in Figure 237. In the first, used for cross cutting only, the material which is being cut remains stationary on the table while the revolving saw is drawn across it. The second type, where the material is fed past the revolving saw, is suitable for both rip and cross cutting.

The three main types of circular saw are:

Type	Main use
Cross cut saw	cutting to length
Rip saw	cutting to width and thickness
Dimension saw	precision cutting of sheet material and prepared timber

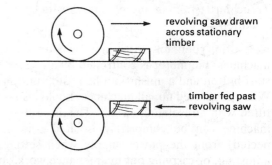

Figure 237 *Circular saws (basic methods)*

Figure 238   *Cross cut saw*

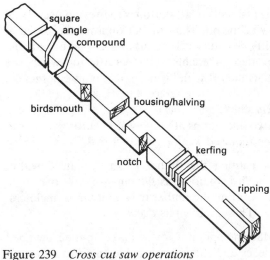

Figure 239   *Cross cut saw operations*

Cross cut saw (Figure 238)
The saw unit is drawn across the material cutting it to length. Adjustable length stops may be fitted where repetitive cutting to the same length is required.

With most models it is also possible to carry out the following operations (see Figure 239):

Cross cutting
Compound cutting
Cutting birdsmouths
Cutting housings
Cutting notches
Cutting halving joints
Kerfing
Ripping (with riving knife fitted)
Trenching, tenoning and ploughing with special
    cutters

Note: In common with most woodworking machines, the motor is controlled by a recessed start button and a mushroom-head stop button. When connected up, all machines should also be fitted with an isolating switch. This is so that a machine can be completely isolated (disconnected) from the power supply when setting, adjusting, or carrying out maintenance work on the machine (see Figure 240). The purpose of

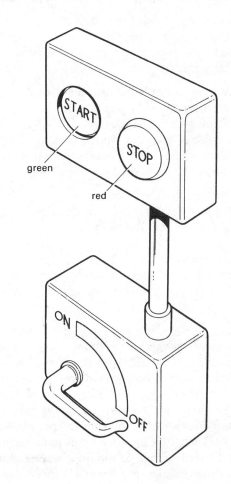

Figure 240   *Control and isolating switches*

recessing the start button is to prevent accidental switching on. The stop button is mushroomed to aid positive switching off and should be suitably located to enable the operator to switch the machine off with his/her knee in an emergency.

Rip saw (Figure 241)
Two operations are involved in cutting timber to the required section (see Figure 242) as follows:

1 Cutting the timber to the required width. This is known as *flatting*.
2 Cutting the timber to the required thickness. This is known as *deeping*.

Machine operators often make up their own bed pieces and saddles to enable them to carry out bevel and angle ripping as shown in Figure 243.

Figure 241 *Rip saw*

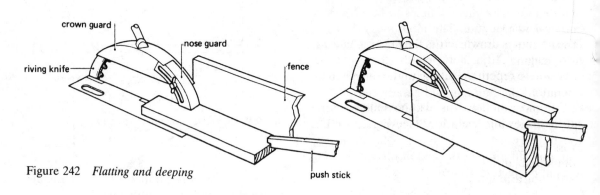

Figure 242 *Flatting and deeping*

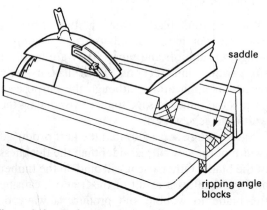
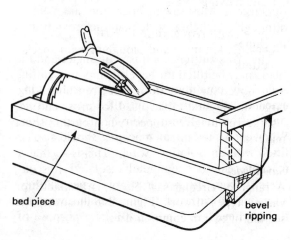

Figure 243 *Bed pieces and saddles*

Figure 244   *Dimension saw*

Some saws have a recess on each side of the blade where it enters the table. These recesses are to receive felt packings and a hardwood mouthpiece. The packing helps to keep the saw cutting in a true line. The mouthpiece helps to prevent the underside of the timber breaking out or 'spelching'.

When setting the machine up for any ripping operation, the fence should be adjusted so that the arc on its end is in line with the gullets of the saw teeth at table level. Binding will occur if it is too far forward and, if it is too far back, the material will jump at the end of the cut, leaving a small projection.

Dimension saw (Figure 244)

This is used for cutting material to precise dimensions. Most sawing operations are possible although on a lighter scale than the previous two machines.

The cross cut fence adjusts for angles and the blade may be tilted for bevels/compound cutting and moved up and down for trenching. The large sliding side table, used for cross cutting, also serves to give support when cutting sheet material.

Saw blades

A range of circular saw blades is available for various types of work. Figure 245 illustrates the section of two in common use:

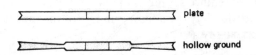

Figure 245   *Circular saw blades (section)*

Plate, also known as parallel plate for straight-forward rip and cross cutting work.
Hollow ground for dimension sawing and fine finished work.

Other section blades with a thin rim are available but have limited uses, for example, swage, ground off and taper. They are used for rip sawing thin sections. Each has its own particular application, although the purpose of each is the same: to save timber by reducing the width of the saw kerf.

Saws require setting so that the kerf produced (width of the saw cut) is wider than the thickness of the blade. Otherwise it will bind on the timber and overheat as a result of the friction, causing the blade to wobble and produce a wavy or 'drunken' cut.

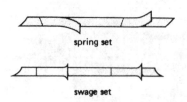

Figure 246   *Circular saw blades (set)*

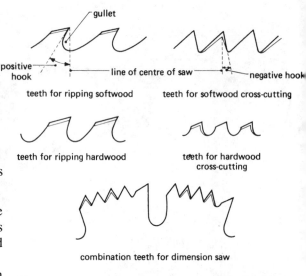

Figure 247   *Circular saw blades (part elevation)*

The teeth can be set in two main ways as shown in Figure 246:

1 Spring set teeth, where adjacent teeth are sprung to the opposite side of the blade. This is the same method as that used for hand saws.
2 Swage set teeth, mainly used for setting thin rim rip saws. The point of each tooth is spread out evenly on both sides to give it a dovetail-shaped look.

Note: Hollow ground and tungsten tipped saws do not require setting as the necessary clearance is provided by the hollow grinding or the tip side overhang respectively.

For efficient cutting the shape of the saw teeth must be suitable for the work being carried out (see Figure 247).

Rip saws require teeth with chisel edges which incline towards the wood (they have positive hook). Teeth for ripping hardwood require less hook than those for ripping softwood.

Cross cut saws require needle-point teeth which incline away from the wood (they have negative hook). The needle-point teeth for hardwood cross cutting must be strongly backed up.

Dimension sawing ideally requires a blade with a combination of both rip and cross cut teeth, although, as dimension saw benches are rarely used for ripping, a fine cross cut blade is often fitted.

The use of wear-resistant tungsten carbide tipped teeth saws (Figure 248) is to be recommended when cutting abrasive hardwoods, plywood and chipboard. This reduces excessive blunting, extending the period before re-sharpening is required.

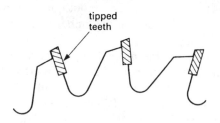

Figure 248   *Tungsten carbide tipped saw blade*

Band saw (Figure 249)

This machine, as its name implies, has a fairly long, endless narrow blade. Its main function is for cutting curves and general shaping work, although it is also capable of ripping and bevel cutting.

Figure 250 shows a close-up view of the thrust wheel and guides, which are fitted above the table. There is also a similar arrangement below the table.

The purpose of the thrust wheel is to support the back of the blade and stop it from being pushed back during the cutting operation. These should be set up approximately 1 mm away from the back of the blade when it is stationary. The guides are set up to just clear the blade. Their

Figure 249   *Band saw*

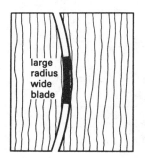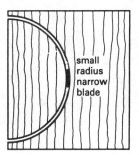

Figure 251   *Band saw widths*

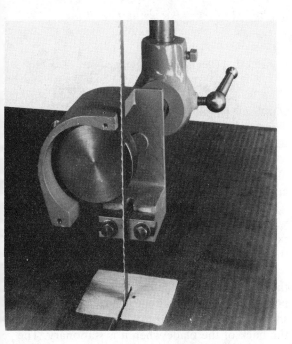

Figure 250   *Thrust wheel and guides*

purpose is to stop any sideways movement of the blade and keep it running true on its intended path.

Also shown is the hardwood mouth where the saw passes through the table.

Various width band saw blades are available and in general the narrower the blade the tighter the curve that can be cut, i.e. widest blades for straight cuts and large sweeping curves, and the narrowest blades for small radius curves as illustrated in Figure 251.

Planing machines

The cutter block of a planing machine is normally circular. Square blocks are only permitted on mechanically fed machines, with a block containing two cutters, revolving at between 4000 and 6000 r.p.m. A series of cutter marks or ripples, two per revolution, are produced on the timber surface. The distance between the marks is called the pitch. True flatness of a surface is approached as the pitch is reduced to a minimum.

A slow feed speed produces a small pitch (large number of short cutter marks) and, as a result, a smooth finish. A fast feed speed, on the other hand, produces a long pitch (small number of long cutter marks), which results in an irregular surface. This principle is illustrated in Figure 252. Acceptable cutter mark pitches for items of joinery work are:

External and general – 2.5 mm and less
High quality and cabinet – 1.25 mm and less

Much time in sanding and hand finishing can be

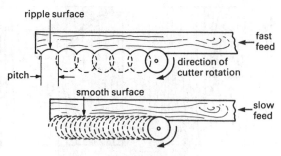

Figure 252   *Effect of feed speed*

Figure 253   *Surface planer*

saved if timber is planed at the outset to a high standard.

Surface planer (Figure 253)

This machine has two main uses:

1   To produce a smooth, flat and straight face side on a piece of timber. This is called surfacing.
2   To produce a smooth, flat and straight face edge which is at right angles to the face side. This is called edging.

In addition this machine can also be used for bevel edging. This is carried out by fitting a pressure guard and canting the fence (shaw guard).

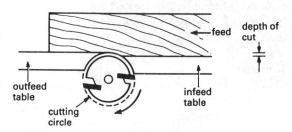

Figure 254   *Section through surface planer*

A section through a surface planer is shown in Figure 254. The outfeed table should be level with the top of the cutting circle of the block, while the infeed table is adjusted below the cutting circle to determine the depth of the cut.

Note: The timber should be fed so that its grain runs with the cutter, otherwise the grain may be 'picked up' leaving a poor irregular finish. Distorted timber should be surfaced convex side up so that its ends, where possible, make contact with the table. Badly distorted timber should be cross cut into shorter lengths before surfacing.

Panel planer (Figure 255)

This machine is also known as a thicknesser. Its purpose is to plane timber, which has previously been surfaced and edged, to the required width and thickness. This is known as thicknessing.

Figure 255   *Panel planer*

Combination planer (Figure 256)

Combination machines combine the functions of both the surface and panel planer.

When planing timber to width and thickness on a panel or combination planer, the timber should be planed to width before being planed to thickness. This is so that the tendency for the timber to tip over in the machine and distort is reduced to a minimum.

A section through a combination planer is shown in Figure 257. A panel planer has the same design although without the top table.

The timber is mechanically fed through the machine at a constant rate by the power-driven feed rollers, the first of which is serrated to grip the sawn surface. Either side of the cutter block is a spring-loaded pressure bar/chipbreaker to keep the timber in contact with the bottom friction rollers and provide a breaking edge for the wood chips.

Mortisers

There are two main ways of machining mortises (see Figure 258):

With a *hollow chisel mortiser* the mortise is cut by a hollow chisel, inside which an auger bit rotates. The auger bit drills a round hole, thereby removing most of the waste, leaving the chisel to square up the hole

Chain mortisers use a cutting chain that runs around a guide bar. A chipbreaker is required on the upward running (exit) side of the chain to prevent the edge of the mortise breaking out.

The chisel mortiser is to be preferred where neatly cut mortises are required. But in production situations, the chain mortiser is often used because of its ability to cut mortises at a much greater speed.

Combined machines are also available on which either cutting action can be selected as required.

Hollow-chisel mortiser (Figure 259)

Various sized chisels and bits are available, from 6 mm square up to 25 mm square. In order to accommodate this range of chisels and bits,

Figure 256   *Combination planer*

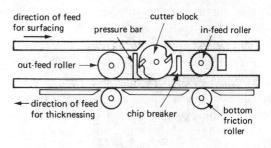

Figure 257   *Section through a combined planer*

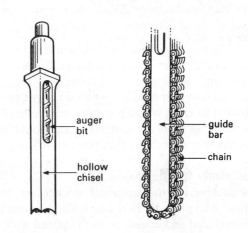

Figure 258   *Machining mortises*

different size collets must be fitted to both the chisel and bit, so that they can be tightened correctly.

When correctly set up, the bit should project 1 mm to 2 mm below the chisel. The machine edges of these chisels are sharpened by either a conical grinding stone which is fitted to some machines, or a steel reamer which is used in a carpenter's ratchet brace. Figure 260 shows both the conical grinding stone and steel reamer for sharpening hollow mortise chisels.

Chain mortiser (Figure 261)

Various sized chains and guide bars are available to cut mortises in one penetration, from 4.5 mm wide and 18 mm long to 32 mm wide and 75 mm long. Most chain machines are fitted with a grinding attachment to facilitate the semi-automatic sharpening of the chain cutting edges.

The start and stop control of both mortising machines normally works in conjunction with the hand lever which starts the cutting action as it is pulled downwards and stops the cutting action when it is raised.

As with the hand method of mortising, through mortises are better cut from both sides in two operations, reversing the timber between them. When carrying out this operation, it is essential to keep the same side of the timber against the fence, to avoid stepped mortises and twisted frames. For this reason it is common practice to position the face side of the timber against the fence of the machine.

Figure 259   *Hollow chisel mortiser*

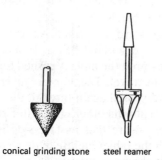

conical grinding stone   steel reamer

Figure 260   *Grinding stone and reamer*

Figure 261   *Chain mortiser*

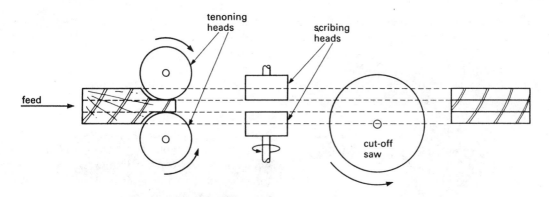

Figure 262 *Section through tenoning machine*

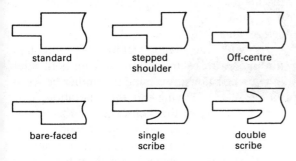

Figure 263 *Various types of tenon*

The tenoning heads are fitted with small shoulder cutters or spurs to cross cut the shoulders just before the tenon cutters. These spurs give a clean shoulder without any breakout.

Scribing heads are vertically mounted behind the tenoning heads to form where required single or double through scribed shoulders.

Finally a cut off saw is positioned at the rear of the machine to allow prepared tenons to be cut to the required length.

Various types of tenons which tenoners may produce are shown in Figure 263.

Single ended tenoner (Figure 264)

Once the cutters have all been set up correctly the member can be placed face side down on the sliding table and secured, after moving it into contact with the guide fence and shoulder length stop. The table is then moved forward by the operator so that the timber passes between the rotating cutter heads.

Further forward movement of the table is required for the scribing heads. Where the cut off saw is required the table is pushed forward to the limit of its travel. The member must then be reversed and passed again through the machine in order to tenon its other end. After reversing the member ensure that its face side is still in contact with the table. Failure to do so may lead to the faults shown in Figure 265.

Double ended tenoners, that process both

Note: Mortises are cut before tenons as chisels and chains are fixed sizes. A tenoning machine can be adjusted to fit a mortise, but not the other way round.

Tenoning

The cutting of tenons on a typical machine can utilize two cutting blocks, two scribing blocks and a cut off saw as illustrated in Figure 262. The two main cutter blocks or tenoning heads are mounted one above the other on horizontal motors. Once these are set and revolving the timber is passed between them to form the tenon. The tenoning heads have vertical adjustment to vary the tenon thickness and horizontal adjustment to enable the cutting of tenons with unequal shoulders (long and short shoulders for rebated framing).

Figure 264   *Tenoner*

tenon shoulder profile reversed, through not
keeping face side on table

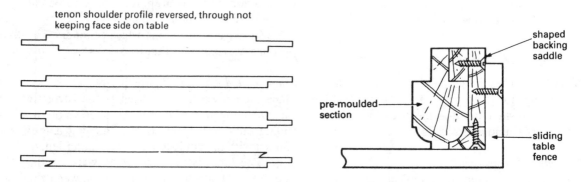

Figure 265   *Possible tenoning faults*

Figure 266   *Saddle to prevent spelching*

ends of the member at one pass through the
machine, are available.

It is normal practice to mortise and tenon
timber before any moulding operations have
been carried out, although it is sometimes
necessary to tenon pre-moulded sections. In
these circumstances it is necessary to prepare
and fix to the fence a shaped backing saddle.

This must be the reverse profile of the moulding
and prevents the member spelching out as the
cutters leave it (see Figure 266).

Spindle moulder (Figure 267)

This is a most versatile machine capable of
edging, rebating, grooving and moulding both
straight or curved members. In addition this

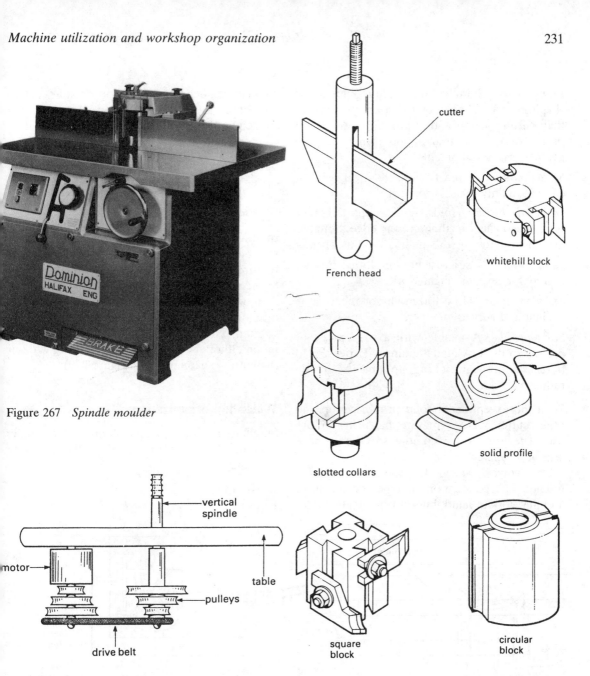

Figure 267   *Spindle moulder*

cutter

French head

whitehill block

slotted collars

solid profile

vertical spindle

motor

table

pulleys

drive belt

Figure 268   *Vertical spindle moulder*

square block

circular block

Figure 269   *Spindle moulder cutter heads*

range of operations may be increased by the fitting of attachments to facilitate dovetailing, corner locking joints, stair string trenching and tenoning.

Basically the machine consists of a vertical spindle which is driven at its lower end by a belt from the motor (see Figure 268). Set spindle speeds from 3000 to 15000 revolutions per minute are achieved by motor switching and moving the drive belt on to different diameter pulleys.

The upper end of the spindle which projects through the work table, is designed to accept various different cutter heads. The main cutter heads in common use are shown in Figure 269 and listed below:

French head   Suitable for all light moulding and shaping work. The cutter has a scraping rather than cutting action and is ground to the exact profile of the required mould (others require geometrical development).

Slotted collars   Used to hold identical pairs of cutters, mainly for curved work.

Whitehill block Holds and supports small cutter heads near to their cutting edge. Suitable for most operations except small radius work.

Square block   Used with bolt on slotted cutters. Mainly for heavy straight work.

Circular block   Used for edging or rebating of straight and curved members.

Solid profile   Available with a wide range of profiles in-built by manufacturers. Expensive to purchase although setting up time is greatly reduced.

With the exception of solid profile cutters, all other cutter set ups require balancing before use. The greater the spindle speed the more crucial balancing becomes.

The correct speed to operate a spindle moulder is dependent on the type of cutter head and the work in hand, but in general, the larger the cutter head or the longer the cutter projection, the slower the speed. Higher speeds are required for curved than for straight work.

Note: Excessive speed is potentially dangerous. Always consult the machine handbook and cutter manufacturers for specific information.

The standard straight fences illustrated and shaw type pressure guards are suitable for use when running straight work, although these are not suitable for curved work, which normally requires a template (usually 9 mm plywood) cut to the shape of the member. This is fixed to the member and kept in contact with a ring fence or other suitable guide while the member is worked. The template itself should have a 'lead in' on either end to enable safe working without the cutters snatching (see Figure 270).

Workshop organization

Small to medium joinery shops will normally contain the majority if not all of the following machines:

Cross cut saw
Rip saw

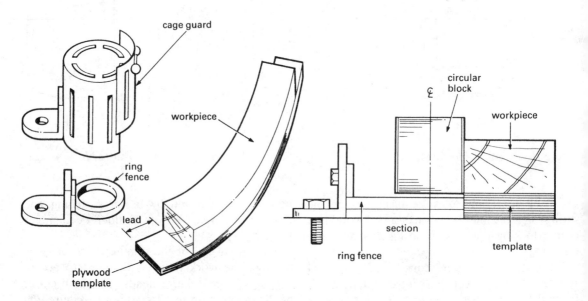

Figure 270   *Guards and fences for curved work*

Dimension saw
Band saw
Surface planer $\Big\}$ or a combined machine
Panel planer
Mortiser
Tenoner
Spindle moulder

The layout of a woodworking machine shop is most important to its efficient running. A shop must be planned to keep the timber moving, as far as possible, in a continuous flow with the minimum of back tracking from the timber store right through all the machine operations to the finishing, assembly, painting and dispatch areas.

Figure 271 illustrates a typical layout and work flow for a woodworking machine shop.

The movement of component parts from one machine or area to another is normally done with the help of trolleys. Component parts are taken off one trolley, passed through the machine, stacked on another trolley and then moved on to the next stage.

The work flow or stages for producing a typical item of joinery would be as follows:

Cross cut all timber to the required or manage-
able length in the timber store. This does

away with the need to bring long lengths of timber into the shop.

Rip saw all the timber to the approximate section.

Machine face side and edge on the surface planer

Plane to the required width and thickness on the panel planer (thicknesser).

Mark out the timber for joints and mouldings etc., on the marking out bench.

Cut plywood, blockboard, etc., and follow by fine dimensioning to length, if required, on the dimension saw.

Cut joints on the mortiser and the tenoning machine.

Cut any curved work to the required shape on the band saw.

Run the required rebates, grooves and mould-ings, etc., on the spindle moulder.

Pass all components to the finishing and assembly shop for joiners to finish, assemble and clean up the joinery items.

In larger shops more than one of each machine may be found, particularly the mortiser and spindle moulder. Sanding and more specialist advanced machines may also be installed.

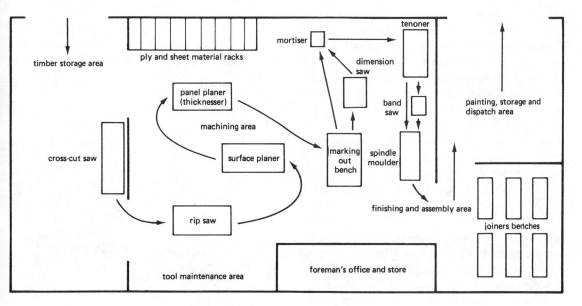

Figure 271 *Typical woodworking machine shop layout and work flow*

Portable powered hand tools

Power tools, in addition to their use in a joiner's shop, are often used by joiners for the on-site installation of purpose-made joinery and specialist items. Therefore the full range of tools and details of the main sources of power supply have been included in this section.

Power supply

Electricity

Electricity is virtually indispensable in this mechanized age. Although an invaluable aid to productivity, it is also a major safety hazard which, unlike most other hazards, is invisible and instantaneous in effect. Its degree of hazard is directly related to the level of current and the duration of contact. Low levels of current may only cause an unpleasant tingling sensation, but the consequent momentary lack of concentration may be sufficient to cause other injury (contact with moving parts, or fall etc.). Medium levels of current result in muscular tension and burning. Higher levels of current, in addition to the burning, affect the heart and often result in death.

Since the lower the voltage, the lower the risk, reduced voltage schemes are the accepted procedure for safe working. Reduced voltage equipment operates on 110 volts supplied through step down transformers with a centrally tapped earth so that, in the event of a fault, the maximum shock that the operator should receive would be 65 volts on the three phase circuit and 55 volts on the single phase circuit. In addition, most power tools are now manufactured using the double insulated principle whereby the motor and other live parts are isolated making it impossible for the operator to receive a shock, should a fault occur. Double insulated tools which bear the BS 2769 (kitemark) and the double-squares symbol do not require an earth wire, although the risk of shock is still present if the cable is damaged.

Moisture is a good conductor of electricity, so the risk of an electric shock in moist conditions is greatly increased, not only from the machine or power tool, but also from the supply flex which may be frayed, damaged or jointed.

Mains supply

The electricity board will provide a supply to a lockable covered incoming unit which houses a meter, main fuses and master switch. This unit is connected to a mains distribution unit from which distribution cables connect up to transformer units, outlets units and extension outlet units, providing a supply at the correct voltage.

The use of supply outlets, plugs and couplings complying to BS 4343 make it impossible for a piece of equipment operating on one voltage to be plugged into an outlet of a different voltage. This is achieved by keys and keyways in different positions in the plugs and sockets and a colour coding. Figure 272 illustrates one of these plugs and sockets.

Red	415 volts
Blue	240 volts
Yellow	110 volts
White	50 volts
Violet	25 volts

All electrical installation including the wiring up of plugs to individual items of equipment must be carried out and regularly inspected by a competent electrician.

When power tools are being used in the joiner's shop or an existing building from the 240 volts mains supply, a 110 volt portable step

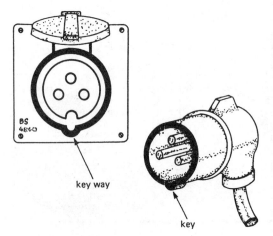

key way

key

Figure 272   *Keyed plug and socket*

down transformer should be used. In cases where an extension lead is required these should be used on the 110 volt side, be kept as short as possible and routed safely out of the way, to prevent risk of tripping or damage. If the extension lead is stored on a drum, it must be fully unwound before use in order to prevent over-heating.

Generators

Where electricity is provided by a portable generator, care must be taken in its siting, in order to minimize any nuisance from the emission of fumes and noise.

Figure 273 shows a portable petrol 110 volt single phase generator with an output of four kilowatts.

In damp, confined or isolated conditions it is well worth considering the use of rechargeable battery powered hand tools.

Compressed air

Air above the atmospheric pressure of 1 bar is used as the power source for a range of pneumatic tools. The majority of these tools operate at pressures of between 5 and 8 bar. This is normally produced by a mobile compressor unit as illustrated in Figure 274. This may be powered either by a petrol/diesel motor or by an electric motor.

Reciprocating type compressors are normally used for this type of work, where the air is

Figure 274   *Mobile compressor unit*

sucked through a filter into a cylinder, compressed by a piston and passed on into an air receiver. A single stage compressor draws in the air and compresses it by a single stroke of the piston. Two stage or multi-stage compressors, compress the air in successive stages until the final pressure is achieved.

Air receivers are incorporated into compressors to even out the pulsating delivery and provide a store of air that is available for discharge at a constant pressure. A system of hoses is used to transport the compressed air to the required working position. The size of the air hose must be compatible with the tool being used: any variation in the bore of the hose will result in a variation of the power supplied to the tool.

Ideally the compressor should be positioned as closely as possible to the work. Long runs cause pressure drop through friction and create hazards. Where long air hose runs are unavoidable, large bore air hoses should be run to the work area, where a shut-off valve can be fitted.

Figure 273   *110 V portable generator*

In addition to reducing the bore of the air hoses to that compatible with the tool, this allows the tool to be isolated when not in use.

In order to work efficiently, prevent overheating through friction, and avoid excessive wear, it is most important that compressed air tools are supplied with clean air and constant correct lubrication. Therefore every air hose should be equipped with an efficient air filter and lubricator to provide a supply of clean constantly lubricated air.

Safety procedures

Compressed air equipment can, if correctly used, be perfectly safe. However, if misused, they can cause severe personal injury. Compressed air entering the body causes painful swelling. If it is allowed to enter the bloodstream it can make its way to the brain, burst the blood vessels and cause death.

The following safety points must be observed whenever compressed air equipment is used.

1 The compressor must be in the control of a fully trained competent person at all times.
2 All equipment must be regularly inspected and maintained.
3 Training must be given to all persons who will use compressed air equipment.
4 Position the compressor in a well ventilated area.
5 Ensure all hose connections are properly cramped.
6 Route all air hoses to prevent snaking, risk of persons tripping or traffic crossing them, as any squeezing of the hose causes excess pressure on the couplings.
7 Always isolate the tool from the air supply before investigating any fault.
8 Never disconnect any air hose unless protected by a valve.
9 Never use an air hose to clean away waste material or anything else that may result in flying particles.
10 Never use compressed air to clean down yourself or anyone else, as this carries a great risk of injury to the eyes, ears, nostrils and rectum.

In many circumstances there is little to choose between the various power sources available, although some particular advantages and disadvantages are associated with each type. Table 29 gives a comparison of these.

Table 29 **Comparison of power sources**

Electricity	Compressed air	Rechargeable battery
Advantages		
Power supply readily available	Tools are lighter	Suitable for use in damp condition
Wide range of tools	Suitable for use in damp conditions	No leads or hoses
	Certain tools may be used under water	Ideal for use in isolated or confine conditions where there is no powe supply
	No risk of motor burning out under load	
	Normally more powerful	
Disadvantages		
High risk of motor burning out under load	Limited range of tools	Limited range of tools
Trailing cables	Requires use of compressor	Limited motor power
Risk of shock	Compressor noise and fumes	Need to recharge batteries
Not suitable for use in damp conditions	Long trailing air hoses limit access	

Power tool safety

Although each type of power tool has its own individual safe working procedures, the following basic safety rules should be followed when using any powered tool.

1 Never use a power tool unless you have been properly trained in its use.
2 Never use a power tool unless you have your supervisor's permission.
3 Always select the correct tool for the work in hand (if in doubt consult the manufacturer's instructions).
4 Ensure that the power tool and supply are compatible.
5 Ensure that the cable or air hose is:
   (a) Free from knots and damage
   (b) Firmly secured at all connections
   (c) Unable to come into contact with the cutting edge or become fouled during the tool's operation.
6 Before making any adjustments, always disconnect the tool from its power supply.
7 Always use the tool's safety guards correctly and never remove or tie them back.
8 Never put a tool down until all the rotating parts have stopped moving.
9 Always wear the correct protective equipment for the job. These may include:
   (a) Safety goggles
   (b) Dust mask
   (c) Ear protectors
   (d) Safety helmet

Note: Loose-clothing and long hair should be tied up so that they cannot be caught up in the tool.

10 All power tools should be properly maintained and serviced at regular intervals by a suitably trained person. Never attempt to service or repair a power tool yourself. If it is not working correctly or its safety is suspect, return it to the storeman with a note stating why it has been returned. In any case it should be returned to the stores for inspection at least once every seven days.
11 Ensure that the material or workpiece is firmly cramped or fixed in position so that it will not move during the tool's operation.
12 In general compressed air tools must be started and stopped under load, whereas electric tools must not.
13 Never use an electric tool where combustible liquids or gases are present.
14 Never carry, drag or suspend a tool by its cable or hose.
15 Think before and during use. Tools cannot be careless but their operators can. Most accidents are caused by simple carelessness.

Drill

This is the most common type of portable power tool. The two main types available are:

The palm grip type
The heavy duty back handle type.

Both are available in two or multi-speed versions which are more versatile as they allow the user to adjust the speed to suit the size of hole and material being worked.

In general use a fast speed for drilling small diameter holes and a slow speed for larger diameter ones.

Figure 275 shows a drill with a palm grip handle. This design ensures the pressure is exerted directly in line with the drill bit, thus assisting the cutting action.

Figure 275 • *Drill*

Figure 276   *Back handle drill*

Figure 277   *Drill stand*

Figure 276 shows a back handle heavy-duty drill which is designed for two-handed operation. This type is often fitted with a percussion or hammer action for drilling masonry and concrete, with special percussion tungsten carbide tipped drills.

Twist drills and bits
Only high quality twist drills and bits capable of withstanding the pressure and heat generated when drilling at speed should be used. They must be fully inserted into the jaws of the chuck and tightened using a chuck key in all three positions, so that the jaws grip the shank of the drill evenly.

A useful hint is to tape the chuck key to the power tool flex, near the plug, thus ensuring that the chuck is tightened and the key removed before the drill is plugged in and operated.

Drill stand
For repetitive work and light mortising a drill can be fitted into a drill stand as illustrated in Figure 277, thus combining accuracy and speed of production. In order to comply with safety requirements the stand is fitted with a retractable chuck and drill guard which must always be in position when drilling.

Operation

During use:
1 Hold the drill firmly.
2 Cramp the workpiece.
3 Do not force the drill, allow it to work at its own pace.
4 Withdraw the drill from the hole frequently to clear the dust and allow it to cool.
5 Drill a small pilot hole first to act as a guide when drilling large holes.
6 Reduce the pressure applied on the drill as it is about to break through, to avoid snatching or twisting.

Screwdriver
When large numbers of screws have to be driven, or nuts tightened, the use of a power screwdriver will greatly speed up the process. Figure 278 shows a power screwdriver. The body and motor is similar to that of an electric power

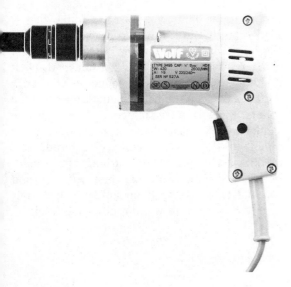

Figure 278 *Screwdriver*

drill, although a reduction gear is fitted to give the correct speed for screwdriving. Where a two-speed tool is used, the slow speed should be used for wood screws and the high speed for self-tapping screws. Most tools are manufactured with a reverse gear to enable screws to be removed as well as inserted.

The front housing of the tool holds the screwdriver bits and contains a clutch assembly. This operates in two stages:

1 The tool's motor will run but the screwdriver bit will not rotate until sufficient pressure is exerted to enable the clutch to operate and engage the main drive.
2 When the screws are tight and in the required position, the second stage of the clutch operates and stops the screwdriver bit rotating.

The clutch can be adjusted by tightening or loosening the spring as required. If the adjustment is not suitable for the work in hand, the clutch spring can be changed for a weaker or stronger one. Four strengths are normally available. The weakest is used for driving smaller screws or screws which are to be left proud of the surface, and the strongest for large or deeply driven screws. The two intermediate

strength springs are used for a variety of operations in between these two extremes.

Screwdriver bits and sockets
Various screwdriver bits and sockets are available to suit different types and sizes of screws. It is a simple operation to change the type of bit when required. The hexagonal shank of the bit is simply pushed into the front housing of the tool and retained in position by a spring-loaded steel ball which locates in a groove around the top of the shank. The bit is removed by simply pulling it out of the front housing.

Operation of screwdriver

During use:
1 Select a screwdriver bit that is compatible with the tool being used.
2 Drill a pilot hole, clearance hole and countersink, where required before screwing, to avoid overloading the motor and splitting the material.
3 Maintain a steady, firm pressure on the screwdriver so that the bit cannot jump out and damage the screwhead or the workpiece.

Sanders
The two main types of sander in use are the orbital sander and the belt sander.

Orbital sander (Figure 279)
This type is also known as the finishing sander as it is mainly used for fine finishing work. The sander's base has a 3 mm orbit which operates at 12,000 r.p.m.

Various grades of abrasive paper may be clipped to the sander's base. It is best to start off with a coarse grade to remove any high spots or roughness and follow on with finer grades until the required finish is obtained, although where the surface of the timber has machine marks or there is a definite difference in the levels of adjacent material, the surface should be levelled by planing before any sanding is commenced.

Belt sander (Figure 280)
This is used for jobs requiring rapid stock

Figure 279   *Orbital sander*

Figure 280   *Belt sander*

removal. When fitted with the correct grade of abrasive belt they can be used for a wide range of operations such as smoothing and finishing joinery items, block flooring, and even the removal of old paint and varnish finishes.

The sanding or abrasive belt is fitted over two rollers. The front roller is spring-loaded and can be moved backwards and forwards by the belt-tensioning lever. This movement allows the belt to be changed easily and it also applies the correct tension to the belt. When changing the belt it is necessary to ensure that it will rotate in the correct direction. This is indicated on the

inside of the belt by an arrow. If the belt is inadvertently put on the wrong way round the lap joint which runs diagonally across the belt will tend to peel. This could result in the belt breaking, with possible damage to the work surface. To keep the belt running central on the rollers, there is a tracking control knob on the sander which adjusts the front roller by tilting it either to the left or right as required. The tracking is adjusted by turning the sander bottom upwards with the belt running and rotating the tracking knob until the belt runs evenly in the centre without deviating to either side.

Operation of sanders

During use:

1 Always start the sander before bringing it into contact with the work surface and remove it from the work surface before switching off. This is because slow moving abrasive particles will deeply scratch the work surface.
2 Do not press down on a sander in use. The weight of the machine itself is sufficient pressure. Excessive pressure causes clogging of the abrasive material and overheating of the motor.
3 For best results lightly guide the sander over the surface with parallel overlapping strokes in line with the grain.
4 Always use the abrasive belts and sheets specifically recommended by the manufacturer for the particular model as makeshift belts and sheets are inefficient and dangerous.
5 Always use the dust collecting bag where one is fitted. In any case always wear a dust mask as inhaling the dust from many species of wood causes coughing, sneezing and running eyes and nose.

Saws

There are two main types of portable saw in common use by the joiner, each with its own specific range of functions: the circular saw and the jig saw.

Figure 281 *Circular saw*

Figure 282 *Jig saw*

Circular saw (Figure 281)

This is often known as a 'skill' saw and can be used by the joiner for a wide range of sawing operations. The saw is capable of cross cutting, rip sawing, bevel cutting and compound bevel cutting, and is particularly useful for cutting sheet material.

The use of tungsten-carbide-tipped saw blades is preferable in all situations, but particularly when cutting plywood, chipboard, fibreboard, plastic laminates and abrasive timbers.

Operation of circular saw

1 Select and fit correct blade for the work in hand (rip, cross cut, combination or tungsten tipped etc.).

2 Adjust depth of cut so that the gullets of the teeth just clear the material to be cut.

3 Check blade guard is working properly. It should spring back and cover the blade when the saw is removed from the timber.

4 Set the saw to the required cutting angle. This is indicated by a pointer on the pivot slide.

5 Insert rip fence (if required) and set to the width required.

Note: When cutting sheet material or timber where the rip fence will not adjust to the required width, a straight batten can be temporarily fixed along the board to act as a guide for the sole plate of the saw to run against.

6 Check to ensure that all adjustment levers and thumbscrews are tight.

7 Ensure that the material to be cut is properly supported and securely fixed down.

Note: As the saw cuts from the bottom upwards, the face side of the material should be placed downwards. This ensures that any breaking out which may occur does not spoil the face of the material.

8 Rest the front of the saw on the material to be cut and pull the trigger to start the saw.

9 Allow the blade to reach its full speed before starting to cut. Feed the saw into the work smoothly and without using excess pressure.

Note: The blade guard will automatically retract as the saw is fed into the work.

10 If the saw binds in the work, ease it back until the blade runs free.

11 When the end of the cut is reached, remove the saw from the work, allowing the blade guard to spring back in place and then release the trigger.

Note: Do not release the trigger before the end of the cut has been reached.

Jig saws (Figure 282)

These are also known as reciprocating saws.

Although they may be used with a fence for straight cutting they are particularly useful for circular, shaped and pierced work. In addition many models have adjustable sole plates which allow bevel cutting to be carried out.

A range of different blades are available, suitable for cutting a wide variety of materials.

Operation of jig saw
1 Select the correct blade for the work in hand.
2 Select the correct speed, slow speed for curved work and high speed for straight cutting.
3 Ensure that the material to be cut is properly supported and securely fixed down.
4 Rest the front of the saw on the material to be cut and pull the trigger to start the saw.
5 When the blade has reached its full speed, steadily feed the saw into the work, but do not force it.
6 When the end of the cut is reached release the trigger, keeping the sole plate of the saw against the workpiece, but making sure the blade is not in contact.

Pocket cutting
Both the circular saw and the jig saw may be used for pocket cutting. The circular saw is suitable for cutting access traps in completed floors. The jig saw is useful for cutting sink top holes in worktops etc. without the need for templates. See *Carpentry and Joinery for Building Craft Students 2* for pocket cutting techniques.

Planer (Figure 283)
The portable planer is mainly used for edging work although it is capable of both chamfering and rebating. On site it is extremely useful for door hanging and truing up the edges of sheet material. Surfacing and cleaning up of timber can be carried out when required but it tends to leave ridges on surfaces which are wider than the length of the cutters.

Operation of planer
1 Check that the cutters are sharp and set correctly.

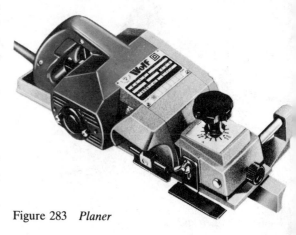

Figure 283 *Planer*

2 Adjust the fence to run along the edge of the work as a guide.
3 Rest the front of the plane on the workpiece, ensuring that the cutters are not in contact with the timber.
4 Pull the trigger and allow cutters to gain speed.
5 Move the plane forward keeping pressure on the front knob.

Note: The depth of the cut can be altered by rotating this knob.

6 Continue planing, keeping pressure both down and up against the fence.
7 When completing the cut, ease the pressure off the front knob and increase the pressure on the back.

Note: This prevents the plane tipping forward, causing the cutter to dig in when the end of the cut is reached

8 Allow the cutters to stop before putting the plane down; otherwise the plane could take off on the revolving cutters.

Rebating and chamfering is carried out using a similar procedure. When surfacing, a number of overlapping strokes will be required.

Router (Figure 284)
This is a very versatile tool which is capable of performing a wide variety of operations includ-

Figure 284   *Router*

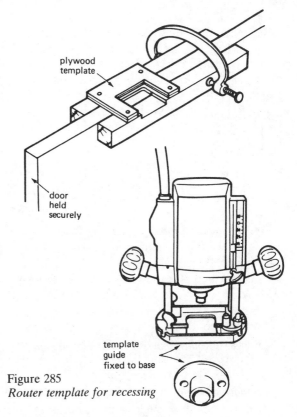

Figure 285
Router template for recessing

ing rebating, housing, grooving, moulding, slot mortising, dovetailing and, on many types, drilling and plunge cutting.

Mechanically the router is a fairly basic piece of equipment. It consists of a motor driving a central shaft with a chuck at one end. The cutters are held in the chuck by a tapered collet which grips the shank of the cutter as the locking nut of the chuck is tightened.

Cutters

High speed steel cutters are suitable for most softwoods, although tungsten tipped cutters are recommended when working with abrasive timbers, laminates, plastics, plywood, chipboard and fibreboard.

Operation of router

Recessing

This operation requires the fitting of a template guide to the base plate of the router and a template of the recess required.

When making the template an allowance must be made all round equal to the distance between the cutting edge of the bit and the outside edge of the template guide. Figure 285 shows a typical template for recessing a hinge.

1 Fix the template in the required position.
2 Place the router base on the template, taking a firm grip on the router, start the motor and allow it to attain maximum speed. Plunge the router to the pre-set depth and lock.
3 Applying a firm downward pressure, move the router around the edge of the template before working the centre. It is most important to feed the router in the opposite direction to the rotation of the cutter.
4 On completion, retract the cutter, switch off the motor and allow the cutter to stop rotating before putting the router down.

Note: Rounded corners will be left by the cutter which can easily be squared up with a chisel.

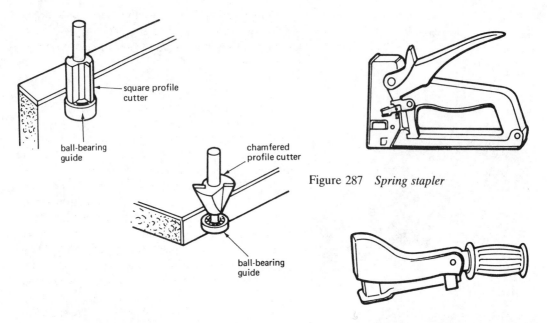

Figure 287   *Spring stapler*

Figure 286   *Router cutters for laminate trimming*

Figure 288   *Hammer-action stapler*

Laminate trimming

Small routers for single hand operation are manufactured specifically for laminate trimming, although it is possible to fit a ball-bearing guided, laminate trimmer to a standard plunging router.

Figure 286 shows two router cutters suitable for laminate trimming. The square profile is used for trimming the edging strip and the chamfered one for trimming the top.

Automatic drivers

Various types of automatic driver are available to suit a wide range of fixings. The smaller drivers are usually operated by spring power and the larger ones by compressed air, although a limited range of electric tackers are available.

Operation of automatic drivers

This will vary depending on the type being used but the following are a number of general points:

1 Do not operate the trigger until the base plate is in contact with the fixing surface.
2 Keep fingers clear of the base plate.

3 Maintain a firm pressure with the fixing surface during use. Failure to do so can result in kickback of the tool and ricochet of the nail or staple.
4 On tools with a variable power adjuster, carry out trial fixings at a low setting and gradually increase until the required penetration is achieved.

Figure 287 shows a spring stapler that is useful for fixing thin material, paper, plastic sheet, hessian and tiles etc. To operate, the tacker is placed firmly in position and the operating lever pressed downwards.

Figure 288 illustrates a heavier type spring operated stapler that is designed to drive a staple when swung against a surface in a hammer-like fashion.

Figure 289 illustrates a pneumatic nailer/stapler that is capable of firing nails and staples of up to 75 mm in length, thus making it suitable for a wide range of fixings.

Cartridge-operated fixing tools (Figure 290)

The cartridge operated fixing tool is an invaluable aid to making fast and reliable fixings to a

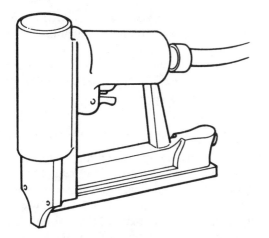

Figure 289   *Pneumatic nailer*

Figure 290   *Cartridge tool*

variety of materials including concrete, brick and steel. The two types of tool in use are the direct acting and the indirect acting.

Direct acting

In this type of tool the expanding gas from the detonated cartridge acts directly on the fastener, accelerating it from rest down the barrel to strike the base material at a velocity of up to 500 m/s (metres per second). At no time are the fastener's propulsion or depth of penetration controlled. Should for any reason the base material be inconsistent, there is a danger that the fastener could through-penetrate or ricochet and cause untold damage in the surrounding area.

Direct-acting tools are also known as high-velocity tools. They are operated by pulling a trigger which releases a spring to detonate the cartridge.

Indirect acting

This type of tool has a piston in its barrel. When the cartridge is detonated, the released gas acts on the piston, accelerating it from rest to drive the fastener into the base material at a maximum velocity of up to 100 m/s. The piston is held captive in the tool and once the piston stops so will the fastener. This virtually eliminates the risk of through-penetration or ricochets, even if the base material is inconsistent. Indirect-acting tools are also known as low-velocity tools. They may be operated in one of two ways, depending on the make and type of tool being used. The cartridge may be detonated by an externally applied blow. This blow is normally from a club hammer. Alternatively, the cartridge is detonated by a spring which is released when the trigger is pulled.

Indirect-acting low-velocity tools are considered to be the safest types of cartridge operated tool available.

Operation of cartridge operated fixing tools

Safe working procedures are most important when using cartridge tools and these can never be over-emphasized. Before operating a tool, run through the following dos and don'ts checklist.

Dos

Do ensure the tool is in good repair (cleaned and serviced daily).
Do ensure you have had the correct training.
Do ensure you understand the misfire procedure (given in the manufacturer's handbook).
Do wear recommended safety equipment (goggles, helmet and ear protectors).
Do ensure the base material is suitable (try the hand hammer test).
Do ensure the tool is used at right angles to the fixing surface.
Do ensure the fixing surface is free from cracks and damage.
Do insert fixing device before inserting cartridge.

Do ensure correct pin, piston and cartridge combination is used.

Do ensure you understand the handling and storage of cartridges (stored in a metal box, in a secure store, to which only authorized persons have access).

Don'ts

Don't use a suspect tool (if in doubt return to the manufacturer for overhaul).

Don't use a tool you have not been trained for (manufacturers provide on-site training for operators).

Don't use force when loading a cartridge (it could detonate in your hand).

Don't load a cartridge before you need it.

Don't leave a loaded tool lying about.

Don't point the tool at any person.

Don't drive into brittle material.

Don't drive into very soft material.

Don't drive less than 63 mm from the edge of brick and concrete.

Don't drive less than 13 mm from the edge of steel.

Don't drive within 50 mm of a weld.

Don't drive into a damaged surface.

Don't drive where another fixing has failed.

Don't strip the tool without checking that it is unloaded.

Don't use the tool without recommended safety equipment.

Don't use other manufacturer's cartridges.

Don't use other manufacturer's fixing devices.

When cartridge fixing into a suspect material the best procedure to follow is to carry out the hand hammer test. This is carried out by attempting to hand hammer a fastener into the material. A cartridge fixing is not suitable if any of the following occurs:

The point of the fastener is blunted.

The fastener fails to penetrate at least 1.6 mm.

The surface of the material cracks, crazes or is damaged.

Where the strength of the material into which a fixing is being made is not known, a test fixing should be carried out in order to establish the required cartridge strength. Always make test fixings using the lowest strength cartridge first, increasing by one strength each time until the required fixing is achieved.

Further information on cartridge-operated fixing tools is given in *Carpentry and Joinery for Building Craft Students 2*.

Health hazards associated with wood dust

The wood dust created when machining certain timbers has a known irritant effect. The most harmful effects are created by the fine airborne dust produced when sanding or sawing in confined, poorly ventilated areas, although the severity of the effect will depend on the sensitivity of the individual concerned.

The common timbers that are known to have irritant properties are listed in Table 30 along with its type and degree of effect.

Precautions

Since it is the dust that causes the problems, the most effective precaution is the use of dust extraction equipment. However, this is only part of the answer, as a certain amount of airborne dust cannot be avoided. Therefore when working with a timber that has irritant properties, the following precautions should be taken.

1 Always use a dust mask or respirator.
2 Wear properly designed dust-proof protective clothing.
3 Use barrier cream or disposable plastic gloves.
4 Thoroughly wash or shower as soon as possible after exposure to remove all traces of dust.

Maintenance

In order to function efficiently and with safety, woodworking machines and portable power tools require adequate maintenance. If this is not carried out, the result will be premature wear, breakdowns and damage, which could be very costly in terms of repairs, lost production time and missed delivery dates in addition to the potential source of danger it creates for all workshop personnel.

Table 30 **Common irritant timbers**

	Severity			Harmful effect	
	Highly irritant	Irritant	Mildly irritant	Respiratory irritation: coughing, sneezing, inflamed and running eyes and nose, nosebleeds and in severe cases breathing difficulties	Skin irritation: dermatitis, reddening of skin, itching, swelling, dry flaking skin and in severe cases blisters and weeping sores
Idigbo			*		*
Obeche			*	* .	
Western red cedar	*			*	*
Mahogany African	*				*
Keruing		*			*
Yew		*		*	*
Afrormosia		*			*
Agba			*		*
Iroko	*				*
Teak		*			*
Makore	*			*	
Rosewood		*			*

It is preferable to operate a planned maintenance programme rather than an unplanned emergency one. Planned maintenance is where all of the equipment is checked and serviced at, say, weekly intervals. This might consist of general cleaning, oiling, greasing and adjustment, the checking and replacing as required of worn strained or distorted parts. The main advantages of planned maintenance which is also known as preventative maintenance are:

The reduction in repair costs, as minor faults can be identified and remedied before they develop into major items.

Equipment lasts longer.

Increased production rates because there is less likelihood of equipment breakdowns.

During the maintenance inspection a note should be made of items which are worn due to normal wear and tear but which do not require immediate replacement. This is so that replacement parts may be obtained in advance and their fitting planned to be carried out at a convenient time. This may be the shut-down period, after normal work has finished or during a meal break, depending on the nature of the fault and its priority.

Unplanned or emergency only maintenance is where worn or damaged parts are only replaced when the equipment breaks down. This method is costly, dangerous and totally inefficient: the workshop simply muddles through from one breakdown to another.

Self-assessment questions

1 List *four* operations where the use of eye protection is statutory.

2 Electricity or compressed air may be used as the power source for powered hand tools. State *one* advantage and *one* disadvantage of using *each*.

3 List *five* safety points to be observed when using electrically powered hand tools.

4 Briefly state with the aid of a sketch the requirements of the Woodworking Machines Regulations 1974 applicable to a circular saw bench.

5 Sketch the position of the bridge guard when facing and edging a piece of 45 mm × 100 mm timber in consecutive operations.

6 List *three* main requirements relating to the floor around woodworking machines.

7 What do the Woodworking Machines Regulations state with regard to the temperature in work areas?

8 Name and sketch *two* cutting blocks that may be used on a spindle moulder.

9 List in production order the sequence of operations required to manufacture a curved head casement window with the aid of woodworking machines and portable power tools.

10 (a) Describe the personal safety hazards created by wood dust.
   (b) State the precautions that should be taken.

chapter 10

Joinery components

After reading this chapter the student should be able to:

1 State the principles involved in the following joinery components:
Doors
Windows
Panelling
Suspended ceilings
Seating
Fitments
Partitions
Lectern/litany desk
Stairs
Structural members

2 Identify the component parts of these various items.

3 Produce sketches to show typical working details of these various items.

4 State any Building Regulations that are relevant to a given item of joinery.

5 Select the most suitable detail or method of construction for a given job.

Doors

A door can be defined as a movable barrier used to cover an opening in a structure. Its main function is to allow access into a building and passage between the interior spaces. However, a door must be carefully designed and detailed so that it is capable of doing this while at the same time maintaining its other various performance requirements, such as weather protection, fire resistance, sound and thermal insulation, security, privacy, ease of operation and durability.

A door will rarely be expected to fulfil all of these performance requirements. In most situations doors are only expected to maintain a limited number of them. The priority given to each requirement will differ depending on the situation in hand.

Weather protection

This requirement applies to external doors. These may be exposed to wind, rain, snow, sunlight and the extremes of temperature and must provide the same degree of weather protection as the remainder of the building. Openings are the weak point in a building as far as weather protection is concerned. Therefore careful consideration of materials to be used, construction details, glazing and ironmongery is critical.

Fire resistance

Building elements that have a separating, compartment or other fire protection role must be able to contain a possible fire and provide protection to the side remote from the fire for a given period of time. Doors that permit passage through this element must provide the same degree of protection in order to ensure a safe means of escape for the building's occupants. Doors in industrial buildings may also be required to protect the contents of the area until the fire has been extinguished.

Sound and thermal insulation

In general as the size of the door is relatively small in relation to the surrounding wall area, doors are rarely designed specifically for these requirements. Although the use of draught stripping, sealed unit double glazing and solid rather than hollow construction can all be used to an advantage.

Security

Door security depends on the materials used, soundness of construction, selection of suitable ironmongery and positioning. Only external door security is normally required for domestic dwellings, although internal door security is often necessary for offices, shops and factories etc.

Privacy

Unglazed doors provide total privacy when closed and if the layout has been carefully designed the door can still provide this privacy when partly opened. For this reason it is normal for doors in domestic dwellings to swing into the room rather than the wall.

Glazed or partly glazed doors are used either to provide additional light through the doorway or provide through vision for safety purposes. Partial privacy may be obtained by the use of obscure glass where through vision is not required.

Ease of operation

A door's size, weight and position in a building will determine its method of operation, so correct selection of ironmongery is a most important design consideration.

Durability

A door, or any item of joinery for that matter, must be capable of giving satisfactory service, for a reasonable length of time, in the situation for which it was designed. In addition to the normal opening and closing, doors must also stand up to the occasional slamming and other misuse. Thus there is a need for sound, stable materials, rigid construction, suitable protection and again the selection and positioning of suitable ironmongery.

Door classification

Doors are classified by both their method of construction and method of operation.

Methods of door construction

The form of construction used to make a timber door may be listed under one of the four main groups. These are:

Panelled and glazed doors
Flush doors
Fire-check doors
Matchboarded doors

The quality of a door will obviously affect its useful life (length of time that it is able to give satisfactory service). The majority of doors are therefore graded as being of either an internal or external quality. In general internal doors have a finished thickness of either 35 mm or 40 mm, while the thickness of external doors is increased to 44 mm, in order to withstand the extra stresses and strains that they are subjected to. While the type of adhesive used in manufacture is a significant factor to be considered, in practice it is of less significance when using standard doors as most manufacturers use a synthetic adhesive for both grades. In addition, external doors should be preservative treated against fungal decay.

Panelled and glazed doors

The design and construction of panelled doors are very similar to those of glazed doors. They consist of a frame which has either a plough groove or rebate run around it to receive the panels or glazing. The framing members for these doors vary with the number and arrangements of the panels. They will consist of horizontal members and vertical members.

All horizontal members are called rails. They are also named according to their position in the door, such as top rail, middle rail, bottom rail, intermediate rail. The middle rail is also known as the lock rail and the upper intermediate rail is sometimes called a frieze rail.

The two outside vertical members are called stiles, while all intermediate vertical members are known as muntins.

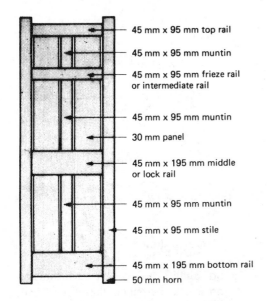

Figure 291   *A typical panelled door*

45 mm x 95 mm top rail

45 mm x 95 mm muntin

45 mm x 95 mm frieze rail
or intermediate rail

45 mm x 95 mm muntin

30 mm panel

45 mm x 195 mm middle
or lock rail

45 mm x 95 mm muntin

45 mm x 95 mm stile

45 mm x 195 mm bottom rail

50 mm horn

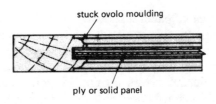

stuck ovolo moulding

ply or solid panel

Figure 292   *Panel detail (plough groove)*

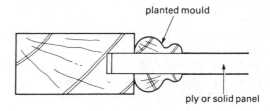

planted mould

ply or solid panel

Figure 293   *Panel detail (planted mould)*

Figure 291 shows a typical panelled door, with all its component parts named. The middle and bottom rails are of a deeper section as they serve to hold the door square and thus prevent sagging. Muntins are introduced in order to reduce the panel width, therefore reducing the unsightly effect of moisture movement and the likelihood of panel damage.

It is normal to leave at least a 50 mm horn on each end of the stiles. This serves two purposes:

1 It enables the joints to be securely wedged without fear of splitting out.
2 The horns protect the top and bottom edges of the door before it is hung.

Figure 292 shows a ply panel which is held in a plough groove that is run around the inside edge of the framing. Two ovolo mouldings are also worked around the inside edges of the framing for decorative purposes. They are known as stuck mouldings. The plough groove should be at least 2 mm deeper than the panel. This is to allow for any moisture movement (shrinkage and expansion).

Figure 293 again shows a solid or plywood panel which is held in a plough groove that is run around the inside edge of the framing. Here a planted or bed mould has been applied around the panel for decoration. This method avoids the need to scribe or mitre the shoulders of the rails which applies with stuck mouldings.

Planted moulds must not be allowed to restrict panel movement. Therefore they should be pinned to the framing and not the panel.

Figure 294 shows a timber panel which is tongued into a plough groove in the framing.

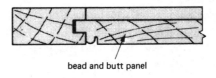

bead and butt panel

Figure 294   *Panel detail (bead butt)*

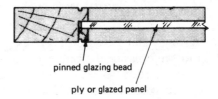

pinned glazing bead

ply or glazed panel

Figure 295   *Panel detail (planted bead)*

This type of panel is known as a bead butt panel because on its vertical edges a bead moulding is worked, while the horizontal edges remain square and butt up to the rails.

Figure 295 shows a thin plywood or glazed panel which is located in the rebate. It is held in position by planted beads, which are pinned into the framing. Where this type of door is used externally the planted beads should be placed on the inside of the door mainly for security reasons but also because when glazing beads are used externally water tends to get behind them. This makes both the beads and framing susceptible to decay.

For a neat finish planted beads or moulds should not finish flush with the framing.

Figure 296 shows a planted mould that is rebated over the framing in order to create an enhanced feature. This type is known as a bolection mould. In general bolection moulds are fitted on the face and planted bed moulds on the reverse, although in the case of top quality work bolection moulds could be used on both faces.

The bolection mould is fixed through the panel with screws. The holes for the screws should be slotted across the grain to permit panel movement without risk of splitting. The planted bed mould used on the other side to

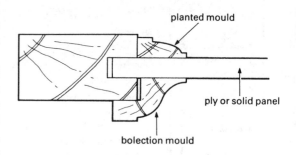

Figure 296   *Panel detail (bolection mould)*

cover the screws should be skew nailed to the framing.

In good quality joinery, refurbishment or restoration work, the panels themselves may be decorated by working various mouldings on one or both of their faces. The portion around the edge of a panel is called the margin and the centre portion is known as the field. The small flat section around the edge of the panel is to enable its correct location in the framing.

Figure 297 illustrates the section and part elevation of the main types of decorated panels.

(a)   Shows a raised or bevel raised panel.
(b)   Shows a raised and fielded panel, also known as bevel raised and fielded, where

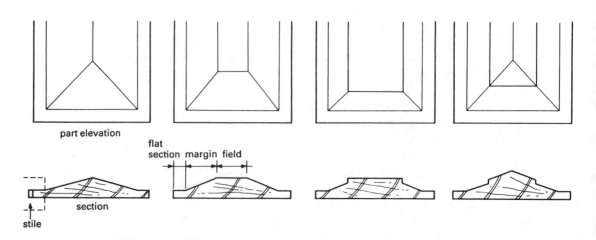

Figure 297   *Decorated panels*
(a)   *Raised*   (b)   *Raised and fielded*   (c)   *Raised, sunk and fielded*   (d)   *Raised, sunk and raised fielded*

the margin has been bevelled to raise the field.

(c) Shows a raised, sunk and fielded panel, also known as bevelled, raised sunk and fielded. In this case the margin has been sunk below the field to emphasize it.

(d) Shows a raised, sunk and raised fielded panel, also known as bevelled raised, sunk and bevelled raised fielded panel, where the field itself has been bevelled as a further enhanced detail.

Note: When bolection moulds or planted moulds are used to finish decorated panels, the small flat section around the panel edge must be extended to provide a flat surface that will accommodate the mouldings.

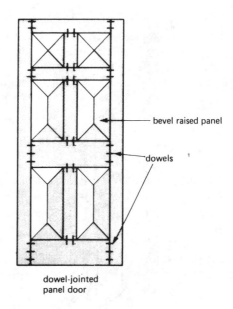

dowel-jointed panel door

Figure 298   *Dowel-jointed panel door*

Joints

Traditionally the mortise and tenon joint was used exclusively in the jointing of panelled and glazed doors, but today the majority of doors are mass produced and in order to reduce costs the dowelled joint is used extensively. The use of the dowelled joint reduces the cost of the door in three ways:

1   The length of each rail is reduced by at least 200 mm.
2   The jointing time is reduced as holes only have to be drilled to accommodate the dowel.
3   The assembly time is reduced as no wedging etc. has to be carried out.

Figure 298 shows a six-panel door which has been jointed using dowels. These dowels should be 16 mm × 150 mm and spaced approximately 50 mm centre to centre. The following is the minimum recommended number of dowels to be used for each joint.

Top rail to stile	two dowels
Middle rail to stile	three dowels
Bottom rail to stile	three dowels
Intermediate rail to stile	one dowel
Muntin to rail	two dowels

Figure 299 shows an exploded view of a dowelled joint between a top rail and stile. In

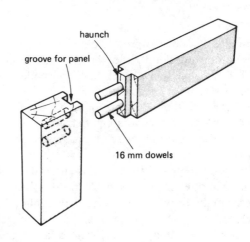

Figure 299   *Exploded view of a dowelled joint*

addition to the dowel, a haunch is incorporated into the joint. This ensures that the two members finish flush. Its use also overcomes any tendency for the rail to twist.

Note: A small groove should be cut along each dowel. This is to let any excess glue and trapped air escape when the joint is cramped up.

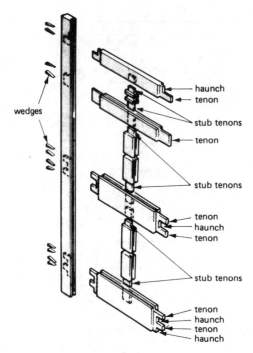

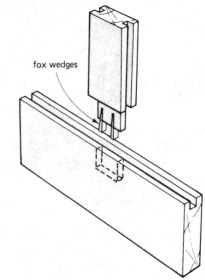

wedges

haunch
tenon

stub tenons

tenon

stub tenons

tenon
haunch
tenon

stub tenons

tenon
haunch
tenon
haunch

Figure 300   *Exploded view of joint details*

fox wedges

Figure 301   *Fox wedged joint*

Although the dowel joint is extensively used for mass-produced doors, the mortise and tenon joint is still used widely for purpose-made and high-quality door construction.

Figure 300 shows an exploded view of the framework for a typical six-panel door. Haunched mortise and tenons are used for the joints between the rails and stiles.

For joints between the muntins and rails, stub mortise and tenons are used. As these joints do not go right through the rails, they cannot be wedged in the normal way. Instead fox wedges are used (see Figure 301). These are small wedges which are inserted into the saw cuts in the tenon. When the joint is cramped up the wedge expands the tenon and causes it to grip securely in the mortise.

A traditional half-glazed door is shown in Figure 302. It is constructed with diminishing stiles, in order to provide the maximum area of glass and therefore admit into the building the maximum amount of daylight. This type of door is also known as gun stock stile door because its stiles are said to resemble the stock of a gun.

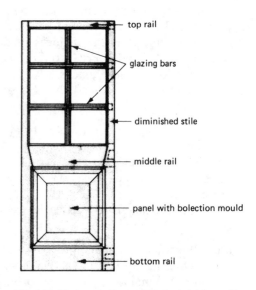

top rail

glazing bars

diminished stile

middle rail

panel with bolection mould

bottom rail

Figure 302   *Half-glazed door with diminishing stiles*

The mortise and tenon joints used in the construction of this door are indicated in the drawing.

Note: The middle rail has splayed shoulders to overcome the change in width of the stiles, above and below the middle rail. An exploded view of this joint is shown in Figure 303.

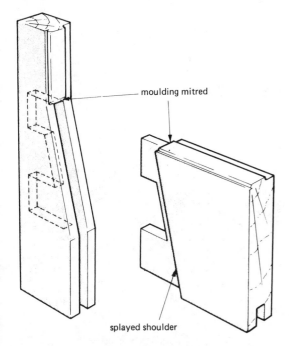

Figure 303   *Diminished stile joint detail*

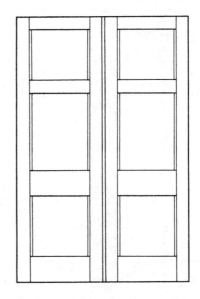

Figure 305   *Double margin door*

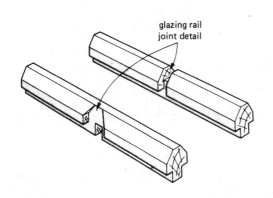

Figure 304   *Glazing rail or bar joint detail*

The top half of the door can either be fully glazed or subdivided with glazing bars as shown in Figure 302. When glazing bars are used they are normally stub tenoned into the stiles and rails. The joints between the glazing bars themselves could either be stub tenoned or halved and scribed. The halved and scribed method is shown in Figure 304. The bottom half of the door normally consists of a bevel raised sunk and fielded panel with planted bolection mouldings.

Double margin door

This is a pair of narrow doors joined together at their meeting stiles to make a single door, with the appearance of a pair (see Figure 305). It is used for very wide openings where a single door would give an ill-proportioned, awkward appearance and where each half of a double door would not allow easy pedestrian passage. The correct procedure for assembly is to glue and wedge the rails to the meeting stiles and then join together the two stiles with folding wedges. The panels are inserted from either side before assembling the outer stiles, cramping up and wedging. Figure 306 shows an exploded view of the framework for a typical double margin door. For additional stiffness, a flat metal bar is housed and screwed across the joint at both the top and bottom edges. Traditionally the top and bottom rails would be continuous across the whole door width, with the meeting stiles bridle jointed to them.

Figure 307 shows a section through the meeting stiles. It illustrates the positioning of the

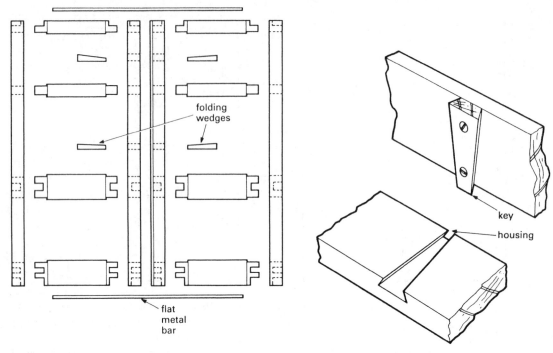

Figure 306   *Exploded view*

Figure 308   *Dovetail key*

Figure 307   *Meeting stile detail*

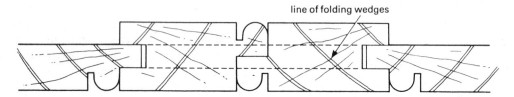

folding wedges. In addition, it shows that the stiles are rebated together and a stuck bead is used to break the joint between the stiles. Alternatively the two stiles can be tongued together with a loose tongue and the joint masked with either stuck or planted beads.

Double faced doors

In certain situations (particularly in prestigeous public buildings and stately homes etc.) adjacent rooms or corridors may be panelled in a different timber or to a different detail. In these cases it is necessary for the face of the door to match in timber and design the room or corridor in which it is situated. With flush veneered panelling all that is required is the application of different veneer. Where a framed panel door is required the solution is to use two thin doors, each about 28 mm thick, which are fitted to each other with dovetail keys to form a door that matches its respective location. The dovetail keys are screwed at intervals to the backs of the framing of one door and housed into the framing of the other (see Figure 308). The corresponding members (stiles, rails etc.) of each door face are paired, glued and keyed together before the

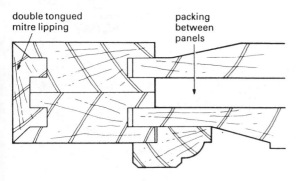

Figure 309   *Double-faced door finishing detail*

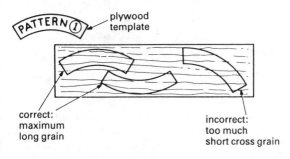

Figure 310   *Marking out curved members*

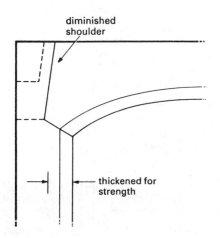

Figure 311   *Shaped rail joint detail*

door itself is assembled. After assembly the edges of the door must be finished with a veneer or mitred lipping (see Figure 309). The closing stile lipping should be matched to the room in which it opens, while the hanging stile should be matched to the other.

Curved rail doors

The main problem encountered with the construction of curved work is that of short graining. This causes a weakness in the member because of a marked tendency to sheer along the short grain. This risk can be reduced by taking care when marking out the member to ensure that there is as little short grain as possible (see Figure 310). The design of the joint is also important as this is often the area most affected. Figure 311 illustrates the joint between a shaped top rail and stile. It shows how the shoulder is diminished in order to thicken up the short grain section of the rail.

Figure 312 shows the elevation of a semi-circular headed door. The door head is formed in two parts. Traditionally hammer-headed joints would have been used (see Figure 313). A

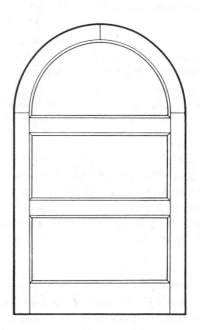

Figure 312   *Semi-circular headed door*

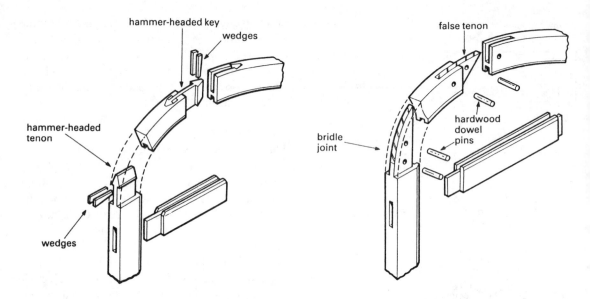

Figure 313 *Traditional joint details, semi-circular headed door*

Figure 314 *Alternative joint details*

double-ended hardwood hammer-headed key is used at the crown. The wedges secure the joint and draw the two parts together. A hammer-headed tenon is used to join the stile and curved head. This is the same as one end of the key except that it is formed on one end of the stile. An alternative method of jointing which reduces the amount of handwork is illustrated in Figure 314. This shows how the crown can be jointed using a false tenon insert and a bridle joint between the stile and rail. Both joints are secured using hardwood draw pins.

Note: Whichever method is used to construct the semi-circular headed door the immediate rail should be kept about 50 mm below the head/stile joint. This is in order to ensure sufficient strength and minimize the possibility of shearing along the short grain between the mortise and shoulder.

Louvred doors
The frame of this type of door is similar in construction to that of a panel door i.e. mortise and tenons or dowels are used to join the rails to the stiles. Traditionally louvres were only used

as a means of ventilation, but now their use is increasing because of their pleasing appearance.

When used externally, the louvre slats or blades are normally set at an angle of 45°. They should also project beyond the face of the framing for weathering purposes. Figure 315

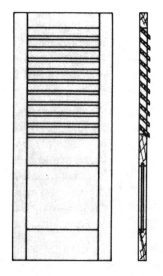

Figure 315 *Louvre door*

shows an elevation and section of an external half-louvred door.

There are two methods by which the projecting louvre slats can be jointed to the stiles. Figure 316 shows the first method where the stiles have been mortised to receive the tenons which have been formed on the ends of the louvred slats. Figure 317 shows the second method. Here the stiles have been through-housed to accommodate the full thickness of the louvre slats.

Note: In all cases the slats should have an overlap of 6 mm to prevent through vision.

Where louvre doors are used internally it is not necessary for the louvre slats to project beyond the face of the framing. The internal slats are normally set at an angle of 60° for two main reasons: more of the face of the slat is visible, adding to the decorative appearance, and fewer slats are required, giving a more economical door.

Figure 318 shows the method which is normally used for jointing the louvre slats of an internal door to the stiles. The stiles are stop-housed on a high speed router using a purpose-made jig. The housing must be cut to exactly the same size as the louvre slat, otherwise the slat will be a slack fit, or time will be wasted easing the housing to fit each individual slat.

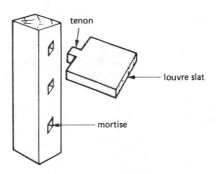

Figure 316 *Louvre slat joint detail (mortise and tenon)*

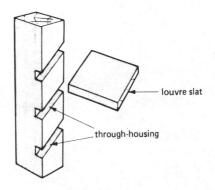

Figure 317 *Louvre slat joint detail (through housing)*

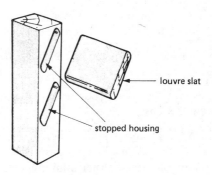

Figure 318 *Louvre slat joint detail (stopped housing)*

Door sets

Many manufacturers are now able to supply mass-produced door sets. These sets consist of a door frame or lining, door, architraves and ironmongery.

Figure 319 illustrates a horizontal and vertical section of a storey height door set showing the arrangement of members.

The doors are prehung on loose pin or lift-off hinges for easy door removal. The ironmongery, including locks and handles are factory fitted. Architraves are normally fixed on one side of the frame and loose pinned on the other. If required the door sets can be supplied completely predecorated (painted or polished).

The fixing of door sets should not be carried out until at least the second fixing stage. This is to avoid the possibility of any damage during the building process. The main advantage of using door sets is the considerable saving in time and labour on site.

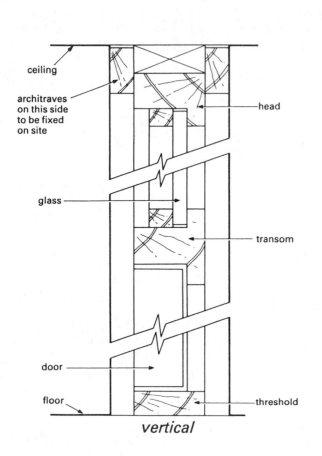

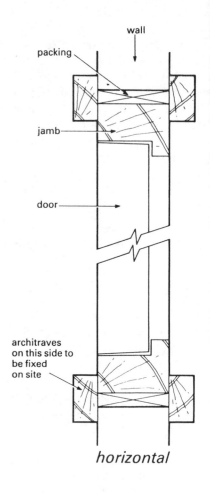

Figure 319   *Storey height door set*

Flush doors

These are used in modern buildings for the following two reasons:

1 They can be mass produced at a comparatively low cost.
2 They provide a plain, dust-free surface, which is easy to clean and decorate.

Flush doors consist of either a hollow or a solid core which is faced with sheets of hardboard or plywood.

Note: An exterior grade (WBP) plywood or oil-tempered hardboard should be used for the facings of external doors.

Flush doors are produced in two thicknesses: 35 mm for internal use and 44 mm for external use, although some manufacturers are now producing doors which have a thickness of 40 mm.

Hollow core

Hollow core doors are normally the cheapest type of flush door to produce and purchase. There are many ways in which the hollow core can be made. The two main methods are the skeleton core or the lattice core.

Both types of hollow core have the same disadvantage: there is a tendency for the facing to deflect between the compartments of the core. This produces a ripple effect which is especially noticeable when the facings are finished with a gloss coating such as paint or varnish.

Note: Ventilation holes or grooves must be incorporated between each compartment. This is to prevent air becoming trapped in the compartment when the door is assembled. If this were not done the facings would have a tendency to bulge.

Figure 320 shows a skeleton core door. It consists of 28 mm × 70 mm stiles and top, bottom and middle rails; and 20 mm × 28 mm intermediate rails are used to complete the framework.

Very simple joints can be used in this type of construction, as its main strength is obtained by firmly gluing the facings to the framework. The rails are usually either tongued into a groove in the stiles or butt jointed and fixed with staples or corrugated fasteners.

Figure 321 shows a lattice core door. It consists of 28 mm × 30 mm framework which is simply stapled together. The core is made from narrow strips of hardboard which are simply slot jointed to produce the lattice. As with other types of flush door construction the strength of the door is obtained by firmly gluing the facings to both the framework and the core.

Note: A lock block should be provided in all hollow core doors to accommodate a mortise lock or latch. The block also serves to provide a fixing for the lock furniture. The position of the lock block is normally indicated on the edge of the door.

Solid core

Solid core flush doors are considered to be of a better quality than hollow flush doors. There are three main reasons for this view:

1 Their facing remains flat, so they have no tendency to produce the ripple effect.
2 Their increased rigidity.
3 Their increased sound insulation.

Figure 322 shows a laminated core door. It consists of 25 mm strips which are firmly glued together along with the two plywood facings.

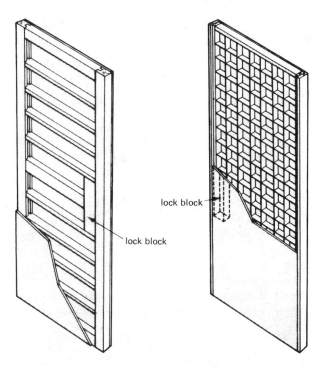

lock block

lock block

Figure 320 *Skeleton core*

Figure 321 *Lattice core*

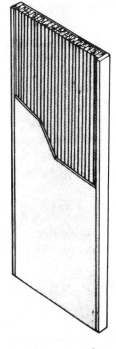

Figure 322 *Laminated core*

Note: The strips should be laid alternately in order to balance any stresses.

Figure 323 shows a flaxboard core door. A door with this type of core is not considered to be a true solid core flush door and is only slightly more expensive to produce than the hollow core. It consists of the flaxboard core which is surrounded by a simple 30 mm framework. The framework is normally stapled together at the corners. The door is completed by gluing the facings to either side.

Lippings

These are narrow strips of timber which are fixed along the edges of better quality flush doors. Their purpose is to mask the edges of the facings and provide a neat finish to the door. External doors should have lippings fixed to all four edges for increased weather protection.

Figure 324 shows a plain lipping which is used for internal doors.

Figure 325 shows a lipping which is tongued into the edge of the door. It is used for both

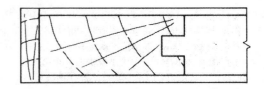

Figure 324   *Flush lipping*

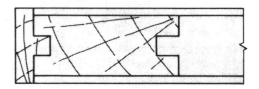

Figure 325   *Tongued lipping*

internal and external doors. It is more expensive than plain lippings as the door has to be assembled, then passed through a spindle moulder a number of times to produce the groove for the lipping.

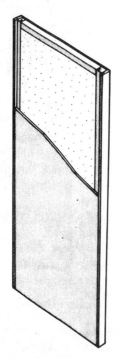

Figure 323   *Flaxboard core*

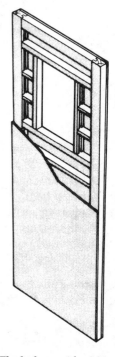

Figure 326   *Flush door with vision panel*

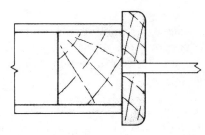

Note: Lipping should be glued in position and not fixed with panel pins.

Vision panels

When vision panels are required in flush doors the opening should be framed out as shown in Figure 326. Additional blocking out pieces can be used where other shaped vision panels are required (see Figure 327). This framing and blocking is normally done during the construction of the door, although it is possible to form the opening at a later stage. The glass is held in place by glazing beads.

Figure 328 *Internal glazing beads*

Figure 328 shows internal glazing beads for an internal door. Figure 329 shows rebated glazing beads. These are suitable for external doors as they provide a more weather-resistant finish.

Figure 330 shows a better method for fixing glazing into external flush doors. It provides far greater security than the previous method.

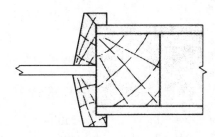

Figure 329 *Internal or external glazing beads*

Note: Glazing beads for doors are normally fixed using countersunk brass screws and recessed cups. This is to enable the glazing beads to

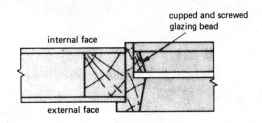

Figure 330 *Alternative external flush door glazing detail*

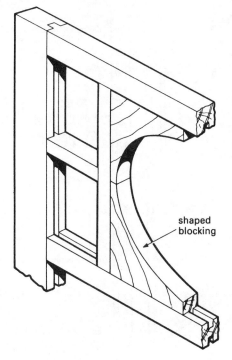

Figure 327 *Blocking for circular vision panel*

be easily removed in the event of the glass needing replacement.

Hinges

Each door must be of a suitable construction to receive hinges in the normal position. Where only one edge of the door is suitable to receive hinges this must be indicated on the edge of the door.

Locks

Each door must be of a suitable construction to receive a mortise lock in the normal position. Where the lock can only be fitted in a certain position, e.g. in the lock block, this position must be indicated on the edge of the door.

Letter plates

Each door for exterior use must be of a suitable construction to receive a letter plate in the normal position.

Fire resisting doors

The main function of this type of door is to act as a barrier to a possible fire by providing the same degree of protection as the element in which it is located. They should prevent the passage of smoke, hot gases and flames for a specified period of time. This period of time will vary depending on the relevant statutory regulations and the location of the door. For instance, it is significant if the door is providing access through a separating or compartment wall, opening on to a protective shaft, or separating a hazard (attached garage, boiler house etc.). Therefore, consultation with the Local Authority's Fire Prevention Officer is advised in order to determine their specific requirements at the design stage.

As stated previously, the fire resistance of a building element and thus the performance of a fire resisting door can be defined by reference to the following criteria:

Stability	Resistance to the collapse of the door
Integrity	Resistance to the passage of flames or hot gases to the unexposed face
Insulation	Resistance to the excessive rise in temperature of the unexposed face

All fire doors can be called 'fire resisting doors', although they should be prefixed by their stability and integrity rating respectively. Thus a 60/45 fire resisting door has a minimum 60 minutes stability rating and a 45 minutes integrity rating.

Note: Although the insulation resistance of a door may be recorded during a fire test, this is not a normal requirement.

The more commonly used terms for fire doors are 'fire check' and 'fire resisting'. 'Fire check' is used to signify doors with a reduced integrity.

Table 31 **Requirements of fire doors**

Door type	Stability	Integrity
Half hour fire check	30	20
Half hour fire resisting	30	30
One hour fire check	60	45
One hour fire resisting	60	60

Table 31 lists the minimum requirements of fire check and resisting doors.

Note: For fire resisting requirements in excess of one hour metal doors are normally specified.

Fire check doors are usually constructed in accordance with BS 459 Part 3 which gives details of half hour and one hour rated doors.

Half hour construction (Figure 331)

Size

The standard widths are 838 mm or 914 mm, with a standard height of 1981 mm. The finished

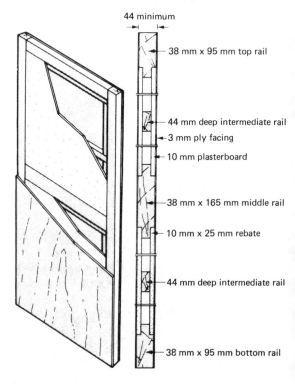

44 minimum

38 mm x 95 mm top rail

44 mm deep intermediate rail

3 mm ply facing

10 mm plasterboard

38 mm x 165 mm middle rail

10 mm x 25 mm rebate

44 mm deep intermediate rail

38 mm x 95 mm bottom rail

Figure 331 *Half hour fire-check door*

thickness of the door should not be less than 44 mm.

Framing

The stiles and top and bottom rails should not be less than 38 mm × 95 mm. The minimum size of the middle rail should be 38 mm × 165 mm.

Note: The stiles, top, bottom and middle rails must have a 10 mm × 25 mm rebate on both sides to receive the protective plasterboard infill.

Protective infill

This is 10 mm plasterboard which must be fixed in the rebate of the framing at 225 mm centres.

Facing

This is 3 mm plywood or hardboard which must be fixed with glue over the whole area of the door face. No metal fasteners should be used when fixing the facings.

Lippings

When used they can be fixed with glue to one or both of the stiles or all four edges of the door. They can either be tongued into the framing or fit flush to it. No metal fasteners must be used when fixing the lippings.

Frame

This must have a 25 mm deep rebate to receive the door. Where this is a planted stop it must be fixed with 38 mm No. 8 countersunk screws spaced 75 mm from each end of the stop and at intervals of not more than 600 mm (see Figure 332).

One hour construction (Figure 333)

Size

This is the same as for the half hour construction, except that the finished thickness of the door shall be not less than 54 mm.

Framing

This is the same as for the half hour construction.

Protective infill

10 mm plasterboard is used in the same way as for the half hour construction.

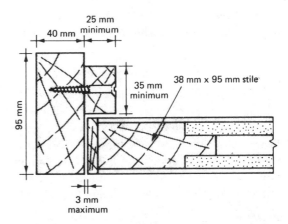

Figure 332 *Frame for half hour fire-check door*

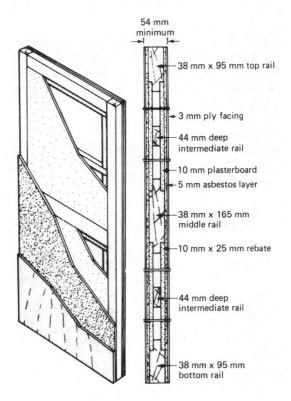

Figure 333 *One hour fire-check door*

Asbestos layer

An asbestos layer must be incorporated under the facing. It must be not less than 4.5 mm thick and must be fixed with glue over the whole area of the door face. No metal fasteners should be used when fixing the asbestos layer.

Facing
This is 3 mm hardboard or plywood as for the half hour construction.

Lipping
Doors may be used with or without a lipping. Where they are used, they must be tongued to the edges of the door and glued. The lipping must be not more than 9 mm thick. No metal fixings should be used when fixing the lippings.

Frame
This is the same as for half hour construction except that the rebate must be formed from the solid. No planted stops are permitted (see Figure 334).

Impregnation
The frame must be pressure impregnated with a 15–18 per cent solution of monoammonium phosphate in water. This is a fire-inhibiting solution.

External fire doors
For external doors, whether of half hour or one hour construction, the following conditions also apply to facing, adhesives and lippings.

Facing
The plywood or hardboard must be of an exterior quality.

Adhesives
The construction of the door must be carried out using a synthetic resin adhesive.

Lippings
Lippings for external doors must continue around all four edges.

Hanging fire-check doors
When hanging fire-check doors a 3 mm maximum joint should be used between the frame and the door. One pair of hinges will suffice for the half hour type door, while the one hour type door requires one and a half pairs.

   In order to fulfil their function, fire-check doors must be kept closed. Therefore, self-closing springs or similar fittings must be used.

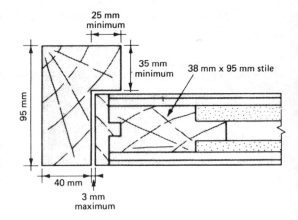

Figure 334   *Frame for one hour fire-check door*

Although the British Standard only specifies two types of timber fire door, any door and frame, however constructed, may be called a fire door if one of the following conditions is fulfilled:

It has been proved by tests in accordance with BS 476 Part 1 *Fire Tests on Building Materials and Structures* before 31 August 1973 to give a similar performance to that of the half hour or one hour fire check doors specified in the standard.

It has been tested to the more rigorous BS 476 Part 8 and issued with a test report or certificate stating the time the door assembly (door, frame, ironmongery and surrounding wall) satisfied the requirements of stability and integrity.

Where purpose-made fire doors are concerned it is clearly advantageous to use, where possible, either the standard designs or proven proprietary products, although in certain situations it may be necessary to design and construct the one-off or limited run special. In these situations it is possible to submit the design to a reputable test laboratory for an assessment of its probable fire resistance performance. This assessment is normally accepted in place of a fire resistance test report or certificate.

   Figure 335 illustrates a solid hardwood door that is constructed in the traditional way. It consists of stiles, rails, muntin and panel which have a minimum finished thickness of 44 mm. If this type of door were constructed from a dense hardwood (oak, teak etc.) and hung in a suitable hardwood frame with 25 mm stops it should at least give half hour resistance.

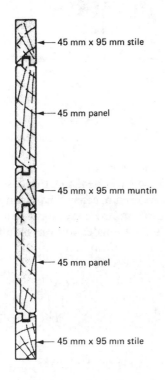

Figure 335 *Solid hardwood fire-check door*

Vision panels

Vision panels in fire doors have several advantages. In general use they enable a person to see if the passage is clear on the other side. In fire use they provide a warning of fire before the door is opened.

Figure 336 shows a number of suitable fire door glazing details. Doors with a 30/20 rating may use untreated softwood beads with the glass bedded in intumescent putty, although it is safer also to coat the bead with intumescent paint. Two coats of intumescent paint or capping with a metal angle is required for 30/30 doors.

Non-combustible glazing systems are recommended for one hour fire resisting doors, as timber beads are not normally suitable.

A maximum glazed area of 1.2 m^2 for half hour and 0.5 m^2 for one hour timber fire doors is recommended, when using either 6 mm thick wired glass or a proprietary plain fire resisting glass, although any glazing system can exceed these sizes provided it has been proved suitable by tests.

Door seals

The weak point in fire door construction is the joint between the door and frame. This is where the fire and smoke will penetrate first. As stated previously, intumescent strips may be fitted around the door opening. When activated by heat in the early stages of a fire these strips

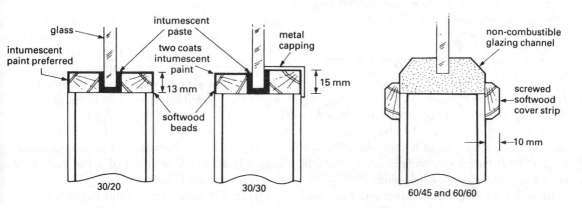

Figure 336 *Fire door glazing details*

expand, sealing the joint and prolonging the door's integrity.

Although the intumescent strip is designed to seal the joint around the door, it must not have a cramping action that might prevent the door being opened for escape or rescue purposes.

Figure 337 shows an intumescent seal that is contained in an aluminium channel. As the channel is a good conductor it has the advantage of assisting the activation of the strip.

Some doors are required to have a cool smoke control function, that is, they are intended to prevent the passage of cool smoke. Intumescent strips are of little use for this as they are not activated until a temperature of about 200 °C is reached.

Frames with 25 mm door stops provide some degree of smoke control but good quality draft seals give far greater resistance. Figure 338 details an aluminium channel intumescent seal that incorporates a neoprene rubber blade to act as a cool smoke seal, in addition to a draft seal in normal use. This strip is suitable for both single and double action doors.

Matchboarded doors

This group of doors involves the simplest form of construction. They are suitable for use both internally and externally, although they are mainly used externally for gates, sheds and industrial buildings.

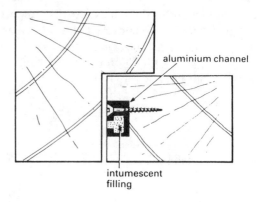

Figure 337 *Intumescent seal*

The basic type of door consists of matchboarding, which is held together by ledges. This type is little used because it has a tendency to sag and distort on the side opposite the hinges (Figure 339). In order to overcome this, braces are usually incorporated in the construction (Figure 340). The use of braces greatly increases the rigidity of the door. The bottom ends of the braces should always point towards the hinged edge of the door in order to provide the required support. Where these doors are used externally, the top edge of the ledges should be weathered to stop the accumulation of rainwater and moisture.

Three ledges are used to hold the match-

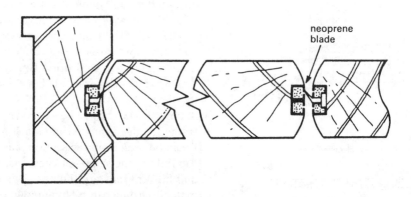

Figure 338 *Combined intumescent and smoke seals*

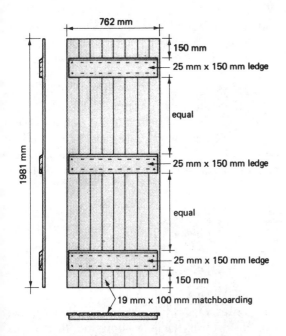

Figure 339   *Ledged and matchboarded door*

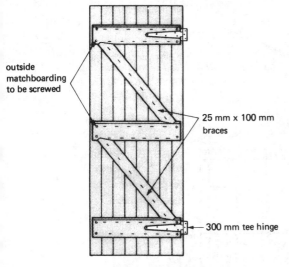

Figure 340   *Ledged, braced and matchboarded door*

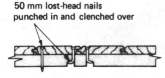

Figure 341   *Clenching over*

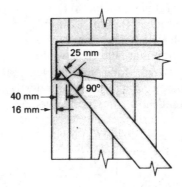

Figure 342   *Joint detail between ledges and braces*

boarding together. The outside pieces should be fixed with screws, while the remaining lengths of matchboarding are nailed to the ledges. Lost-head nails 6 mm longer than the thickness of the door are used for this purpose. The nails should be punched in and clenched over. Clenching over simply means bending the protruding part of the nails over and punching the ends below the surface (see Figure 341).

The two braces, when used, are also fixed with losthead nails which are clenched over. The joint detail between the ledges and braces is shown in Figure 342.

Framed, ledged, braced and matchboarded doors
These are an improvement on the ledged, braced and matchboarded door, as they include stiles which are jointed to the top, bottom and middle rails with mortise and tenons.

The use of the framework increases the door's strength, and resists any tendency which the door might have to distort. Braces are optional when the door is framed, but their use further increases the door's strength.

Figure 343 shows the rear view of a typical framed, ledged, braced and matchboarded door. It can be seen from the section that the stiles and top rail are the same thickness, while the middle and bottom rails are thinner. This is so that the matchboarding can be tongued into the top rail, over the face of the middle and bottom rails, and run to the bottom of the door. As the middle and bottom rails are thinner than the stiles, bare-faced tenons (tenons with only one shoulder) must be used. This joint is shown in Figure 344. These joints are normally wedged, although for extra strength draw pins can be used.

Large garage, warehouse and industrial doors are often made using the framed, ledged, braced and matchboarded principles. This is because this type of door is ideal in situations where strength is more important than appearance. A pair of doors suitable for a garage are shown in Figure 345. The portion of the door which is above the middle rail is normally glazed to admit a certain amount of light into the building. The top, middle and glazing rails must be rebated in order to receive the panes of glass. These panes are held in the rebate by glazing spigs and putty.

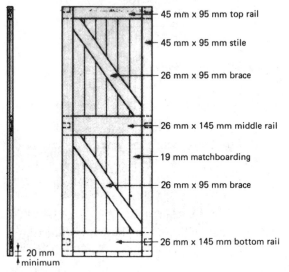

45 mm x 95 mm top rail

45 mm x 95 mm stile

26 mm x 95 mm brace

26 mm x 145 mm middle rail

19 mm matchboarding

26 mm x 95 mm brace

26 mm x 145 mm bottom rail

20 mm minimum

Figure 343 *Framed, ledged, braced and matchboarded door*

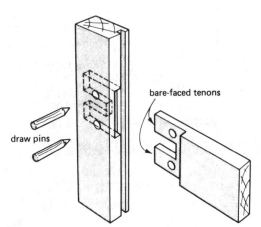

bare-faced tenons

draw pins

Figure 344 *Bare-faced tenons joint detail*

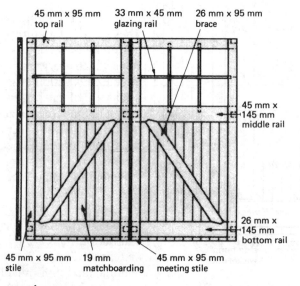

45 mm x 95 mm top rail

33 mm x 45 mm glazing rail

26 mm x 95 mm brace

45 mm x 145 mm middle rail

26 mm x 145 mm bottom rail

45 mm x 95 mm stile

19 mm matchboarding

45 mm x 95 mm meeting stile

Figure 345 *Part glazed garage doors*

Note: In this case the middle rail is the same thickness as the stiles. Therefore bare-faced tenons are only used on the bottom rail.

The joint normally used at the intersections of the glazing rails is scribed cross-halving. Another joint which can be used is a stub tenon, but as the glazing rails are of a small section the joint is not as strong as the halving.

Figure 346 shows a section through the meeting stiles of a pair of garage doors. Figure 346 also shows how the matchboarding may be jointed to the stiles or rails. An alternative detail is shown in Figure 347.

Very large industrial doors are normally made to slide rather than be side hung, because of their increased tendency to sag as weight and size are increased.

Figure 348 shows a part inside and part outside elevation of a pair of large industrial doors. A small side-hung wicket door has been included to enable personal access without the need to open the main doors, although this is not common to all such doors. The main difference in the construction of these large doors is the

Figure 346 *Rebated meeting stiles*

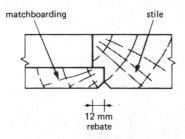

Figure 347 *Alternative matchboarding to stile detail*

increased sectional size of the members. In addition, since they are designed to slide, they are cross-braced to resist the tendency to distort when sliding in either direction.

A pair of external gothic design doors often made of oak and used in churches is illustrated in Figure 349. The internal and external

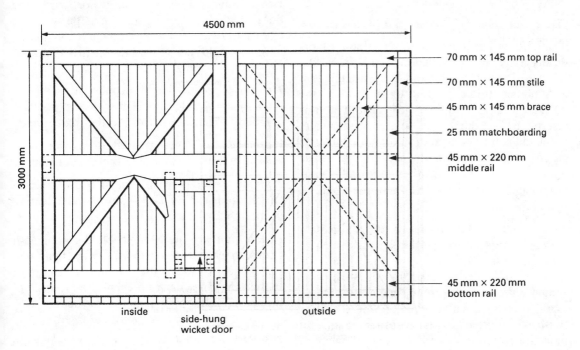

Figure 348 *Industrial sliding doors*

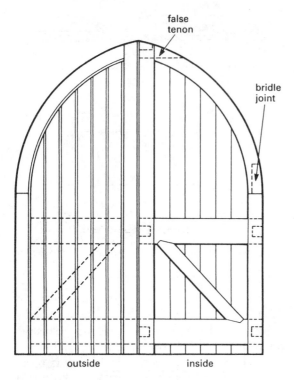

Figure 349 *Gothic head doors*

elevations of each leaf are indicated in the one illustration. The construction of these doors differs only in the shaped head from the standard framed, ledged and braced details.

A pinned bridle joint is used between the outside stile and top rail. A false tenon is inserted to join the top rail to the meeting stile, as the rail's short grain at this point discounts the use of a normal tenon. In addition, the false tenon considerably strengthens the rail's short grain and minimizes the possibility of it shearing.

Note: Before the assembly of all match-boarded doors, all concealed surfaces, such as the tongues and grooves of the matchboarding, back of rails, ledges and braces should be coated either with a priming paint for painted work, or with a suitable sealer where a clear finish is required. This is in order to prevent moisture penetration and subsequent decay of the timber.

Methods of operation
A door's method of operation will be determined by its location, construction and desired performance requirements. Figure 350 illustrates various methods of door operation.

Swinging
This method is the most suitable for pedestrian use and also the most effective for weather protection, fire resistance, sound and thermal insulation.

The most common means of swinging a door is to side hinge it, although top-hung pivots are more effective where constant use is expected e.g. shops and office reception areas etc. The hands of doors are required to enable the correct items of ironmongery to be selected. To determine the hand of a door, it must be viewed from the hinge knuckle side; if they are on the left, the door is left handed, whereas if they are on the right, the door is right handed. They may also be defined as either anti-clockwise or clockwise closing (see Figure 351).

Figure 352 illustrates a range of hinges which are readily available in a variety of materials. Brass hinges should be used for hardwood doors. Steel hinges should not be used in external locations and aluminium or plastic hinges should not be used for fire check or fire-resistant doors.

The butt hinge is suitable for most applications. As a general rule the leaf with the greatest number of knuckles is fixed to the door frame.

Washered butt hinges are used for heavier doors to reduce knuckle wear and prevent squeaking.

Parliament hinges have extended knuckles to enable doors to fold back against a wall, clearing deep architraves etc.

Rising butts are designed to lift the door as it opens to clear any obstruction e.g. mats and rugs. They also give the door some degree of self-closing. In order to prevent the top edge of the door fouling the frame as the door closes, the top edge of the door must be eased.

Double and single action spring hinges are designed to make a door self-closing. Their large

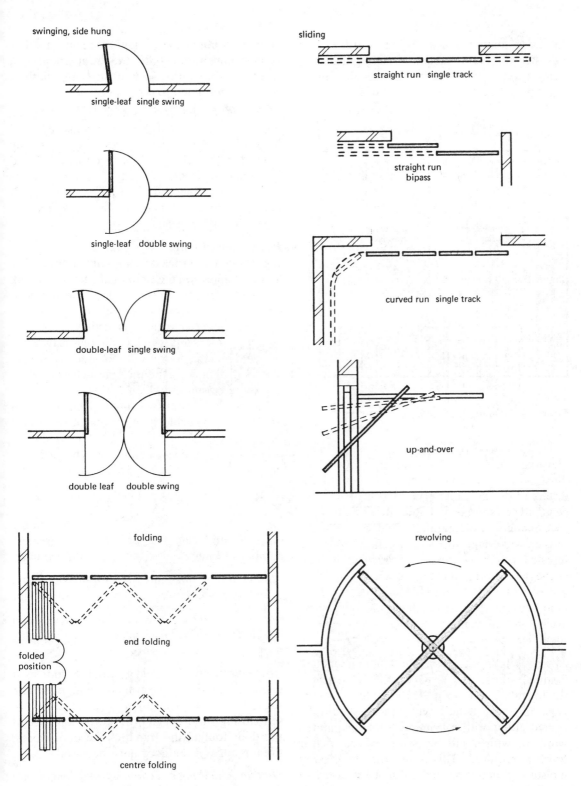

swinging, side hung

single-leaf single swing

single-leaf double swing

double-leaf single swing

double leaf double swing

sliding

straight run single track

straight run bipass

curved run single track

up-and-over

folding

end folding

folded position

centre folding

revolving

Figure 350 *Methods of door operation*

knuckles contain helical springs which can be adjusted to give the required closing action by using a tommy bar and moving the small pin at the top of the knuckles into a different hole.

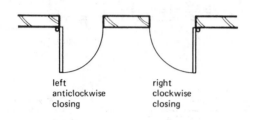

left
anticlockwise
closing

right
clockwise
closing

Figure 351 *Typical handing diagram*

Where double-action hinges are used, they should not be cut into the door frame but screwed to a planted section the same width as the door and fixed to the frame.

Hawgood hinges are another type of spring hinge and are suitable for industrial and heavy-duty double-swing doors. The spring housed in the cylinder is mortised and recessed into the door frame, while the moving shoe fits around both sides of the door. A twin-spring Hawgood hinge is available for use as the top hinge of very heavyweight doors.

Positioning of hinges
Lightweight internal doors require one pair of 75 mm hinges while glazed, half hour fire-check

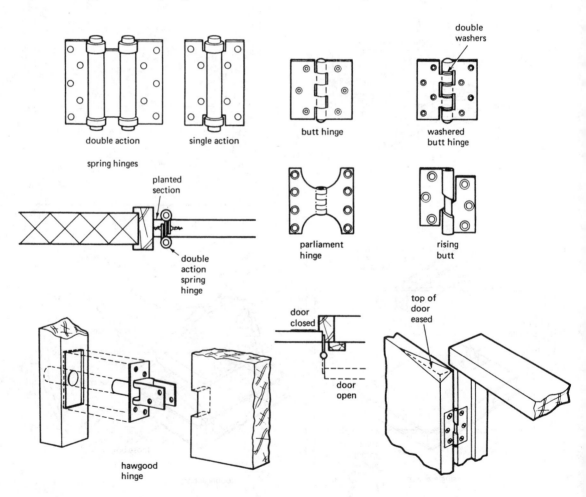

double action   single action

spring hinges

butt hinge

double
washers

washered
butt hinge

planted
section

double
action
spring
hinge

parliament
hinge

rising
butt

door
closed

top of
door
eased

door
open

hawgood
hinge

Figure 352 *Range of hinges*

and other heavyweight doors need one pair of 100 mm hinges. All external doors and one hour fire-check doors require one and a half pairs of 100 mm hinges.

Figure 353 illustrates the standard hinge positions for flush doors although on glazed and panelled doors the tops of the hinges are often fixed in line with the rails to produce a more balanced effect.

Pivoted floor spring

Pivoted floor springs are the best method of swinging and controlling both single and double-action doors, although their use is restricted mainly to shops and offices etc. because of their expense.

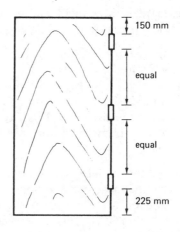

Figure 353   *Hinge positions for flush doors*

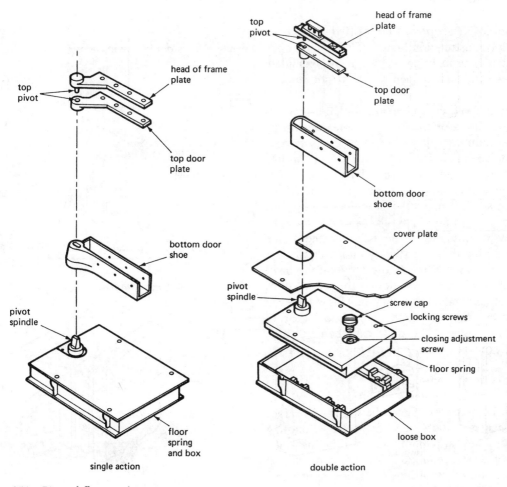

Figure 354   *Pivoted floor springs*

Figure 354 illustrates single and double floor springs. Both consist of:

1 A spring contained within a metal box which is bedded into the floor screed.
2 A shoe which is fixed to the bottom of the door and locates over the pivot spindle.
3 A two part top pivot which is fixed to the head of the frame and top of the door respectively.

It is essential for the later smooth operation of the door that the loose box and floor spring are set into the floor at the correct position to the frame (see Figure 355). This is determined by the finished thickness of the door plus an allowance between the door in its opening position and the frame of between 3 mm and 6 mm.

The closing action of a door fitted with a floor spring is illustrated in Figure 356. A stand open position, normally at 90°, can be included, although the stand open device is not suitable for fire doors.

The delayed closing action over the first few degrees can delay the closing of the door for up to one minute before it reverts to its normal closing speed. It is suitable for doors through which goods and trolleys etc. have to pass. The closing action may be varied by turning the closing adjustment screw in the floor spring. The single action doors may be removed from the frame by unscrewing the head of the frame plate, tilting the door slightly outwards to clear the frame and lifting it off the bottom pivot spindle. Double-action doors are removed by first retracting the top pivot pin. This is achieved by turning the adjustment screw in the head of the frame plate. The door can then be tilted slightly outwards and lifted off the bottom pivot.

Door closers (Figure 357)
These are mainly used in offices, shops and industrial premises to give their normally larger and heavier doors a controlled self-closing action. They also hold the door in the open position when required. The speed of closing may be altered by turning the adjustment screw which is normally under the main cover. Certain

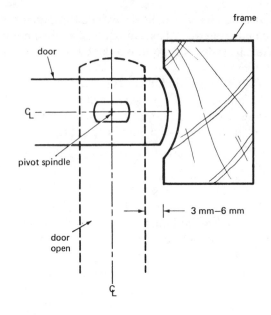

Figure 355   *Floor spring loose box*

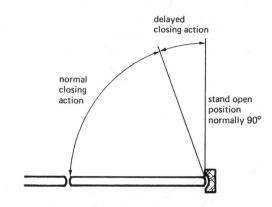

Figure 356   *Action of door with floor spring*

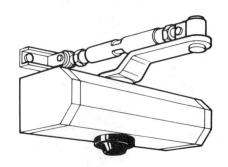

Figure 357   *Overhead door closer*

types of closer are fitted with a temperature-sensitive device that automatically closes the door from the held-open position in the event of a fire.

Others are available with:

1 A delayed closing action the same as floor springs
2 A snap action over the last few degrees of travel to ensure the door closes fully into the latch
3 A back check action, which controls the last few degrees of opening travel, thus preventing the door from slamming into a return wall adjacent to the opening

Figure 358 shows another type of spring door closer which is concealed when the door is closed. The cylinder which contains the spring is mortised into the edge of the door and the plate recessed flush. The anchor plate is recessed in and screwed to the frame. Adjustment to the closing action is achieved by inserting the metal plate near the cylinder plate to hold the chain, unscrewing the anchor plate and turning it either clockwise to speed the action or anti-clockwise to slow the closing action.

The hydraulic door check and holder shown in Figure 359 can be used in conjunction with door closers or spring hinges to control the last few degrees of closing travel. This prevents slamming and holds the door firmly closed against strong winds.

In order to ensure that self-closing double doors with rebated stiles close in the correct sequence, a door selector must be fitted (see Figure 360).

Locks and latches
Cylinder rim latches are mainly used for entrance doors to domestic property but, as they

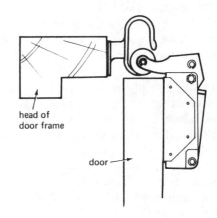

Figure 359 *Hydraulic door check and holder*

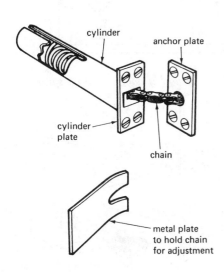

Figure 358 *Concealed door closer*

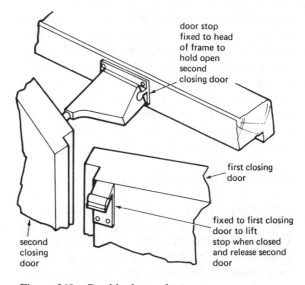

Figure 360 *Double-door selector*

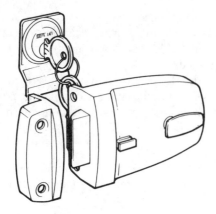

Figure 361   *Cylinder rim latch*

are only a latch, provide little security on their own. When fitted, the door can be opened from the outside with the use of a key and from the inside by turning the handle. Some types have a double locking facility which improves its security (see Figure 361).

Mortise deadlock provides a straightforward key-operated locking action and is often used to provide additional security on entrance doors where cylinder rim latches are fitted. They are also used on doors where simple security is required, e.g. storerooms (see Figure 362).

Mortise latch is used mainly for internal doors that do not require locking. The latch which holds the door in the closed position can be operated from either side of the door by turning the handle (see Figure 363).

Mortise lock/latch is available in horizontal and vertical types (Figure 364). The horizontal type

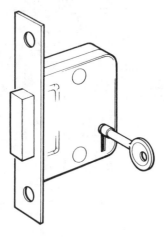

Figure 362   *Mortise deadlock*

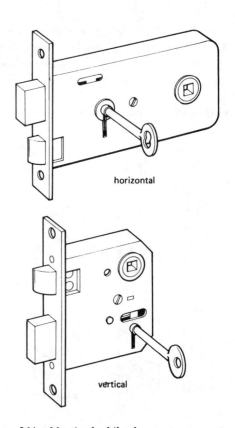

horizontal

vertical

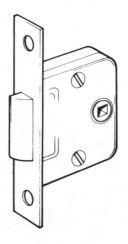

Figure 363   *Mortise latch*

Figure 364   *Mortise lock/latches*

is little used nowadays because of its length, which means that it can only be fitted to substantial doors. The vertical type is the more modern type and can be fitted to most types of doors. It is often known as a narrow stile lock/latch.

Both types can be used for a wide range of general purpose doors in various locations. They are, in essence, a combination of the mortise deadlock and the mortise latch.

Rebated mortise lock/latch should be used when fixing a lock/latch in double doors that have rebated stiles. The front end of this lock is cranked to fit the rebate on the stiles (see Figure 365).

Knobset consists of a small mortise latch and a pair of knob handles that can be locked with a key, so that it can be used as a lock/latch in most situations both internally and externally. Knobsets can also be obtained without the lock in the knob for use as a latch only (see Figure 366).

Knob furniture is for use with the horizontal mortise lock/latch. It should not be used with the vertical as hand injuries will result (see Figure 367).

Keyhole escutcheon plates are used to provide a neat finish to the keyhole of both deadlocks and horizontal mortise lock/latches (see Figure 368).

Lever furniture is available in a wide range of patterns, for use with mortise latches and mortise lock/latches (see Figure 369).

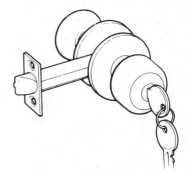

Figure 366   *Knobset*

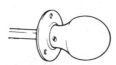

Figure 367   *Knob furniture*

Figure 368   *Escutcheon plate*

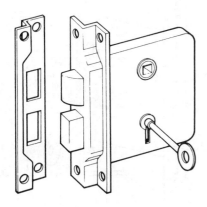

Figure 365   *Rebated mortise lock/latch*

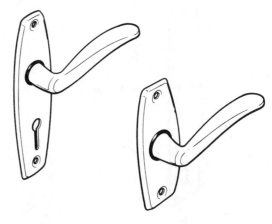

Figure 369   *Lever furniture*

Barrel bolts are used on external doors and gates to lock them from the inside. Two bolts are normally used, one at the top of the door and the other at the bottom (see Figure 370).

Flush bolt is flush fitting and therefore requires recessing into the timber. It is used for better quality work on the inside of external doors to provide additional security and also on double doors and French windows to bolt one door in the closed position. Two bolts are normally used, one at the top of the door and the other at the bottom (see Figure 371).

Security chains can be fixed on front entrance doors, the slide to the door and the chain to the frame. When the chain is inserted into the slide, the door will only open a limited amount until the identity of the caller is checked (see Figure 372).

Door holders are foot-operated and hold doors and gates in the open position. They are particularly useful for holding side-hung garage doors open, while driving into or out of the garage (see Figure 373).

Panic bolts are used on the inside of emergency exit doors to bolt them closed. Pressure applied to the push bar will disengage the bolts. They can be fitted with an audible alarm to deter unauthorized use (see Figure 374).

Figure 375 illustrates the recommended fixing height for various items.

Figure 370   *Barrel bolt*

Figure 371   *Flush bolt*

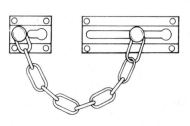

Figure 372   *Security chain*

Figure 373
Door holder

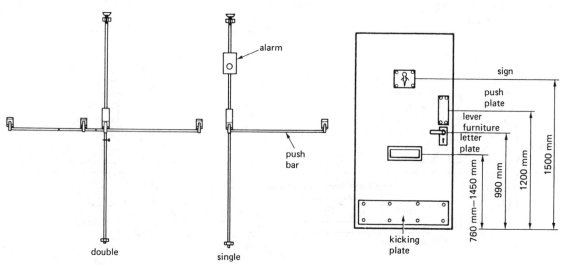

double

single

Figure 374   *Panic bolts*

Figure 375   *Fixing heights*

Sliding

Sliding doors may be used either to economize on space where it is not possible to swing a door or where large openings are required that would be difficult to close with swinging doors.

Various types of sliding gear are available, for straight sliding, by-passing and around-the-corner arrangements. In general, top sliding gear is used for lightweight doors and bottom sliding gear is used for heavier doors.

Figure 376 shows typical details and sections of an internal sliding door which is top hung. The bottom of the door is controlled by a small nylon guide that runs in a channel, set in the bottom of the door.

Sliding doors require special locks and latches with hook-shaped bolts which prevent the door being slid open. The furniture is usually flush fitting, so that the doors can be slid without fouling (see Figure 377).

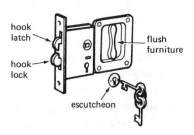

Figure 377 *Sliding door mortise lock/latch*

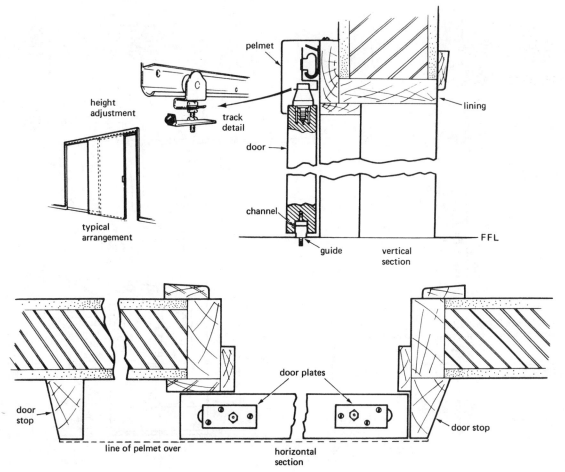

Figure 376 *Internal sliding door*

Folding

Folding doors are in fact folding sliding doors. They can either be used as movable internal partitions to divide up large areas or as commercial folding doors for warehouse and showroom entrances etc., and may be either end folding or centre folding. Top hung or bottom roller gear is available for both types.

End folding

End folding units should consist of an even number of leaves, up to six hinged on either jamb of the frame. For extra wide openings, additional floating units of four or six leaves not hinged to either jamb may be added. An extra leaf can be added if a swinging access door is required. A leaf width of between 600 mm and 900 mm is recommended. These must have solid top and bottom rails so that a firm fixing for the edge fitting hangers and guides can be achieved.

Figure 378 shows the arrangement and section of an external end folding top hung unit.

Centre folding

Centre folding units are of a similar construction to edge folding units except that there will always be a half leaf hinged to the frame to permit the centre folding arrangement. From one and a half to seven and a half leaves may be hinged together, on either jamb of the frame.

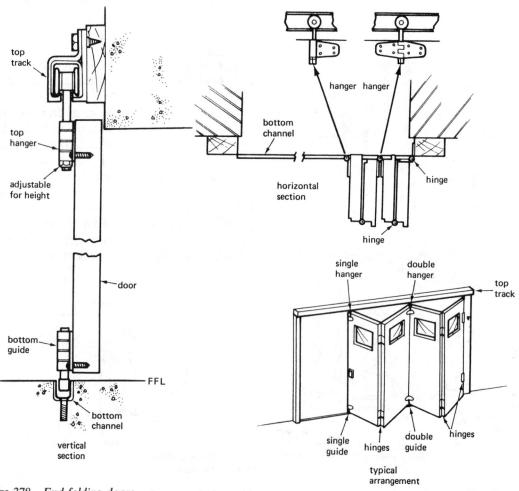

Figure 378 *End-folding doors*

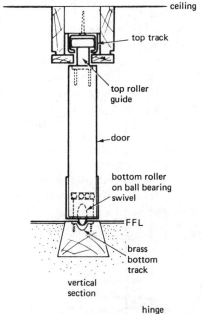

vertical
section

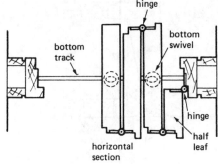

horizontal
section

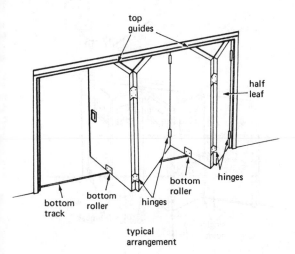

typical
arrangement

Figure 379   *Centre-folding doors*

An extra leaf can be added if a swinging access door is required.

Figure 379 shows details and sections of an internal centre folding, bottom- running partition. The half leaf hinged to the door frame is equal to half the width of a full leaf less half the door thickness.

Revolving doors
Revolving doors may be used as main entrances to hotels, offices and shops etc. They allow a fairly constant flow of traffic, while at the same time reducing draughts and heat loss. They are often adjacent to swinging doors in order to accommodate extra traffic and goods.

The design, construction and installation of revolving doors is normally carried out by a specialist firm.

Door frames and linings
Doors can be hung on frames or linings which have been built up, or fixed into an opening in a wall or partition.

Door frames are usually made from substantial rectangular section timber, with the door normally accommodated by a 12 mm deep stuck rebate, although both deeper stops and planted stops are sometimes used (see Figure 380). Frames are used for most external doors and heavy internal doors.

Door linings are made from 25 mm or 32 mm boards which cover the full width of the wall, including the plaster. Planted door stops are

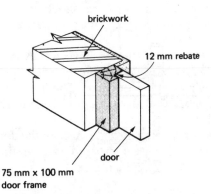

Figure 380   **Door frame**

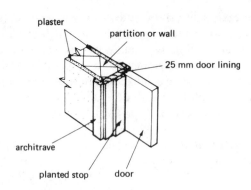

Figure 381   *Door lining*

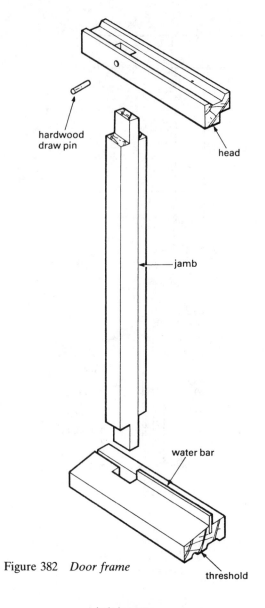

Figure 382   *Door frame*

normally used to accommodate the door. Architraves are fixed around the door lining to cover the joint between the plaster and the wood. Door linings are used for the majority of internal doors (see Figure 381).

Unlike door frames which are normally fully assembled in the workshop, it is common practice to produce linings in a knock-down form to be assembled on site by the carpenter.

Frames

Standard door frame (Figure 382)
This consists of a head, two jambs and, where required for external use, a sill or threshold. These components are jointed together with draw-pinned mortise and tenon joints.

Draw pins are used in preference to wedges, as they will hold the joint even if the horn is cut off. In addition, by off-setting the hole in the tenon slightly towards the shoulder, the joint will be drawn up tight as the pin is driven in (see Figure 383).

The threshold should have a galvanized or fibre water bar fitted to prevent the passage of driving rain under the door. The door will have to be rebated along its bottom edge to fit over the bar. As an additional protection against rainwater running down the face of the door and underneath, a weatherboard can be fitted to throw it clear (see Figure 384).

Storey height door frames (Figure 385)
These are used for door openings in thin

Figure 383   *Draw pinning*

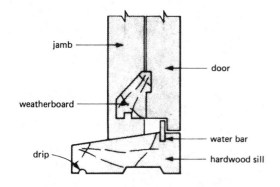

Figure 384   *Threshold detail*

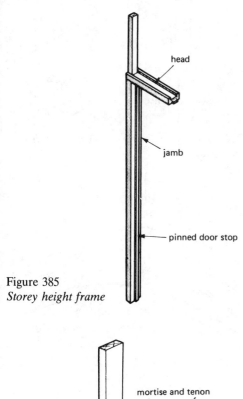

Figure 385
Storey height frame

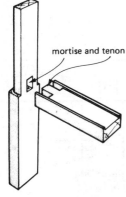

Figure 386   *Joint detail (storey height frame)*

non-loadbearing blockwork partitions. The jambs and head which make up the frame are grooved out on their back face to receive the building blocks. A mortise and tenon joint is used between the head and the jambs (see Figure 386).

The jambs above the head are cut back to finish flush with the blockwork. These should be covered with expanded metal before plastering.

Storey height frames with fanlights
Two common types are available. Figure 387 shows a frame for internal use, and Figure 388 a frame for external use. Both types consist of two jambs, a head and a transom. The external frame also has a hardwood sill with a galvanized water bar which has been bedded into a plough

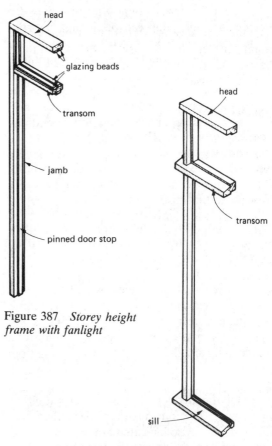

Figure 387   *Storey height frame with fanlight*

Figure 388   *External storey height frame*

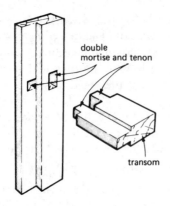

Figure 389   *Transom joint for internal storey height frame with fanlight*

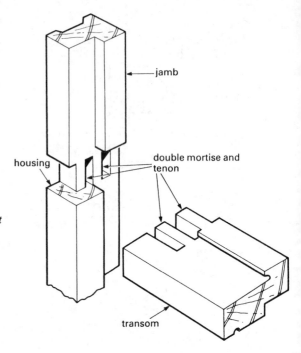

Figure 390   *Transom joint for external storey height frame with fanlight*

groove with mastic. The joints used for both frames are mortise and tenons.

For a plain internal frame the joint between the transom and jamb can be a single mortise and tenon but where a rebated frame is used, the joint should be a double mortise and tenon as shown in Figure 389.

On external storey height frames where the transom extends beyond the face, the joint will also be a double mortise and tenon and the overhanging edge of the transom should be housed across the face of the jambs (see Figure 390).

Curved head frames

It is normal to form the head of curved door frames from solid sections which are jointed together to produce the required shape. Alternatively, the curved member may be built up using a number of layers with end joints staggered and glued together (see Figure 391).

A third method of forming the curved head is by glulam construction. However, this is not often used as it is the most expensive, requires a cramping jig and the grain pattern resulting from the thin laminations may not be suitable for high quality work.

Curved head door frames are classified by their shape. The four main types are illustrated in Figure 392. Also indicated are suitable joints.

The main methods used to join the members are either bridle joints and draw pins, or

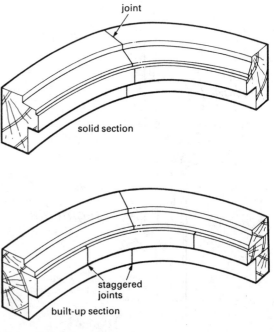

Figure 391   *Curved members*

handrail bolts and dowels (see Figure 393). Where a transom is required near the springing point, it should be jointed to the jamb using two tenons in order to minimize short graining

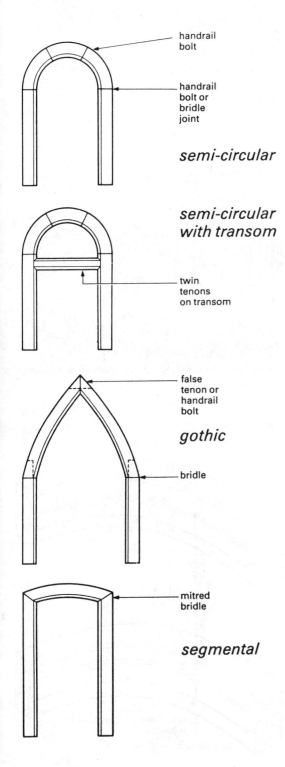

Figure 392 *Curved head door frames*

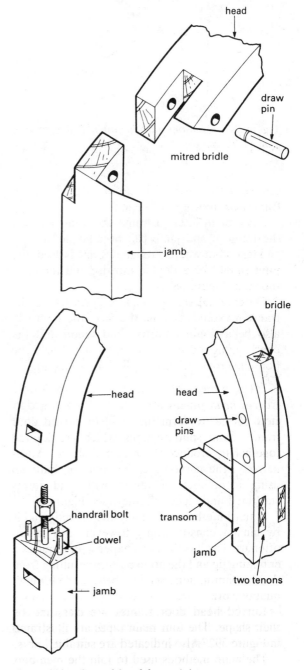

Figure 393 *Curved head frame joints*

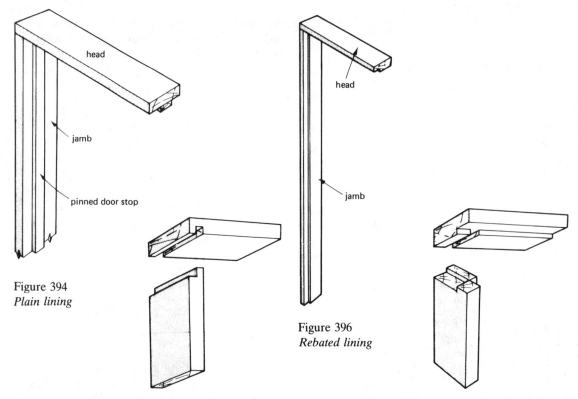

Figure 394
Plain lining

Figure 395   *Joint detail (plain lining)*

Figure 396
Rebated lining

Figure 397   *Joint detail (rebated lining)*

problems. Hammer-headed tenons and keys could also be used to join the curved members together, although they are less popular, as they are not suitable for machine production methods.

Linings

Plain linings (Figure 394)
These consist of two plain jambs and a plain head. The pinned stop is fixed around the lining after the door has been hung. The joint used for plain linings is shown in Figure 395.

Rebated linings (Figure 396)
Rebated linings are used for better quality work. They consist of two rebated jambs and a rebated head. The rebate must be slightly wider than the width of the door so that when the door is hung it will finish flush with the edges of the lining, but still have a working clearance of 1.5 mm between the door and the stop in order to

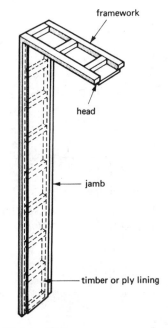

Figure 398   *Skeleton lining*

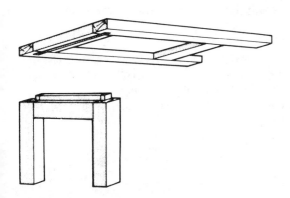

Figure 399   *Joint detail (skeleton lining)*

prevent binding and rubbing. The joint used for rebated linings is a shouldered housing which is shown in Figure 397.

Skeleton linings (Figure 398)
These are only used for deeper reveals e.g. where the brickwork is too thick for a normal lining to be used. Skeleton linings consist of a basic framework which is stub tenoned together. The housing joint used between the head and the jambs is shown in Figure 399. A ply or solid timber lining is used to cover the framework and form the rebate to receive the door.

Panelled linings (Figure 400)
These are normally used in conjunction with

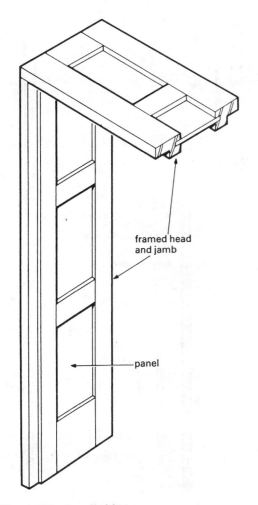

framed head
and jamb

panel

Figure 400   *Panelled lining*

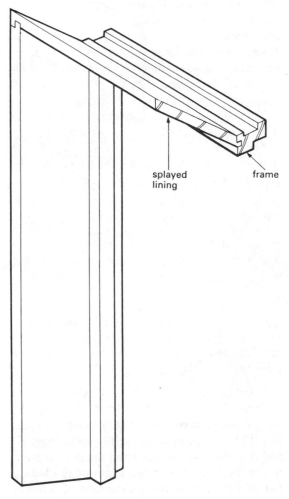

splayed
lining

frame

Figure 401   *Splayed lining*

wall panelling. Their construction is similar to skeleton linings except that the framed jambs and head are grooved out to receive the panels and the stop is normally stuck on the solid.

Splayed linings (Figure 401)
These are mainly used in conjunction with a door frame to finish deep reveals. They give a lead into the open and create a distinctive feature. The linings which may be plain, rebated, skeleton or panelled are housed or mitred together at their head and tongued into the frame. In order to construct the lining the true shape and bevels will have to be geometrically developed (see Chapter 7).

Fixing of frames and linings
Door frames are usually built in as the brickwork proceeds, using galvanized frame cramps which are fixed at intervals on the backs of jambs. However, in order to protect the door frames from damage, they are sometimes fixed at a much later stage in the building process. In this case they are screwed through the jambs and into plugs or pads inserted by the bricklayers.

The later fixing of frames mainly applies to expensive hardwood frames. The holes for the screws should be counterbored and later filled using cross-grained plugs or pellets of a matching timber.

Linings are normally nailed or screwed in position after an oversized opening in the wall has been formed, projecting twisted timber

plugs, pads or folding wedges being used to plumb the lining and take up the tolerance.

Glazed screens
The elevation of a glazed screen that incorporates a double-action door is illustrated in Figure 402. This type of frame is sometimes called a combination frame as it incorporates both door

Figure 402   *Glazed screen with door*

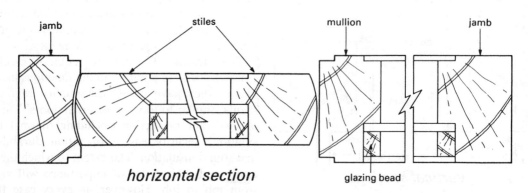

horizontal section

Figure 403   *Glazed screen details*

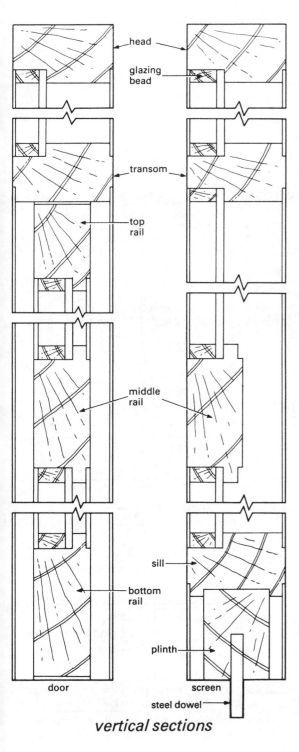

head

glazing bead

transom

top rail

middle rail

sill

bottom rail

plinth

door

screen

steel dowel

vertical sections

and glazing. Although the illustration shows a door, this could be omitted and the same detail used to construct a glazed partition.

The middle rail of the door has been continued across the side screen (also known as a side light). This continues the feature and also serves to break up the area of glass and provide protection at a vulnerable point.

The general arrangement of members is shown in the vertical and horizontal sections (see Figure 403). When the frame is fixed the mullion and plinth on the side screen must be secured with the aid of galvanized steel dowels grouted into the floor.

Entrance lobbies

It is fairly common for a lobby or vestibule to be built at the entrance to public buildings, banks, offices etc. Figure 404 shows a plan of such a lobby. It consists of a pair of single action entrance doors leading to a pair of double-action doors. The entrance doors are only intended to be closed when the building is locked up out of business hours, so they are often referred to as night doors. During the day they are kept open to give the impression of a panelled lobby. A pictorial sketch of this lobby with the entrance doors in the open position is shown in Figure 405. The actual walls of the lobby may be constructed in various ways, including brickwork, as shown in the plan, or timber framing.

Windows

A window is essentially a glazed opening in a wall. Its main functions are to provide natural lighting and natural ventilation, and also to give the building's occupants an outside view.

The design of windows requires careful consideration. In addition to the functions listed above, they have other performance requirements, similar to those of external doors. These are weather protection (including thermal insulation), security, ease of operation, durability and sound insulation. The extent to which these apply and their order of importance will vary from job to job. However, in every case the following points should be borne in mind. They

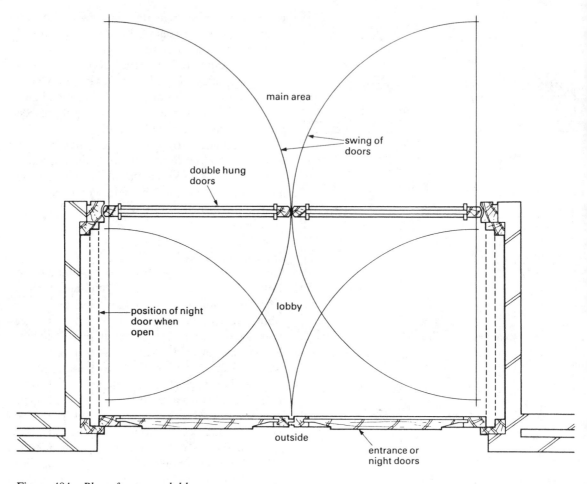

Figure 404   *Plan of entrance lobby*

can be considered the principles of window design.

1 Use only durable, preservative-treated timber with a suitable moisture content.
2 Ensure all framing joints are tight fitting and use a synthetic resin adhesive.
3 Prime or seal, preferably directly after manufacture.
4 All external horizontal surfaces to be weathered.
5 The horizontal surfaces of projecting sills and transoms must be provided with a drip.
6 The opening joint must be a tight fit for draught-proofing, but must open out within rebate to avoid capillarity.

7 Incorporate anti-capillary grooves and throatings around the opening.
8 External glazing in painted work may be secured with weathered face putty and spigs.
9 External glazing in clear finished work and internal glazing should be bedded in a suitable material but secured with cupped and screwed glazing beads from the inside of the building.

Note: Putty should be used externally and wash leather, rubber seal or a proprietary non-shrinking bedding mastic internally.

10 Considerable additional protection is

Figure 405   *Entrance lobby*

achieved by setting the window well back from the wall face.

All of these points are further emphasized and illustrated in the following examples.

Windows are normally classified by their method of opening. The majority of windows come under one of the following three groups. These groups are illustrated in Figure 406.

1 *Casements* which are either top or side hung on hinges.
2 *Pivot hung* which can be either horizontally or vertically hung.
3 *Sliding sashes* which can slide either horizontally or vertically.

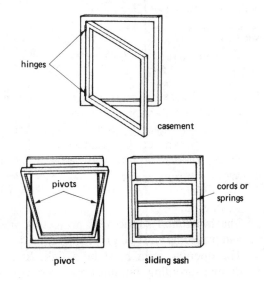

Figure 406   *Types of window*

The recommended method of indicating on a drawing the type of window and its method of opening is shown in Figure 407.

Figure 408 illustrates the principle of setting out rectangular window openings, with well balanced proportions. The method used is to draw a square with sides equal to the smallest dimension and then to swing the diagonal down to give the longest side. This method is equally suitable to determine the proportions of other items of joinery where a pleasing balanced effect is required.

Casement windows

Casement windows are comprised of two main parts:

The frame which consists of head, sill and two jambs. Where the frame is subdivided, the intermediate vertical members are called mullions and the intermediate horizontal member is called a transom.

The opening casements which consists of top rail, bottom rail and two stiles. Where the casement is subdivided, both the intermediate vertical

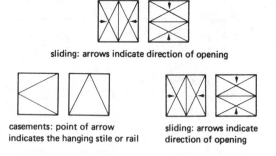

sliding: arrows indicate direction of opening

casements: point of arrow indicates the hanging stile or rail

sliding: arrows indicate direction of opening

Figure 407   *Direction of opening doors and windows*

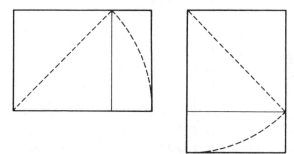

Figure 408   *Setting out rectangular openings*

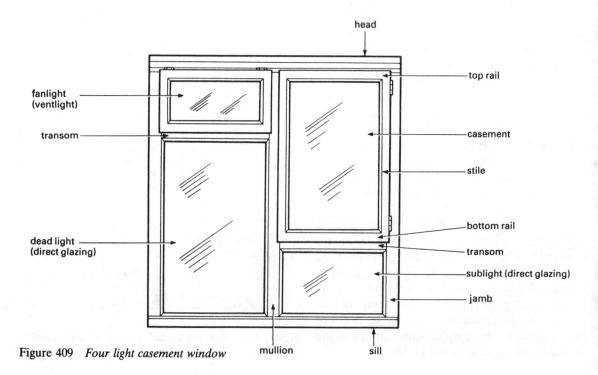

head

top rail

fanlight (ventlight)

transom

casement

stile

dead light (direct glazing)

bottom rail

transom

sublight (direct glazing)

jamb

mullion

sill

Figure 409   *Four light casement window*

and horizontal members are called glazing bars. Opening casements which are above the transom are known as fanlights. Fixed glazing is called a dead light and glazing at the bottom of a window, normally below a casement is a sublight. Where glass is bedded in main frame itself, it is called direct glazing.

Figure 409 shows the elevation of a four-light casement window with all the component parts named. The 'four' refers to the number of glazed openings or lights in the window.

Casement windows can further be divided into two types, traditional and stormproof depending on their method of construction.

Traditional casements

Figure 410 shows a vertical section through a traditional casement window. Anti-capillary grooves are incorporated into the frame and the opening casements, in order to prevent the passage of water into the building. Drip grooves are made towards the front edges of the transom and sill to stop the water running back underneath them.

A mortar key groove is run on the outside face of the head, sill and jambs. The sill also has a plough groove for the window sill to tongue into. Both the transom and sill incorporates a throat to check the penetration of wind-assisted rain. In addition this feature may be continued up the jambs. Finally the front of the transom and sill is weathered: it has a 9° slope for the rainwater to run off.

Figure 411 shows part of a horizontal section through a traditional casement window. It also shows the sizes and positions of the rebates, grooves and moulding in the jambs, mullion and the casement stiles.

All joints used in traditional casement window construction are mortise and tenons. Standard haunched mortise and tenons are generally used for the actual casements, although a sash haunch is preferable where smaller sections are used. As a matter of good practice, the depth of the rebates should be kept the same as the depth of the mouldings. This simplifies the jointing as the shoulders of the tenons will be level.

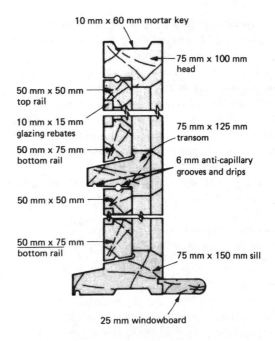

Figure 410   *Traditional casement*

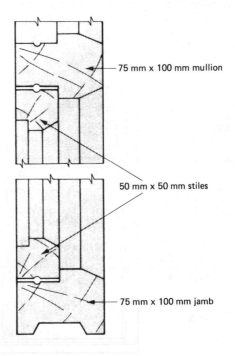

Figure 411   *Part horizontal section of traditional casement*

Figure 412 shows the jointing of head, jamb and sill of the main frame. These joints are normally wedged, although the use of draw pins or star dowels is acceptable and even preferable where the horn is to be later cut off.

Figure 413 shows an exploded isometric view of the joint between the transom and jamb. In order to make a better weatherproof joint, the front edge of the transom is housed across the jamb.

Figure 414 illustrates the mortise and tenon joints used for casements.

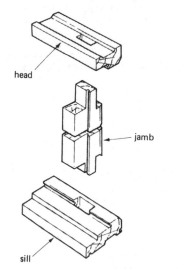

Figure 412   *Jointing the frame*

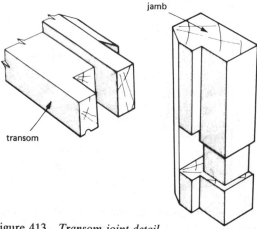

Figure 413   *Transom joint detail*

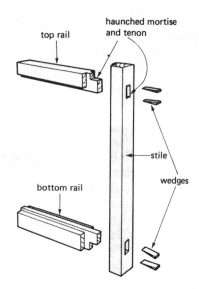

Figure 414   *Haunched mortise and tenon joint, secured with wedges*

Stormproof casements

Figure 415 shows a vertical section through a stormproof casement window. Stormproof casement windows incorporate two rebates, one round the main frame, and the other round the casement. These rebates, in conjunction with the drip, anti-capillary grooves and throat make this type far more weatherproof than traditional casements.

Figure 416 shows an alternative sill which must be used in conjunction with a stone, concrete or tiled sub-sill. This type is normally only used where the window is set well back from the brickwork face.

Figure 417 shows part of a horizontal section of a stormproof casement. It shows the jambs, mullion and casement stiles.

The jointing of the main frame of the stormproof casement window is often the same as that of the traditional casement, except for the transom which is not housed across the face of the jambs since it is usually of the same width. Comb joints can also be used, although they leave no horn for building in. Comb joints fixed with metal star dowels are normally used for jointing the actual casements (see Figure 418) although mortise and tenon joints can be used.

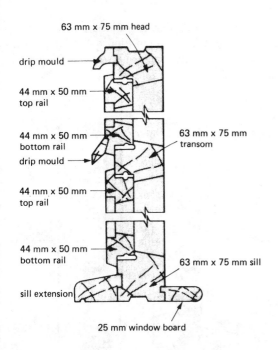

Figure 415   *Stormproof casement*

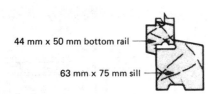

Figure 416   *Alternative sill*

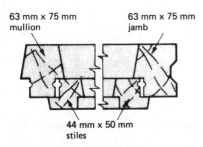

Figure 417   *Part horizontal section of stormproof casement*

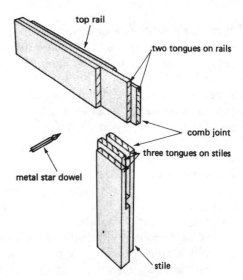

Figure 418   *Comb joint secured with a metal star dowel*

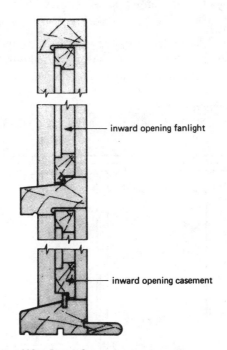

Figure 419   *Inward-opening casement*

Inward opening casements

Inward opening casements are rarely used as they are very difficult to weatherproof. They also present problems for the occupier of the building, because they obstruct the curtains.

Figure 419 shows a typical vertical section through an inward opening casement with a bottom hung inward opening fanlight. The bottom rail of the casement is rebated over a galvanized water bar which is set in the sill. This prevents the passage of water into the building between the bottom rail and the sill.

Timber sub-frames for metal casements

Metal casements can be fixed directly into the opening in the wall. However, as these windows are produced from light section material, they are better fixed in timber sub-frames.

The timber frames are manufactured using mortise and tenons or comb joints. Double rebates are incorporated around the frame to provide a suitable bedding and weather protection. A vertical and horizontal section of a metal casement in a timber sub-frame is shown in Figure 420.

Note: The metal casement is bedded in mastic and screwed through the holes provided into the rebate of the timber frame.

Combination frame

These combine in one frame a door and window.

They are often used as entrance frames and shop fronts. The one shown in Figure 421 includes an outward opening external door, fixed glazing and side hung casement. Typical vertical and

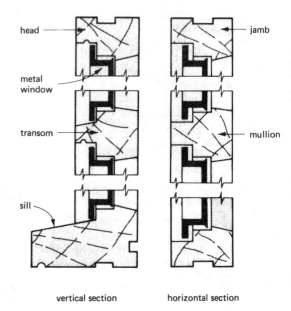

vertical section   horizontal section

Figure 420   *Metal casement in a timber sub-frame*

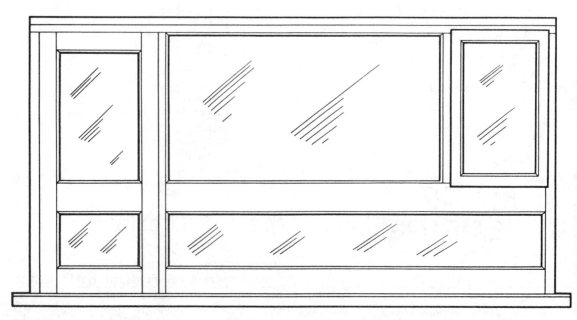

Figure 421   *Combination frame (door/window)*

horizontal sections of a combination frame are illustrated in Figure 422. Where an inward opening door is required the rebates for this will have to be reversed and a water bar ploughed into the sill. Figure 423 shows an alternative to the solid middle rail. This is built up from two sections with a plywood panel ploughed between them.

Bay windows

A bay window is normally incorporated into a building for one or a combination of three reasons:

1 To increase the amount of daylight and ventilation admitted into a room.
2 To increase room size.
3 To provide an architectural feature for the house.

Figure 422 *Combination frame details*

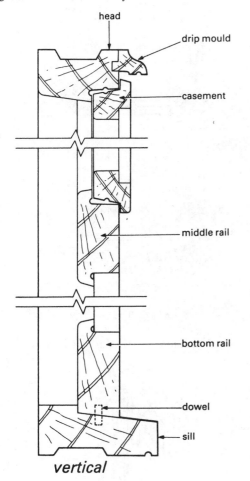

vertical

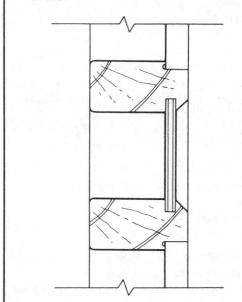

Figure 423 *Alternative built-up middle rail*

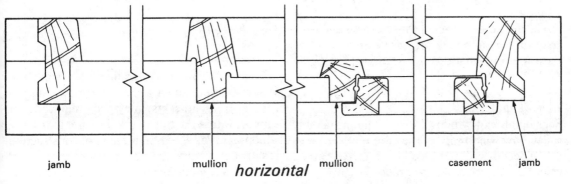

horizontal

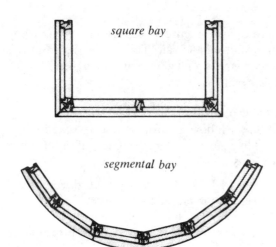

square bay

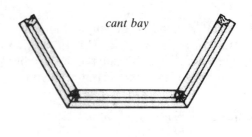

cant bay

segmental bay

combination bay

Figure 424   *Types of bay window*

The majority of bay windows are constructed using outward opening casements. The main construction details vary little from the standard casement windows covered above.

Bay windows are classified according to their shape on plan. The four main types of bay are illustrated in Figure 424:

Square bays
Cant bays
Segmental bays
Combination of square and cant

A bay window which projects from an upper storey only is known as an oriel window.

The angled intersections of the head and sill are normally mitred. These mitres are drawn up tight using handrail bolts. Two hardwood dowels are also used for each joint to overcome any tendency which the joint has to twist (see Figure 425).

The mullions or angle posts can be made from solid timber, although for ease of manufacture these are often made in two sections (see Figure 426).

Bow window
Segmental bay windows are often mistakenly called bow windows, but they are really a series of flat sections joined together to give a curved effect.

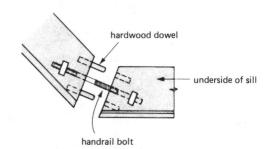

hardwood dowel

underside of sill

handrail bolt

Figure 425   *Joining head and sill*

Figure 426   *Two piece mullion*

Figure 427 is an illustration of a true bow window, often called a Georgian bow. Shaped cantilevered brackets may be required for support where the brickwork does not follow the window curve. A typical method of construction is shown in Figure 428. It consists of a head and sill vertically glulaminated to the required curve.

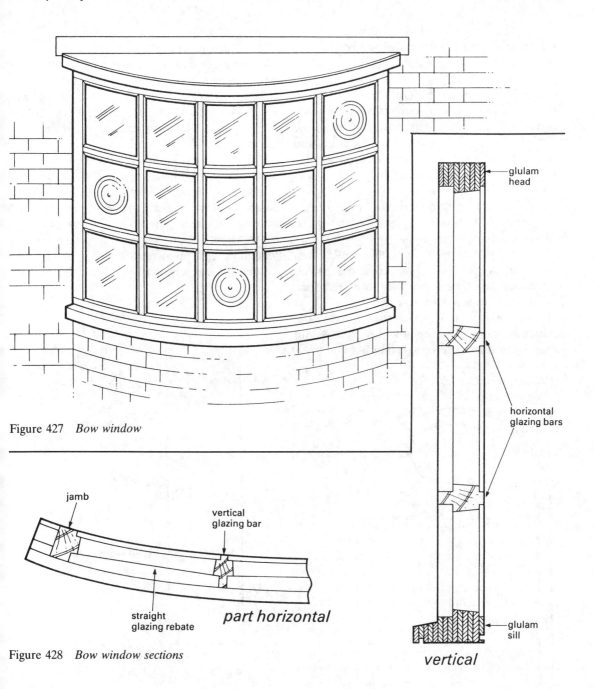

Figure 427   *Bow window*

Figure 428   *Bow window sections*

part horizontal

jamb

vertical
glazing bar

straight
glazing rebate

glulam
head

horizontal
glazing bars

glulam
sill

vertical

Jambs and vertical glazing bars are mortised and tenoned into the head and sill. The horizontal glazing bars can be jointed to the jambs and vertical glazing bars using short stub tenons. Where the horizontal bars have a large curvature short graining will weaken the tenons. In such cases they may be simply housed into the vertical members, or alternatively they may be also vertically glulaminated.

The glazing rebate in the head, sill and horizontal bars is worked flat to avoid the necessity of using expensive special order curved glass.

In cheaper quality work often only the head

and sill are curved leaving the horizontal bars straight.

Curved head casement windows

Where curved head casement windows are required, they can be constructed using the same method as that used for curved head doors and frames. Curved members are built up from a number of pieces to avoid short grain, and jointed together with handrail bolts, false tenons, hammer headed key and tenons or bridle joints.

Figure 429 illustrates a semi-circular headed window with direct glazing.

Glazing bars are used to subdivide the area into seven lights. These bars are cross halved and scribed together where they intersect, then stub tenoned to the main frame.

Figure 430 is an enlarged section through the semi-circular boss showing how it is cut over and dowel jointed to the cross-glazing bar.

Centre hung pivot windows

This type of window is often used for high rise buildings, as both sides of the glass can be cleaned from the inside of the building with ease. The main disadvantage of this type is that, when opened, the top of the sash interferes with the curtains.

Figure 431 shows the vertical and horizontal sections of a traditional pivot window. Both the surrounding frame and the pivoting sash are constructed using mortises and tenons. The sash is hung on pivot pins about 25 mm above its centre line height to give it a self closing tendency. The pivot pin usually is fixed to the frame and the socket to the sash. The planted

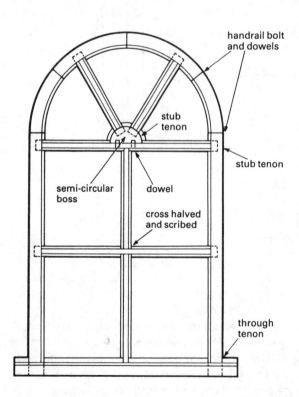

Figure 429 *Direct glazed semi-circular headed window*

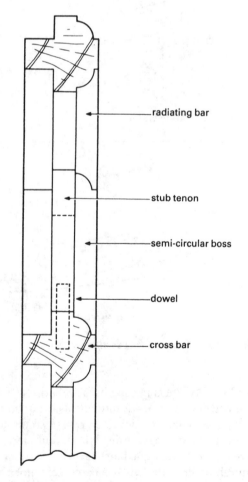

Figure 430 *Section through boss*

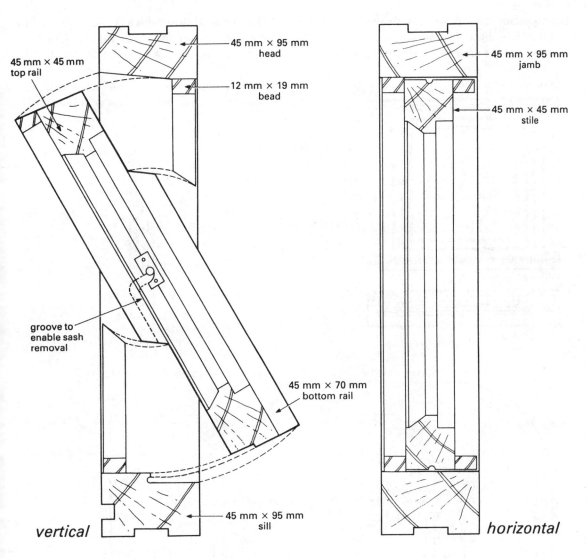

45 mm × 45 mm
top rail

45 mm × 95 mm
head

12 mm × 19 mm
bead

45 mm × 95 mm
jamb

45 mm × 45 mm
stile

groove to
enable sash
removal

45 mm × 70 mm
bottom rail

45 mm × 95 mm
sill

vertical

horizontal

Figure 431   *Traditional pivot window sections*

stops which form the rebates serve to weatherproof the window. Those above the pivots are nailed or screwed to the frame on the outside and the sash on the inside, whereas those below are fixed to the frame on the inside and the sash on the outside. The actual positions of intersection of the beads needs to be precisely determined, especially where the sash is required to be removable without taking off any beads (for details of the method see Chapter 7).

This is shown in the vertical section. The sash stile and its planted top bead must be grooved as shown to allow removal of the sash.

The head and top rail is splayed to give sufficient opening clearance. This is provided at the sill by its weathering.

Figure 432 shows an elevation and width section of a stormproof centre hung pivot window, which is an improvement on the type described above. The joints used in the frame are mortise and tenons. Comb joints are used for the sash. Face fixing friction pivots or back flap hinges are used for hanging the sash.

The moulded stop, which is mitred around the frame and cut on the pivot line, is glued and pinned to the top half of the frame and the bottom half of the sash.

The partially opened sash is shown as a broken line on the height section in Figure 433.

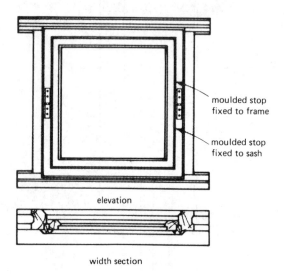

Figure 432   *Centre-hung pivot window*

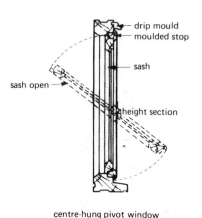

centre-hung pivot window

Figure 433   *Centre-hung pivot window*

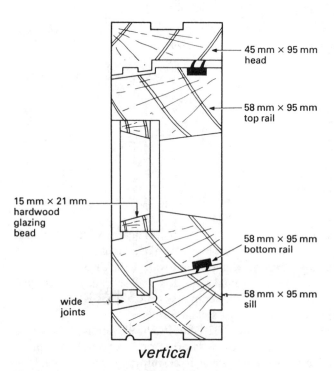

vertical

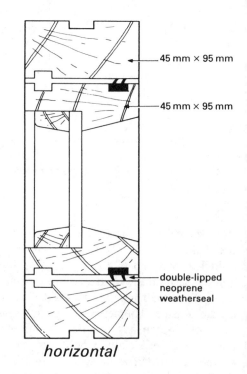

horizontal

Figure 434   *Proprietary pivot window sections*

Various other proprietary designs of pivot windows are used by specialist window manufacturers. Figure 434 illustrates a typical section of such a window. Wide joints are used between the frame and the sash throughout to combat capillarity. This is sealed with double lipped neoprene strips. External glazing beads have been used but at least these are weathered and normally of hardwood.

Hanging is by special friction pivots, housed into the edge of both the frame and sash, the knuckle of which is normally visible on the inside of the building.

Vertically pivot hung windows may be constructed using similar details to those of the horizontal type. Although as the bottom pivot takes all of the sash weight a special pivot is required which normally incorporates some form of ball race mechanism.

Bull's eye windows
These are circular windows consisting of a main frame which can be glazed direct or contain a

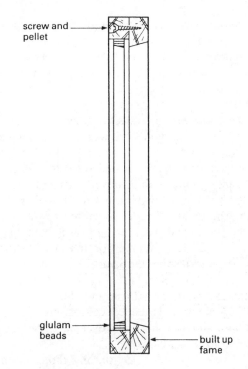

Figure 436 *Bull's eye window section (direct glazed)*

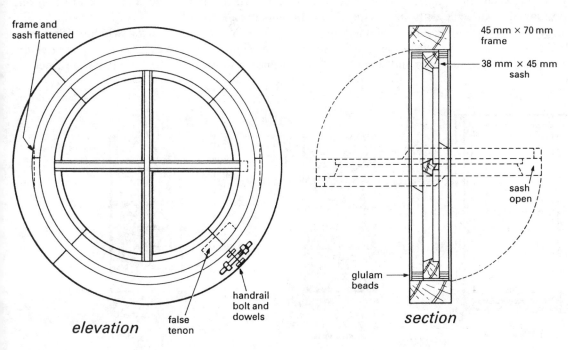

elevation

Figure 435 *Bull's eye window (pivot hung)*

section

sash. The sash itself may be either fixed or pivot hung.

Figure 435 shows an elevation and section of a bull's eye window with a pivot hung sash that has been subdivided with glazing bars into four lights.

There are various ways (already described in the section on curved work with doors) in which the frame and sash can be made. In this case they have both been formed from four curved segments, joined with handrail bolts and dowels on the main frame with false tenons used for the sash. The planted beads, which are fixed partly to the frame and partly to the sash, have been glulamed using a number of thin laminations bent around a suitable former. Both the frame and sash will require flattening around the pivot positions on the inside to enable it to pivot without binding. Threaded centre screw pivots are normally used for bull's eyes, as these allow easy removal of the sash.

Figure 436 shows a section of a direct glazed bull's eye window. In this case it has been built up in two layers with end joints staggered. The joint between the layers, which has been positioned to coincide with the rebate, is glued, screwed and pelleted. The glulamed glazing bead run around the inside of the frame is secured with recessed cups and screws.

Sliding sash window

These may be classified into two groups according to their direction of opening:

Vertical sliding sash
Horizontal sliding sash

Vertical sliding sashes

These consist of two sashes which slide up and down in a main frame. They are also known as double hung sliding sash windows. There are two different forms of construction for these types of window:

Those with boxed frames
Those with solid frames

Boxed frames

This type of window is the traditional pattern of sliding sashes and for many years has been superseded by casements and solid frame sash windows. This was mainly due to the high manufacturing and assembly costs of the large number of component parts. An understanding of their construction and operation is essential as they will frequently be met in renovation and maintenance work.

The double hung boxed window consists of two sliding sashes suspended on cords or chains which run over pulleys and are attached to

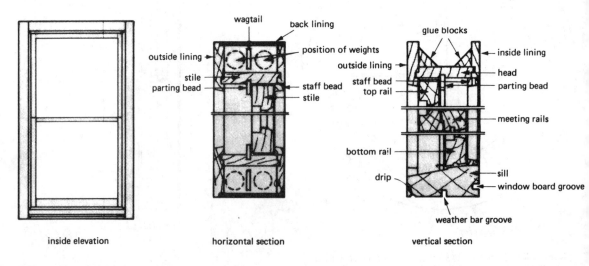

Figure 437   *Boxed frame sliding sash window*

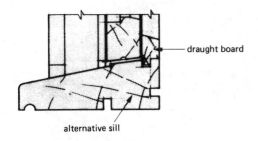

Figure 438 *Alternative sill detail*

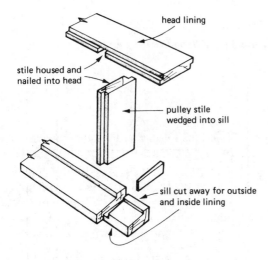

Figure 439 *Boxed frame joint details*

counterbalanced weights inside the boxed frame.

Figure 437 shows an elevation and horizontal and vertical section of a boxed frame sliding sash window. It shows the make up of this type of window and names the component parts.

Figure 438 shows an alternative sill detail, with a draughtboard tongued into the sill. This allows the bottom sash to be partly opened to provide ventilation without causing a draught.

Figure 439 shows how the pulley stiles are jointed to the head and sill. The inside and outside linings are tongued and nailed to the head and stiles.

Figure 440 illustrates how the outside lining and parting bead should be cut away in order to prevent water and dirt being trapped at this point. A pocket piece is cut in the pulley stiles to provide access to the weights. It is cut out by making saw cuts as shown in Figure 441 and then firmly tapping out from the back of the stile.

Figure 442 shows the mortise and tenon joint which is used between the sash stile and rail. The sash haunch or reverse franking is used instead of a normal haunch. If this were not done, the joint would be seriously weakened by the sash cord groove which is run into the edge of the stile.

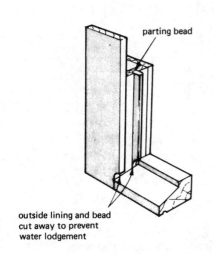

Figure 440 *Cutting away of outside lining and parting bead*

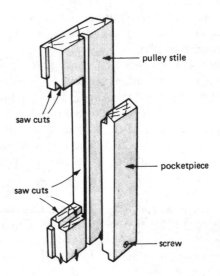

Figure 441 *Pocket piece*

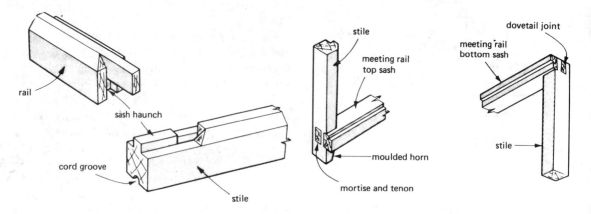

Figure 442 *Joint detail (sash haunch)*   **Figure 443** *Alternative meeting rail joint details*

Figure 443 shows two alternative methods used for the joints between the stiles and meeting rails. Where the horn is left, a mortise and tenon joint can be used. The horn is usually moulded as shown. A dovetail joint should be used where no horn is required.

Where a window is more than one sash wide, boxed double mullions shown in Figure 444 are introduced to accommodate the four weights. These have a wide bulky appearance, so they were often concealed on the outside with ornamental stone mullions or pilasters.

Venetian windows, shown in Figure 445, do not require boxed mullions as normally only the middle sashes slide. The narrow side sashes are screwed in position.

Figure 446 shows a section through the solid mullion of a Venetian window. The method used to hang the centre sashes is shown in Figure 447. The pulleys are fixed to the pulley stiles as high as possible. The cords fixed at one end to the sashes, pass over the mullion pulleys, across the heads of the side sashes, then, finally, over the side pulleys to the weights.

Figure 448 shows how the cords are concealed across the top. The top rail of the side sash is grooved out to receive the outer cord. The inner cord is concealed by a grooved cover mould that also incorporates the top staff bead. Both the cover mould and the fixed top sash must be made removable for cord replacement.

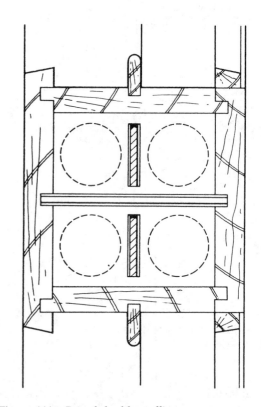

Figure 444 *Boxed double mullion*

Curved head sashes

The inside elevation of a semi-circular headed vertical sliding sash window is shown in Figure 449. The construction details of this sash window

Figure 445   *Venetian window (inside elevation)*

are the same as those of a standard sash up to the springing line. Above this a number of alternative methods may be used to construct the frame and sash.

Figure 450 shows the curved head built up in three layers with joints well staggered and glued together. The middle layer, often of plywood, also forms a fixed parting bead. Below the springing line a removable parting bead is used.

Also shown in Figure 450 is how the sash stile to curved rail joint (handrail bolt with dowels) is positioned beyond the springing to enable a shoulder to be formed. The shoulder stops on the projecting edge of the built up head when

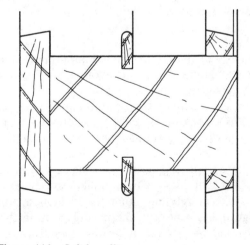

Figure 446   *Solid mullion*

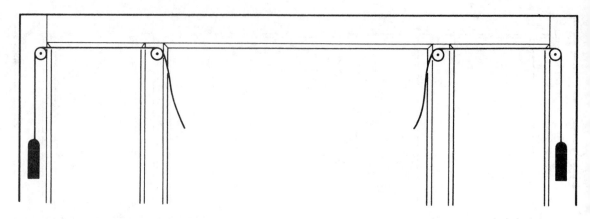

Figure 447   *Cording a Venetian window*

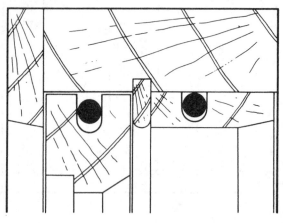

Figure 448   *Concealing sash cords across head*

the sash is lifted. This prevents jamming and impact at the crown, thus avoiding the risk of sash damage and breaking glass.

An alternative method of forming the curved head is shown in Figure 451. In this case the head has been glulamed from thin solid laminates or thin plywood. Blocks are glued around the head to provide a fixing for the curved inner and outer linings, which, unlike the straight ones, are merely butt jointed and pinned, not tongued and grooved. The parting bead in this case would be shaped from ply or solid timber and grooved into the head.

Figure 449   *Semi-circular headed sash (inside elevation)*

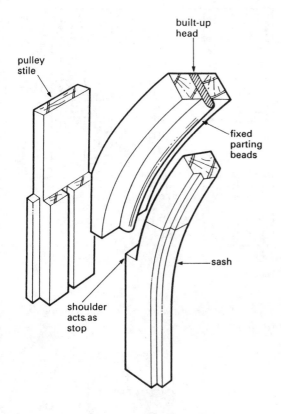

Figure 450 *Semi-circular headed sash details*

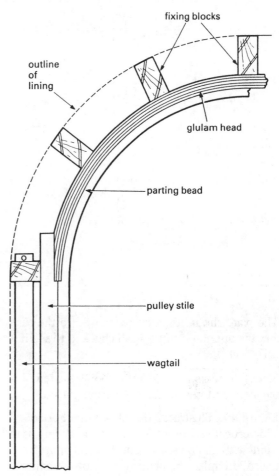

Figure 451 *Alternative method of forming curved head*

For all forms of boxed sash windows, two cast iron or lead weights are required to balance each sash. To determine the size of these weights the fully glazed sashes can be weighed with a spring balance. The weights for the top sash should each be half the sash weight plus about 250 g and the bottom sash weights half the sash weight less 250 g. Using this principle, both sashes are counterbalanced, but will have the tendency to remain closed in their respective positions, firmly against the head or sill.

Solid frame sash window

For many years balances have been manufactured for use in place of sash cords and weights. The use of the sash balance does away with the need for boxed frames, thereby reducing the number of component parts and simplifying the construction of sliding sash windows.

Two balances are required for each sash.

Where the sashes are the same size, the longer balances are for the bottom sash and the shorter balances are for the top. The balances (one is shown in Figure 452) are fixed to the tops of the jambs with a screw. The plate on the other end is attached to the bottom rail of the sash. As each sash is raised or lowered the spring is tensioned. The sash is then supported or balanced by the tension of the springs. If the sash is not balanced both springs on the sash should be adjusted. The tension of the springs may be adjusted by unscrewing the sash plate and twisting it one turn in a clockwise or anticlockwise direction.

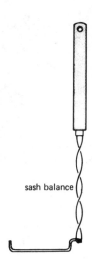

sash balance

Figure 452   *Balance*

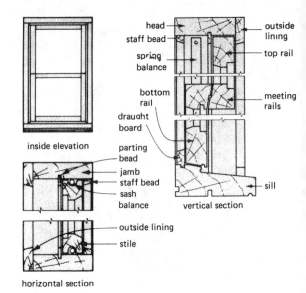

head
staff bead
spring balance
bottom rail
draught board
parting bead
jamb
staff bead
sash balance
outside lining
top rail
meeting rails
sill
outside lining
stile

inside elevation

vertical section

horizontal section

Figure 453   *Solid frame sliding sash window*

The plate should then be rescrewed to the sash and the operation of the sash checked to see if it is correct.

Note: Springs should not be adjusted for balance until the sashes have been glazed.

Figure 453 illustrates the elevation, horizontal and vertical section of a solid frame sliding sash window. It can be seen from this that apart from the solid jambs, the arrangement of the component parts is similar to that of the boxed frame sash window. The frame and sashes can be jointed using mortise and tenon joints, although modern mass-produced windows are now exclusively manufactured using comb joints with metal star dowels.

Note: For lightweight domestic sashes, the spring balances are accommodated in grooves run in the back of the sash stiles. The spring balances for heavyweight industrial sashes are accommodated in grooves which are run in the actual jamb of the frame as shown in Figure 454.

Fixing sash windows
Solid frame sash windows are usually built-in in the normal manner using galvanized frame cramps. Boxed frame sash windows are normally fixed into a prepared opening in the wall by

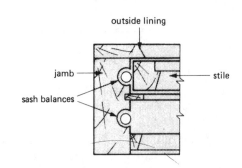

outside lining
jamb
sash balances
stile

Figure 454   *Part horizontal section*

driving wedges in behind the jambs (see Figure 455).

Horizontal sliding sashes
The elevation and sectional details of a window with horizontally sliding sashes is shown in Figure 456. The main frame is simply constructed from rectangular section material, using mortises and tenons. It has planted staff beads and grooved parting beads. The sashes, which are also framed using mortises and tenons, have rebated meeting stiles to prevent draughts. Both sashes may be made to slide on a track or waxed hardwood runners.

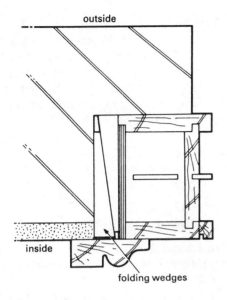

Figure 455 *Fixing boxed frame sash windows*

Larger three or four sash windows can be constructed, using similar details to those shown. Normally only the middle sash or sashes slide, while the outer ones are fixed to the main frame.

Ventilators

These are used where permanent ventilation only is required and not daylight or a view. They consist of a main frame into which louvre slats are housed. The slats which are normally set at 45° should project beyond the face of the frame to throw rainwater clear. The top and bottom edges of adjacent slats should overlap to prevent through vision and restrict the passage of driving rain (see Figure 457).

The elevations of the two most common ventilators are illustrated in Figure 458. The triangular frame may be jointed using dovetails

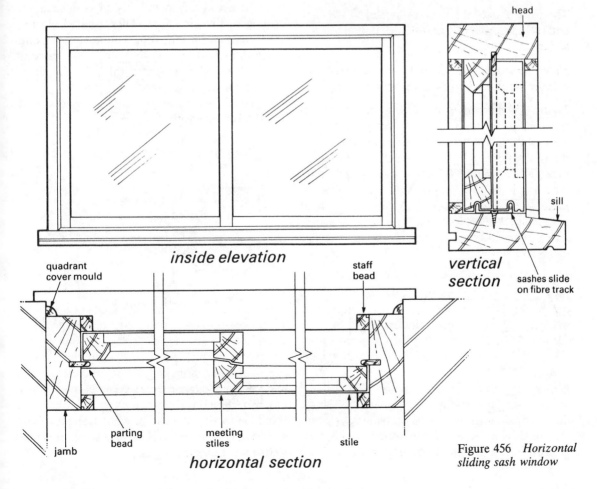

Figure 456 *Horizontal sliding sash window*

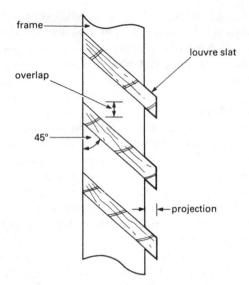

Figure 457   *Typical ventilator (vertical section)*

or pinned bridles and the circular one built up using any of the methods covered previously. The true shapes of the louvre slats and the housings in the frame must be determined geometrically (see Chapter 7). This is because the slats are inclined and do not intersect with the frame at right angles.

Double glazing

Double glazing is carried out for two main reasons:

Thermal insulation
Sound insulation

Modern sealed glazing units are often used to double glaze windows for thermal insulation. These consist of two panels of glass with an air space of up to 25 mm between them. The edges are hermetically sealed in a clean dry atmosphere to avoid any possibility of condensation forming in the air space. These sealed glazing units are fitted into the rebates of casements and sashes in the normal way. Where the rebate is too small to take the extra thickness of glass, stepped units can be used.

Figure 459 shows normal and stepped sealed glazed units in position.

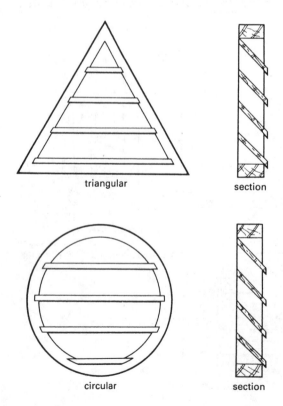

Figure 458   *Louvre ventilators*

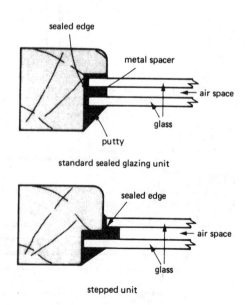

Figure 459   *Sealed glazing units*

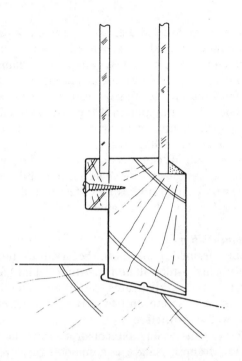

Figure 460 illustrates a method of double glazing that is similar in effect to sealed units. This is achieved by fixing a second pane of glass on the inside of the sash or casement with the aid of rebated beads. A distinct disadvantage of this method is the very high risk of condensation occurring between the two panes of glass.

While sealed units do provide a certain amount of sound insulation, this is often insufficient for noisy locations, e.g. near busy roads or airports. In general, the sound insulation properties of a window increase as the air space between the two windows increases. For efficient sound insulation, the air space should be between 100 mm and 200 mm. In order to achieve this air space, a second window can be built on the inside of the reveal behind the existing window. This type of double glazing is known as secondary double glazing.

Figure 461 shows a secondary double glazing detail. As a further improvement, the reveals between the two frames can be lined with a

Figure 460 *Double glazing*

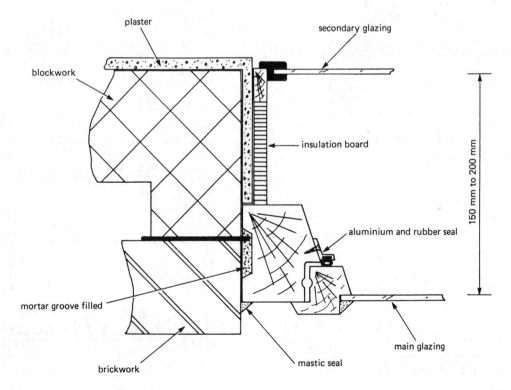

Figure 461 *Secondary double glazing*

sound absorbent material, such as strips of insulation board.

Linked casement windows provide an alternative method of double glazing which is popular in Europe (see Figure 462). The two casements are hinged and screwed together. The outer one is normally hinged to the frame. Where the casements are screwed together, the fixings should be accessible as the inner faces of the glass will require cleaning occasionally. This can be reduced to a minimum if the two casements are sealed together with an air permeable but dust excluding sealing strip.

Condensation can occur between the two panels of glass where this space is not ventilated. However, ventilation has the effect of reducing the window's insulating value.

Curtain walling

Timber framed panels can be used as non-loadbearing in-fill wall units (curtain walling) for skeleton frame structures of either steel or reinforced concrete and for brick or concrete cross wall construction.

These panels may be constructed as large window frames using a combination of glazed

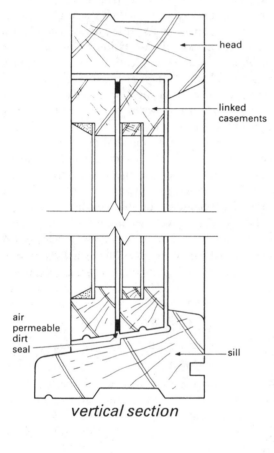

vertical section

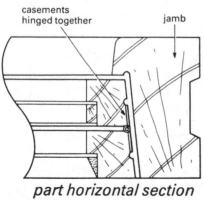

part horizontal section

Figure 462   *Linked casements*

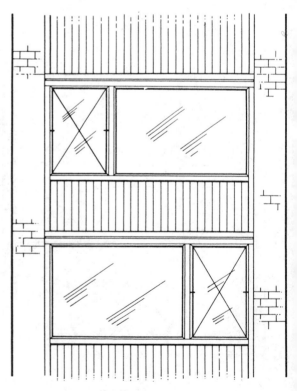

Figure 463   *Curtain walling*

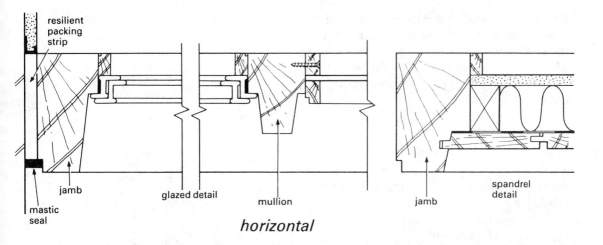

resilient packing strip

jamb

glazed detail

mullion

jamb

spandrel detail

mastic seal

horizontal

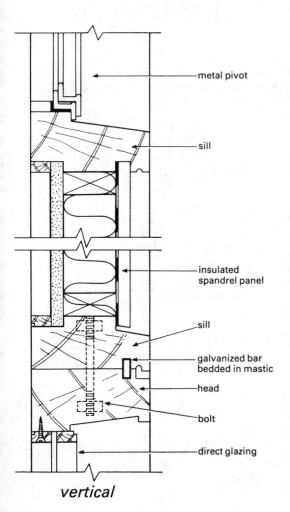

metal pivot

sill

insulated spandrel panel

sill

galvanized bar bedded in mastic

head

bolt

direct glazing

vertical

Figure 464 *Curtain walling sections*

openings and insulated in-fill sections as illustrated in Figure 463.

Typical vertical and horizontal details are shown in Figure 464.

The curtain walling frames are broken down into units bolted together at the head and sill. These horizontal joints incorporate a galvanized water bar bedded in mastic to produce an effective seal. A similar detail can be used to join frames side by side in order to form a long run of curtain walling.

Standard in-fill panels extend from head height of one frame to the normal window sill height of the frame above. An alternative to the insulated timber clad panel shown, is the insulated, enamelled steel and GRP faced panels used in proprietary curtain walling systems.

Ventilation is provided by metal pivot hung windows which are bedded in mastic and screwed to the main frame. The direct fixed glazing shows the use of both internal and external beads. The external ones should be permanently fixed with a suitable synthetic resin adhesive and pins. The internal beads are recess cupped and screwed in place, thus permitting the glazing to be carried out from the inside of the building.

The panels must be securely fixed to the structural frame or cross walls, normally using metal brackets, straps, or expanding bolts.

Careful detailing is required in order to allow

for the differential movement between the curtain walling and the main structure while at the same time maintaining a weatherproof joint. This can be achieved by filling the joint with a resilient strip and sealing with a compressible mastic.

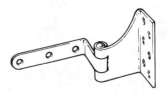

Figure 466   *Offset hinge*

Window ironmongery

Cranked hinge (Figure 465)
The cranked hinge is also known as the stormproof hinge as it is used for hanging rebated stormproof casements.

Offset hinge (Figure 466)
These are used for hanging casement windows. When open they allow an arm to be passed through the gap between the frame and the casement in order to clean the outside of the window from the inside, hence the popular name 'easy clean' hinge.

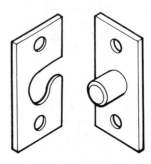

Figure 467   *Window pivot*

Window pivot (Figure 467)
These pivots are recessed into the edge of the window jamb and stile. They are used for the concealed hanging of pivot windows.

Friction pivot (Figure 468)
This is a modern type of hinge used for hanging pivot windows. It screws on to the face of the window and also contains a friction action, allowing the window to remain open in any position.

Figure 468   *Friction pivot hinge*

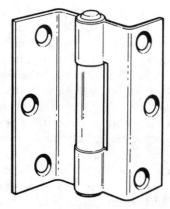

Figure 465   *Cranked hinge*

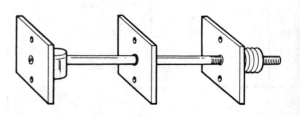

Figure 469   *Centre screw pivot*

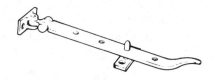

Figure 470   *Casement stay*

Figure 471   *Casement fastener*

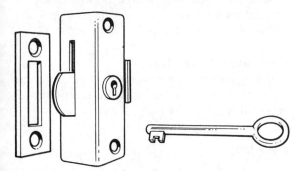

Figure 472   *Window lock*

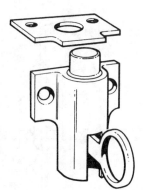

Figure 473   *Fanlight catch*

Centre screw pivot (Figure 469)
These pivots allow the sash to be easily removed. The threaded steel pin passes through the first two plates which are recessed either side of the sash stile and screws into the final plate that is fixed to the jamb of the outer frame.

Casement stay (Figure 470)
This is also known as a peg stay. It is used to hold the window in various opening positions.

Casement fastener (Figure 471)
This is also known as a cock spur and is used to secure a casement window in the closed position.

Window lock (Figure 472)
A key operated lock fitted to casements and fanlights for additional protection.

Fanlight catch (Figure 473)
Fitted to the top rail of horizontal pivots and inward opening fanlights to secure them in the closed position. For high level windows the ring pull may be operated with a window pole or cord system.

Quadrant stay (Figure 474)
Used in pairs to limit travel of inward opening fanlights.

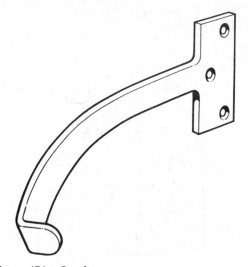

Figure 474   *Quadrant stay*

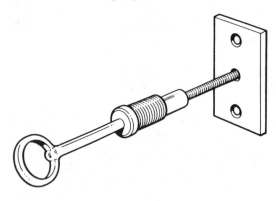

Figure 475   *Sash fasteners*

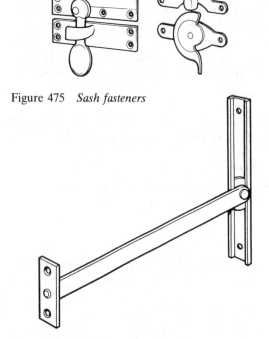

Figure 476   *Retaining stay*

Figure 477   *Security screw*

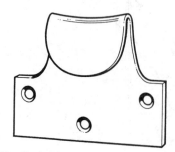

Figure 478   *Sash lift*

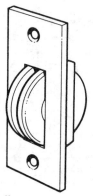

Figure 479   *Sash pulley*

Sash fasteners (Figure 475)
These are available in a number of types and are used to hold the meeting rails of a sash window together, thereby securing the sashes in a closed position.

Retaining stay (Figure 476)
Used to limit the travel of horizontal pivots and fanlights.

Security screw (Figure 477)
Fitted mainly to the meeting rails of sliding sash windows for extra security. The threaded screw passes through the socket drilled into the inner meeting rail and locates in the plate fixed to the outer meeting rail. It can also be used to secure casement windows by passing through the casement stile and into the jamb.

Sash lift (Figure 478)
One or two are fixed to the bottom rail of a vertical sliding sash to act as a finger grip when lifting or lowering the sash.

Sash pulley (Figure 479)
Various patterns are available to take different sized cords and chains. They are mortised and recessed flush into the top of pulley stile.

Panelling

Wall panelling is the general term given to the covering of the internal wall surface with timber or other materials to create a decorative finish. All panelling may be classified in one of two ways, either by its method of construction or height.

Dado height panelling (Figure 480)
Panelling that extends from the floor up the walls to the window sill level or chair back height, i.e., about 1 m, is known as dado panelling.

Three-quarter height panelling (Figure 481)
This type of panelling is also known as frieze height panelling. It extends from the floor up the

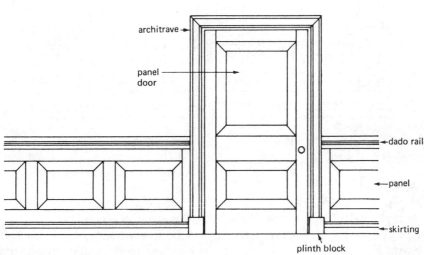

Figure 480   *Dado-height panelling*

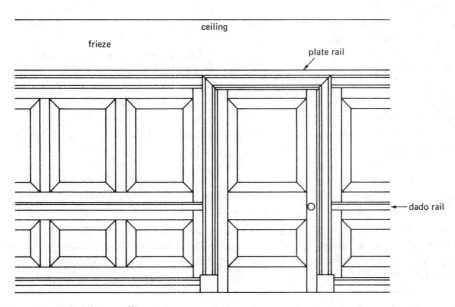

Figure 481   *Three-quarter-height panelling*

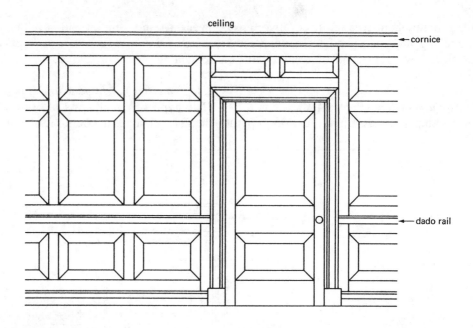

Figure 482   *Full-height panelling*

walls to the top of the door, i.e., about 2 m. Traditionally a plate shelf was incorporated on top of this type of panelling to display plates and other frieze ornaments.

Full height panelling (Figure 482)

This, as its name suggests, covers the whole of the wall from floor to ceiling.

Methods of construction

Traditionally all panelling was made up from solid timbers. It consisted of framing, mortised and tenoned together to receive decorative, flat or raised panels and other solid mouldings. However, the modern practice is to utilize sheet materials as far as possible, either in a traditional framed surround or without framing giving a flush appearance. This flush appearance can be given a traditional look by tacking planted mouldings to its surface to form mock panels. In addition to framed or sheet panelling, strip panelling made from narrow strips of boarding (tongued and grooved and vee jointed) are also used.

Vertical and horizontal sectional details of

three-quarter traditional framed panelling are illustrated in Figure 483.

Different panel and mould details have been included to show the various treatments possible. For example, panels are sometimes fitted into rebates and beaded rather than plough grooves. This method enables the polishers to work on the panels and framing before they are finally put together. Also shown are finishing details at door and window openings.

In this type of work it was common for the large architraves to be halved, and mitred together at their top joint and bare faced tenoned into the back of the plinth block at the bottom (see Figure 484). The whole set of architraves and plinth blocks are glued and screwed together prior to fixing. The purpose of the plinth blocks is to take the knocks and abrasions at floor level, which would easily damage the large moulded section architraves if they were continued down. In addition they also ease the fixing problems and provide a neat finish when the skirting is thicker than the architrave.

Skirtings should be mitred at external angles,

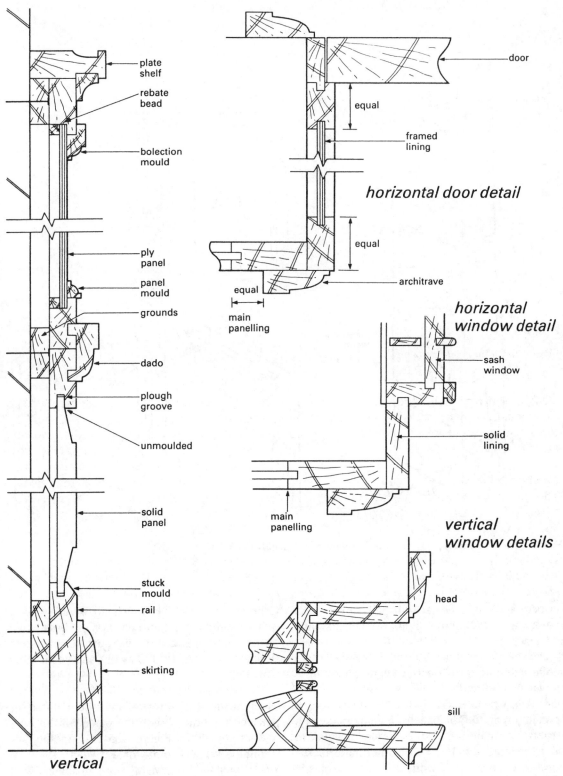

plate
shelf

rebate
bead

bolection
mould

ply
panel

panel
mould

grounds

dado

plough
groove

unmoulded

solid
panel

stuck
mould

rail

skirting

vertical

door

equal

framed
lining

horizontal door detail

equal

architrave

equal

main
panelling

*horizontal
window detail*

sash
window

solid
lining

main
panelling

*vertical
window details*

head

sill

Figure 483   *Framed panelling details*

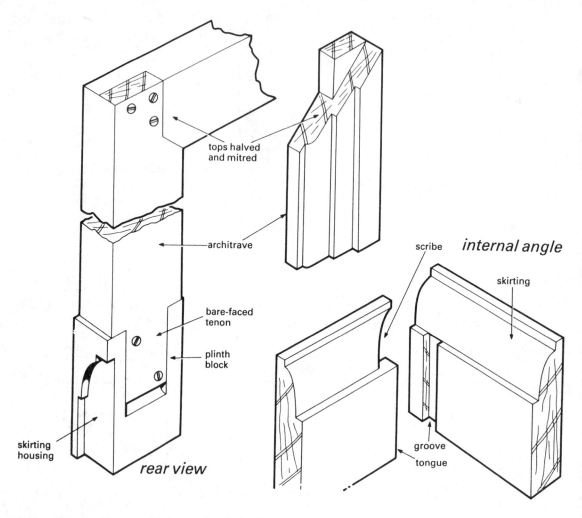

Figure 484 *Architrave, skirting and plinth block details*

scribed and tongued at internal angles and housed into the plinth block to conceal any movement.

The elevation and sectional details of a modern design, three-quarter height panelling is shown in Figure 485. This is formed of sheet panelling which is fixed on the surface of a framed surround. The panels could be made of a variety of material, for example, insulation board covered with hessian or other material for good acoustics, ply with a veneer, plastic laminate, cork, lino or PVC applied finish.

Other sheet materials which are suitable have either a chipboard, hardboard or ply base and a factory finished decorative surface including simulated stonework, brickwork and vee jointed matching.

The simple framework, the bottom rail of which forms the skirting, may be painted or polished to contrast with the panel finish.

Also shown in Figure 485 is a method of forming a vertical joint, for use where the total length of panelling might cause problems with handling or access.

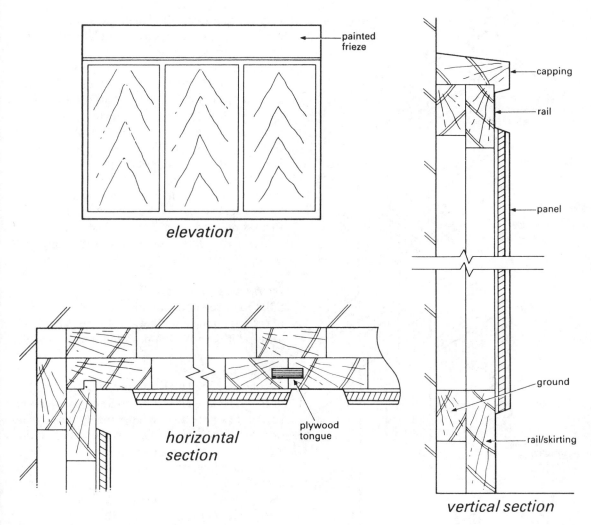

Figure 485   *Sheet panelling details*

Fixing panelling

Grounds

Probably the most important requirement of panelling is a straight and level surface on which to fix it. Any distortion will be exaggerated in the finished panelling and mar its appearance. This straight and level surface can be provided by battening out the walls with grounds. These are normally preservative-treated softwood. They may have been framed up using halvings or mortise and tenon joints or alternatively sup-

plied in lengths for use as separate grounds or counter battening (see Figure 486).

The method used to fix the grounds will vary depending on the material they are being fixed to (for example, brick, block, concrete, steel) but will be either by plugging and screwing, nailing into twisted timber plugs, nailing direct to the wall with cut or hardened steel nails or by using a cartridge fixing tool.

Uneven wall surfaces will require packings behind the grounds to achieve a flat surface. A level and straight edge can be used to test the

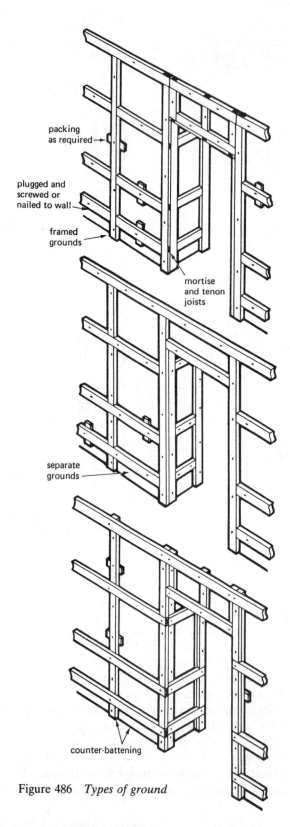

packing
as required→

plugged and
screwed or
nailed to wall

framed
grounds

mortise
and tenon
joists

separate
grounds

counter-battening

Figure 486   *Types of ground*

wall in order to find any high spots. The grounds can then be fixed, packed out and lined in to this level. As framed grounds are made up with the panelling in the joiner's shop, they will have been planned to suit each other, but when separate grounds or counter battens are used it is essential that these are correctly positioned in order to provide the desired fixings for the panelling. These positions will be shown on the full size setting out rods of the panelling supplied by the joiner's shop.

The fixing of panelling to the grounds should be concealed as far as possible. There are various methods of achieving this.

Figure 487 illustrates the following concealed or secret fixings.

Interlocking grounds
Splayed or rebated grounds are fixed to the back of the panelling and the wall. As the panelling is lowered it is hooked in position on the grounds.

Slot screwing
Key hole shaped slots are prepared in the back of the panelling and corresponding countersunk head screws are driven into the grounds. The slots are then located over the projecting screws and the panelling tapped down so that the head is driven along the slot to provide a secure completely secret fixing. This method was widely used in traditional panelling for fixing skirtings, architraves and plinth blocks.

Slotted and interlocking metal plates
The use of key hole slotted plates is similar to slot screwing. The plates are recessed in the back of the panelling. Interlocking plates are similar in principle to interlocking grounds. The cranked plate is fitted in corresponding positions in the back of the panelling and the face of the grounds. Alternatively, the plates may be fitted so that the panels can slide in sideways.

Pellets
Screw holes are counterbored and cross grained pellets made from the same material as the panelling are glued and inserted in the hole. Care must be taken in matching the grain and

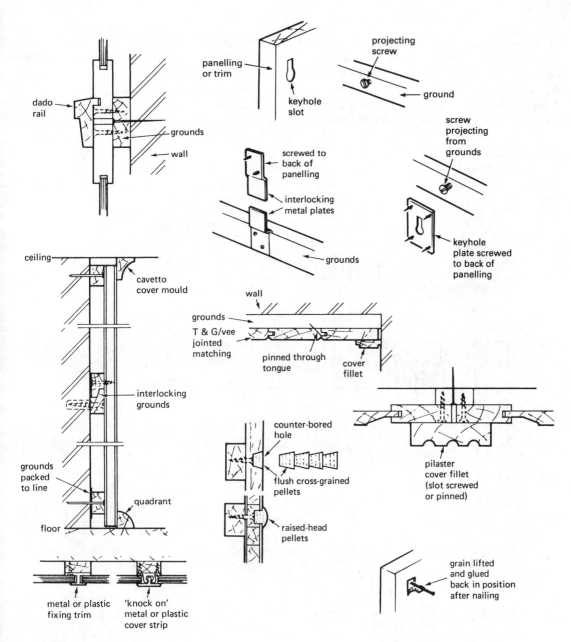

Figure 487 *Concealed fixings*

cleaning the pellet back flush with the surface. Dome-headed pellets are also available to provide a featured fixing.

Cover fillets
Panelling can be surface screwed to the grounds and then covered with a fillet pinned in place.

This may be moulded to form a feature or may in fact be the skirting, cornice, frieze rail, dado rail or pilaster.

Nailing
Strip panelling such as tongued and grooved matchboarding may be secret fixed by pinning

through the tongue. In other sections the nails may be partly concealed by pinning through a quirk in the moulding and filling with a matching stopping or secret fixed through the surface by lifting a thin sliver of grain with a chisel, nailing behind this and gluing the grain back in position.

Metal or plastic trim

These are mainly used to fix sheet material panelling and usually provide a raised feature joint.

Corner details

The method of forming internal and external angles will depend on the type of panelling but in any case they should be adequately supported by grounds fixed behind. Figure 488 illustrates various details.

Tongue and groove joints, loose tongues, rebates or cover fillets and trims have been used to locate the panelling members. At the same time these will conceal the effects of moisture movement.

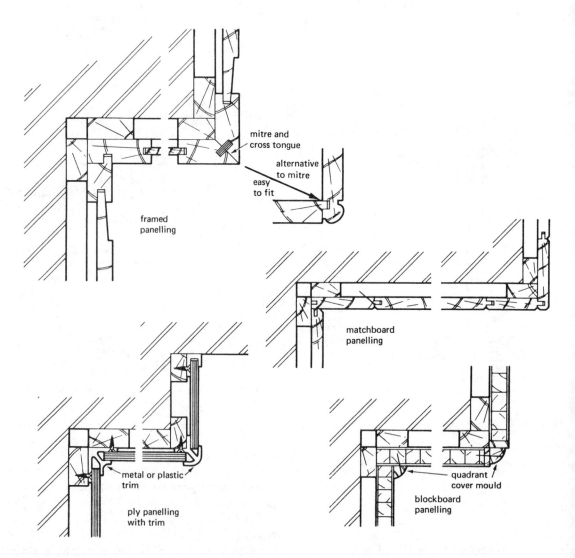

Figure 488   *Corner details*

Panel moulds

Where bolection mouldings are used, these should be slot screwed through the panel from behind. The length of the slot must be at right angles to the grain in order to allow panel movement without any possibility of splitting (see Figure 489).

Also shown in Figure 489 is a method used to fix planted panel moulds. They should be pinned to the framing only and not the panel. This again allows a certain amount of panel movement without splitting.

General requirements of panelling

1 Before any panelling commences it is essential that the wall construction has dried sufficiently.
2 All timber should be of the moisture content required for the respective situation (equilibrium moisture content).
3 The backs of the panelling sections should be sealed prior to fixing, thus preventing moisture absorption.
4 Timber for grounds should be preservative-treated.
5 A ventilated air space is desirable between the panelling and the wall.
6 Provision must be made for a slight amount of moisture movement in both the panelling sections and trim.
7 The positioning of the grounds must be planned to suit the panelling.
8 The fixing of the panelling to the grounds should be so designed that it is concealed as far as possible.

Suspended ceilings

These are also known as false ceilings. They are used mainly in concrete or steel frame buildings, such as offices, shops, factories and schools, to provide a decorative finished ceiling.

The main reasons for the installation of suspended ceilings are as follows:

1 To improve the thermal insulation and so reduce heat loss.
2 For sound insulation purposes

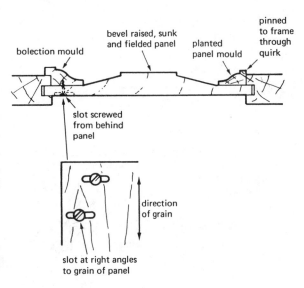

Figure 489 *Bolection moulds and planted panel moulds*

3 For structural fire protection
4 To conceal structural beams
5 To route and conceal services, heating ventilation ducts and sprinkler systems etc.
6 To create integrated lighting.

In addition, suspended ceilings may be used in houses, particularly in older houses with high ceilings. This may be to reduce the height of the ceiling, thus creating a better proportioned room, or to conceal an existing ceiling in a bad state of repair.

Joiners may be expected to fix strip, panelled or proprietary ceilings in conjunction with the fixing of wall panelling, or other joinery items.

A timber and stripboarded suspended ceiling is shown in Figure 490. This consists of ceiling joists spanning the shortest dimension and skew nailed between the wall pieces which have been previously fixed at the required height. Binders are hung at intervals from the main structure to provide intermediate support to the ceiling joists and prevent them sagging. The method used to hang the binders will depend on the type of main structure and the distance between it and the suspended ceiling. This arrangement gives a suitable framework on which to secret fix the

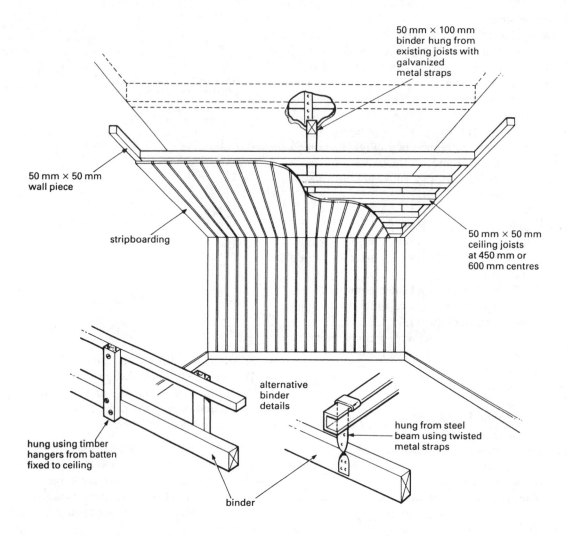

50 mm × 100 mm
binder hung from
existing joists with
galvanized
metal straps

50 mm × 50 mm
wall piece

stripboarding

50 mm × 50 mm
ceiling joists
at 450 mm or
600 mm centres

alternative
binder
details

hung from steel
beam using twisted
metal straps

hung using timber
hangers from batten
fixed to ceiling

binder

Figure 490   *Timber and stripboarded suspended ceiling*

stripboarding. A cover mould can be pinned in place to mask the joint between the wall and ceiling.

Alternative binder details are also given in Figure 490.

A counter battened suspended ceiling is shown in Figure 491. This method, which is also known as brandering, is used when the existing ceiling surface is not level enough or is otherwise unsuitable for the application of the required ceiling finish. The counter battens are fixed to the ceiling base surface, lined in and packed down as required to provide a level surface on which the stripboarding can be fixed.

Framed panelled ceilings may be formed in the same way as wall panelling and fixed to a supporting framework similar to that shown in the previous examples, although a more straightforward method, giving a similar appearance, is shown in Figure 492.

This is a timber framed drop-in panel suspended ceiling. It consists of polished hardwood ceiling joists spanning the shortest dimension of the area cut over hardwood wall pieces,

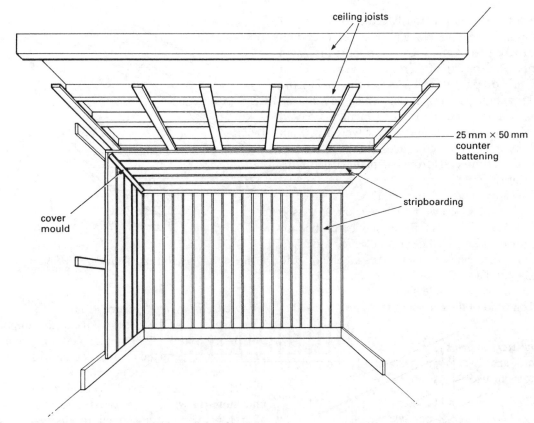

Figure 491 *Counterbattened stripboarded ceiling*

Figure 492 *Panelled ceiling*

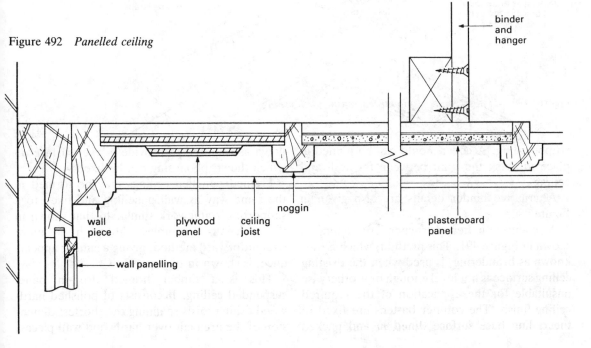

which have been previously fixed to the top of the wall panelling. Noggins are cut over and inserted between the joists to support the panel joints. The spacing of members is dependent on the size of panels, 650 mm centres being the most suitable. The panels, which lay in the rebate run around the framing members, could be of plywood or plasterboard covered with an embossed paper or acoustic tiles. Again, binders are hung at intervals from the main structure to prevent sagging.

The advantage of this method is that it is simply pocket screwed together on site (see Figure 493). Also each panel may be pushed up to provide access to the services which are often run in the ceiling void. As much of the preparation work as possible should be carried out in the workshop, leaving only the wall pieces and one end of the ceiling joists to be cut on site.

Proprietary systems

There are two main suspended grid ceiling systems in use, which are:

1 The exposed grid system.
2 The concealed Z bar system.

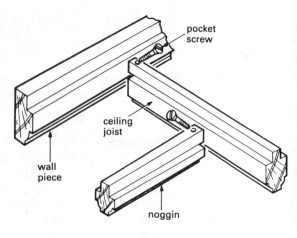

Figure 493 *Panelled ceiling assembly details*

Exposed grid system (Figure 494)

The exposed grid system is used to support either 600 mm × 1200 mm or 600 mm square plasterboard, acoustic or other decorative in-fill tiles. The grid consists of galvanized steel, main T section runners spaced at 1200 mm centres and hung on wires from the structural soffit or alternatively on straps fixed to timber joists.

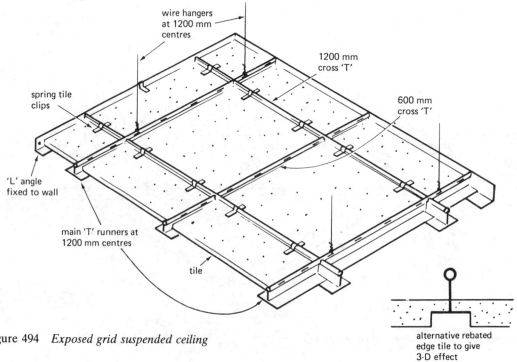

Figure 494 *Exposed grid suspended ceiling*

1200 mm long cross tees interlock into the main runners at 600 mm centres. Where 600 mm square tiles are to be used, 600 mm long cross tees are interlocked into the centre of the 1200 mm cross tees. An L sectioned angle is fixed around the perimeter of the room to support and finish the edge.

The exposed parts of the grid are stove enamelled or capped in aluminium. A wide variety of finishes are available including white, black, silver and timber effect.

The tiles are simply dropped in place, between the T sections, and secured using spring clips. A number of tiles are normally left unclipped in order to provide a convenient access to the space above. The ceiling may be given a three dimensional effect by using rebated edge tiles.

Concealed Z bar system (Figure 495)
This is a concealed grid system for supporting various types of grooved edge tiles. The system consists of galvanized main channels which support the Z sections. The Z sections are clipped to the main channels at either 300 mm or 600 mm centres (depending on the tile size).

The bottom flanges of the Z section provide support for the two opposite sides of the tiles. The other sides of the tiles are joined by a metal splice or noggin tee.

L section angles are used to support the tiles and finish the ceiling where it abuts the walls.

Before fixing, the layout of the components must be planned, so that the tiles are centralized and any cut tiles around the perimeter are the same width on opposite sides of the room.

Levelling
The levelling of suspended ceilings is extremely important as any distortion or misalignment will be evident in its finished appearance.

To achieve a level ceiling the first operation is to establish the position and fix the wall pieces. All of the other components must then be lined into these. The position of the wall pieces may be marked out by measuring up a set distance from a datum line. Usually this will have been previously established using either a water level or an optical levelling instrument. However, specialist erectors fixing proprietary systems are increasingly using electronic and laser levelling instruments to establish datums.

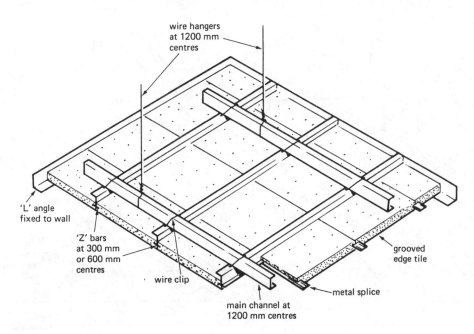

wire hangers at 1200 mm centres

'L' angle fixed to wall

'Z' bars at 300 mm or 600 mm centres

wire clip

grooved edge tile

metal splice

main channel at 1200 mm centres

Figure 495   *Concealed Z-bar suspended ceiling*

Seating

Normally the manufacture of seating is more of an area for specialist furniture or upholstery concerns than the joiner, although purpose-made joinery works may be involved with the timber framework for upholstered seats and other continuous public seating.

A typical upholstered seat suitable for use in bars, hotels, office reception areas and restaurants is illustrated in Figure 496. This type of seating can be used on its own free standing, backing against a wall, or in pairs back to back. The basic framework to take the sprung or foam upholstery work is normally made in beech. It consists of a number of simple mortised and tenoned framed standards spaced at about 500 mm centres (the amount of space allowed for each person). The rails which tie the whole unit together are housed and screwed to these standards (see Figure 497).

Figure 498 illustrates another upholstered bench seat. It can be clearly seen from the section shown in Figure 499 that this is a more basic form of construction, where the seat and

supports are framed from 45 mm × 45 mm softwood.

The seat is formed using a removable upholstered foam cushion which is supported by 18 mm plywood. The foam backrest is upholstered around 12 mm plywood and is fixed through the veneered plywood back. A matching hardwood edging and capping are used to finish both the seat and back rest. These are screwed and pelleted in place. The capping may also require scribing to an irregular wall surface. The space under the seat is closed by pinning 6 mm veneered plywood in place.

This type of seating is suitable for fixing against a wall. Alternatively, two units can be fixed back to back forming island seating as shown in Figure 500, in which case a wider capping would be used to cover the joint between them.

Church seating (pews) are invariably unupholstered and little attention is paid to making them comfortable, although the use of sloping backs and seats are an improvement to straight backs and flat seats.

Traditionally, they were made from oak or

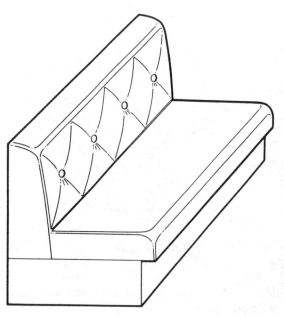

Figure 496   *Upholstered bench seat*

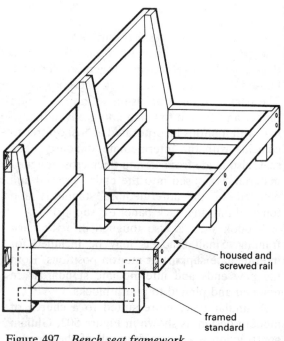

housed and
screwed rail

framed
standard

Figure 497   *Bench seat framework*

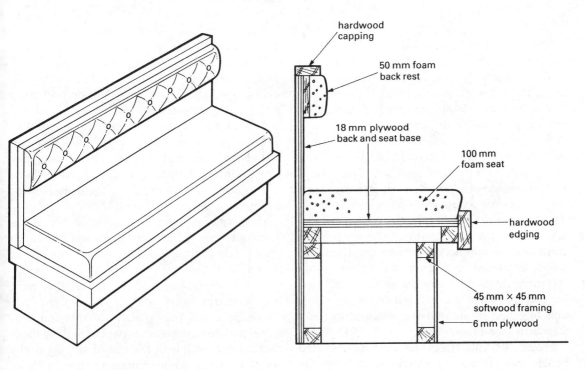

Figure 498 *Upholstered bench seat*

Figure 499 *Bench seat section*

pitch pine, and the pew ends often decorated with ornate carvings.

Figure 501 illustrates a traditional style pew. The pew ends are built up from four 45 mm thick boards, cross tongued together. They are housed to receive the seat back and book shelf. The back is framed up using 45 mm × 95 mm timber and 19 mm tongued and grooved boarding, with muntins incorporated at 1 m centres to coincide with the intermediate standards. The seat, also made from 45 mm thick cross tongued material, is housed into the ends, screwed and pelleted to the intermediate standards and tongued into the back panel for support.

A book shelf is also tongued into the back framing. Small brackets may be included for intermediate support at muntin positions. Both the pew ends and intermediate standards are tenoned and pinned to plinth blocks.

A similar pew, more suited to a church of modern design, is shown in Figure 502. Glulam construction is used to form all of the compo-

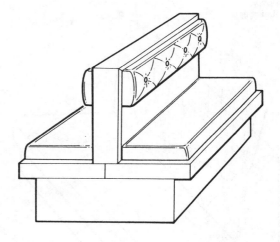

Figure 500 *Island seating*

nents, which are housed and screwed and pelleted together.

Figure 503 shows an outdoor seat with a hardwood seat and backrest supported by

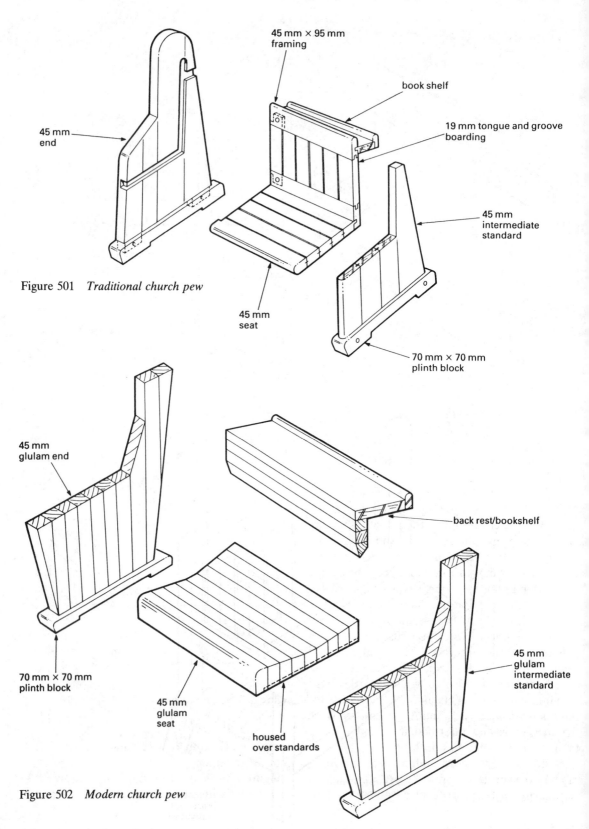

45 mm
end

45 mm × 95 mm
framing

book shelf

19 mm tongue and groove
boarding

45 mm
intermediate
standard

45 mm
seat

70 mm × 70 mm
plinth block

Figure 501   *Traditional church pew*

45 mm
glulam end

back rest/bookshelf

70 mm × 70 mm
plinth block

45 mm
glulam
seat

housed
over standards

45 mm
glulam
intermediate
standard

Figure 502   *Modern church pew*

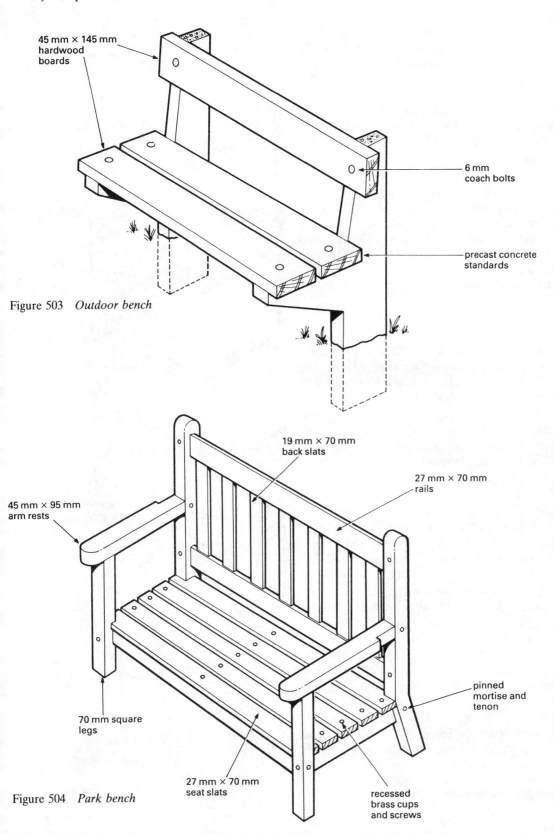

45 mm × 145 mm
hardwood
boards

6 mm
coach bolts

precast concrete
standards

Figure 503   *Outdoor bench*

19 mm × 70 mm
back slats

27 mm × 70 mm
rails

45 mm × 95 mm
arm rests

pinned
mortise and
tenon

70 mm square
legs

27 mm × 70 mm
seat slats

recessed
brass cups
and screws

Figure 504   *Park bench*

precast concrete standards spaced about 1.8 m apart. Intermediate standards could be introduced where longer seats are required. The hardwood boards forming the seat and backrest are coach bolted to the standards.

A traditional outdoor park bench is illustrated in Figure 504. Typically framed up in teak, it uses pinned mortise and tenon joints. The seat slats are fixed to the end frame and intermediate cross rails with brass recessed cups and screws. The back legs have been shaped from 75 mm × 225 mm section which gives a slope to the back rest and reduces the likelihood of the seat toppling over. Other suitable sectional sizes have also been indicated.

Fitments

Fitments can be constructed as built in fixtures or independent freestanding units. There are many forms of fitment in common use each designed to suit its own particular purpose, for example, shelves, cupboards, counters and display units. A large amount of these fitments is provided by the specialist manufacturers who offer mass produced standard ranges of units.

The main fitments used are domestic kitchen, bedroom and lounge units; office storage units; counters, shelving and racks for supermarkets, multiple stores or clothes' shops.

Purpose-made fitments are extensively used for bank, building society, reception and bar counters, as well as one-off items or fitments with special design features.

Traditionally, fitments were made either from wide timber boards joined together to form standards and shelves, or as a framed carcass with in-fill panels of thin plywood or timber. However, modern methods of construction utilize sheet materials to a large extent.

An exploded view showing the typical arrangement of members in a freestanding shelf unit is illustrated in Figure 505. This could be made from either 18 mm thick solid timber or sheet material. The joints used are simple housings stopped before the front edge to give a neat appearance.

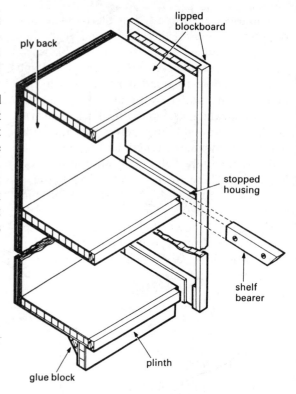

Figure 505   *Shelf unit*

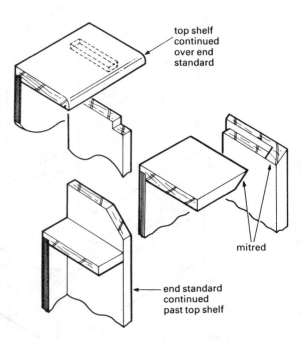

Figure 506   *Alternative top shelf details*

A plinth is incorporated at the base to raise the bottom shelf off the ground and enable the unit to be scribed to an uneven floor surface. This has been set back from the face of the unit to allow people to stand close when selecting items off the shelves without risk of damage through kicking. The plywood back, which is glued and screwed to the shelves and standards, is tidy and provides strength and rigidity.

Alternative top shelf details are illustrated in Figure 506. These are more suitable for low level shelves where the visible end grain of the joint may be unacceptable.

Figure 507 shows that the plinth may be framed up and fitted to the base as a separate item. This is fixed by pocket screwing from behind. Glued angle blocks are used to provide extra rigidity between the two parts. Figure 507 also shows how the intermediate standards are housed into the base or pot board.

Note: The lower member of a unit is historically named a pot board after a low board or shelf raised just off the floor on which pots were stored. Cupboards are so named because they derive from the simple open boards or shelves on which cups, silver plate and other items could be displayed.

In situations where the sizes of the items to be stored are not known or where they are subject to change, some form of shelf adjustment must be incorporated.

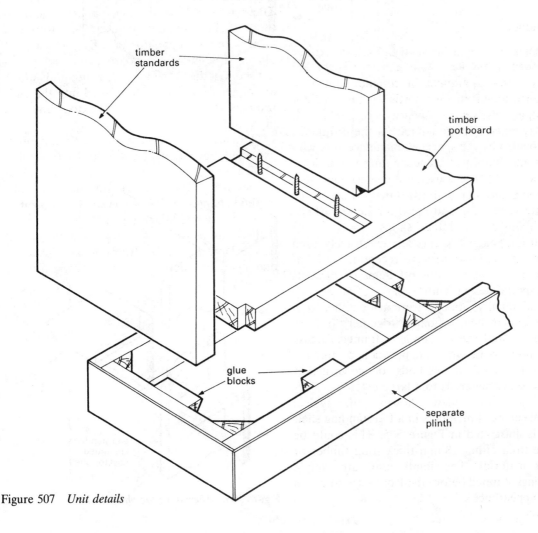

Figure 507   *Unit details*

Figure 508 illustrates three of the many methods in use. The traditional solution is the use of saw tooth supports and splayed end push-in shelf bearers, that can be fitted at any desired height.

The most popular and a very efficient method is the use of 'tonks': bookcase strips and studs which allow height adjustment in 25 mm units. The flush strip is designed to be recessed into the standards and a smaller, deeper groove must also be run to give clearance for inserting the tongues of the studs. Alternatively, a surface fixed strip can be used. This overcomes the need for grooving out and weakening members, but results in an inferior finish.

Sockets tapped into blind holes which have been drilled at intervals down the standards, and used with push-in studs, are suitable for a lighter range of applications.

Cupboard units

These are constructed using similar methods to those of shelving units. Figure 509 illustrates a basic form of cupboard unit. This consists of blockboard ends, pot board shelf and plinth housed together. The two horizontal rails which are either dowelled or dovetailed into the ends provide a fixing for the worktop and the plywood back.

The sides and worktop of a unit are often extended beyond its back. This is to enable service pipes to be accommodated in the space created (see Figure 510). In addition, this method enables the unit to be scribed and cut to fit uneven or irregular wall surfaces.

In situations where the length of a unit would be too large to handle, transport and install in one section, it should be constructed as a range

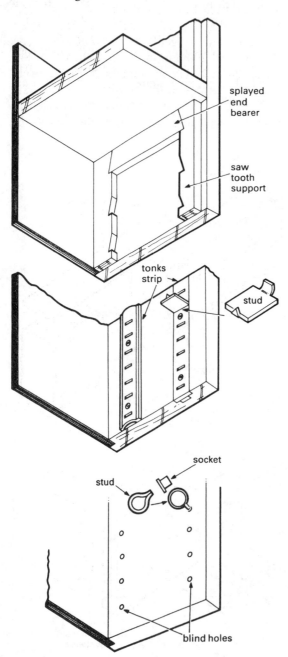

Figure 508   *Adjustable shelf details*

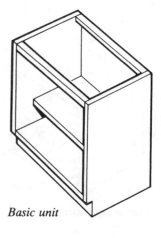

Figure 509   *Basic unit*

of independent units placed together and joined with a continuous worktop (see Figure 511). The units have been spaced apart and bridged by the worktop to create a free area under the worktop, which may be used as a knee space for a work station, dinette etc., or to accommodate an item of equipment, such as a washing machine, fridge or filing cabinet.

Drawers may be incorporated into units in order to provide storage and security (when fitted with a lock) for smaller items. The size of a drawer will be related to the items it is intended to store, but in general will range between 100 mm and 200 mm in depth. When they are vertically stacked in one unit the deeper drawers should be located at the bottom.

Figure 512 illustrates a traditional method of drawer construction which uses through dove-

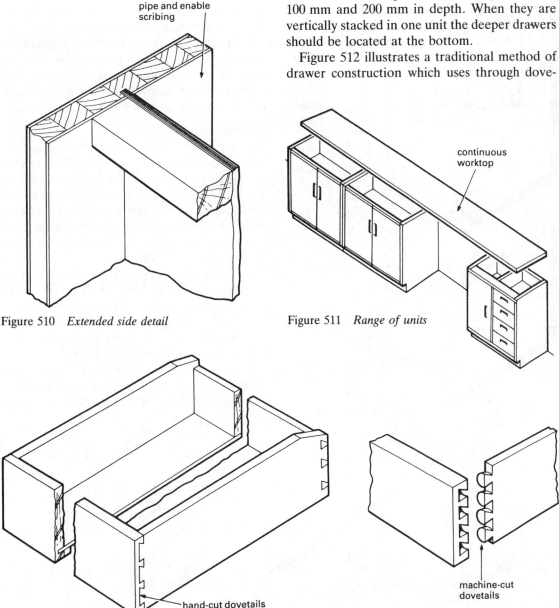

side extended to accommodate service pipe and enable scribing

Figure 510   *Extended side detail*

continuous worktop

Figure 511   *Range of units*

hand-cut dovetails

machine-cut dovetails

Figure 512   *Drawer construction*

tails at the back and lapped dovetails at the front. The plywood bottom is grooved into the front and sides and is pinned to the bottom of the drawer back. Small glue blocks are positioned under the bottom to provide additional rigidity and assist sliding. Rounded machine-made dovetails, produced on a router or spindle moulder, are a more economic alternative where repetitive production is required. These are also illustrated in Figure 512.

Various methods can be used to suspend and slide drawers. Figure 513 shows how framed drawer rails may be incorporated into a unit for this purpose. The dustboard shown grooved into the rails is mainly used on better quality work.

Its purpose is to separate the drawer and cupboard spaces. A drawer kicker is fitted between the top rails to prevent the front of the drawer falling downwards as it is pulled out.

When closed, the drawer front should finish flush with the unit. This can be achieved by pinning small plywood drawer steps to the front drawer rail.

Another common method of suspending and sliding drawers is shown in Figure 514. This uses grooved drawer sides, preferably of a hardwood with good wearing qualities, which slide on hardwood runners glued and screwed to the unit's sides or standards. Where this method is used, the drawer is often fitted with a false front

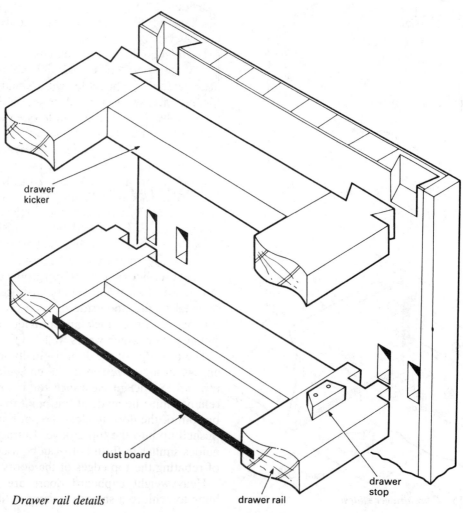

drawer
kicker

dust board

drawer rail

drawer
stop

Figure 513   *Drawer rail details*

screwed from the inside of the drawer. This front has projecting ends to conceal the runner from view. Alternatively, fibre drawer slides may be used (see Figure 515), one part fixed to the side of the drawer and the other to the unit.

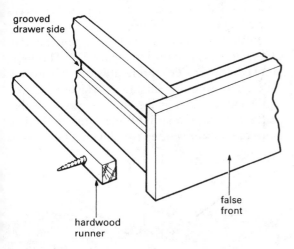

Figure 514 *Drawer slide detail*

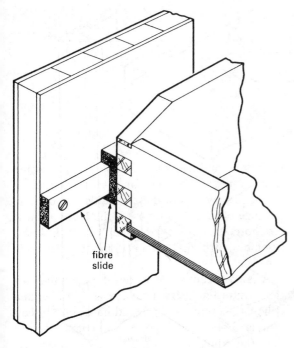

Figure 515 *Fibre drawer slides*

Doors can be incorporated to close the front of open units, for reasons of tidiness, protection or security. They may be either side-hung or sliding. Side hung doors allow maximum access, but when they are open, they project into the room, which can be restrictive and even hazardous in confined spaces.

Figure 516 illustrates three methods of side hanging cupboard doors.

In detail A the door is set flush within the unit and hung on butt hinges. The use of flush hinges avoids the need for recessing and provides the necessary clearance joint.

Rebated doors (detail B) hung on cranked hinges were at one time popular for mass produced units. These doors do not require any individual fitting, as the rebate which laps over the face of the unit conceals the very large clearance joint.

Doors hung on the face of a unit are probably the simplest to make and fit. Although this arrangement is possible with standard butt hinges, the use of cranked or special extended pivot hinges permits the door to open within the width of the unit (detail C).

There are various methods available for making cupboard doors slide. Glass and thin plywood doors are often made to slide in nylon or fibre tracks (see Figure 517). The deeper channel track is used at the top, so the doors can be inserted and removed by pushing them up into the top track, clearing the bottom one.

Figure 518 shows how a cupboard door may be made to slide on fibre tracks grooved into the pot board. Two nylon sliders are recessed and screwed to the underside of each door. These run on the fibre track and provide a smooth sliding action which wears well.

The top edge of the door is usually rebated to engage in a groove run in the underside of the top rail. Sufficient clearance for insertion and removal must be made at this point to allow the bottom of the door to clear the pot board when pushed up into the top groove. Retractable top guides similar to flush bolts can be used instead of rebating the top edges of the doors.

Heavyweight cupboard doors are best top hung to achieve a smooth running action.

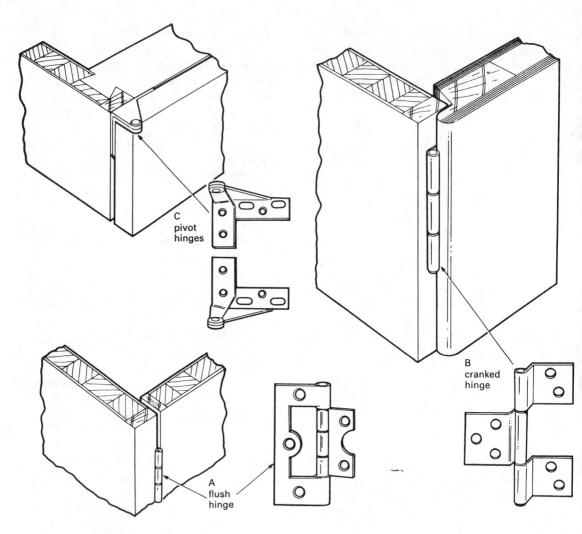

Figure 516   *Side-hung cupboard door details*

Figure 519 illustrates one of the simplest types of top hung cupboard door sliding track. It consists of a surface fixed aluminium top track and bottom guide. The door is suspended by two nylon hangers/sliders fixed to its top edge.

The handle position of bottom sliding doors is best kept nearer the bottom of the door for a smooth sliding action. There will be a tendency for the door to tip and judder if the handle is positioned higher than a distance equal to the door's width. The best action is achieved with top hung doors when the handle position is kept as high as possible.

Shelves and cupboards can be constructed using veneer- or melamine-faced chipboard, although they do present difficulties in jointing. A range of joint fittings are available, but these are more associated with cheap flat pack, home assembly furniture rather than purpose-made joinery.

A fairly recent method, developed mainly for the furniture industry, uses a power groover and diagonal, compressed grained hardwood biscuit dowels. These biscuit dowels are compressed so that the application of glue gives them the tendency to expand in the slot when absorbed,

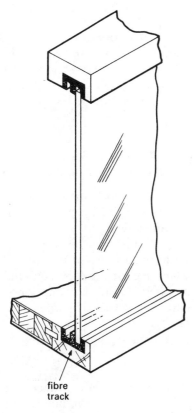

fibre
track

Figure 517   *Glass sliding doors*

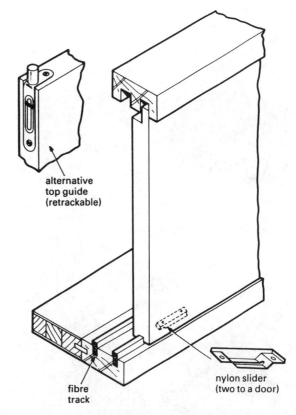

alternative
top guide
(retrackable)

fibre
track

nylon slider
(two to a door)

Figure 518   *Sliding cupboard doors*

producing an easy fitting but tight joint. The purpose of the grain running diagonally is to minimize the risk of splitting and maximize the joint's strength. In addition to the jointing of particle board, this method can be used to produce an economic and acceptable joint when using other sheet materials or solid timbers. Biscuit joints can be used for end to end, edge to edge, end to face and mitre joints.

Figure 520 shows a mitre joint with a biscuit inserted in one piece ready for gluing.

Figure 521 illustrates a biscuit groover used to prepare the joint between the pot board and the end of the cupboard unit. The base plate of the tool is positioned against the marks and when pressure is applied the rotary cutter emerges to cut the slot to receive the biscuit. Accurate and rapid positioning of the slots is achieved by lining up a centre mark on the tool with the centre line marked on the material.

In addition to cutting short slots for the

aluminium
track

Figure 519   *Top-hung door*

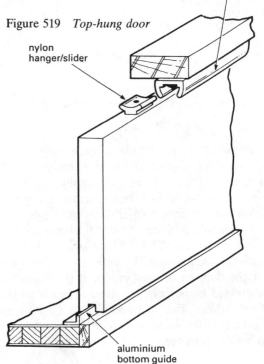

nylon
hanger/slider

aluminium
bottom guide

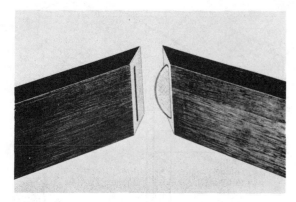

Figure 520   *Mitre joint with biscuit*

Figure 521   *Biscuit groover (cupboard construction)*

Figure 522   *Biscuit groover (drawer construction)*

biscuits, the same tool can also be used to run continuous grooves. Figure 522 shows a biscuit groover being used to join the corners of a drawer as well as grooving out the front and sides to receive the drawer base.

Worktops

The type of worktop used will depend upon the function of the unit. The most common are:

Plastic laminated, blockboard or particle board, where an easily cleaned, hygienic, hard-wearing top is required.
Solid timber finished with french polish or polyurethane varnish, for furniture and other tops where a clear finish is required.
Solid untreated teak for laboratory use.
Blockboard or particle board covered with leather, PVC or lino, for writing surfaces, desks and bank or building society tops.

Counters

Although there are many variations to suit a wide range of retail outlets, hotels, bars, office receptions etc, they may all be constructed using a similar carcass. The main differences are size, front treatment and worktop or counter top treatment.

Figure 523 is a pictorial impression of a modern bank or building society counter. Wide counter tops and glass screens are used as a security measure. They separate persons (i.e., staff and customers) and property, ensuring each remains on their respective side.

A section through a typical bank/building society counter is shown in Figure 524. Veneered blockboard lipped with a matching hardwood on exposed edges and housed together has been used for the main carcass. This sits on a separately framed plinth. The counter top, which is also made from block-board, has a boxed-out overhanging front edge, finished with a deep hardwood edge trim. Leather, PVC, lino or plastic laminate could be used for the actual top finish. The top rails are continuous over the intermediate standards which should be cut out to receive them. The front of the counter has been given a decorative

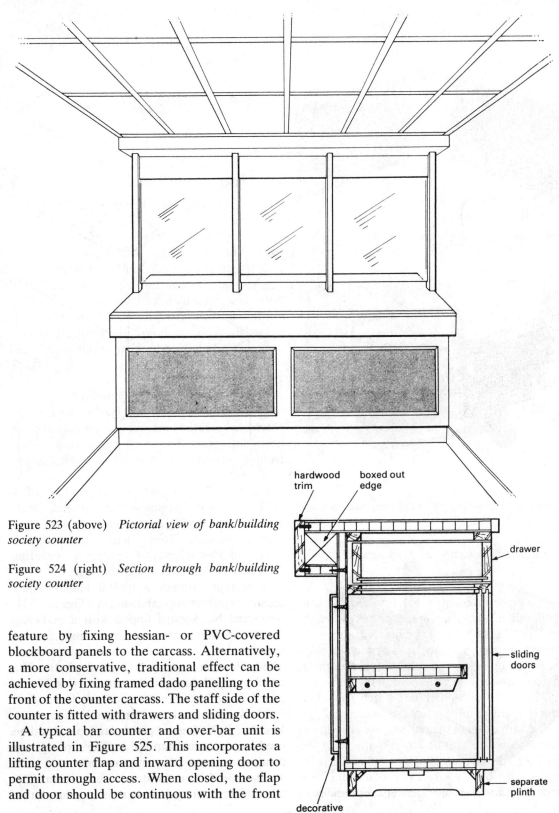

hardwood trim

boxed out edge

drawer

sliding doors

separate plinth

decorative panel

Figure 523 (above) *Pictorial view of bank/building society counter*

Figure 524 (right) *Section through bank/building society counter*

feature by fixing hessian- or PVC-covered blockboard panels to the carcass. Alternatively, a more conservative, traditional effect can be achieved by fixing framed dado panelling to the front of the counter carcass. The staff side of the counter is fitted with drawers and sliding doors.

A typical bar counter and over-bar unit is illustrated in Figure 525. This incorporates a lifting counter flap and inward opening door to permit through access. When closed, the flap and door should be continuous with the front

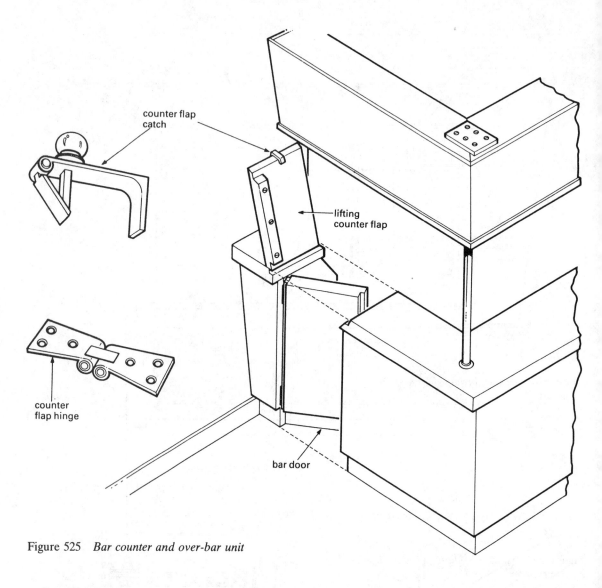

counter flap
catch

lifting
counter flap

counter
flap hinge

bar door

Figure 525   *Bar counter and over-bar unit*

and top surface so that they are hardly noticeable. Counterflap hinges are used to hang the flap. These have no projection above the counter surface when the flap is closed and allow the flap to open through 180° to rest flat on the counter top when required. When the flap opens against a wall a counter flap catch should be fitted to hold it in the open position.

A section through the bar counter showing its construction is illustrated in Figure 526. The inside of this counter and any other used for food should have easily cleaned hygienic surfaces. In this case, all internal surfaces have

been covered with plastic laminate including the faces of the plinth. Also indicated is how a washing up sink can be incorporated below the bar.

The bar top itself has been formed from a solid piece of 32 mm thick hardwood thickened at its front edge to give a deeper impression. This would be fixed to the main carcass using shrinkage plates and finished with polyurethane varnish or other suitable treatment to give a heat, water and spirit resistant surface.

Solid timber bar tops and other counter tops of any width will probably require a number of

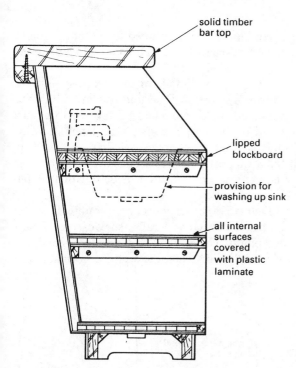

solid timber
bar top

lipped
blockboard

provision for
washing up sink

all internal
surfaces
covered
with plastic
laminate

Figure 526   *Section through bar counter*

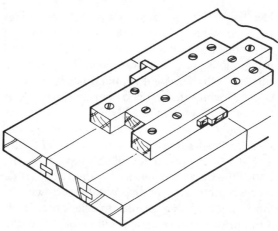

Figure 528   *Counter cramp for heading joint*

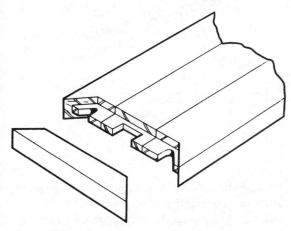

Figure 527   *Mitred counter end cramp*

pieces to be edge jointed together, normally by a
well glued joint incorporating a loose tongue for
strength and to keep the faces flush during
assembly. The ends can be cramped as shown in
Figure 527. This mitred cramp, into which the
top is tenoned, serves to keep the top flat and
prevents any unsightly end grain showing.

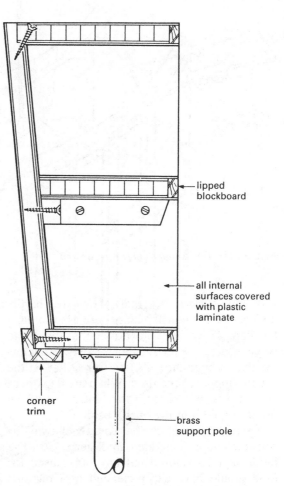

lipped
blockboard

all internal
surfaces covered
with plastic
laminate

corner
trim

brass
support pole

Figure 529   *Over-bar unit*

Heading joints in a worktop are sometimes required where long runs or a change of direction are necessary. These can be formed using a loose tongue or dowels to keep the top surface flush. The joint is pulled up tight with a counter cramp that remains permanently under the counter (see Figure 528).

It can be seen that the cramp consists of three short pieces mortised to take wedges. They are screwed to the underside of the top across the joint initially at one end only, the two outside pieces to one half, and the middle piece with its mortise slightly off centre to the other half. After driving the wedges to pull up the joint, the remaining screws can be driven. Alternatively

small blocks could be fixed to the underside of the top and a sash cramp then used to pull up the joint.

Construction details of the over-bar unit are shown in Figure 529. Again this utilizes lipped veneered blockboard housed together and surfaced on the inside with plastic laminate. This unit is positioned above the bar and held by brass support poles. The ends are fixed back to the structure in order to provide it with a degree of stability.

Figure 530 shows how curved counters may be formed using curved rails, shelves, pot board and plinth. The ends and intermediate standards are positioned so that they radiate normal to the

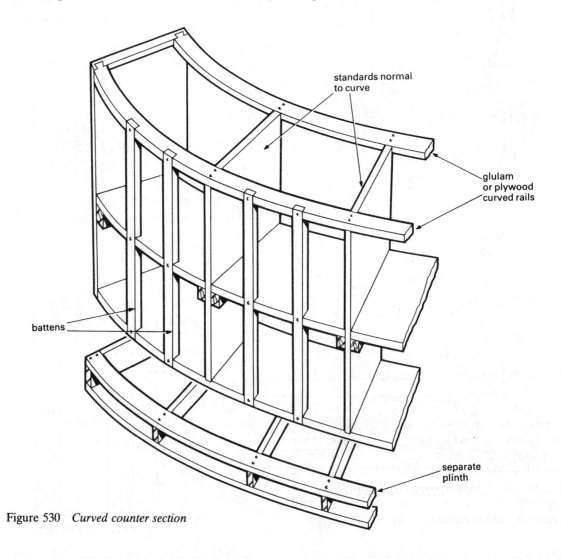

standards normal
to curve

glulam
or plywood
curved rails

battens

separate
plinth

Figure 530   *Curved counter section*

curve. For obvious reasons (short graining) both the rails and the plinth cannot be cut in the usual way from solid timber. Instead they may be made from plywood or formed using glulam methods. The counter front could be finished in 6 mm plywood bent around the curve. This would be glued and pinned to the main carcass. The facing may be built up using a double layer of 3 mm ply on tight curves.

Partitions

Partitions or screens, less than the full height of a room, are used in a variety of buildings to provide visual separation between adjacent areas. Figure 531 shows an elevation and sectional details of a fixed dwarf partition about a metre in height. It consists of a framed panelled section fixed between two built-up end posts. This is topped by a grooved capping for additional stiffening. A skirting to match that of the room has been fixed on both sides.

Where the partition is continuous between two walls, a door or wicket gate may be provided for access. The hanging and closing edges would be rebated to prevent a through joint and also act as an effective stop for the closed position. A radiused rule joint, as shown in Figure 532, will have to be used on the hanging edge of the overhanging cap to prevent binding on opening. Alternatively parliament

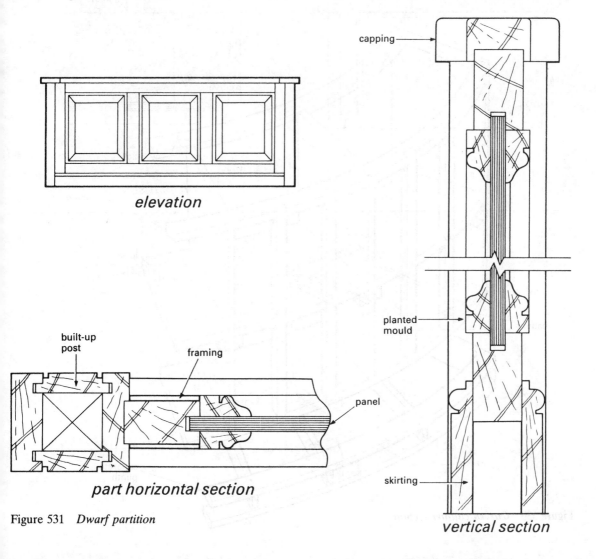

elevation

built-up post

framing

panel

part horizontal section

capping

planted mould

skirting

vertical section

Figure 531 *Dwarf partition*

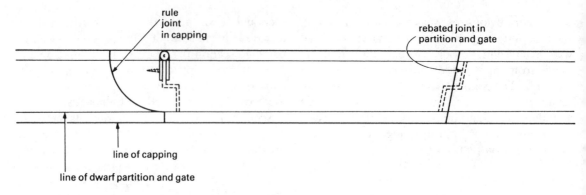

Figure 532   *Wicket gate*

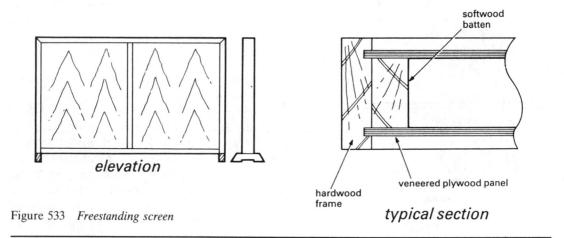

Figure 533   *Freestanding screen*

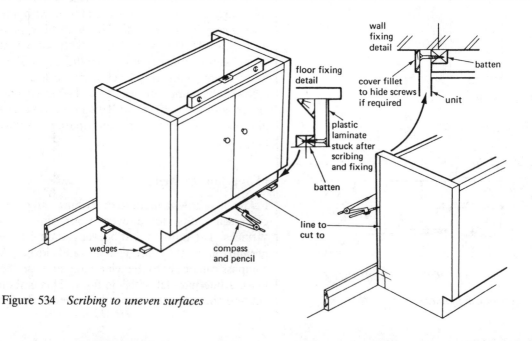

Figure 534   *Scribing to uneven surfaces*

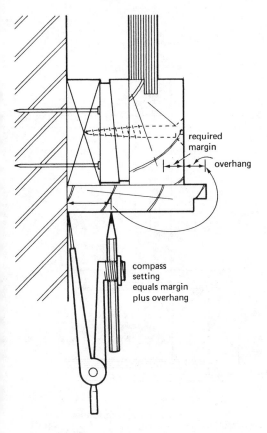

required
margin

overhang

compass
setting
equals margin
plus overhang

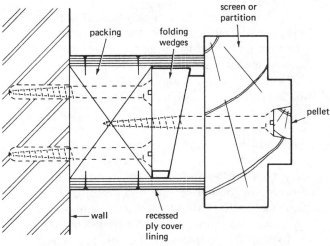

screen or
partition

packing

folding
wedges

pellet

wall

recessed
ply cover
lining

hinges could be used, as these would extend the pivot point outside the capping.

Figure 533 illustrates details of a typical freestanding movable screen often used to divide up and give a degree of privacy to open plan offices. The framework, which incorporates the feet, is of polished hardwood, while the in-fill panels fixed to softwood battens may be of veneered plywood (as shown) or plywood covered with PVC, hessian or similar material. Alternatively, the in-fill panels can be made of softboard or other acoustic material with the hollow core between them filled with fibre glass or rockwool. This would give them excellent sound absorption qualities, making them ideal for screening with noisy machinery, for instance, typewriters, computer printers and telex terminals. In addition this type of screen is suitable as a pin board for poster or information display purposes.

Fixing joinery items

Figure 534 shows a method of scribing and fixing cupboard units to uneven floor and wall surfaces. The units should be wedged up off the ground until they are plumb and level. A compass can be set to the widest gap and used to mark a line parallel with the floor. This is then cut and the operation repeated to scribe to the

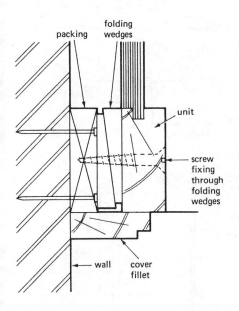

packing

folding
wedges

unit

screw
fixing
through
folding
wedges

wall   cover
fillet

Figure 535   *Fixing joinery*

wall. The unit can then be screwed to battens fixed to the wall and floor. Plastic laminate is often cut and glued to the plinth after fixing to provide a neat, easily cleaned finish.

Partitions, screens and units are normally made slightly smaller than the opening in which they are to fit. They can then be packed or wedged out and suitable cover strips or linings applied to conceal the joint (see Figure 535).

Figure 536 shows how a framed dwarf screen may be fixed to the floor by inserting steel dowels into the bottom rail and grouting these into holes in the floor. Often the free end of this type of screen terminates with a post. This may be fixed to the floor in a similar way to a newel post, either by inserting a steel dowel partly into the bottom of the post and grouting it into the concrete, or, in the case of a timber floor, continuing the post through the floor and bolting it to a joist. Alternatively, L shaped metal brackets screwed to both the framing and floor can be used to stiffen and secure the screen at an open end or door position.

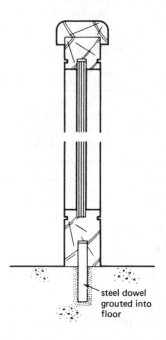

steel dowel grouted into floor

Figure 536   *Fixing a dwarf screen*

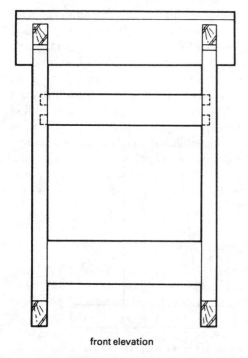

front elevation

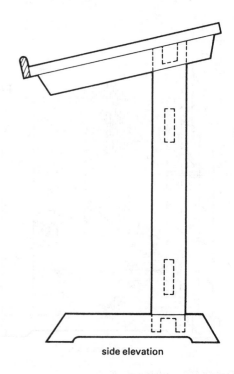

side elevation

Figure 537   *Lectern*

Lectern

This is a reading desk or book stand, normally used in churches and lecture halls by readers in a standing position.

Figure 537 shows a modern type of lectern standing up to 1.2 m in height to the lower edge of the sloping top, which is angled at about 25°. The side support frames and cross rails are mortised and tenoned together. The sloping top, which is fixed by screwing up through the sloping bearers, has a raised lipping on the edge nearest the reader, to prevent books and papers slipping off.

Litany desk

This is similar to a lectern but lower in height, as it is intended for church use with the reader in a kneeling position. Figure 538 illustrates a litany desk consisting of two framed sides joined by a framed front panel and a sloping book top. Often the front panel is decorated with carved tracery or linenfold pattern as shown in Figure 539. Linenfold panels, also known as drapery panels are intended to imitate folded or draped curtains.

Stairs

A stairway can be defined as a series of steps (combination of tread and riser) giving floor to floor access. Each continuous set of steps is called a flight. Landings are introduced between floor levels either to break up a long flight, giving a rest point, or to change the direction of the stair where there is a restricted going.

Stairs can be classified according to their plan shape. The main ones are:

Straight flight stairs
Quarter-turn stairs
Half-turn stairs
Geometrical stairs

In addition, each type can be further classified by its method of construction, for instance, close

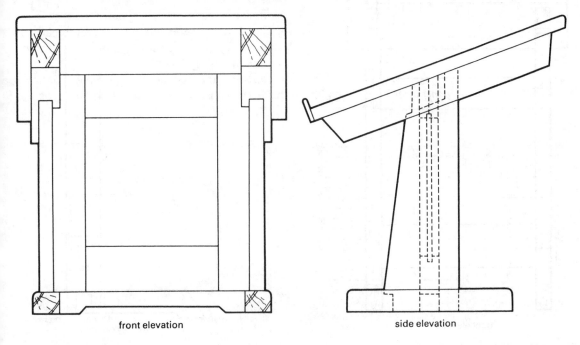

front elevation   side elevation

Figure 538 *Litany desk*

tracery

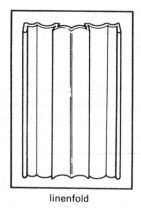

linenfold

Figure 539 *Alternative panel details*

string, open string, open riser, carriage beam, and spine beam.

Straight flight stairs

These run in one direction for the entire length. Figure 540 shows three different variations.

The flight which is closed between two walls (also known as a cottage stair) is the simplest and most economical to make. Its handrail is usually a simple section fixed either directly on to the wall or on brackets.

The flight fixed against one wall is said to be open one side. This open or outer string is normally terminated and supported at either end by a newel post. A balustrade must be fixed to this side to provide protection. The in-filling of this can be either open or closed and is usually capped by a handrail. Where the width of the flight exceeds one metre a wall handrail will also be required.

Where the flight is freestanding, neither side being against a wall, it is said to be open both sides. The open sides are treated in the same way as the previous flight.

Quarter-turn stair

As its name suggests this type of stair changes direction, 90° to the left or right by means of either a quarter space landing or tapered steps (see Figure 541).

Tapered steps economize on space because the extra steps are introduced in place of the

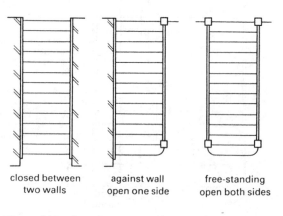

closed between   against wall   free-standing
two walls   open one side   open both sides

Figure 540 *Straight-flight stairs*

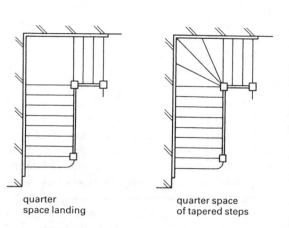

quarter   quarter space
space landing   of tapered steps

Figure 541 *Quarter-turn stairs*

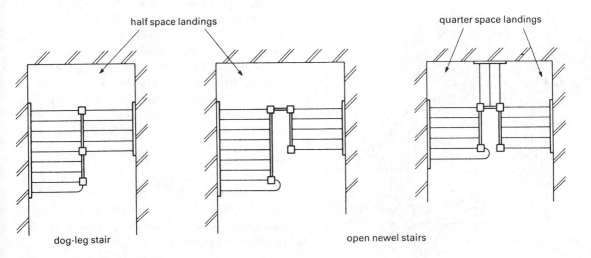

Figure 542   *Half-turn stairs*

landing, but they are potentially dangerous, due to the narrowness of the treads on the inside of the turn. They should therefore be avoided where possible, especially in situations where they are likely to be used by young children or elderly persons, or at least be located at the bottom rather than the top of the flight.

Half-turn stair

This stair reverses its direction through 180°, normally by a half-space landing. Figure 542 illustrates the two main types. One is the dog-leg stair, where the outer strings of the upper and lower flights are joined into a common newel immediately above each other. This stair takes its name because of the appearance of its sectional elevation.

The other type is the open-newel stair (also known as an open-well stair). Two newels are used at landing level. These separate the string of the upper and lower flights, thus creating a central space or well. A short flight is often introduced between the two newels at landing level thereby creating two quarter space landings and at the same time economizing on space.

Tapered steps could be used instead of landings to negotiate turns in both dog-leg and open-newel stairs.

Geometrical stair

The previous more robust types of stair utilize newels to change direction and also to terminate and support the outer strings. This gives them an image of more strength and rigidity, whereas a geometrical stair, as shown in Figure 543, presents a graceful more aesthetical appearance. They have an outer string and handrail that are continuous from one flight to another throughout the entire stairway. As both the string and handrail rise to suit the stairs throughout the curve they are said to be 'wreathed'.

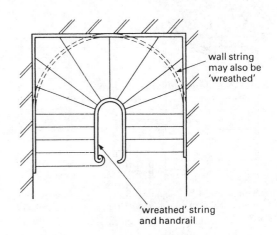

Figure 543   *Geometrical stair*

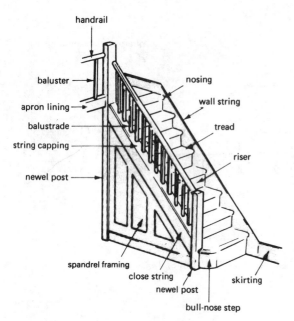

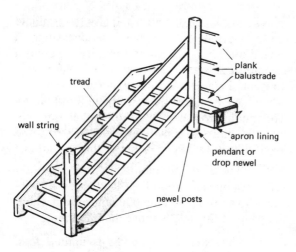

Figure 544   *Stairway terminology*

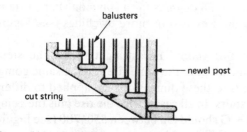

Figure 545   *Open plan stairs*

Figure 546   *Cut string*

Although newels are not essential, they are sometimes used at the top and bottom of a stair to support the scrolled handrail above. This type of stair is the most expensive and thus rarely encountered in new work, except for the one-off, very high quality situation.

In addition to the stair illustrated, an infinite variety of designs for geometrical stairs may be devised, including helical (often misnamed spiral), and elliptical stairs.

Terminology (Figures 544, 545, 546, 547, 548)

Apron lining
The boards used to finish the edge of a trimmed opening in the floor.

Balustrade
The handrail and the in-filling between it and the string, landing or floor. This can be called either an open or closed balustrade, depending on the in-filling.

Baluster
The short vertical in-filling members of an open balustrade.

Bull-nose step
The quarter-rounded end step at the bottom of a flight of stairs.

Carriage
This is a raking timber fixed under wide stairs to support the centre of the treads and risers. Brackets are fixed to the side of the carriage to provide further support across the width of the treads.

Commode step
A step with a curved tread and riser normally occurring at the bottom of a flight.

Curtail step
The half-rounded or scroll-end step at the bottom of a flight.

Newel
The large sectioned vertical member at each end

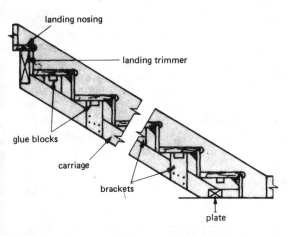

Figure 547 *Stair carriage*

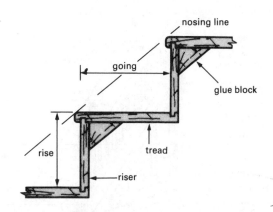

Figure 548 *Stairway definitions*

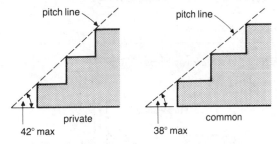

Figure 549 *Pitch*

of the string. Where an upper newel does not continue down to the floor level below it is known as a pendant or drop newel.

Nosing
The front edge of a tread or the finish to the floorboards around a stairwell opening.

Riser
The vertical member of a step.

Spandrel
The triangular area formed under the stairs. This can be left open or closed in with spandrel framing to form a cupboard.

String
The board into which the treads and risers are housed or cut. They are also named according to their type, for example, wall string, outer string, close string, cut string, and wreathed string.

Tread
The horizontal member of a step. It can be called a parallel tread or a tapered tread, etc., depending on its shape.

Building Regulations
The design and construction of stairs is very closely controlled by the Building Regulations:

1985: Part K. These lay down different requirements for stairs depending on the use of the building, these are summarized as follows and illustrated in Figures 420 to 427.

Note: These requirements do not apply to stairways outside a building; ladders; or a stairway with a rise of less than 600 mm, except where the drop at the side is more than 600 mm.

Pitch The pitch or steepness is limited to a maximum of 42 degrees for a private stair (a stairway used only by one dwelling) and a maximum of 38 degrees for a common stair (a stairway used by two or more dwellings (see Figure 549).

Rise and going For straight flights the steps should all have the same rise and the same going. Limits to these dimensions are applied to different stairs. In all cases twice the rise plus the going 2 R + G should fall between 550–700 (see Figure 550 and Table 32).

Table 32 **Specific requirements for stairs: rise and going**

Description of stair	Max. rise (mm)	Min. going (mm)	Range (mm) (to meet pitch limitation)
Private stair	220	220	155–220 rise used with 245 to 260 going or 165–200 rise used with 220 to 305 going
Common stair	190	240	155–190 rise used with 240–320 going
Stairway in institutional building (except stairs only used by staff)	180	280	
Stairway in assembly area (except areas under 100 m²)	180	280	
Any other stairway	190	250	

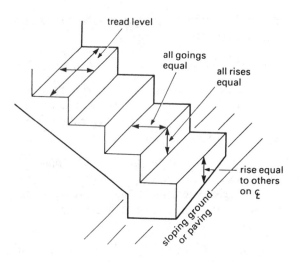

Figure 550   *Risers*

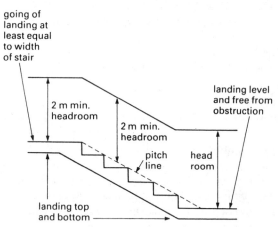

Figure 551   *Headroom and landing*

The rise is measured from the top surface of one tread to the top surface of the next tread. Goings are measured from face of riser to face of riser, and where there are not any risers from nosing to nosing.

Headroom A minimum headroom of 2 m is required over the pitch line of all flights and over landings (see Figure 551).

Steps All steps should have level treads, where steps have open risers the treads should overlap each other by at least 15 mm. The gaps in open riser steps must not permit the passage of a

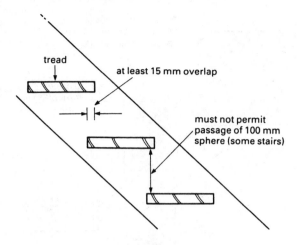

Figure 552   *Open-risers stairs*

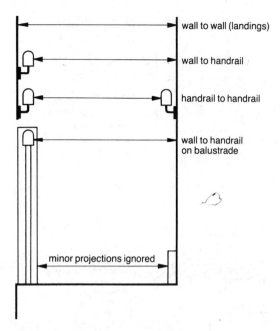

Figure 553   *Measuring minimum width*

100 mm diameter sphere when the stairway is in a dwelling (private and common); any other residential building; or an institutional building (where it is likely to be used by children under five years of age) (see Figure 552).

Width   Minimum widths for stairways depend on the type of stair, as showing the Table 33.

These minimum dimensions are unobstructed widths (see Figure 553), although minor projections such as skirting strings and newels are ignored. Wide flights over 1.800 m should be sub-divided in width to form separate flights.

Length   No more than 36 risers are permitted in consecutive flights unless there is a change of direction of at least 30 degrees. Flights forming part of the stairway in a shop or an assembly area are limited to a maximum of 16 risers.

Landings   Landings are required at both ends of any flight. They should be free of obstruction and be at least equal in width and depth, to the width of its adjoining stairway. All landings should be level except where they are firm made-up or paved ground, when a slope up to 1 in 12 is permitted (see Figures 550 and 551).

Door swings should not obstruct a landing except at the bottom of a flight if it still leaves at least 400 mm clear across the full width of the bottom riser.

Tapered treads   These must conform to the previously mentioned rise and going restrictions,

Table 33 Specific requirements for stairs: minimum width

Description of stair	Minimum width (mm)
Private stair giving access to one room only (except kitchens and living room)	600
Other private stair	800
Common stair	900
Stairway in institutional building (except stairs only used by staff)	1000
Stairway in assembly area (except areas under 100 m²)	1000
Other stairway serving an area that can be used by more than 50 people	1000
Any other stairway	800

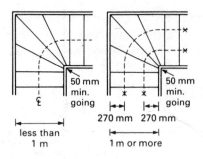

Figure 554 *Tapered tread details*

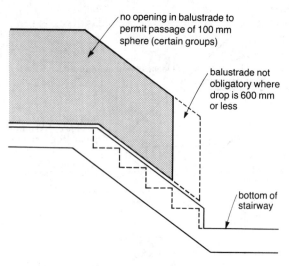

Figure 556 *Guarding of stairways*

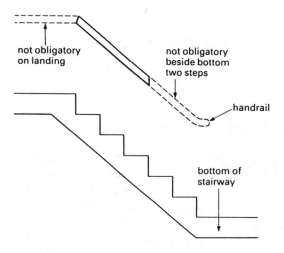

Figure 555 *Handrails*

measured as follows: flights less than 1 m wide in the middle; flights 1 m or wider, 270 mm in from each edge (see Figure 554). The minimum width of tread at the narrow end is 50 mm. All consecutive tapered treads should have the same taper.

Handrails All flights less than 1 m wide require a handrail on one side, wider flights should have a handrail on both sides. These should be fixed between 840 mm and 1 m measured vertically above the pitch line. Handrails are not required; beside the bottom two steps of the stairway (see Figure 555).

Guarding A balustrade or other suitable guard is required at the open sides of all flights and landings. Except where the drop is 600 mm or less. For all private and common stairways, those

in institutional buildings likely to be used by children under five years of age, and any other residential building, openings in balustrades must not permit the passage of 100 mm diameter sphere; in addition its design should prevent children readily climbing up it. See Figure 556 and Table 34.

Note: The purpose of prohibiting the passage of a 100 mm diameter sphere, through open risers and openings in balustrades, is to prevent children from getting their heads stuck in them.

The height of the balustrade depends on the type of stair.

Alternative approach An alternative approach to the stairway design requirements given in the Building Regulations AD: K is to use BS 5395 stairs, ladders and walkways. The BS is more comprehensive in that it states optimum sizes in addition to the minimum ones.

In certain aspects the BS is more restrictive

Table 34 **Specific requirements for stairs: minimum balustrade heights**

Description of stair	Minimum balustrade height (mm)	
	Flight	Landing
Private stairway	840	900
Common stairway	900	1000
Other stairway	900	1100

than the AD and in others it is more lenient. Stairways must be designed in their entirety to conform with either the BS or AD. It is not permissible to pick the best requirements from both and mix them.

Means of escape   Stairways that are in offices, shops, dwellings of three or more storeys, or form part of the only means of escape for disabled persons, may need to conform to additional requirements. See mandatory rules for means of escape in case of fire published by HMSO.

Setting out stairs

Before setting out a flight of stairs, it is necessary to determine the individual rise and going for each step.

The rise of each step is determined by dividing the total rise (vertical measurement from finished floor to finished floor) by the number of risers required.

The going of each step is determined by dividing the total going (horizontal measurement from bottom step nosing to landing nosing) by the number of treads required (one less than the number of risers).

Example

Internal flight for a dwelling house with a total rise of 2574 mm and a restricted going of 2805 mm, assuming that the minimum number of steps are required:

Minimum number of risers
= total rise ÷ maximum permitted rise for purpose group
= 2574 mm ÷ 220
= 11.7
(say) = 12 (each measuring less than the maximum permitted)

Individual rise
= total rise ÷ number of risers
= 2574 mm ÷ 12
= 214.5 mm

Individual going
= total going ÷ number of treads
= 2805 mm ÷ 11 = 255 mm

Carry out the following checks to ensure compliance with the Building Regulations.

$$2R + G = 550 \text{ mm to } 700 \text{ mm}$$
$$(2 \times 214.5) + 255 = 684 \text{ mm}$$

Pitch maximum: 42°. Draw rise and going full size and check the angle with a protractor. In this case it measures 40° which is permissible.

In cases where the checks prove unsuccessful alternative measures will have to be taken. For example, where $2R + G$ is more than 700 mm, the individual going can be reduced. Where $2R + G$ is less than 550 mm, the total going is too restrictive. Therefore, the stairs must be redesigned, possibly by the introduction of a landing to change the direction on plan.

Where the pitch is greater than 42° the individual rise can be reduced by introducing an extra rise and going, thereby slackening the pitch. However, this will increase the total going, so stairs with restricted goings (such as a doorway at the bottom of the stairs) will again require redesigning to comply.

Once the rise and going of the stairs has been decided, they can be set out. In order to do this, a number of templates can be made out of thin plywood. These are shown in Figure 557. The pitchboard and margin template are used to mark out the face of the treads and risers. The housing for the tread and risers is marked out with the tread and riser templates. These templates are equal to the shape of the tread and

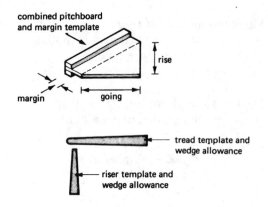

Figure 557 *Setting out templates*

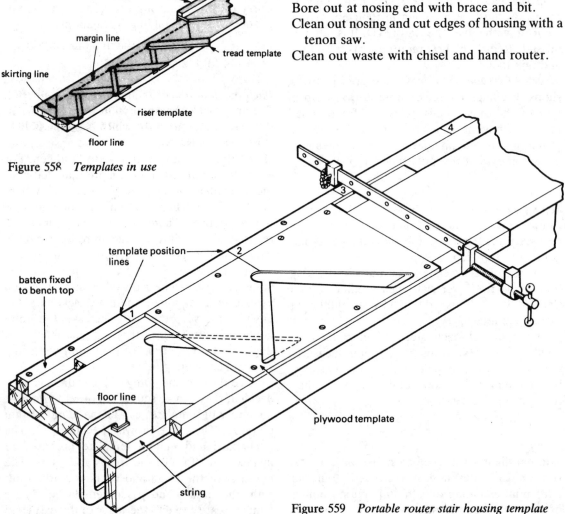

riser plus an allowance for wedging. The use of the templates to mark out the strings is shown in Figure 558.

Close strings
The construction of any staircase with close strings follows the same basic procedure, with slight variations depending on the particular type of stair.

The housings in the string can be cut out on a spindle moulder or by using a portable router and a stair housing template (see Figure 559). Where neither of these is available, they can be cut by hand using the sequence of operations shown in Figure 560.

Bore out at nosing end with brace and bit.
Clean out nosing and cut edges of housing with a tenon saw.
Clean out waste with chisel and hand router.

Figure 558 *Templates in use*

Figure 559 *Portable router stair housing template*

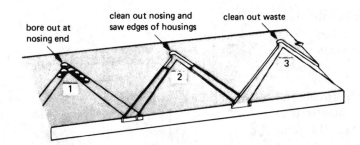

Figure 560   *Sequence of operations*

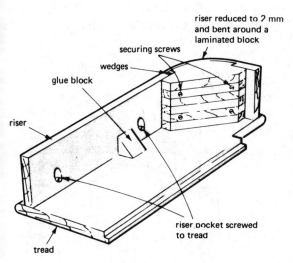

Figure 561   *Forming a bull-nose step*

Figure 561 shows a method of forming a bull-nose step. The curved section of the riser is reduced to a 2 mm thickness and bent around a laminated block. The wedges tighten the riser around the block and hold it there until the glue has set. The reduced section of the riser should be steamed before bending. It can then be bent around the block fairly easily without risk of breaking. The same method of construction is used to form other shaped steps.

Figure 562 shows a curtail step. The shaped riser may alternatively, be glulamed. Splayed end steps are sometimes used in cheaper quality work with the riser mitred and tongued at the joints (see Figure 563).

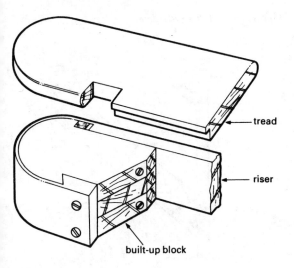

Figure 562   *Round end step (curtail)*

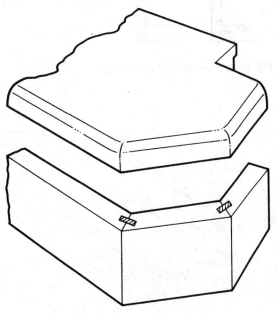

Figure 563   *Splayed end step*

Figure 564 shows three alternatives for tread and riser details. The tread can be made from 25 mm timber and the riser from 19 mm timber or, as is increasingly the case, risers are made from 9 mm plywood.

Figure 565 shows how each step (tread and riser) is made up in a jig before being fixed to the strings. Glue blocks strengthen the joint between the tread and riser. The absence or loosening of these often results in squeaky stairs.

Figure 566 gives a part view of the steps fixed into a string. The treads and risers are glued and securely wedged into their position in the string housing.

Balusters may be either stub tenoned into the string or fitted into a groove run into the string capping. At their upper end they are normally pinned into the groove run on the underside of the handrail (see Figure 567).

Figure 568 shows that the outer string and handrail are normally mortised into the newels at either end. The newels also require housing

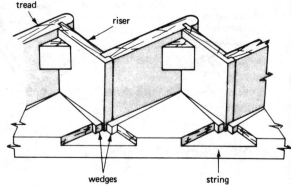

Figure 566   *Fixing of steps into string*

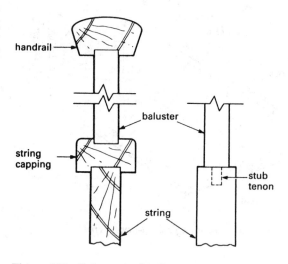

Figure 567   *Balustrade details*

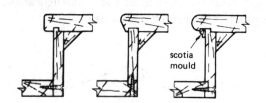

Figure 564   *Tread and riser details*

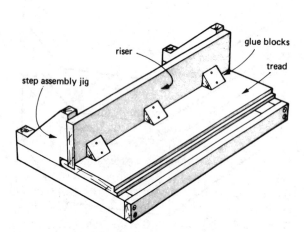

Figure 565   *Step assembly jig*

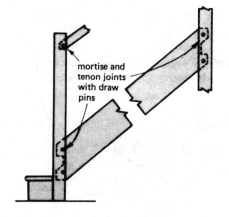

Figure 568   *String and handrail joints*

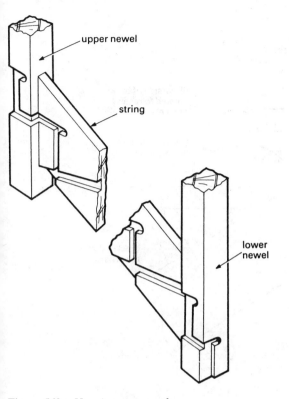

Figure 569 *Housing out newels*

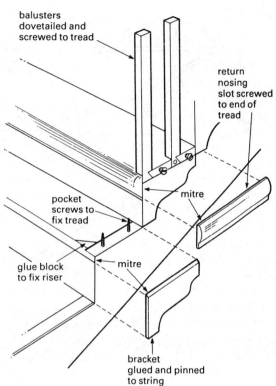

Figure 570 *Cut-and-bracketed stair*

out to receive the treads and risers (see Figure 569).

Cut string

Figure 570 shows the construction details of a cut and bracketed string. This type is used as the outer string of more decorative flights. The string is cut to the shape of the step and the treads are pocket screwed to them. The risers extend past the face of the string and are mitred with thin plywood brackets which are glued and screwed in place.

Most of the assembly will be completed in the workshop with the exception of the following which will be completed on site: the balusters, which are dovetailed and screwed to the tread, and the return nosings, which are slot screwed to the end of the tread.

Open riser stairs

Shown in Figure 571 is a method used to join the

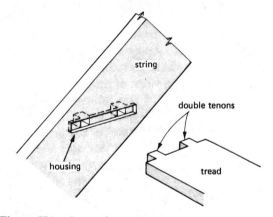

Figure 571 *Open plan stairs*

treads to the strings in a riserless flight of stairs (open plan). The through tenons should be wedged on the outside of the string. Alternatively, the treads could be simply housed into the string, and metal ties used under every third or fourth tread to tie the flight together.

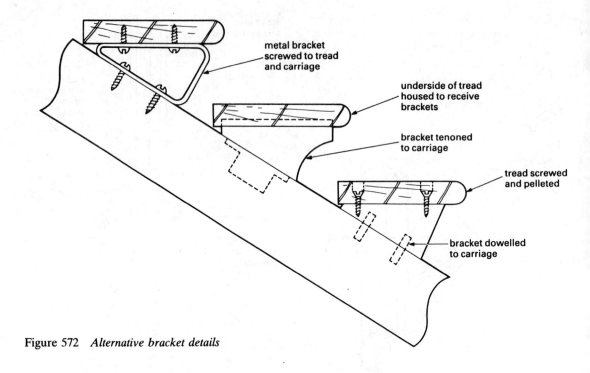

metal bracket
screwed to tread
and carriage

underside of tread
housed to receive
brackets

bracket tenoned
to carriage

tread screwed
and pelleted

bracket dowelled
to carriage

Figure 572   *Alternative bracket details*

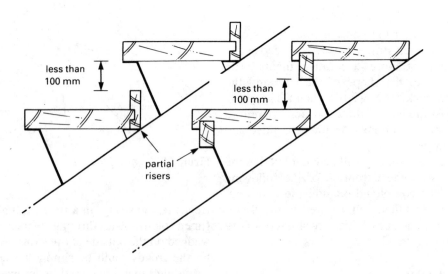

less than
100 mm

less than
100 mm

partial
risers

Figure 573   *Partial risers*

Where carriages instead of strings are used in an open plan flight, the treads are supported by two timber brackets, which are either dowelled or tenoned into the carriage as shown in Figure 572. Alternatively, these may be replaced by purpose-made metal brackets.

The balustrade of open plan flights is often of the straightforward ranch style. This is a number of planks either screwed and pelleted directly to the inside stair face of the newels or mortised and tenoned between them.

On certain flights where the gap between the treads is restricted a partial riser tongued to either the top or underside of the tread can be used. Figure 573 illustrates these two alternative methods.

Tapered steps

Before marking out tapered steps they should be set out full size on a sheet of ply, as shown in Figure 574. This enables the shapes of the strings and tapered treads to be determined. The risers must normally radiate from a point outside the stair width in order to achieve the 50 mm minimum going. Shaped easing pieces are glued and tongued on to the string where the extra width is required. The two wall strings should be tongued and grooved together where they join.

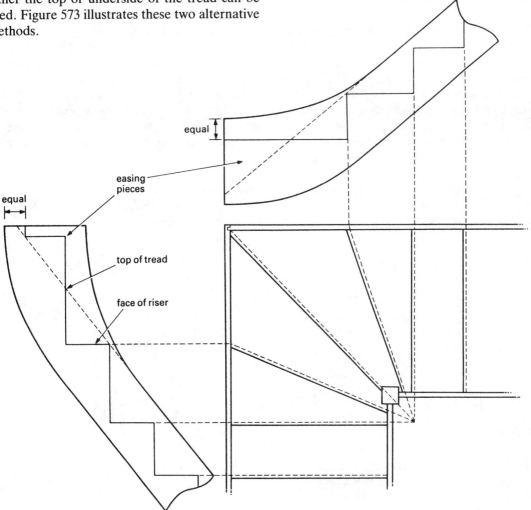

Figure 574 *Setting out tapered steps*

The increased width of tapered steps necessitates them being made up from a number of pieces tongued together. Care should be taken when cutting to ensure that the nosing is kept parallel to the grain. Alternatively, the treads may be cut from 25 mm blockboard with solid timber nosing glued to their front edge.

Geometric stairs

Geometric stairs have wreathed outer strings which are normally cut and bracketed to receive the treads and risers. These strings consist of straight sections, joined either side of a curved section which rises and turns to suit the change in direction.

The two main methods of forming these wreathed strings are by glulam construction or staving.

Staving involves reducing the curved section to about 2 mm so that it may be easily bent around a former or drum to the required shape. After bending, timber staves are glued to the reduced section, thus building up the string to a uniform thickness and retaining it in its bent position.

Figure 575 shows a quarter turn wreathed string fixed around a drum ready for staving. After the staves have cured sufficiently the string may be removed from the drum, cut to the shape of the steps and prepared for jointing to the straight strings (see Figure 576).

These are jointed one rise past the turn with a cross grained or loose tongue. A counter cramp can be used to pull the two ends tightly together as shown in Figure 577. This also has the effect of stiffening the stair and preventing movement at the joint. The cramp consists of three short pieces mortised to take the wedges. They are screwed to the strings initially only at one end. The two outside pieces are screwed to the wreathed string and the middle piece with its mortise slightly off centre to the straight string. After driving the wedges to pull up the joint, the other ends can be screwed.

The handrail associated with a geometric stair also requires wreathing to follow the line of the string below. The setting out and construction of wreathed strings and handrails is a very highly skilled operation, carried out in general by only a few joinery works who specialize in staircase manufacture. The geometrical setting out of such work is covered in Chapter 7.

Installation

Many joiners, especially those working for firms who are staircase specialists, are often required

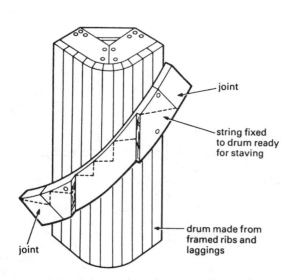

Figure 575   *Forming wreathed string*

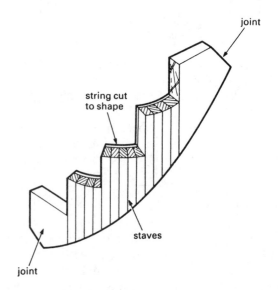

Figure 576   *Wreathed string (staved and cut)*

Figure 577 *Counter-cramp for fixing geometrical stair*

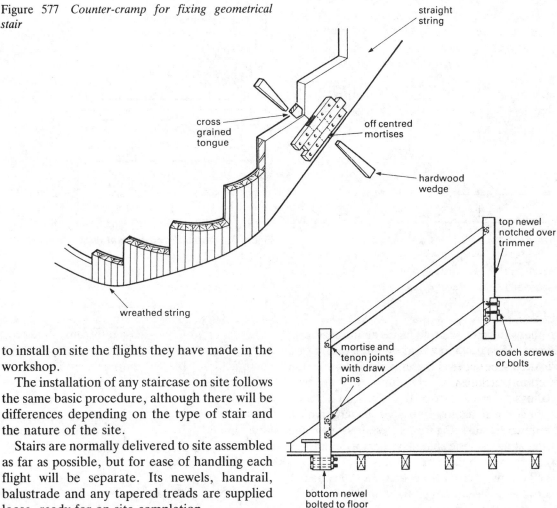

to install on site the flights they have made in the workshop.

The installation of any staircase on site follows the same basic procedure, although there will be differences depending on the type of stair and the nature of the site.

Stairs are normally delivered to site assembled as far as possible, but for ease of handling each flight will be separate. Its newels, handrail, balustrade and any tapered treads are supplied loose, ready for on-site completion.

For maximum strength and rigidity the stairs should be fixed as shown in Figures 578–80. The top newel is notched over the landing or floor trimmer and either bolted or coach screwed to it. The lower newel should be carried through the landing or floor and bolted to the joists (see Figure 578). The lower newel on a solid ground floor can be fixed by inserting a steel dowel partly into the newel and grouting this into the concrete (see Figure 579).

Figure 579 shows that the outer string and handrail are mortised into the newels at either end. With the flight in position, these joints are glued and then closed up and fixed using hardwood draw pins. The wall string is cut over the trimmer at the top and cut-nailed or screwed

Figure 578 *Fixing outer string and handrail*

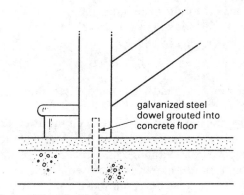

Figure 579 *Newel fixing*

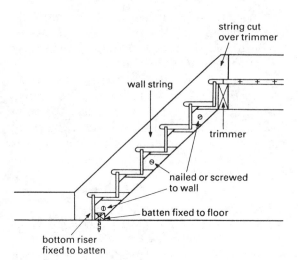

Figure 580   *Fixing wall string*

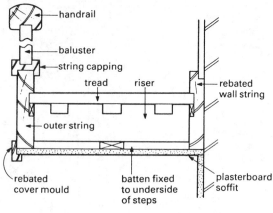

Figure 581   *Section across flight open one side*

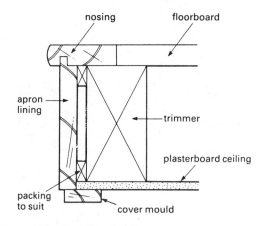

Figure 582   *Landing detail*

to the wall from the underside as illustrated in Figure 580. Also shown is how the bottom of a flight may be secured by screwing it to a batten fixed to the floor.

Illustrated in Figure 581 is a section across a flight fixed up against one wall showing typical finishing details. Figure 582 shows how the trimmer around the stairwell opening is finished with an apron lining and nosing.

Where the width of the stair exceeds about 1 metre, a carriage may be fixed under the flight to support the centre of the treads and risers. To securely fix the carriage it is birdsmouthed at both ends, at the top over the trimmer and at the bottom over a plate fixed to the floor. Brackets are nailed to alternate sides of the carriage to provide further support across the width of the treads (see Figure 583).

Tapered treads

Any tapered treads are fixed after the main flights are in position. They should fit in place fairly easily as they will have been prefitted dry in the joiner's shop and disassembled for transportation, although in practice a certain amount of adjustment is often required to take account of on-site conditions, for example, slightly out of square or out of plumb brickwork.

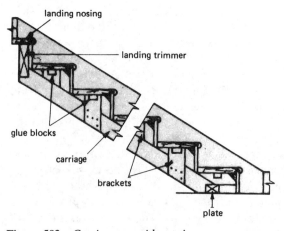

Figure 583   *Carriage on wider stairs*

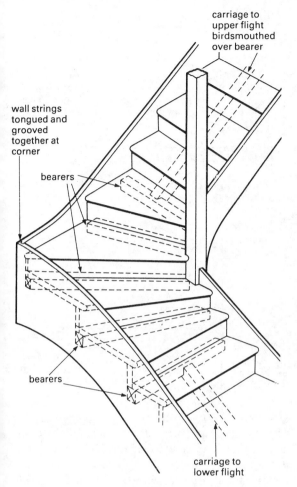

Figure 584   *Tapered treads*

After fitting the tapered treads and riser into the housings in the string, they should be wedged up and screwed. Because of their extra length some form of support is normally required under the tapered treads. This can be provided as shown in Figure 584 by bearers under the riser of each step. These are fixed between the two strings or between the string and the newel. Also shown is how the carriages of the main flights are birdsmouthed over these bearers.

Landings

The construction of landings and the materials used are normally similar to the upper floor.

Figure 585 shows details of a half space landing. The trimmer joist spans between two walls and supports the ends of the trimmed joists spanning across the landing.

The free end of the trimmer for a quarter space landing is normally supported by extending the newel post down to the floor, as shown in Figure 586. Alternatively, either a landing frame or some form of cantilever landing could be used.

Figure 587 shows a typical landing support framework. This would be subsequently boxed

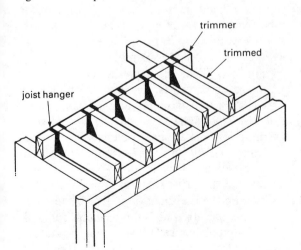

Figure 585   *Half-space landing details*

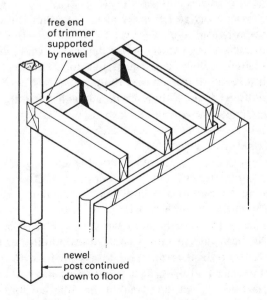

Figure 586   *Quarter-space landing details*

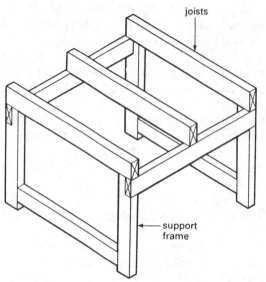

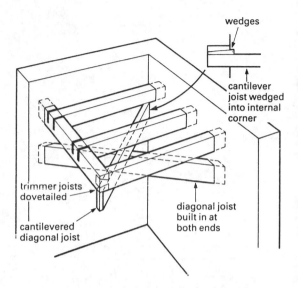

Figure 587   *Landing support framework*   Figure 588   *Cantilever landing*

in or made into a cupboard to create extra storage space.

The cantilever landing shown in Figure 588 consists of a diagonal joist built in to the wall at both ends. This provides a bearing midway along the cantilevered joist which is built in to the internal angle of the wall. The landing trimmer joists are dovetailed together and supported on their free end by the cantilevered joist. This method of support has the advantage of giving a clear space under the stair. However it is essential that the timber used is well seasoned as even slight shrinkage will cause the landing to move and creak in use.

Geometric stairs
These should be delivered partly assembled in a number of easily handled sections. The tapered treads are assembled on site as described above. The main difference in the installation is the fixing of the wreathed portion of the string. This will have been previously formed and permanently fixed at one end to a straight string. The other end of the wreathed string has to be fixed to its adjoining string on site. These will be jointed one rise past the turn with a cross

grained or loose tongue and counter cramped as previously mentioned.

Open riser stairs
The fixing of open riser or open plan stairs with close strings and newels is the same as the stairs previously mentioned. Where carriage or spine beam stairs are concerned the method of installation differs. Both types can be completely prefabricated in the joiner's shop, requiring only fixing at the top and bottom on site. Alternatively, they can be delivered in knock-down form for on-site assembly.

Figure 589 illustrates a typical open riser stair supported on carriages. The upper ends of the carriages are birdsmouthed around the trimmer while the lower ends of the carriages are fixed to the floor with metal angle brackets. The treads are supported by and screwed and pelleted to timber brackets, which are themselves glued and dowelled to the carriages. Newel posts are fixed at either end of the flight on to which the ranch style plank balustrading is screwed and pelleted.

Illustrated in Figure 590 is a spine beam stair which is also known as a mono carriage stair. The spine beam is a large glulam section that is

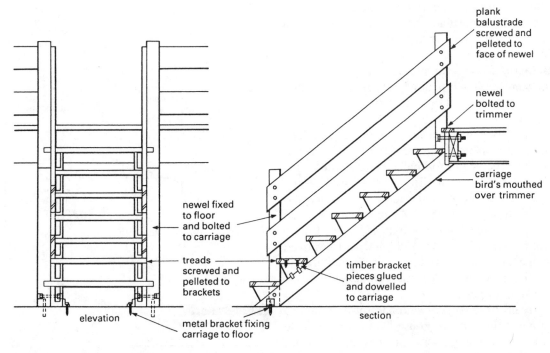

Figure 589 *Open-riser stair*

Labels for Figure 589:

plank
balustrade
screwed and
pelleted to
face of newel

newel
bolted to
trimmer

carriage
bird's mouthed
over trimmer

newel fixed
to floor
and bolted
to carriage

treads
screwed and
pelleted to
brackets

timber bracket
pieces glued
and dowelled
to carriage

elevation

section

metal bracket fixing
carriage to floor

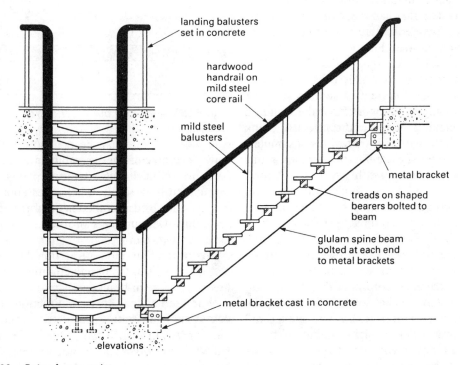

Figure 590 *Spine beam stair*

Labels for Figure 590:

landing balusters
set in concrete

hardwood
handrail on
mild steel
core rail

mild steel
balusters

metal bracket

treads on shaped
bearers bolted to
beam

glulam spine beam
bolted at each end
to metal brackets

metal bracket cast in concrete

elevations

often tapered or curved on its underside to reduce its somewhat bulky appearance. Both ends of the spine beam are fixed to metal brackets that have been cast in the concrete. Because of the great stresses and likelihood of movement at the junction between the tread and beam, it is essential that these are securely fixed. The shaped bearers would be bolted, screwed or fixed with metal brackets to the beam. The treads can then be screwed and pelleted on to the bearers. Metal rod balusters are often used for this type of stair. They are secured at one end to the tread. A mild steel core rail is used to secure the tops of the balusters. This is fixed using set screws into the baluster after drilling and tapping. The hardwood handrail is grooved on the underside to conceal the core rail through which it is screwed. An enlarged detail of this is shown in Figure 591.

Treads of open riser stairs are often found to be noisy and slippery in use. They can be made safer by fitting non-slip nosings to the front edges of the treads. Alternatively, to cut down on the noise and at the same time make them less slippery, carpet may be wrapped around the treads between the carriages and tacked, or fitted into recesses that have been cut into the top of each tread (see Figure 592).

Balustrade

Balustrading to stairs and landings can be formed in many ways, apart from the standard balusters, metal balusters and ranch style plank balustrading covered in previous examples. Other methods of forming balustrades range from framed panelling with a variety of in-fill including laminated or toughened glass to decorative wrought iron work in various designs.

Handrails

Handrails to straight flights with newels as illustrated in previous examples are tenoned into the face of the newel posts. In better quality work they will also be housed into the face of the newel by about 6 mm so that any shrinkage will not result in an open, unsightly joint.

Wall handrails may be fixed by either plugging, screwing and pelleting directly to the

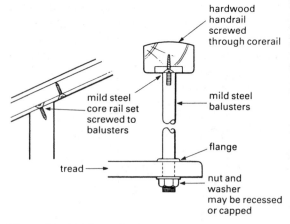

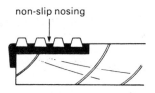

Figure 591   *Balustrade detail*

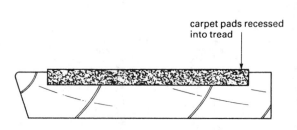

Figure 592   *Carpeting open-riser stairs*

wall, or stand clear of the wall on metal brackets fixed at about 1 metre centres. They can be terminated by a scroll or other suitable means: For economy this often takes the form of simply returning the handrail's profile across the end grain.

Figure 593 illustrates a traditional section and a modern built-up section fixed direct to the wall as well as one on brackets.

Where a handrail changes direction around a corner or from rake to level the section fixed directly to the wall may simply be mitred. Handrails on brackets are not normally mitred but change direction with the aid of short tangential curved sections, jointed to the main straight lengths with handrail bolts and dowels. The nuts are set from the underside of the rail and the mortises plugged with grain matched inserts. Figure 594 illustrates a number of these curved sections.

A quadrant is used to turn a level handrail around a 90° bend. Ramps are either concave or convex and are used to join raked to level handrails. Wreaths are double curvature sections. They are used where a raking handrail turns a corner (e.g. in stairs with tapered steps) or where a raking handrail turns a corner and changes to a level handrail (e.g. at the junction of stair and landing). Alternatively, a ramp and mitre, also known as a swan neck, may be used in conjunction with quadrant. A half newel can be used to give support to the handrail and

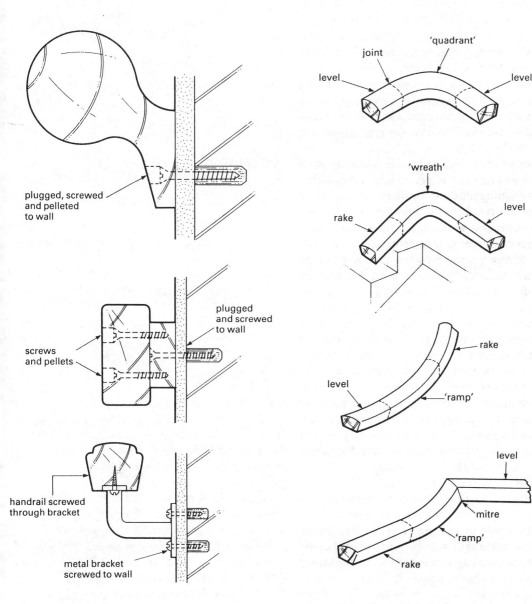

Figure 593   *Handrail sections*

Figure 594   *Curved handrail sections*

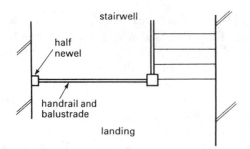

Figure 595   *Use of half newel*

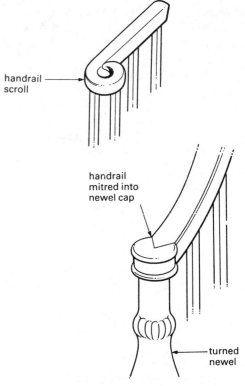

Figure 596   *Geometrical handrail*

balustrade where it meets the wall or a landing (see Figure 595).

The end of a handrail in a geometrical stair is supported by the balusters and may either terminate in a scroll or be mitred into the top of a decorative turned newel post as shown in Figure 596.

Where the balustrading is of metal, as is often the cast in present day, non-domestic construction, the handrail is fitted to a metal core rail. It is common practice for the handrail to be wreathed, grooved and jointed and then given to the metalworker to produce a suitable core rail. Details of fixing metal balustrades and core rails have been illustrated in previous examples. Wall handrails may also be fixed to core rails for additional strength. Figure 597 shows a detail of a hardwood handrail that has been fitted to a metal core rail, welded on brackets and set in the wall.

Timber facings

Concrete stairs can be given a more pleasing appearance by the addition of hardwood treads as shown in Figure 598. These are screwed and pelleted to dovetail blocks that have been cast into the concrete. The landings may be given the same finish by secret fixing hardwood tongued and grooved flooring to dovetail bearers that have again been cast into the concrete.

In situations where the riser is also to be faced, the detail shown in Figure 599 could also be used. In certain circumstances, a hardwood cut string is also used to finish the edge of a stair. This can be screwed and pelleted to fixing blocks.

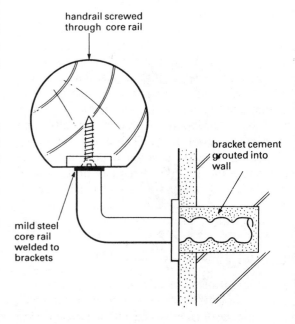

Figure 597   *Metal core rail and brackets*

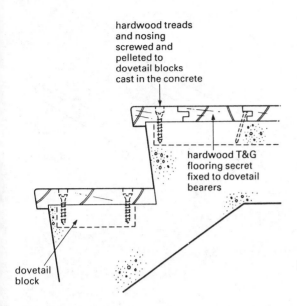

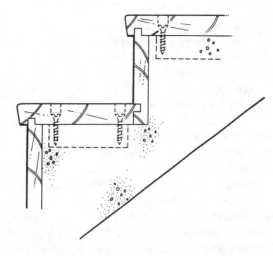

hardwood treads and nosing screwed and pelleted to dovetail blocks cast in the concrete

hardwood T&G flooring secret fixed to dovetail bearers

dovetail block

Figure 599 *Hardwood risers for concrete stairs*

Figure 598 *Hardwood treads for concrete stairs*

Protection of completed work

After a new staircase has been installed a short period of time spent taking measures to prevent damage during subsequent building work saves much more than it costs.

False treads made from strips of hardboard or plywood as shown in Figure 600 are pinned on to the top of each step. The batten fixed to the strips ensures the nosing is well protected. On flights to be clear finished the false treads should be held in position with a strong adhesive tape, as pin holes would not be acceptable.

Strips of hardboard or plywood are also used to protect newel posts. These can either be pinned or taped in position depending on the finish (see Figure 601). Adequate protection of handrails and balustrades can be achieved by wrapping them in corrugated cardboard held in position with adhesive tape.

Structural members

In addition to the glulam methods of construction previously mentioned, structural members may also be formed using either stressed skin panels or built-up beams.

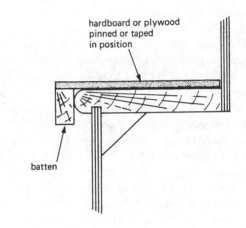

hardboard or plywood pinned or taped in position

batten

Figure 600 *Temporary protection of treads*

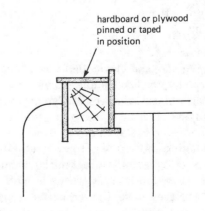

hardboard or plywood pinned or taped in position

Figure 601 *Temporary protection of newels*

Stressed skin panels

Stressed skin plywood panels consist of timber framing members called webs, on to which a skin of plywood is fixed. The panels can be single skin for most situations or double skin for use in high loaded conditions.

A double skin panel is illustrated in Figure 602. They are used as prefabricated floor or roof panels, especially where long uninterrupted spans are required.

Stressed skin panels differ from normal joists and boarding in that the plywood, in addition to supporting the load between the framing, contributes to the strength and stiffness of the framing itself. This is because the plywood is

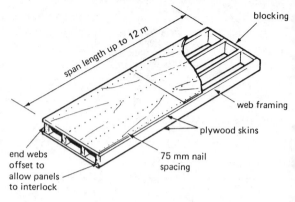

Figure 602   *Stressed skin panel*

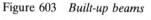

Figure 603   *Built-up beams*

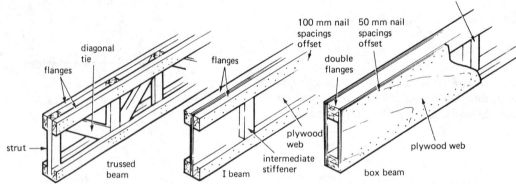

glued and nailed to the framing. The panels therefore function as an efficient structural unit transmitting the stresses between the plywood and framing.

Built-up beams

Built-up, nailed and glued beams have a distinct advantage over solid timber sections or glulam. Figure 603 illustrates typical details of three different methods of forming built-up beams. Each consists of top and bottom flanges, spaced by either ties and struts or plywood webs and stiffeners. It is possible to use built-up beams for far greater spans than is possible with solid timber and they have a much better weight to strength and stiffness ratio than either solid timber or glulam sections. They may be used as

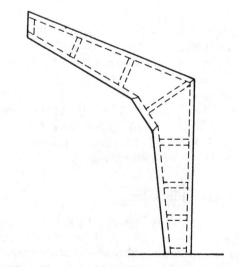

Figure 604   *Plywood portal frame*

purlins or support beams in roof construction and as binders or main support beams in double or framed floors. It is possible to manufacture portal frames using either the I or box beam method of construction as illustrated in Figure 604.

Self-assessment questions

1 Produce a sketch showing an exploded view of the joint between the diminished stile and middle rail of a half glazed door.

2 State the requirements of the Building Regulations applicable to the following:
   (i) Tapered steps in private residence
   (ii) Openings in the balustrade to a flight used by children under five

3 (a) Sketch a section through the vision panel of a 30/30 fire resistant door.
   (b) State the type of glass to be used.

4 Describe with the aid of a sketch *two* alternative methods of supporting adjustable height shelves in a bookcase unit.

5 (a) State the purpose of sealing the backs of panelling.
   (b) Sketch *two* methods of secret fixing framed panelling to softwood grounds.

6 A pair of curved head entrance doors are shown in Figure 605.
   (i) Sketch suitable joints for (A) and (B)
   (ii) Sketch section C–C.

7 The centre sashes of a Venetian window with solid mullions are to be counterbalanced using cords and weights.
   (i) Describe with the aid of sketches the method of accommodating these cords and weights
   (ii) State an alternative method by which the sashes could be counterbalanced

8 Sketch *two* alternative fittings for hanging horizontal pivot sashes.

9 (a) List *four* reasons for the installation of suspended ceilings.
   (b) Sketch *two* alternative methods of forming built-up timber beams:

10 Sketch the plan arrangement of a centre folding, bottom running partition with four leaves.

11 Sketch the following details:
   (i) A section through the recessed plinth and pot board of a cupboard unit
   (ii) A method of tightening the heading joint between two pieces of solid timber counter top
   (iii) A non-slip nosing for an open plan stair tread

12 State the purpose of the following:
   (i) A binder in a suspended ceiling
   (ii) A stair carriage
   (iii) A wreathed handrail
   (iv) A stressed skin plywood panel

Figure 605

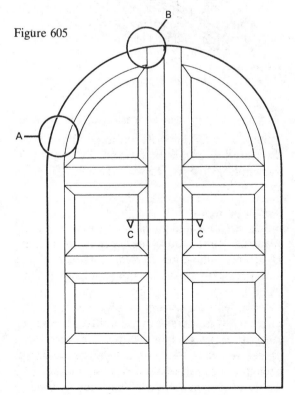

A guide to advanced examinations and study

The main purpose of an advanced craft course of study is to develop practical ability in, and theoretical knowledge of your chosen craft. Examinations are set to measure your achievement of the course objectives. In setting an examination question, examiners give you the opportunity to demonstrate your knowledge and understanding of a particular topic. Their aim is to obtain a true assessment of your abilities, not to confuse, mislead or fail you.

How examinations are set and marked

Setting

Subject experts from education or industry set draft question papers, based on an examination specification. These draft papers are submitted to a meeting of the subject moderating committee, who are also subject experts. At this meeting the draft paper is discussed as a whole and each question considered individually in detail. As a result of discussion between the examiner and moderators, questions may be replaced or amended. This process should ensure that the final version of the examination conforms to the specification and is clear, straightforward and valid.

Types of question

There are three main types of question that appear in an advanced craft examination:

1 Short-answer questions
2 Structured questions
3 Long-answer questions

Short-answer questions

This type of question consists of one or more problems to which you are required to give a limited written answer. The length of this answer may vary, depending on the topic, from one or two words to a short paragraph. In certain circumstances a sketch or simple calculation may be all that is required.

Example

State the meaning of the following abbreviations:

(a) HMSO
(b) BSI
(c) BRE
(d) BWF
(e) TRADA
(f) HASAWA
(g) JCT
(h) BEC
(i) SMM
(j) HSE

Typical answer

(a) Her Majesty's Stationery Office
(b) British Standards Institution
(c) Building Research Establishment
(d) British Woodworking Federation

(e) Timber Research and Development Association

(f) Health and Safety at Work etc. Act

(g) Joint Contractors Tribunal

(h) Building Employers' Confederation

(i) Standard Method of Measurement

(j) Health and Safety Executive

Structured questions

These normally start with a statement which gives a certain amount of information, followed by a series of subquestions in logical order. The length of your answer for each subquestion may again vary depending on the topic from one or two words to a short paragraph, a labelled sketch, scale drawing, detailed calculation or a combination of these, but at each stage the question will make it clear what is required.

Example

After felling, timber is converted into usable sizes and then seasoned ready for use.

(a) Produce large end grain sketches to show:
   (i) A radial sawn plank
   (ii) A tangential sawn plank

(b) Show the shape that each plank is likely to take up as a result of shrinkage.

(c) State what is meant by the term 'equilibrium moisture content'.

(d) Name *two* methods of determining the moisture content of a plank.

(e) State *four* reasons for seasoning timber.

(f) Name *two* distortions that can occur during seasoning.

(g) State the probable causes of the defect.

Typical answer

(a)

(i) Radial cut. Annual rings at 45° or more

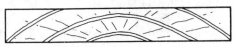

(ii) Tangential cut. Annual rings at less than 45°

Figure 606

(b)

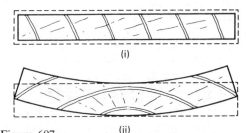

(i)

(ii)

Figure 607

(c) When a piece of timber has a moisture content that is equal to the surrounding atmosphere, it is said to have an equilibrium moisture content.

(d) (i) Oven-drying method
   (ii) Electric moisture meter

(e) (i) To ensure the moisture content of the timber is below the dry rot safety line of 20 per cent.
   (ii) To ensure that any shrinkage takes place before the timber is used.
   (iii) Using seasoned timber, the finished article will be more reliable and less likely to split or distort.
   (iv) Wet timber will not readily accept glue, paint or polish.

(f) (i) Bow
   (ii) Twist

(g) Distortions can be caused as a result of poor stacking or bad air circulation.

Long-answer questions

This more 'traditional' form of question calls for an extended unguided answer to a particular problem, thus requiring the students to structure their answers. This may consist of either an essay, or a scale drawing, or a geometrical development. Questions requiring this type of answer, especially the essay, are rarely set at this level, preference being given to short-answer or structured questions.

Example

To a scale of 1:20 draw the elevation of a 3 m high × 4.5 m wide, framed, ledged, braced and matchboarded pair of sliding industrial doors. One door is to include a small side-hung wicket for personal access. Show the inside of one door and the outside of the other. Suggest suitable component sizes.

Typical answer

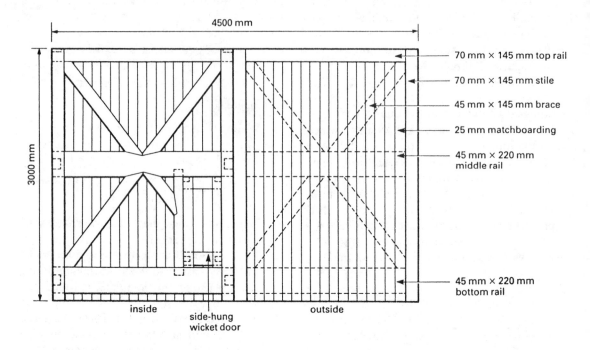

Figure 608

Marking

Completed examination scripts are marked by a team of examiners under the supervision of a chief examiner, who ensures the marks from each member of the team are standardized. At the moderating meeting where the draft paper was discussed an outline solution and marking scheme for each question will have been agreed. A typical question, outline solution and marking scheme is shown in the following example.

Example

Define briefly *each* of the following joinery terms:

(a) Potboard
(b) Weathering
(c) Commode step
(d) Spandrel
(e) Handrail quadrant

Outline solution	*Possible marks*
(a) *Potboard* Lower board or shelf of a unit	2
(b) *Weathering* Splayed or sloping external section	2
(c) *Commode step* Step with curved tread and riser	2
(d) *Spandrel* Triangular area formed under stairs	2
(e) *Handrail quadrant* Section used to turn a level handrail around 90° bend	2
Maximum total	10

Before marking commences the team of examiners will meet to decide on a common approach to marking. During the marking each examiner will have to forward to the chief examiner samples of their marking. From these samples the chief examiner can tell if any particular examiner is marking too strictly or too easily and advise them accordingly.

You should remember that:

1 Marks can only be given for correct information that is relevant to the question.
2 Marks are not taken away for wrong information.
3 Marks are not deducted for poor spelling or ungrammatical expressions.
4 Marks are awarded for each question separately. Care is taken not to let a poor performance or a good performance in one answer reflect in the marks for the rest of your paper. Each answer gets the marks it deserves!
5 A few days after the examination an examiner will receive several batches of papers; one of these will be yours. An impression comes across immediately: is the paper neatly laid out and the sketches well proportioned, or is the paper untidy and the sketches scrappy? One thing is certain: anything you can do to make the examiner's job easier will be appreciated.

Examination preparation

Examination papers are not set with the intent of tricking you. It is not the examiner's fault if you fail to understand or misread a question and give an answer that has not been asked for. The main causes of student failure in examinations are:

1 Lack of preparation
2 Lack of topic knowledge or understanding
3 Bad examination technique

The first two of these causes can be overcome by following a sensible revision programme.

Revision
Revision is an extremely important part of study. Unless facts and information are repe-

ated, used or revised they will quickly be forgotten. Ideally revision should be a continual process, starting from the very beginning of your course, not just at the end of it, although it will, of course, become more concentrated as the examination approaches. Revision is an individual thing; it is impossible to define the 'ideal method'. What suits one person may not be suitable for another.

Revision techniques
As a guide some of the following revision techniques could be incorporated into your personal study programme.

1 Rewrite rough class written notes after each lesson.
2 Underline main or key points in notes, class handouts and textbooks, as remembering these words can bring back to mind the whole topic.
3 Write brief revision notes. These condense a lot of information into a skeleton of a topic that can be recalled at a later date.
4 Read textbooks, magazine articles and technical brochures to supplement your class lectures and notes. Condense this information and add to your revision notes.
5 Answer the self-assessment questions in this book and repeat them periodically; this will show up your weak areas which you should list for more concentrated revision.
6 Research topics on your concentrated revision list.
7 Reread notes and textbooks periodically. This recalls facts and reinforces them in your mind.
8 Mentally ask yourself questions on a particular topic. This can be done anywhere, even on a bus or train when travelling to work. Decide if your answer was suitable: if not add the topic to your concentrated revision list.
9 Read past question papers and attempt timed answers. This is often done in class as a run-up to the examination.
10 In addition, use any technique you have found successful in your previous studies.

Examination technique

As the examination day approaches, anxiety is normally the main problem to be encountered. Much of this can be overcome by the confidence derived from the knowledge that you have studied the course to the full and have undertaken a comprehensive revision programme. However, do not be overconfident; a little anxiety is required to help you do your best. The use of the following checklist will aid you both prior to and during the examination itself.

Examination checklist

1 Arrive at the examination in good time, ensuring that you have everything you are likely to need – examination card or number, pens, pencils, drawing equipment and electronic calculator.
2 Listen carefully to the invigilator's instructions.
3 Read the instructions at the top of the paper carefully.
4 Read through the whole paper. Many students at this stage underline key words in each question. In addition to the subject matter, look for words that indicate the length and precision of the expected answer.

   (i)   Questions or parts of a question that start with 'name', 'list', 'suggest' or 'state' normally require a fairly brief answer of one or two words or a sentence at the most.
   (ii) Words such as 'define', 'describe' or 'explain' require a longer answer, although these can also be shortened by the inclusion of 'briefly'; for example, 'briefly describe' etc.
   (iii) 'Sketch' or 'find' call for less accurate answers than required from 'draw', 'develop' or 'calculate'.
   (iv) Look out for questions that contain two indicating words; for example, 'explain with the aid of sketches' etc.

5 Divide up the available time evenly between the number of questions to be answered, allowing say ten minutes reading time at each end of the examination. For example, for a three-hour paper with ten questions to be answered, the time would be divided up as follows:

Reading time at the start   10 minutes
Reading/correction time
at the end   10 minutes

Time for each question
$$(180–20)/10 = 16 \text{ minutes}$$

6 Attempt your best answer first as this will give you confidence to tackle the rest of the paper.
7 Attempt the remaining questions in increasing order of difficulty. This gives you more time to think about and plan the harder questions subconsciously while you are completing the easier ones.
8 Keep to your time plan. When you reach the end of the time allocated to each question, stop writing even if you have not finished the answer. Leave a space before starting the next question so that if time permits you may come back and complete the answer later. It is far better to have attempted all the questions even if some of the answers are incomplete than to run out of time and leave out the last four or so questions, which could happen if you spent five or ten minutes longer on each question.
9 If time is short, your final question can be put down in a condensed skeleton form; this will obtain you some marks at least.
10 Read through your paper at the end of the examination. This gives you a chance to spot and correct errors. Also you may have time at this stage to complete any unfinished answers.
11 Finally ensure you have put your name and student examination number on all your answer sheets and drawing paper.

Specimen examination papers

You should now be ready to tackle the following examination papers.

Read the front page of each paper carefully. It will tell you what you need for the examination, and from the information given you can calculate the length of time to be spent on each question.

Each examination is designed to be completed within a three hour period, so before starting make sure that you have this amount of time available.

Good luck!

CITY AND GUILDS OF LONDON INSTITUTE

PAPER NUMBER **5 8 5 – 2 – 1 1**	EXAMINATION **CARPENTRY AND JOINERY ADVANCED CRAFT**	**Sample Paper 1985 Onwards**
SERIES	PAPER **GENERAL CARPENTRY AND JOINERY**	**14 00 – 17 00 3 hours**

YOU SHOULD HAVE THE FOLLOWING FOR THIS EXAMINATION
**one answer book
1 sheet A3 drawing paper
drawing instruments
drawing board and tee square
metric scale rule**

SAMPLE QUESTIONS FOR EXAMINATIONS FROM MAY–JUNE 1985 ONWARDS

This question paper contains 10 compulsory structured questions to be answered in 3 hours.

ALL questions carry equal marks.

1   (a)   State clearly the responsibilities of the employee in respect of The Health and Safety at Work Act.
     (b)   List FIVE safety checks which should be made on an independent scaffold before commencing work.
     (c)   Give TWO examples of the work done by the Timber Research and Development Association.

2   (a)   Sketch a suitable method of supporting 2440 × 1220 × 12 plywood sheeting placed 2440 in height
        when being used as a security hoarding around a small building site.
     (b)   Prepare a list of materials using the information in (a) if the site measures 20 m × 30 m and is
        completely enclosed.

3   Fig. 1 shows the top portion of a fully glazed semi-circular hardwood external door one metre wide.
     (a)   Choosing suitable dimensions for head, stile and rail, sketch the jointing arrangement at X.
     (b)   Draw to a scale of 1:1 the section through A – A to show the method of jointing the small curved boss to
        the straight horizontal rail clearly indicating how the glass is held in position.

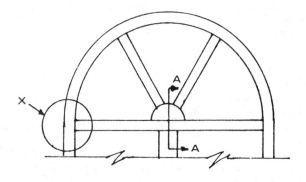

FIG. 1

See next page

4   The octagonal plan of a pyramid turret roof on an architect's drawing indicates the length of each side as
     3500 and the rise 6000.
     (a)   To a scale of 1:50
           (i)   develop the true shape of the boarding for one side
           (ii)   determine the backing angle of one of the hip rafters.
     (b)   Sketch the jointing arrangement of the rafters at the apex.

5   (a)   Sketch sufficient detail to indicate the method of construction of a one hour fire resistant internal door
           and frame.
     (b)   List the ironmongery for two such doors hung as a pair.

6   (a)   Sketch and describe a method of improving the sound resisting qualities of an existing solid concrete
           floor in a multi-storey block of flats.
     (b)   Define with illustrations the difference between air and structure borne sound.

7   (a)   Describe the meaning of the following terms in relation to a structural timber beam
           (i)   compression
           (ii)   tension
           (iii) neutral layer
           (iv)   shear stress
           (v)   factor of safety.
     (b)   Determine the reactions for the simply supported beam in Fig. 2.

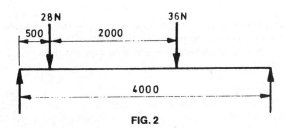

FIG. 2

8   (a)   List and describe briefly FIVE essential items of equipment required in a workshop producing
           structural laminated timber sections.
     (b)   Name an adhesive suitable for use in the construction of a laminated timber beam which is to be used
           in an exposed position
     (c)   List and give a brief explanation of FOUR factors that affect the bond between the timber laminates.

9   (a)   To which document would a carpenter refer for information on sizes and grades of timber for floor
           joists?
     (b)   Name TWO methods of stress grading.
     (c)   Describe ONE method of stress grading.
     (d)   Sketch a typical section through a timber dead shore and explain the reasons for its shape.

10   (a)   Suggest TWO possible structural defects which may give rise to wet rot in timber floor joists.
     (b)   Describe how to recognize wet rot.
     (c)   What remedial treatments can be made for timber subject to wet rot.
     (d)   Name TWO types of preservative which can be used on timber joists.
     (e)   Describe briefly the process of the 'full cell' method of timber impregnation.

CITY AND GUILDS OF LONDON INSTITUTE

PAPER NUMBER	EXAMINATION	Sample Paper
585—2—18	CARPENTRY AND JOINERY ADVANCED CRAFT	1985 Onwards

SERIES	PAPER	
	PURPOSE MADE JOINERY	14 00 — 17 00 3 hours

YOU SHOULD HAVE THE FOLLOWING FOR THIS EXAMINATION

one answer book
2 sheets A3 drawing paper
drawing instruments

drawing board and tee square
metric scale rule.

SAMPLE QUESTIONS FOR EXAMINATIONS FROM MAY— JUNE 1985 ONWARDS

This question paper contains 8 structured questions (with a choice of 6 from 8) to be answered in 3 hours.

ALL questions carry equal marks.

1   The semi-circular brick archway shown in Fig. 1 is to be filled with framing to include a pair of doors, side lights and small opening transom light

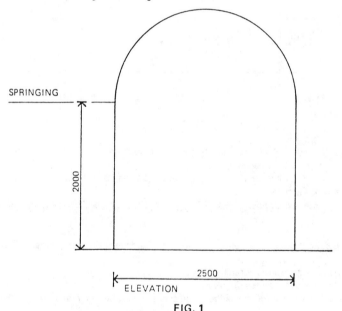

SPRINGING

2000

2500

ELEVATION

FIG. 1

(a) Draw
   (i)   an outline elevation of the finished framing and doors. Scale 1:20
   (ii) vertical and horizontal sections for a setting out rod. Scale 1:10.
(b) List the ironmongery requirements for the doors and transom light.
(c) Produce a cutting list showing sawn sizes only.
(d) State a method of fixing the frame to the existing opening, listing the tools and materials required.

2   (a)   Describe, using sketches where appropriate, EACH of the following associated with timber
          (i)   equilibrium moisture content
          (ii)   natural seasoning
          (iii) natural timber defects giving FIVE examples
          (iv)   two methods of timber conversion from log to sawn stock.
    (b)   Specify
          (i)   a suitable hardwood for a wood frame to aluminium windows
          (ii)   an alternative hardwood for external panelled doors.
    (c)   State THREE main characteristics of each hardwood specified in (b).

3   Fig. 2 shows the elevation of one of a number of laminated beams to support the roof of a spectators'
    stand. The beams are to be made in pairs by manufacturing a rectangular beam 16.5 m long x 2500 mm
    wide x 200 mm in thickness.

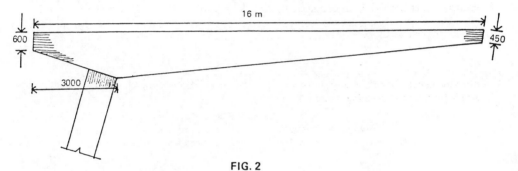

FIG. 2

    (a)   Describe fully a method of manufacture of the beam.
    (b)   State
          (i)   the maximum size of laminate
          (ii)   a method of jointing the laminates in their length
          (iii) a suitable adhesive and its application
          (iv)   a type of preservative and its application
          (v)   a suitable protective finish.
    (c)   Calculate the volume of timber required for one pair of beams before shaping.

4   A circular louvre ventilator of 100 mm x 75 mm cross section has an external diameter of 1000 mm.
    (a)   Draw to a scale of 1:10
          (i)   an elevation
          (ii)   a vertical section on the centre line.
    (b)   Develop the shape of both faces of any one louvre board.
    (c)   Show a method of marking out the housings on the inside face of the frame.

5   (a)   List the sequence of operations involved in the setting up of a single ended tenoning machine to
          produce a tenon with square stepped shoulders on a number of rails for an item of joinery.
    (b)   Describe and sketch a false fence to prevent spelching when producing a tenon with square
          shoulders on pre-moulded stock having an ovolo mould and rebate on both edges.

6   A number of glazed and louvred frames are to be manufactured as shown in Fig. 3

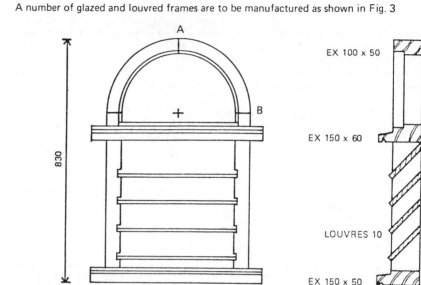

ELEVATION   SECTION

EX 100 x 50

EX 150 x 60

LOUVRES 10

EX 150 x 50

830

500

FIG. 3

(a) Sketch a method of jointing the members at A and an alternative jointing arrangement at B.
(b) Sketch a jig for working the louvre housings by means of a powered hand router.
(c) Sketch and describe the preparation of the curved head from sawn stock to ready for jointing.

7   Fig. 4 shows the part plan of an open newel stair with 75 mm x 62 mm deep handrails of hardwood on both sides.

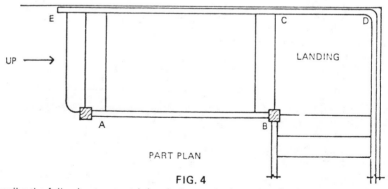

E   C   D

UP →

LANDING

A   B

PART PLAN

FIG. 4

(a) Describe the following terms and sketch the required templets for producing each member
     (i)   ramp to capping on the bottom newel post A
     (ii)   swan neck to capping on the upper newel post B
     (iii) knee to rail on the wall C
     (iv)   level bend or quadrant on the landing D.
(b) Sketch a suitable finish at E.
(c) Calculate a suitable rise and going, given that the storey height is 2700 mm and available going 3530 mm.
(d) State the formula for checking the rise and going.

8   Flush panelling in the conference room of an office block is 2000 mm high. It is formed with 12 mm hardwood veneered lamin board panels in widths of 750 mm, fixed to grounds, without cover fillets to the vertical joints and finished with a plain capping and 150 mm recessed skirting.
(a)   Draw to a scale of 1:10
       (i)   a 2000 mm run of the elevation showing position of grounds
       (ii)   a vertical section through the grounds and panelling.
(b)   Sketch
       (i)   details of the panels to show fixing to the grounds
       (ii)   horizontal sections of an external and internal angle.

CO890/576/2699. S15. © 1983. City and Guilds of London Institute.

Index

TURN TO PAGE 42